W9-BSV-529

PRAISE FOR SuperBaby

Dr. Jenn's unplugged approach to parenting is a breath of fresh air. In *SuperBaby* she clears the way to good, instinctive, relationship-based parenting.

—**Michele Borba,** EdD, internationally renowned educator, parenting expert, and award-winning author of 23 parenting books, including *The Big Book of Parenting Solutions: 101 Answers to Your Everyday Challenges and Wildest Worries*

Basing her recommendations on the best available evidence, Dr. Jenn provides essential and practical suggestions for 21st century parents.

—**Dr. Susan Linn,** director of the Campaign for a Commercial-Free Childhood and author of *Consuming Kids: The Hostile Takeover of Childhood and The Case for Make Believe: Saving Play in a Commercialized World*

As parents it is our responsibility to seek insightful, credible, and useful information when raising our children—this book has it all!

—**Christopher Gavigan,** CEO and executive director of Healthy Child Healthy World and author of *Healthy Child Healthy World: Creating a Cleaner, Greener, Safer Home*

SuperBaby is the essential roadmap for everything parents need to know about early childhood.

—**Jill Spivack,** LCSW, and Jennifer Waldburger, LCSW, co-creators, The Sleepeasy Solution

With our first child arriving in just weeks I devoured the information in this book, so grateful for the advice… I'll be carrying *SuperBaby* with me for some time to come.

—**Sara Snow,** green living expert, TV host, and author of *Sara Snow's Fresh Living*

Don't let the title intimidate you: Berman isn't interested in creating the perfect baby, but in giving parents the research and support they need to do what they want: help their baby and toddler flourish.

—**Laura Diamond,** editor, *Los Angeles Family* and the Family Magazine Group

This is a profoundly important book. It is not about techniques to push your child too hard, but about learning practices, well grounded in research, that stimulate a baby's cognitive and emotional potential… Read *SuperBaby*, apply its teachings, and become a super parent or grandparent.

—**Nathaniel Branden,** PhD, author of twenty books, including *The Six Pillars of Self-Esteem*

SuperBaby starts with building super parents. Dr. Berman presents all the research and how-to information in this timely book.

—**Donna Holloran,** BABYGROUP™

This book should be required reading for every parent.

—**Dr. Tanya Remer Altmann,** pediatrician, editor in chief of *The Wonder Years,* associate medical editor of *Caring for Your Baby and Young Child, Birth to Age 5* and author of *Mommy Calls: Dr. Tanya Answers Parents' Top 101 Questions About Babies and Toddlers*

Informative, engaging and inspiring, *SuperBaby* will help readers become super parents and empower them to do what is best for their child in the first three years of life.

—**Scott Cohen,** MD, FAAP, author of *Eat, Sleep, Poop: A Common Sense Guide to Your Baby's First Year*

Dr. Jenn helps parents effortlessly integrate signing into their child's life, reducing tantrums and aiding child development in many ways!

—**Dr. Joseph Garcia,** author and creator of the Sign with Your Baby Sign Language Kit

New (and old) parents will appreciate the practical advice in this book, which Dr. Berman bolsters with research findings on diverse aspects of language learning. She covers all the bases for early bilinguals.

—**Dr. Barbara Zurer Pearson,** author of *Raising a Bilingual Child: A Step-by-Step Guide for Parents*

In *SuperBaby*, Dr. Jenn calms parents' anxieties and skillfully demonstrates how to maximize every stage of their children's development to spark learning, curiosity, creativity, and compassion.

—**Donna Corwin,** author of eight parenting books, including *Time Out for Toddlers, The Challenging Child,* and *Give Me, Get Me, Buy Me*

SuperBaby is supremely researched and organized—the charts and lists are fridge-magnet worthy—making it a reliable source of sound developmental advice.

—**Gregory Keer,** award-winning fatherhood columnist and publisher of FamilyManOnline.com

If you use this wonderfully written, intelligently laid out and cleverly helpful book to berate yourself about what you don't know...stop. *SuperBaby* is a book that you will live with for years.

—**Marilyn Kagan,** LCSW, psychotherapist and author of *Defenders of the Heart*

SUPERBABY

SUPERBABY

12 WAYS TO GIVE YOUR CHILD A HEAD START
IN THE FIRST 3 YEARS

Dr. Jenn Berman

STERLING

New York / London
www.sterlingpublishing.com

STERLING and the distinctive Sterling logo are registered trademarks of
Sterling Publishing Co., Inc.

Library of Congress Cataloging-in-Publication Data Available

10 9 8 7 6 5 4 3 2 1

Published by Sterling Publishing Co., Inc.
387 Park Avenue South, New York, NY 10016

© 2010 by Dr. Jenn Berman

Distributed in Canada by Sterling Publishing
c/o Canadian Manda Group, 165 Dufferin Street
Toronto, Ontario, Canada M6K 3H6

Distributed in the United Kingdom by GMC Distribution Services
Castle Place, 166 High Street, Lewes, East Sussex, England BN7 1XU

Distributed in Australia by Capricorn Link (Australia) Pty. Ltd.
P.O. Box 704, Windsor, NSW 2756, Australia

Manufactured in the United States of America
All rights reserved

Sterling ISBN 978-1-4027-7033-3

For information about custom editions, special sales, premium and
corporate purchases, please contact Sterling Special Sales
Department at 800–805–5489 or specialsales@sterlingpublishing.com.

The material in this book is intended for education. No expressed or implied guarantee as
to the effects of the use of the recommendations can be given, nor liability taken. Any advice
provided is not meant to take the place of treatment by a qualified medical practitioner or
therapist. Since every child is different, you should consult your child's pediatrician on
questions specific to your child.

All the vignettes in this book are taken from a combination of the author's clinical experience,
personal experience, media work as a therapist, and letters and emails she has received.
She has changed all names and identifiable details to protect the privacy of her psychotherapy
clients. Any similarity between the names and stories of individuals described in this book,
and those of individuals known to readers, is purely coincidental.

To my superbabies,

Mendez

and

Quincy

You are my inspiration,

my greatest joy,

and the best possible proof

that the SuperBaby approach

produces super children

who are a pleasure to spend time with.

I feel so lucky to be your Mama.

Contents

Foreword

This is a book that goes straight to the heart of parenting. As parents, our deepest instinct is a yearning for our children to thrive. I've seen this instinct surface time and again. Commonly, at the magic moment a new baby emerges into the world, eager parents check to be sure there are ten fingers and ten toes. We want our children to be healthy. But our secret hopes for our children go far beyond good health. We want them to be secure, happy, and connected, to be capable and creative, to excel.

In *SuperBaby*, Dr. Jenn speaks to our hopes and fears with sound, practical wisdom. She takes the overwhelming array of possibilities and problems that could confront today's parents and narrows our attention to twelve tangible, exciting areas for our focus.

These twelve keys are far from arbitrary. They are powerful focal points where science and experience have shown that simple actions can make a big difference in your child's life. Each chapter is filled with specific examples in which you will see yourself and your family and know what to do. With this book to learn from and refer back to, the idea of giving your child a head start becomes not just a hidden desire, but also an achievable reality.

One of the twelve keys is play. Playing—and toys—are among my favorite subjects. Play is not a frivolous distraction, but central to children's growth. Children's joy in playing encourages them to engage in activities that stimulate their growth and development—provided that this mechanism isn't short-circuited by a steady stream of passive entertainment (a likelihood made possible only in the past forty years of human history). Entertainments such as television or fancy toys that perform while children watch can artificially satisfy their inborn desire both for play and adult attention, thus robbing them of joy-filled opportunities for growth (in much the same way that processed, partially-hydrogenated snack foods can replace the magic of a ripe peach).

To find the best toys for your child at any age, I suggest turning off the TV, putting away the passive-play toys, and watching your child. Many kids will begin to play spontaneously, using whatever is at hand; take note of what they choose to play with. Others will be directionless or frustrated; interact with them playfully, and their choices will begin to emerge. Spontaneous play gives parents important clues to the cutting edge of a child's development.

Children put the most energy into newly emerging skills. Activities of moderate novelty tend to be the most interesting and the most fun. Once children have mastered something, they will want to repeat it in order to revel in their success. But eventually they will begin to grow bored and either change the activity slightly to keep it interesting or move on to something else. Activities that are too new, too difficult, or too overwhelming will frustrate children and fail to hold their interest.

One of the joys of parenting is finding that zone of moderate challenge for your children and setting up fun opportunities for them to teach themselves through exploration and play. This zone of moderate challenge is one of my favorite concepts, and it applies far beyond the art of play. As Dr. Jenn guides you through the twelve ways to give your child a head start, she steers you unfailingly to this zone in each area. The opportunities for growth and play in each chapter are just hard enough to be challenging, productive, and fun.

And here's the secret—it's not just your baby who benefits! When you apply the ideas in this book, you become secure, happy, capable, creative parents. You become the kind of parents you long to be.

And perhaps even more exciting, your relationships with your children will also thrive. You'll enjoy a connection of mutual respect—one in which you'll learn to understand and respond to each other's cues. This is a treasure that can last a lifetime, long beyond those fleeting months when your child is a *SuperBaby*.

— DR. ALAN GREENE, MD, FAAP
Author of *Raising Baby Green* and *Feeding Baby Green*

Introduction

SuperBaby is not a book about how to create an *über*baby. It has not been written to burden you with new and expensive things that you have to do to raise the perfect genius-child. What I have put together in this book is a collection of important research about the first three years of life, woven together with my own clinical experience as a therapist and parenting expert, along with the personal stories and truths I have picked up as a mother of twins. In addition, this book includes the wisdom of some of the country's leading parenting experts, whose words of advice, in dozens of "From the Experts . . ." sidebars, cover a range of essential parenting issues from learning how to handle colic and tantrums to communicating effectively with a nonverbal baby and detoxing your home. My goal has been to create a helpful, one-of-a-kind resource that will guide you to do things that can *really* make a difference in your child's development, happiness, and health.

You can read this book from cover to cover, if you like, or you can simply dip into the chapters or topics that interest you. Every chapter has tips you can try at home that will enhance your relationship with your child and further her development. Most are simple, like pointing to the words in a book as you read to your child, while others are more demanding—exposing her to a second language, for example. It is up to you to decide which advice will work best for you and your family; I hope that implementing my suggestions will be an enjoyable, meaningful experience for you and your child.

It has been said that authors are consumed by a particular interest or concern that they are driven to write about and tell others. In my case, that is an understatement. Even before I was a parent, I was feverishly passionate about helping parents and children in my private practice and through my "Dr. Jenn" parenting column. Now that I am a parent myself, my passion for parenting has become an obsession. My first book, *The A to Z Guide to Raising Happy, Confident Kids,* only whetted my appetite for sharing important information with parents. In writing *SuperBaby,* my goal is to wrap up, in one package, all the research and information I have used to help my clients as they navigate the critical early years of their children's development.

The first three years of life are so important in your child's development because it is during this time that she begins to form attachments, develops a sense of self, and learns to trust. In addition, there are other developmental windows that provide parents with opportunities, but only if you are aware of what they are and what to do. Previous generations of parents have been satisfied to meet their children's most basic needs: for food, a clean diaper, and a safe place to sleep. Parents today, however, want to give their children every advantage to be as strong and smart as possible, and to set the foundation for raising happy, healthy babies and toddlers who grow up and flourish as adults.

But we are also faced with obstacles that are quite different and in some ways more challenging than the ones our parents faced. So much of our children's food contains harmful toxic chemicals and additives—many of which didn't even exist when we were children—and the content, format, and availability of television has changed dramatically. There is no question that snap 'n' go baby carriers, strollers, and pack 'n' plays have made our lives much easier, but these conveniences have also created a need for parents to make a conscious effort to touch their children and allow them to interact with their environment. When grandparents say, "We didn't do any of this stuff and you turned out just fine," they are overlooking how dramatically the world has changed. Although there are more challenges for parents now, there are also more resources and information available to us about enhancing our children's development and maximizing their potential.

A recent Baby Center poll found that the number one fear of parents of young children is that their kids won't get the education and opportunities they need to reach their full potential. This fear ranked higher than concerns about sudden infant death syndrome (SIDS), obesity, autism, or accidents. All parents want the best for their children, and today's parents recognize that the greatest opportunity for a child to reach her full potential starts most significantly in the first three years.

Researchers now know that children are born with an IQ range that can vary as much as thirty points, depending upon outside factors. While it is believed that "nature" is responsible for 50 percent of intellectual development, the other 50 percent is a result of "nurture." Whether or not a child reaches her potential depends on her environment, experiences, and relationships. This is something parents can greatly influence, and reading *SuperBaby* will show you how.

There are "critical windows" for different mental abilities. According to Dr. Lise Eliot, a professor of neuroscience at Chicago Medical School, "all of the essential refinements in brain wiring . . . can be influenced by a child's experience. But once a given brain region has passed the refinement stage, its critical period has ended, and the opportunity to rewire it is significantly limited." In this book, I will spell out many of the critical developmental windows that you need to know about, showing you the best way to take advantage of them for your child's benefit.

Raising a *superbaby* is not just about intelligence or admission into the right preschool or college; it is about raising a child who is empathic, resilient, and has what experts call emotional intelligence, the ability to regulate one's emotions and read the cues of others. We know that early relationships and attachment experiences are central in shaping children's social development. Following the suggestions in this book, especially those about parent-child communication, will help create the foundation for these important psychological strengths.

As a therapist, I often tell my clients that I would not ask them to do anything I wouldn't be willing to do myself. As an author, I am no different. I have done everything in this book with my own daughters that I suggest you do with your children. Some of my suggestions will give you instant gratification, while others—like learning baby sign language—will take more time. I must admit I was doubtful myself that all the time I spent signing with my own daughters would ever make a difference. But my doubts quickly disappeared the first time one of my daughters, who wasn't even a year old, signed to me. Her new ability to ask for the "milk" that she wanted opened the door to communication for us and reduced her frustration tremendously. It also helped us get closer and have a better understanding of each other.

When I chose to expose my children to a foreign language, I had the same reservations I had about signing with them, but since I had done the research and believed what I read, I continued to read books and play and listen to music in other languages. I now have three-year-old daughters who speak and understand both Spanish and Mandarin Chinese—and there are no native speakers in the house.

In writing this book about all the things you need to know to help your child's development, I would have been remiss if I had not included chapters on toxins and food. Because of children's developing brains, fast metabolisms, and immature immune systems, they are particularly vulnerable to harmful reactions to chemicals, hormones, and additives. While I am not a toxicologist or a dietician, I have relied on my journalistic skills, research, and interviews with top experts in the field, as well as my own judgment, to write this book. I hope this experience opens your eyes the way it has opened mine.

This is a book that has been designed to educate and enlighten parents. I wrote it to help you enjoy and connect with your children and create experiences that are essential to the growth of their mind, psyche, and spirit. But my greatest hope is that it inspires you to enjoy the opportunity to raise a happy, healthy child.

A Note to the Reader

To refer to babies and children, I've alternated between "she" and "he" from chapter to chapter in order to remain gender-neutral. In Chapter 1, for example, the references are to "she" and "her," while Chapter 2 refers to "he" and "him." Chapter 3 returns to mostly female references. This pattern is repeated throughout the book.

To refer to parents, I've used the traditional "mother" and "father" for simplicity's sake, but I want to acknowledge same-sex parents, single parents, and blended families. This book is for *all* families. I hope you will use it to create a stronger bond between you and your children and help them reach their full potential.

—DR. JENN BERMAN

Talk the Talk

Respectful Communication

You would be hard-pressed to find a parent who doesn't want to raise a respectful child. Yet many parents are so focused on receiving respect that they don't realize it's a two-way process that begins on day one. Because babies are so small and totally dependent, it is easy to forget that they're human beings, individuals with preferences, thoughts, and their own feelings.

We often take for granted our infant's experience of the world and us. Caught up in the commotion and turmoil of the day, we pick her up without a word of warning and abruptly put her on the changing table. At other times, we put her in her crib and run out of the room without saying a word because we hear the phone ring. We even get so caught up in our own anxieties about our child being developmentally "on time" that we don't allow her to do her own thing at her own pace. In fact, it seems that often we watch our children without really seeing them for who they actually are.

It's All About Respect

Respectful relationships are built on reciprocity, which creates healthy attachments and helps a child develop trust and self-esteem and feel safe in the world. On a day-to-day level, respectful relationships create an environment in which children can trust their parents to keep their word. In our house we have a rule that a child's hands must be free (with nothing in them) when she goes down the stairs. When my daughter Quincy was as young as fifteen months old, my husband would say to her, "You know the rule: hands must be empty when you go down the stairs. You can put your toy back in your room or you can hand it to me, and I will give it to you when we get to the bottom of the steps." My daughter always handed the toy to my husband because he always kept his word. She knew she could trust him to give the toy back to her. I follow the same routine and, believe me, there are plenty of times when Quincy gets to the bottom of the stairs and I think to myself, "If I give this toy back to her she is going to want to bring it to the kitchen table (we have a no-toy rule at the table), where I am going to have to ask for it again, and I really don't want to face that challenge," or we get to the bottom of the stairs and she has forgotten all about the toy. But no matter what, we always offer her the toy at the bottom of the stairs because this type of respect allows her to trust our words and our actions.

Reciprocity also means having mutually collaborative communication. In other words, your child sends a signal that you understand and respond to—creating a dance of communication that is gratifying to both of you. This responsiveness begins in infancy. When your baby smiles at you and you smile back, she knows she has been seen and responded to, which makes her feel connected and cared for. When a baby first starts to babble and make preverbal sounds, the parent who pauses and listens to those sounds and then replies teaches her baby the give-and-take of dialogue, but more importantly, she sends the message, "I see you, I am listening to you, and I care what you have to say."

Human behavior is motivated by the desire for belonging, understanding, significance, and connection. In the book *Positive Discipline: The First Three Years,* the authors write, "Recent research tells us that children are 'hardwired' from birth to seek connection with others." We know that children who feel connected to their parents, their families, and their communities are less likely to misbehave. When kids feel good, they act "good." When they feel loved, encouraged, and respected, they tend to be cooperative, loving, and respectful themselves.

Oh, Say What You See

A simple but profound interaction I observed revolutionized the way I conceptualize parent-child communication in early childhood. At a Mommy & Me class I was attending, a group of mothers gathered in one corner of the room to chat and called our friend Paige to join us. Before she came over, she kneeled down to make eye contact with her four-month-old son Jackson and said, "Jackson, Mommy is going to go over there to talk to the other moms for a couple of minutes. You will be able to hear me the whole time, and if you need me, you can just let me know and I will come back." When I heard the way she spoke to her son, I knew that this was the kind of parent I wanted to be: a parent who helped her child understand what he could expect, who was respectful enough to tell him what was going to happen next, and who created a sense of safety for him. It was a small gesture that made a huge impact.

Narration is one of the most important tools in developing respectful communication. It generally takes three forms: (1) telling your child what is going to happen ("Now I am going to pick you up," "Now the doctor is going to give you a shot"); (2) narrating her experience ("I see you hit your head," "You really enjoy that toy!"); and (3) letting her know your expectation ("We are going to start putting away the toys in five minutes," "Soon our cuddle time is going to come to an end and it will be time to get in bed").

"But she is only a baby," you may be thinking to yourself. "She doesn't even understand what I am saying." First of all, we don't know for sure when infants really start to understand language, but we believe that even if a child does not yet understand specific words, at the very least she does understand your tone and inflection. Long before she can speak, you will have paved the way for trust and attachment between the two of you through her understanding of you and the respectful communication you've established.

Here are six more advantages to using narration:

1. It gives you something to talk about. Babies are not known for their fascinating conversation. Sometimes new parents, especially fathers, aren't sure what to talk about with their little ones. Narrating gives you the opportunity to engage your child and connect. You can change your child's diaper in silence or you can describe what you are seeing and doing, exposing your child to thousands of words, which will only help her vocabulary later (see Chapter 5 for more on this).

2. It is respectful. Doing things to your child without telling her what you are doing is treating her like an object. Put yourself in her position—having a diaper changed without someone explaining what is going to happen next would make anyone feel vulnerable. It is like being examined by your gynecologist without being told what she is going to do next.

3. It creates good communication habits from the start. If you already talk to your child the way you would talk to another person, you won't have to suddenly change how you speak to her when she is older and becomes verbal. Since you're modeling behavior for her, don't be surprised if she starts talking to you the way you talk to her when she becomes verbal.

4. It provides predictability, which breeds security. When your child knows what is happening next, she feels safe. This safety, in turn, builds trust. She learns to trust you, which only strengthens your attachment to each other.

5. It gives your child a sense of control. Knowing what is going to happen next helps your child prepare herself so she isn't continually surprised. Having the chance to prepare for a transition makes her feel more in control so she is less likely to resist.

6. It helps prevent tantrums. As your child gets older and her will begins to develop, you will be met with more resistance. Respectful communication is one of your best offenses. Just the other day I was at a children's activity center with my daughter Quincy. When it was time to go, literally every child was screaming and kicking. As the parents started to leave, one by one their kids' tantrums erupted, and, understandably, the parents became annoyed and frustrated. Watching these well-meaning moms and dads, I noticed that they all did the same thing: they suddenly said, "It's time to go," which prompted their kids to protest. The parents then picked them up and a battle of wills ensued.

Armed with a long history of respectful communication and the understanding that kids need some transition time, I handled the situation a little differently from the other parents. Five minutes before we needed to leave, my toddler and I had the following conversation:

> **Me:** *We are going to go in five minutes* (letting her know the expectation).
>
> **Quincy:** *I want to play.*
>
> **Me:** *I know you are really enjoying playing* (respectfully acknowledging her desires). *Let me tell you the plan* (preparing her). *You can play for five minutes* (preparing her for the transition); *then we will say good-bye to the toys, wash our hands, and then go to the car. You can walk out holding my hand or I can carry you* (giving respectful choices). *You can pick. You let me know which one you want* (giving her the respect of allowing her to make her own decision within my limits).

I gave her a three-minute warning and then it was time to leave. When she told me she didn't want to stop playing with the toys, I acknowledged her feelings. She told me that she didn't want anyone else to play with the toys, so together we found a high shelf on which to put them, where they were less likely to be touched by other children. Then we washed our hands. Quincy decided that she wanted to walk to the car holding my hand and we left peacefully. I am not a perfect parent by any means, but by using the tools I've shared with you in this chapter I would estimate that I have reduced the tantrums in our household by at least 50 percent. Anyone can use them and it is never too late to start.

The Ten Pillars of Respectful Communication

Your role as a parent should not be one of dictator but rather that of guide and coach. You must constantly recognize the power, influence, and significance of your job. Children are acutely aware of their parents' moods, emotions, words, tone, and messages. Because young children are naturally egocentric, they believe that everything is about them and are constantly looking for clues about themselves in everything you say. In her book *Just Tell Me What to Say,*

Betsy Brown Braun talks about the four types of communication parents have with their children:

- **Verbal communication** is not only what we actually say but also how we say it—our vocabulary, the tone we use, and how loudly or softly we speak.
- **Nonverbal language** is body language—our facial expressions and manner of touch.
- **Listening** is all about how well you hear what your child is trying to express.
- **Modeling** is how you show your kids appropriate behavior as a role model.

The Ten Pillars of Respectful Communication take all four types of communication into account. These tips will enhance your ability to communicate with your children at any age.

1. *REALLY* LISTEN TO YOUR CHILD.

Most parents find it really easy to tell their children what they want but have a much more difficult time listening to their kids' wants and needs. To truly *hear* your child is to understand not only what she is saying but also what the underlying message is and what her needs are. For example, every night after dinner, two-and-a-half-year-old Justin started telling his parents that he was "Baby John," the name of his two-month-old cousin. Instead of just telling him, "No, you're not. You're Justin and you are a big boy," his parents listened, asked questions, and played along. By allowing him to express his need to be "little" and regress, they realized that Justin was in need of more comfort. It is very common for children to regress or become more needy when they experience developmental leaps—crawling, walking, talking, toilet learning, making the transition to a big bed, and the like. Toddlers, in particular, feel a lot of ambivalence about becoming a "big boy" or a "big girl," which they often express through play.

Because children are not born with a ready-made vocabulary, getting a simple sentence out can take a long time for a toddler, especially if she is excited or upset. You can help by getting down on the floor at your child's eye level, being patient, and giving her your full attention. You thus send a message that says, "You are important to me and I care about you." Show your child she is worthy of your attention by turning off the computer, putting down the cell phone, turning off the television, and listening.

2. RESPECT ALL YOUR CHILD'S FEELINGS.

Honor your child's feelings. Whether your infant is expressing herself by kicking her legs during a diaper change to let you know that she does not want to be changed, your eighteen-month-old is throwing a toy that has frustrated her, or your three-year-old is telling you she hates her baby sister, your job as a parent is to hear the feelings your child is expressing and reflect back what you understand. For example, you might make the following statements: "I see you really don't want to have your diaper changed right now," "It looks like that toy really frustrated you," or "It's hard sharing Mommy and Daddy, isn't it?" Too many parents opt for "Cut it out!" "Don't throw your toys," and "You don't really hate her," which completely miss the point and make children feel they can't share their feelings with their parents. Many parents worry that acknowledging their child's negative feelings will only make them worse when, in fact, the opposite is true. Giving a child room to experience her negative feelings often makes those feeling go away.

This does not mean giving children permission to do anything they want. It is never okay to let your child hit, push, or pull another kid's hair. Children need parents to set and enforce these limits so they can feel safe in their own homes. All feelings should be permitted but behaviors should be limited.

Kids learn about feelings when their parents reflect them back. Because children are not born with a "feelings vocabulary," they need help putting words to their emotions. Dr. Haim Ginott, author of *Between Parent and Child,* observes, "Children learn about their physical likeness by seeing their image in a mirror. They learn about their emotional likeness by hearing their feelings reflected to them." Having her feelings understood and normalized frees a child to move forward developmentally so she can concentrate on other tasks. It is comforting for her to know that what she is feeling is a normal part of the human experience.

3. SET YOUR CHILD UP FOR SUCCESS.

It is not respectful to take your child out to dinner after her bedtime and expect her to "behave," to leave a crystal knickknack within your toddler's reach and expect her not to play with it (and break it!), or to give your child spaghetti with tomato sauce and get angry when she stains her clothes. It is important to recognize children's developmental capabilities and limitations and have realistic expectations.

Our kids want to be "good," even though their natural impulses sometimes get the best of them. It is important to understand that your children are not acting out a personal vendetta against you, as a parent, when they act out. In the first few years of life, your child's rational brain is so underdeveloped that her lower, more primitive brain is in control. As parent educator and BABYGROUP™ leader Allison LaTona often says, "Sometimes a child can't stop his body." In other words, sometimes the impulse to do something overrides your child's ability to stop himself, even when you think he should know better.

A perfect example of this was an experience I had at a two-year-old's birthday party. The host family had two big barrels of bottled water, juice boxes, and ice sitting on the ground for guests to take. My daughters were excited about playing with the ice and closed bottles. Next to us was an adorable little girl who was also fascinated by the shiny, slippery ice. When she reached into the barrel for another handful, her mother grabbed the child's hand and screamed, "NO! Hailey, no! Don't do that!" Of course, this extreme reaction scared the little girl. Then, instead of moving her child away from the offending ice bucket, the mother continued to stand there, watching her daughter. The temptation was too strong for poor Hailey, who couldn't stop her body or her impulses and reached for another handful of ice. This time her mother grabbed the child's face and shrieked, "No! I told you no! Look at me when I talk to you. Look at me!"

When I had the chance to speak with this mother, she told me that her daughter Hailey was only eighteen months old and that she thought the child was "out to get her" that day. There are so many things wrong with this picture. First of all, an eighteen-month-old child cannot control her impulses most of the time—even if you've seen a child this age do it on occasion, it is not a fair expectation. Second, screaming "no" at such a young child doesn't teach her anything; it just scares her. Third, the level of concentration it takes for a young child to make continual eye contact is likely to prevent her from hearing what you are actually saying and taking it in. From my point of view, it was relatively harmless to let an eighteen-month-old play with ice in a bucket at a birthday party on a hot summer day. But if the other mother didn't feel that this behavior was acceptable, it was her responsibility to remove her child from the temptation. Instead,

FROM THE EXPERTS . . .

Lousy Local Conditions

While I cannot take credit for inventing the expression *lousy local conditions*, I use it all the time. It's just so right-on-the-button.

Lousy local conditions refers to those times when a child's less than perfect behaviors are magnified or even created by the conditions of his environment. Children who have missed a nap or a meal, who went to sleep late or woke up too early, who have been dragged on too many errands, who have attended one birthday party too many, will reflect those *lousy local conditions* in their behavior, or shall we say, misbehavior. Your two-year-old, for example, isn't so good at "Don't touch!" when you visit your grandmother and her coffee-table china tea set. The environment sabotages his ability to behave. Who can resist touching the sparkly teapot?

Sometimes a child has tantrums, lots of them, because that's the stage he's in. He's learning to assert himself and is intoxicated by his

she yelled at and humiliated her daughter for doing something she instinctually wanted to do and did not yet have the ability to stop herself from doing.

4. HELP YOUR CHILD FEEL CONNECTED.

Children do better when they feel good. They are far more motivated to learn, cooperate, and be loving when they feel connected, cared about, and valued. Some parents mistakenly believe that screaming at, humiliating, hurting, or ordering around their kids will make them behave better. In fact, these tactics create a backlash. Sometimes it comes right away and sometimes it takes a few years, but, in my clinical experience, I've found that it will always haunt you: even if your child obediently follows your instructions when you use one of these harsh methods, be aware that her resentment toward you is building and her perception of you as a safe person has been seriously compromised.

Diana came to see me for a parenting consultation in my private practice. Her own parents had been harsh disciplinarians who never hesitated to scream, spank, or humiliate her. When her two-year-old daughter, Lana, resisted leaving the park, Diana screamed at her, called her a "brat," and threatened to leave her at the park alone. Lana cried so hard that Diana realized she was doing something terribly wrong. The intensity of her daughter's reaction scared Diana into my office. When a child refuses to do something you ask her to do, yelling, name-calling, and humiliation are not the way to make her do what you ask.

own power. When he is frustrated in his quest, look out for a tantrum. But when your child has an uncharacteristic tantrum or meltdown, when he is unusually uncooperative or just plain icky, it is often the result of *lousy local conditions.*

Anticipating your child's thresholds and breaking points will go a long way in avoiding tantrums. Different children have different levels of tolerance for hunger and fatigue, for crowds and new situations, for stimulation of all kinds. Different children have different *lousy local conditions.*

Craft your reasonable expectations for your child around his age, development, and particular temperament. This, coupled with acknowledging the *lousy local conditions,* will bring light at the end of the tantrum tunnel.

—Betsy Brown Braun, child development and behavior specialist, founder of Parenting Pathways, Inc., and author of *Just Tell Me What to Say* and *You're Not the Boss of Me* www.betsybrownbraun.com

Empathy creates connections and is far more likely to work. Telling your child, "I understand you want to stay at the park because you're having so much fun, but we have to go anyway," shows understanding and builds connection while still maintaining a boundary. A child who feels connected in this way is far more likely to want to please her parent than a child who is humiliated. Don't you feel the same way about your spouse? If your husband gets angry with you in public and yells at you, do you feel like working with him and being easygoing? No, you want to strike back and are likely to be too angry to cooperate. Kids are no different.

Ten Reasons Why You Should Not Spank Your Child

Although the American Academy of Pediatrics "strongly opposes striking a child" and cautions parents that spanking is "the least effective way to discipline a child," it has been estimated that 90 percent of American parents spank their children—usually out of frustration or desperation because they don't know what else to do. Here are ten good reasons why spanking your child is a bad idea. Researchers report that the more parents spank, the higher the probability of these harmful side effects:

1. **Spanking children teaches them that it's okay to hit and that hitting is an acceptable means of resolving conflict.** It is hypocritical to tell little Billy that it's not okay to hit his sister and then spank him because he did. The message he receives is that it is justifiable to use force to solve conflict, which only creates more hitting.

2. **Spanking has been shown to be harmful for cognitive development.** A two-year study by Shari Barkin, a pediatrician at the Children's Hospital at Vanderbilt University in Nashville, found that two- to nine-year-olds who were spanked developed less rapidly than other children, based on cognitive testing.

3. **Experiencing pain does not teach children to develop a conscience.** While the pain or shock of a spanking has the potential to extinguish bad behavior in the moment, it has no proven long-term positive effect. Spanking teaches children to fear spanking, not to internalize an understanding of what they did wrong so they can develop their own moral compass that might prevent them from doing the same thing in the future. Hitting your child for taking a cookie from the cookie jar doesn't teach her not to take things—it teaches her to avoid getting caught.

4. Spanking does not teach children to respect parents, but only to fear them. For a child to behave well, she needs to feel a sense of trust and security. Spanking contradicts those goals. It is possible for children to respect their parents without fearing them.

5. Spanking harms children's self-esteem. A child's self-image and self-esteem begin with how she perceives that others see her. Parents are the most important people in a child's world when it comes to the development of self-concept. Children whose parents hit them make the natural assumption that they must not be loved by the people who are "supposed" to love them the most. This harms the development of healthy self-esteem.

6. Spanking teaches children that it is okay to hit the people they love. This message has the potential to harm children's future intimate relationships by leaving them vulnerable to becoming a victim or a perpetrator of domestic violence. Studies of spanking and corporal punishment have found that children who were spanked are more likely to assault their parents, and boys who were spanked to assault their girlfriends, years later.

7. Spanking is associated with aggression and antisocial behavior. In her analysis of spanking studies, Elizabeth Gershoff found convincing evidence that spanking can lead to problems such as delinquent and antisocial behavior in childhood, along with aggression, criminal and antisocial behavior, and spousal or child abuse as an adult. The studies also link spanking with increased rates of fighting in school.

8. Children who are spanked are more anxious and fearful. A 2003 study on how brain chemistry is changed by the use of corporal punishment on children under one year of age found that those who were spanked frequently showed huge spikes in the stress hormone cortisol when subjected to new situations, such as being in the presence of a stranger after their mother had left the room. The researchers concluded that these children were more easily frightened and were generally more fearful.

9. Spanking makes it more likely that children will participate in unprotected and risky sex as an adult. In an analysis of spanking studies, it was found that spanking and other corporal punishment are associated with an increased probability of verbally and physically coercing a dating partner to have sex; risky sex such as premarital sex without using a condom; and masochistic sex such as spanking during sex.

10. Spanking is more likely to lead to abuse by the parent. In a study by the Injury Prevention Research Center, only 2 percent of mothers who didn't spank their children reported physically abusive punishment, compared with 6 percent of mothers who said they spanked their children. Spanking with an object raised the odds of abuse to 12 percent.

5. AVOID POWER STRUGGLES.

Around the age of eighteen months, children start to exert their will. They are now old enough to hold a thought or desire in their minds and are developmentally advanced enough to let those needs be known. Around this time children struggle with the emergent tasks of developing autonomy and initiative. We have all heard the infamous battle cry of the toddler, "I can do it myself!" This stage can be quite challenging for parents.

The more you attempt to control your children, the more likely you are to create power struggles. I am not advocating that you allow your children to make the rules, but I am recommending that you work with your toddler and use techniques and words that invite cooperation rather than resistance. One of the most striking characteristics of toddlers is their desire to please and help Mom and Dad. Knowing parents take advantage of this desire while allowing their children room for autonomy.

Power struggles tend to happen when you take power away from your children instead of guiding them to develop their own power in constructive ways. Your job as a parent is to teach your toddler how to focus her power in positive directions. Punishment and humiliation never accomplish this goal. Here are a few tools that will help:

Give kids the opportunity to make decisions as early as possible. Look for opportunities in infancy to let your child make choices: "Do you want the red blanket or the blue blanket?" "Do you want this pacifier or that one?" As she gets older, opportunities to make choices are constant: "Do you want to walk down the stairs or do you want me to carry you?" "Do you want peaches or pears?" Offering these choices sends a message to your child that you see her as a capable person with opinions and the ability to make decisions for herself. It also gets her into the habit of making these choices—an essential life skill.

Give two acceptable choices whenever possible. Giving your child choices gives her power and makes it much less likely that she'll fight you. It is amazing how willing young children are to cooperate when they feel *they* have the power. At the end of a playdate recently, the visiting mother noticed that her daughter had picked up one of my kid's baby dolls and was growing very attached to it. "She's going to throw a huge tantrum when I take that away from her. Things are about to get very ugly around here," she joked, anticipating her daughter's behavior from previous experiences. Then, trying to avoid a meltdown, she asked me, "Would *you* mind asking her to give the doll back?" Fortunately, she was open to other ideas. "Why don't you try asking her if she wants to hand me the doll or put it back in the toy basket before you leave?" I suggested. The other mom gave it a try and, much to her surprise, her daughter happily put the doll back in the basket and left the playdate smiling.

Remind your child that she has the power. After you have given your child two acceptable choices, remind her that the decision is up to her. Words like "You decide," "The choice is yours," "It's up to you," or "You choose" increase your child's sense of power in a healthy way—and give her less to resist.

Provide opportunities for your child to help. Because toddlers are hardwired to connect with others and to demonstrate autonomy, they often will resist a command but respond happily to requests for help. A command like "Go to the table now" is likely to be met with resistance, whereas a request like "I need your help. Would you please take the napkins to the table for me?" is likely to be met with a positive response.

Try the "as soon as" approach. Instead of the usual "We are not going to breakfast until you get your clothes on," which invites your toddler to test how long you are willing to go without breakfast, try "As soon as you have your clothes on, we can go to breakfast." The "as soon as" technique does not leave a lot for a child to resist.

Provide objective information so your child can make a decision. Instead of barking instructions like "Get your feet off the table" or, worse yet, indulging in character assassinations like "You are so rude! Get your feet off the table!" try providing objective information like "Feet belong under the table, not on the table." You can also use objective information to strengthen your family values—for example, "In our family we don't hit."

6. ESTABLISH CLEAR AND CONSISTENT BOUNDARIES.

Being respectful toward your child does not mean having no boundaries or letting her run the show. It would actually be disrespectful *not* to have rules and boundaries for your child, especially as she grows older. These structures make children feel safe, secure, and cared about while making the world more predictable and manageable. When you are driving on the road, the stop signs, traffic lights, and lines on the road make you feel safe, letting you know where to go and what is expected of you. If these guides were taken away, driving would be terrifying and unpredictable. Boundaries and rules in a family are no different, except that, unlike the rules of the road, the ones at home need to be enforced in a loving way.

Children actually want rules and boundaries. Even though they kick and scream when you enforce them, they help your kids feel that you care. But it is important to let your child know what the rules are *in advance*. As Magda Gerber points out in *Your Self-Confident Baby,* "Respect means setting boundaries for your child and for yourself as a parent, and enforcing these boundaries. It is letting your child know your expectations of her behavior so that she can cooperate and, thus, respect you."

Make sure that you mean what you say and say what you mean. Don't make empty threats. Kids are constantly testing parents to see if they are really going to enforce the rules. When they don't enforce the rules, they send the following messages to their kids:

- I don't mean what I say.
- The rules don't apply to you.
- You can't count on me.

7. DEMONSTRATE GOOD MANNERS.

Using good manners is a developmental task that requires a level of empathy and impulse control that can be quite advanced for young kids. All too often I hear parents urge their children to be polite with comments like "What's the magic word?" or "Say you're sorry!" This approach, however, only encourages the child to repeat words in order to get what she wants, which isn't respectful to anyone. It certainly doesn't teach her gratitude, compassion, or empathy—the foundations of meaningful manners.

On the other hand, *demonstrating* good manners is a great way to teach your child. I have always gone out of my way to let my husband know how much I appreciate it whenever he does something nice for me or goes above and beyond the call of fatherly duty—and I always try to do it in front of the kids. One night after my daughter Mendez, who was about two years old at the time, got sick and threw up in bed, my husband took it upon himself to go into her room, change the sheets, and comfort her. As he was leaving the room, we heard, out of the darkness, Mendez say, "Papa? Thank you for taking care of me." Her reaction was so genuine and unexpected it warmed our hearts.

8. RECOGNIZE THE POWER OF YOUR WORDS.

Parents must be careful with their words. Labels, in particular, can be damaging, disrespectful, or dismissive (e.g., "Joey's always grouchy in the morning," "Oh, that Olivia! She is a devil child!"). Judgments about a child's character often become self-fulfilling prophecies. Children, assuming that adults know more than they do, trust our assessments more than their own: a child who is labeled "shy" may eventually come to believe that she is shy. Labels also overlook a child's strengths. For example, a "shy" child can be very observant, watching people and situations before deciding how and when to act. This child really gets to know people before warming up to them and can develop some valuable attributes from this trait.

Even a seemingly positive label can be restrictive because it doesn't leave your child room to be something different. For example, you tell Emma what a "nice little girl" she is. But sometimes Emma doesn't feel so nice, especially when you bring home her new baby brother and she wants to get rid of him. The disparity between what you tell her (she is a "good" girl) and how she really feels (not so "good") can provoke considerable anxiety in a child.

When your child does something that bothers you, describe the behavior that is troubling you, not the child. You can even add a logical conclusion based on your child's actions. For example, you might say, "You threw your spoon on the floor. That makes me think you are all done with your meal," instead of saying, "You're so careless." This allows your child to differentiate between her behavior and her self-concept and even helps her to understand the consequences of her actions.

The damage done by name-calling and inappropriate nicknames can stay with a child for life. Whenever I talk about this issue during a parenting lecture, inevitably one or two parents admit to using a name or word that is harmful to their child, like the mother who admitted calling her child "stupid" or the father who called his big-boned daughter "The Mack Truck." A parent's words have the power to build and strengthen or they can devastate and destroy a child's self-esteem and sense of self.

9. GIVE KIDS TRANSITION TIME.

Children, especially toddlers, move at their own pace. Their rhythms are much slower than ours, especially when they are absorbed in an activity they enjoy. Giving them two warnings before you stop an activity and start a new one will prepare them for the shift and make the transition much smoother: "In five minutes we are going to stop painting and start putting the supplies away so you can take a bath." Two minutes later, remind the child again: "In three more minutes we are going to stop painting and start putting the supplies away so you can take a bath." Sometimes a child is so absorbed in an activity that she may not hear you or may choose to ignore you. In this case, get down at her eye level and speak to her clearly. If she still is not paying attention, a gentle hand on her back or shoulder can get her attention. When it is time, let her know and give her a moment to transition to the next activity.

Many parents finding that singing a song can smooth transitions from one activity to the next. For example, at our house we sing the "Clean Up" song during clean-up time:

Clean up, clean up,
Everybody, everywhere.
Clean up, clean up,
Everybody do your share.

Many parents create their own songs. A friend of mine sings the "Bye-Bye" song when saying good-bye to one activity and starting another. Once your child is old enough to sing the words, singing can help her feel like she is part of a group experience, making the transition even easier.

10. SAY "NO" WITHOUT SAYING "NO."

Kids need boundaries and limits. Saying "no" to your child helps build her character and provides discipline. It teaches her to tolerate not getting what she wants and to handle delayed gratification—and ultimately it will teach her how to say "no" to herself ("Do I really want that second piece of chocolate cake even though I am full? No, I think I'll pass on that." Or "I'm tired—maybe I'll skip calculus today. No, actually that's not in my best interest. I should go to class"). That said, you should never say "no" to your child just for the sake of saying "no" because that would be disrespectful.

I say "no" twenty times a day but I almost never say the actual word "no." Why? If you say "no" all day long, the word loses its significance and power, and kids start to tune it out. I save "no" for a child who is reaching to touch a hot stove or about to run out into traffic. Used selectively, "no" is taken very seriously.

A study done by Drs. Betty Hart and Todd Risley found that three-year olds who were exposed to constant reprimands such as *"No," "Don't,"* and *"Stop it"* had poorer language skills than kids who received less negative feedback. They also had lower IQs—perhaps because they were exposed to less language. If you just say "no," your child hears one word, whereas if you say, "Please don't do that" or "How about if we play with this toy instead?" you're exposing her to multiple words, increasing both language development and IQ.

Here are ten ways to say "no" without actually saying "no":

- Tell your child what she *can* do instead.
- Try "I won't let you because . . . "
- Distract and redirect.
- Substitute an acceptable object for an unacceptable one.
- Offer two viable choices.
- Clarify the rules.
- Explain your reasoning using age-appropriate language and examples.
- Postpone the request.
- Use humor.
- Validate the desire behind the request without granting the request.

One other tip: Baby-proof the rooms in the house that your child has access to and you won't have to say "no" quite as much.

SuperBaby Paci Tip

A pacifier is not a plug. It should be used to soothe a child and help her calm herself, not shut her up. Crying is how babies communicate, and parents need to give them room to express themselves. Instead of distracting your baby or trying to shut her up, try reflecting back what you see:

"You seem really uncomfortable."

"You really don't want to have your diaper changed right now."

"You didn't want to get out of the bathtub! It's cold."

"The loud noise surprised you!"

You Shouldn't Feel That Way!

Helping your child identify and express feelings verbally is part of a respectful relationship and helps fulfill your duties as your child's emotional coach. Children who are able to express their feelings in words are much less likely to act out in destructive ways.

Many parents worry that listening to their children's negative emotions will validate those emotions and encourage their children to feel bad or hurt others. But validating your child's feelings gives her the freedom to feel without acting on those feelings. It also allows her to have ownership of the experience.

All feelings are valid, even if parents don't understand them—or even accept the underlying emotion. When it comes to feelings, the worst thing a parent can say is "You shouldn't feel that way." In my first book, *The A to Z Guide to Raising Happy, Confident Kids,* I gave five reasons never to say those five nasty words:

- Your child now feels "bad" about having certain feelings.

- Children open up to you, searching for understanding and compassion. Telling them they shouldn't feel a certain way shuts them down and makes them feel misunderstood.

- Feelings that are free to be expressed and explored don't get acted out in destructive ways.

- Being told to stop feeling a certain way doesn't change the fact that that's the way the child is feeling. So now, in addition to feeling bad, your child feels frustrated and guilty about experiencing her natural emotions.

- Energy that is wasted trying to repress feelings is not available for more beneficial activities.

Respectful Communication in Action

The way we communicate with our children is profound. Simple word choices completely change our children's perception. The following are some effective methods for reflecting children's feelings, maintaining boundaries, and communicating respectfully. These easy-to-use scripts can be used over and over again in all kinds of situations that typically arise in the first three years. Start using these scripts from the beginning, to get in the habit, and your child will benefit from this kind of respectful communication as she grows up. All these scenarios and responses come from parents' real-life experiences with their kids.

FROM THE EXPERTS . . .

Toddler-ese

You can translate anything you want into a young child's native language with 3 simple steps: short phrases, lots of repetition, and mirroring about one third of your child's level of emotion with your tone of voice and gestures (you don't want to be too dramatic, or too subdued . . . it's what I call getting in the "sweet spot!"). Speaking in this way is necessary because when a toddler is upset her left brain (the language center of her thinking) shuts down . . . so she can only understand very simple language. In fact, most parents find it quite natural to speak in this more primitive way when their children are very happy. (Have you ever found yourself cheering your child's thrill of accomplishment by saying, "Yea! Yea! You did it! Wow! Wow! Good job!" . . . Well, that is *Toddler-ese)*. But, for some reason we tend to speak almost like bad psychiatrists when our children are upset. Our voices get too calm and monotone . . . and it makes our little kids think we don't really understand how they feel. Save your good, calm explanation and discussion for your child AFTER he begins to calm down.

Here's how Terri, mother of a three-year-old named Billy, describes putting *Toddler-ese* to work in her home:

"Despite my initial embarrassment about looking silly, I have been using *Toddler-ese* to calm Billy's tantrums daily since I learned it six

Situation: Your baby cries as you are changing her diaper.

Instead of saying: "You're okay."

Try this: Narrate what you see. "I hear you crying. You sound really upset. I get the feeling you don't want me to change your diaper. I will try to change it as fast as I can so you are not uncomfortable for long."

Why: In that moment your child isn't okay. If you were upset and your friend told you "You're okay," you would not feel heard. Narrating the experience your child is having allows her to know that you hear and respect her feelings. You are still holding the boundary (i.e., she is still having her diaper changed), but you are doing it with compassion. By reflecting her feelings, you also teach her how to be empathic, which helps in the development of emotional intelligence.

Situation: Your child drops a toy on the ground and has a meltdown.

Instead of saying: "Get over it! It's just a toy!"

months ago. Now, I've gotten so good at it that I can quell most major meltdowns in seconds.

"His tantrums usually follow this pattern: He starts to scream and cry at the top of his lungs. I jump in, almost matching his feelings with a 'broken record' kind of repetition of his words and emotions. If I stop too soon, he starts crying again, and I restart the *Toddler-ese.* 'Billy is still mad, mad, MAD!!!! He's angrrrrrrrry!!! Billy says, No, no, no . . . NO!!!' If he stops screaming and looks puzzled, but remains calm, that's my signal to go to the next step and start distracting him or offering some solutions.

"Initially, Billy's tantrum would last almost five minutes. Now he still needs a couple of minutes of attention when he's upset, but as soon as I start mirroring a bit of his feelings with *Toddler-ese,* he usually stops the tantrum right away!"

These steps may sound a bit bizarre or require a lot of effort, but with a little practice they'll actually save you a ton of time and aggravation. In my experience, by translating your message of caring, attention, and love into *Toddler-ese,* you should be able to quickly settle at least 50% of your toddler's tantrums . . . in a minute or less. And . . . you will quickly boost even the easiest toddler's patience and cooperation!

—Harvey Karp, MD, FAAP, is the author of the best-selling books and DVDs *The Happiest Baby on the Block* and *The Happiest Toddler on the Block* www.happiestbaby.com

Try this: "I see you dropped your toy. You seem really upset! You look like you weren't done playing with it."
Why: Sure, to you or me, it is just a toy that fell on the ground, but to your child, this is genuinely upsetting. Demonstrating empathy is far more likely to help her calm down and to feel heard. By responding to her in this way, you become a safe and understanding source of comfort to her.

Situation: Your toddler does not want to climb into her booster chair.
Instead of saying: "Get in your chair, now!"
Try this: "Do you want to climb in or do you want Mom to put you in?"
Why: This gives the power back to your child while still setting the limit. Now there is less reason for her to resist. If she still refuses to get in the booster chair, you might say, "It looks like you are not hungry. Maybe you are too tired to eat. Your choices are chair or crib. You choose." If she cannot choose, let her know

that if she is unable to reach a decision on her own, Mommy will decide for her. Let her know she has until the count of three (count slowly) and then you will decide for her. She may genuinely be too tired to make a decision.

Situation: You've asked your toddler to come to bed and she is running around her bedroom like a wild child.
Instead of saying: "Settle down! I told you to get in bed!"
Try this: "I see you are having trouble stopping your body. It looks like you need me to help you."
Why: Toddlers are not always able to stop their bodies. Their impulses and need to move are greater than their ability to stop themselves. Sometimes they need some gentle help. It is not fair to get angry with a young child who is not yet equipped with the development skills you're asking her to use.

Situation: You have given your child some cookies and, after finishing what you gave her, she wants more. But you don't want her to have more.
Instead of saying: "No! You can't have any more. You've had enough!"
Try this: "I know you really want more cookies. You can have more tomorrow. If you are still hungry, you can have more of the food on your plate."
Why: You don't want to create a sense of scarcity around food, which can make it

---

FROM THE EXPERTS . . .

Basic *Love* and *Logic*® Consequences

How early in your child's life can you start using Love and Logic?

As soon as she can spit her pureed food and crawl away from you when you are changing her diaper. Fortunately, the basic process is very simple:

Step one: Pray for misbehavior.
Mistakes made early in life have far more affordable consequences than those made later.

Step two: Sing an empathetic "Uh oh."
The fewer words you use when your kids are acting up, the more successful you will be.

Step three: Provide a loving consequence.
There are only three basic consequences for small children. After saying, "Uh, oh," do one of the following:

more likely a child will hoard food or develop an eating disorder later. Also, you don't want to use food to create power struggles. Letting her know that she can have more food if she is still hungry reminds her that eating is about feeding her body and there is still more food available if she wants it.

Situation: Your son does a great job cleaning up after playtime.
Instead of saying: "What a good boy!"
Try this: As a variation of "I see, etc.," you can say, "You put all your toys away! You even put all your books in the basket where they belong!"
Why: The implication is that he is a "good" boy for putting away his toys, so if he doesn't, he must be a "bad" boy. The words "good" and "bad" connote moral judgment. Children are not "bad" because they don't do what we ask. A child who is labeled "good" can feel as if he duped his parents when he does something not so "good." He may also avoid taking a risk, like putting a toy away if he isn't sure where it goes, because he doesn't want to lose the title of "good boy." You are better off describing what you see. This makes your child feel seen and valued.

Situation: On a playdate at Sally's house, your child takes a toy out of Sally's hands.
Instead of saying: "Be nice!"

- Change your location by walking away and paying no attention to them, if appropriate.

- Change the location of the problem object by taking it away, if appropriate.

- Change your child's location by carrying her into her room, or buckling her into her stroller, etc., if appropriate. Expect your child to have a fit over this. It is an indication that the consequence is felt. It is not an indication that she is being hurt or ruined in some way.

Step four: Repeat as needed.
When you repeat this basic process with great consistency, you'll find that you only get to the second step most of the time. Very quickly, your tots learn that "Uh oh" means it's wise to start acting sweet!

—Jim Fay and Dr. Charles Fay,
co-authors of the *Love and Logic* series
www.loveandlogic.com

Try this: "You took that toy from Sally. I don't think she was done with it. Let's give it back and ask Sally if we can play with it when she is done." If your child resists giving the toy back, give her two acceptable options: "Do you want to give the toy back to Sally yourself or do you need my help doing that?"

Why: While some children as young as eighteen months understand the concept of ownership, children don't fully grasp the idea of sharing until they are closer to three years old. To a child, property is an extension of herself. Would you want to share your arm? Shaming your child into sharing only creates negative feelings. Explain that the toy belongs to Sally and that your child needs to ask before taking it.

Situation: Your baby pulled his (breathable) lovey over his eyes and is crying.

Instead of: Just removing it for him.

Try saying: "You pulled your lovey over your eyes and now you can't see. If you take it off your eyes, I think you may feel better."

Why: To respect your child is to believe in his competence. Let him figure things out at his own pace and believe in his ability to solve problems. As long as the lovey is not hurting him, preventing him from breathing, or really frightening him, you should give him a little room to figure out the problem, based on the abilities he has demonstrated. I admit this situation has been challenging for me. It is a parent's natural instinct to jump in and solve problems for their children, but this only teaches them that they have to look to others to solve their problems. Overcoming obstacles makes children stronger and reinforces their belief in themselves. It can help to have a supportive voice cheering them on while they figure things out. Do your best to wait and give your child the room to figure out a problem before stepping in to help. As Magda Gerber says, "If you overreact, it's hard to do less after."

Situation: At a playdate, your child hits another kid over the head with a toy, resulting in tears.

Instead of saying: "Say you're sorry!"

Try this: "You hit Carley over the head with that toy. She looks really upset. What can you do to help her feel better? Let's ask her what we can do to help her."

Why: Forcing a child to say "I'm sorry" does not magically make her feel sorry. Making children say they are sorry when they don't really feel sorry teaches them to be insincere. It teaches them that what matters is saying something that will make people shut up, even if it is a lie. Encouraging your child to help the injured party teaches him about making amends and helping others.

Situation: Your child throws her food on the floor.

Instead of saying: "Stop it!"

Try this: "When you throw food on the floor, it makes me think that you are done eating. It you do it again, the meal will be over."

Why: When children first get to sit in a high chair, they are curious to see what happens when they drop food. By following the recommended script, you let your child know the consequences of the action, you set up a rule, and you put the power back in her court. She can choose to end the meal by throwing food on the floor, but it is her choice. If she has a meltdown after you remove her from the high chair, your job is to hold your ground, but reflect her feelings ("I know you weren't done and you wanted to stay in your chair. We can try again at lunch"). If you follow through with the stated consequence, the odds are that the situation won't happen again for quite some time.

Respectful Communication Don'ts

- **Don't talk about your child when she is in the room with you** as if she were not there. Instead, let her know you are going to share a story about her.

- **Don't threaten your child.** Threats are an invitation for her to misbehave.

- **Don't use bribes.** Your child will come to expect treats for behaving properly.

- **Don't use sarcasm, insults, or criticism.** They prevent learning and erode self-esteem.

- **Don't laugh at your child.** Nobody likes being laughed at, especially by people who are supposed to care about you.

- **Don't make negative comparisons,** especially between siblings. They only create resentment.

- **Don't use baby talk.** It sends the message that you have low expectations for communication from your child.

- **Don't scold or correct improper use of language.** It discourages children from speaking and makes them feel that you are not really hearing them.

- **Don't spell in front of a child** with the intention of keeping her from understanding what you are saying. It is the adult equivalent of people whispering behind your back. The same goes for using a foreign language your child doesn't understand.

- **Don't horseplay with your child.** Throwing children in the air and tickling them is taking advantage of your physical strength and power.

Situation: Your toddler peed in the potty for the first time.

Instead of saying: "I'm so proud of you!"

Try this: "You must be so proud of yourself!"

Why: You want to encourage your child to be internally motivated. Ideally she pees in the potty because she gains a sense of mastery and that makes her feel good, not because she wants to please you.

Internal vs. External Motivation

Most parents raise their child to make choices based on outside approval, fooling themselves into believing that since that approval is geared toward adults—mother, father, teacher, nanny, babysitter, etc.—it must be okay. But by raising kids who are constantly looking for external approval, we hinder the development of their reasoning abilities. It may make your life easier in the short run to have

FROM THE EXPERTS ...

Non-Punitive Discipline

What do you think of when you hear the word "discipline"? Most people think of punishment. I invite you to think a little deeper, starting with the exploration of the long-term results of punishment.

When children are punished they do not learn self-discipline. Punishment provides "external" motivation. Self-discipline requires "inner" motivation. When children are punished they either comply to avoid the punishment (and may become approval junkies), they get sneaky and do all they can to avoid getting caught, or they blatantly rebel—resulting in endless power-struggles with their parents. Then parents complain about the behavior of their children without taking responsibility for their part—how they invited the power struggles by using ineffective discipline methods (punishment).

Positive Discipline does not advocate any form of punishment—no punitive time-out or grounding, no withdrawal of privileges, no yelling, no lectures, no threatening, no spanking, no rewards, no praise.

At this point you may be wondering two things: "What else is there?" and "Wait a minute; praise and rewards aren't punishment." Praise and rewards are not punishment but they are external motivators, which do not teach self-discipline, self-control, and the desire to make a contribution based on inner motivation.

an obedient child, but that obedient child becomes an easily influenced teenager. Barbara Coloroso describes this phenomenon in her book *Kids Are Worth It!*

> From the time he was young, he dressed the way you told him to dress; he acted the way you told him to act; he said the things you told him to say. He's been listening to somebody else tell him what to do. . . . He hasn't changed. He is still listening to somebody else tell him what to do. The problem is, it isn't you anymore; it's his peers. The kid hasn't learned *how* to think.

If that doesn't send chills up and down your spine, I don't know what will.

In the first three years, children's identities are in a fragile state of development. Their ability to judge and their belief systems are just beginning to develop. When we, as parents, push our kids to blindly do what authority tells them to do, we teach them to be compliant; we don't teach them to develop their own inner compass or establish their own sense of right and wrong.

In answer to what else is there, that is what Positive Discipline is all about—providing many non-punitive parenting tools that follow two basic guidelines: 1) Create a connection before correction, 2) Correction usually involves children in focusing on solutions.

There are many specific parenting tools that meet these basic guidelines. I'll mention a few:

- **Family Meetings:** where children learn to give and receive compliments and to brainstorm for solutions to family challenges that have been put on the agenda.
- **Curiosity Questions:** where parents invite children to think instead of telling them what to think.
- **Validating Feelings:** to help children feel supported without needing to be rescued or fixed.
- **Positive Time-out:** to help children learn self-soothing by creating a place that helps them feel better (so they can access their rational brains).
- **Routine Charts:** created by children so they feel motivated to follow the routines they have created (or at least helped create).

These are just a few of the many Positive Discipline tools that invite children to develop a sense of capability and use their personal power in constructive ways.

—Jane Nelsen, EdD, author and co-author of the *Positive Discipline* series
www.positivediscipline.com

The Problem with Praise

I knew I was becoming a praise junkie when I found myself saying, "That was a great fart!" to one of my infants, who shall remain nameless. The truth is, I thought it was great! I still can't believe that a child I made has working parts, so to me every bodily function is a miracle. Not to mention that, just like any parent, I think my kids are extraordinary. But no sooner had I heard the words come out of my mouth than I read a series of studies by psychologist Dr. Carol Dweck of Columbia University that changed my approach to praise.

In a study of fourth graders, Dr. Dweck gave a simple test to the students. When they finished, they were given their scores and a single line of praise. Half were praised for their intelligence ("You must be smart at this") and half were praised for their effort ("You must have worked really hard"). Then the students were given a choice between an easier and a more difficult puzzle for the second round. Of the children who were praised for their effort, 90 percent chose the more difficult puzzle, while the majority of the children praised for intelligence chose the easier one.

In another study done by Dr. Dweck with fifth graders, the children were given a test designed for a much higher grade level and were expected to fail. The researchers found that students who were praised for their effort on this test assumed they simply hadn't focused hard enough, whereas the students praised for their intelligence assumed they weren't really smart at all. When they were given a second round of tests, the group praised for their effort improved by 30 percent and the students praised for intelligence actually did 20 percent worse than they had done on the original test.

Dr. Dweck's studies speak to the importance of parents focusing on process over outcome, as well as the perils of praise. According to Dr. Dweck, "emphasizing effort gives children a variable they can control. They come to see themselves as in control of their success." She believes that labeling a child "smart" doesn't prevent her from underperforming—in fact, it may encourage or predispose her to underperform. Children who are given the "smart" label become so concerned with maintaining that image that they are not willing to take a risk or fail—experiences that are important to the process of learning.

There is mounting concern from experts that the rise in unmerited praise is creating a generation of narcissists. A 2006 study that administered the Narcissistic Personality Inventory to more than 16,000 college students found that two-thirds had above-average scores—a 30 percent hike above a similar sampling taken in 1982. When young people who are accustomed to receiving praise and being constantly rewarded enter the workforce, they are in for a rude awakening. As a result, they are likely to have trouble performing and ultimately keeping a job. More and more employers are finding that the young generations entering the workforce are so accustomed to constant praise, and feel so entitled, that they are difficult to manage. Unwilling to pay their dues and unable to function without constant praise, these young workers have been hindered by a generation of parents who misunderstood the self-esteem movement and thought that praise was the answer.

This doesn't mean that parents should stop offering their children positive feedback altogether. To go to the opposite extreme could be just as detrimental. The key for parents is to give thoughtful praise, which reflects an awareness of their children's efforts and process.

Ten Rules for Effective Praise

1. Be *very* specific. Generalized praise ("Good job!" "Great work!" "Smart thinking!") or praise that is devoid of specific details is useless. In fact, it is actually detrimental because it leaves children hungry for the next parent-approved praise goodie. Instead of creating their own internal motivation, kids focus on getting the next "fix." Children who get a lot of generalized praise grow to rely on it. The litmus test for specific praise is to ask yourself if the words you're using could only be said to *this* person at *this* time. You can say "Good job!" to your garbage collector, your husband, the person bagging your groceries, or even your dog. To say "You were so patient on the potty! You waited until all the pee came out!" is specific and meaningful to your child.

2. Make it about the process or the effort, not the outcome, accomplishment, character, or personality. Use words that describe instead of evaluate. "You made your hand so steady that you were able to pile the blocks really high!"

3. Be genuine and believable. Don't praise for the sake of praise. Kids need to know that they can trust you and that you are giving them an honest appraisal of their actions. When your toddler can barely take two steps without falling, telling her that she is a "great walker" is not sincere—but telling her you see how hard she is working to stay on her feet is.

4. Thank instead of praise. Recognize when your child has done something that has been truly difficult, given her level of development. "Thank you for being patient while I made lunch. I know you were really hungry and it must have been hard to wait so long."

5. Encourage instead of praise. Praise is conditional, but encouragement is unconditional. When your child is first learning to crawl, saying, "That's it! You can do it! Just move your hand forward a little . . . you got it!" is encouraging.

6. Try a "you" statement. This type of statement verbalizes what you have observed. "You handed me the book, just like I asked!"

7. Try an "I" statement, which lets your child know how her behavior makes you feel. "I felt like you really appreciated my cooking when you said you thought breakfast was 'yummy.'"

8. Let her know how her actions affect others. "When your sister was crying and you brought her a teddy bear, that really helped her feel better."

9. Try a nonverbal acknowledgement. Sometimes just a smile or a nod can let your child know that you saw what she did.

10. Overheard praise is the one exception to the "don't talk about your child as if she were not in the room" rule. Overhearing praise from an adult can be particularly powerful. "Bobby knows where every one of his toys belongs and during clean-up time he is able to put them all away by himself!"

Children need their parents to mirror positive, yet accurate reflections of who they are. We owe it to our kids not to pay lip service to them by giving false compliments. Often parents resort to saying things they don't believe to be true because they don't want their child to feel bad, but an important part of developing a sense of self is developing the ability to realistically evaluate situations as well as your self—skills that are best modeled by parents.

You Got Me!

Responding to Cues

S itting at her neighborhood Starbucks with her four-month-old son, Cayden, in her arms, Susan leans toward him and smiles as he starts to fuss. She tickles his chin, calls his name, and waves some toys in front of his face. Instead of returning her gaze, he turns his head away from her, grimacing, and arching his back—an indication that he is overstimulated. Unable to read his cues, Susan continues to add to his distress by trying to engage him instead of removing him from the busy, noisy, brightly lit coffee house.

In a toddler gym class across town, Irina is playing with her eighteen-month-old daughter, Ana, who is having fun pushing herself on a tricycle and playing with toys. When it comes time to put the toys and tricycle away, Ana has a meltdown and starts to cry. Fed up with the tears, Irina ignores Ana's distress and starts chatting with the other mothers in the group instead. When Ana throws herself to the ground at Irina's feet in a tantrum, her mother ignores her blatant cues, missing the opportunity to help her daughter learn to identify and manage her feelings.

Across the street, Janice takes her two-and-a-half-year-old daughter, Alecia, shopping for a new dress. This is the fourth store they have gone to in the last hour and they are running late to get home for Alecia's nap. She is rubbing her eyes and whining about not wanting to go into another store and, after about twenty minutes in this store, she starts pulling clothes off the rack and throwing them on the floor. Having missed the chance to acknowledge her daughter's feelings and take her home for the nap she needs, the frustrated mom loses her cool and yells at her instead.

How you respond to your child, especially in the first three years, is the single greatest determinant of his perception of the world. Is it safe? Can I trust the people who love me? Will my needs be responded to? Do I make a difference? Am I lovable? Children count on a responsive and nurturing relationship with their primary caregiver, usually Mom but sometimes Dad, for healthy emotional development.

Responding appropriately to a child's cues is one of a parent's most important roles. This responsibility can be scary and confusing for first-time parents who often struggle to understand what a preverbal baby is trying to communicate. Children whose cues are responded to and whose needs are consistently met develop secure attachments, which allow them to feel safe in the world. They don't have to waste mental and emotional energy worrying if anyone will feed them, change their diapers, or help them when they are not feeling well. They are able to trust that their basic needs will be met, allowing for more sophisticated learning to take place.

Mirror, Mirror on the Wall

Parents are the psychological mirrors that children use to define themselves. Since infants are born without a sense of self, they need their parents to help them figure out who they are and how they fit in the world. As children grow older and their world becomes bigger, they discover more mirrors, seeing themselves reflected in people they come across every day—friends, relatives, teachers, child-care workers. However, for better or for worse, the parents' words and actions have the most influence in creating the foundation for a child's sense of self.

Human interaction is the essence of a baby's environment. Although most adults don't have conscious memories of their childhood prior to the age of five, we store the general impressions we formed of the world from those crucial, early years deep in our psyche. Babies who are responded to sensitively and consistently grow to expect responsiveness from others. This healthy expectation helps them learn to regulate their emotions because they have the security of knowing that someone can help them bring their intense emotional states (and any parent can confirm that infants have a lot of intense feelings!) back to a comfortable level. For example, when a baby feels overwhelmed and starts to cry, his mother notices his crying, picks him up, and soothes him until he calms down. Through this seemingly ordinary experience of having someone calm him down, the baby learns how to do it for himself.

The experience of being comforted also sends a message to a baby that he is worthy of comforting. Because his parents are so omnipotent in a child's life, he naturally believes that his parents treat him the way he *deserves* to be treated, a message that he internalizes. As Dr. William Sears puts it so succinctly in his book, *The Successful Child,* "What children believe about themselves is at the heart of what they become."

FOUR TYPICAL BABY CUES

Baby's Physical or Emotional State	Signs	
Hunger	• Displays rooting behaviors	• Chews on hand
	• Makes mouth movements	• Puts things in mouth
	• Furrows brow	• Cries
Tiredness	• Rubs eyes	• Fusses
	• Cries	• Clenches fists
	• Yawns	• Pulls on ear*
Interest	• Makes eye contact with you	• Opens eyes wide
	• Looks at objects	• Smiles
	• Reaches for objects	• Makes vocalizations
Overstimulation	• Turns away	• Arches or twists body**
	• Cries or is fussy	• Eyes look glazed
	• Grabs hands or body to comfort self	• Kicks or waves
		• Grimaces
	• Hiccups	• Sticks out tongue

*Rule out an ear infection with your doctor
**Rule out reflux with your doctor

The Chemistry of Love

It is believed that early attachment experiences in life are the most crucial in organizing basic structures of the brain. Early experiences of having our needs accurately responded to not only creates characteristic ways of relating to others, but actually forms psychological and neurological patterns as well. In other words, a child whose cries are consistently responded to in a negative way—he is yelled at, for example, or abused or neglected—is likely to become anxious in anticipation of a negative reaction from his parents. Each time he has a need, it creates a stress response, resulting in an overall elevated level of stress hormones—essentially wiring the child's brain for anxiety. He then becomes an adult who views the world as an unsafe place where his needs are unlikely to be met. On the flip side, a child whose cues are consistently responded to in a loving manner is likely to feel secure and better able to calm himself down and trust people. This child enters the world anticipating that people will be friendly and helpful.

Loving attention from a primary caregiver, like Mom or Dad, decreases the impact of life's stresses on the brain by creating more cortisol receptors. When a baby experiences stress, the adrenal glands release cortisol—which needs receptors to receive it in order to keep the hippocampus from getting flooded with cortisol. An abundance of cortisol receptors means that a child is better prepared for future stressors—wearing a wet diaper too long or taking a difficult test in school—because he is more able to recover. Bonding experiences provided by positive interactions with caregivers enhance the growth and development of neural networks that support attachment relationships, regulate emotions, and assist in problem solving, making those tasks more likely to occur successfully.

Dunstan Baby Language

Priscilla Dunstan, a mother with a special gift for sound, found she was able to pick out certain sound patterns in her baby's cries. Dunstan claims that all babies use five different "words" in the first three months of life to communicate their needs, regardless of race and culture. She says that if the parents do not respond to those sounds, the child will stop using them. Here are the five sounds:

Neh = I'm hungry.

Owh = I'm tired.

Heh = I am in discomfort.

Eairh = I have lower gas.

Eh = I have upper gas (like a burp).

If you are able to hear these subtle sound differences (I was not but my husband was), learning to distinguish between them is a great way to tune in to your child.

Did you ever wonder why it feels so good to both children and parents to have loving interactions? Attachment experiences are correlated with increased production of oxytocin, prolactin, endorphins, and dopamine. If those biochemicals sound familiar, it's because they are the same ones that are activated in addiction. You could even say that your love is addictive for your child, but in a very healthy way! It is through the early dance of interaction—coos, touch, smiles, eye contact, and babbling—that collaborative communication is established, allowing a parent and child to tune in to each other.

Ten Things That Prevent Parents from Responding to Their Baby's Cues

I have to admit, I am not a baby person. I spend my days in my psychotherapy practice talking to people and communicating verbally. This, I like to believe, is what I do best. During my pregnancy, the prospect of dealing with a human being, much less twins, who could not communicate with words and would not be able to understand me sent shivers up and down my spine. I was filled with anxiety that I would not know the difference between hungry, tired, and gassy cries. I think that my anxiety about reading cues properly and being the "perfect parent" was my biggest barrier to reading my daughters' cues. It is important to know what *your* biggest challenges are in this area because, if you are aware of them, you can overcome them. Here are ten of the most common issues:

1. Electronic distractions. Today's children have to compete against Blackberries, televisions, iPods, video games, email, texting, instant messaging, and laptops for their parent's attention. All these distractions prevent parents from tuning in to their children and giving them the one-on-one focus that they need. If you walk into your child's room holding your cell phone, you are not prepared to give him your undivided attention. While I recognize that it might be difficult to never bring a phone into your child's room, it is a good idea to enforce some "no tech" times. As a working mom, I have tried very hard to keep our family's morning time, mealtimes, and nighttime rituals free of distraction. During these times I do not bring a cell phone into my children's room or answer the home phone unless I am expecting an urgent call, in which case I let my kids know in advance that we might be interrupted. It was not easy to make these "no tech" times a habit, but realizing that just about anything can wait an hour or two, until I am done with our family time, has made this commitment easier.

2. Not enough one-on-one time. Getting to know your child and becoming attuned to him means spending quiet time alone together without distractions.

I recommend spending time with each child in your family every day as well as enjoying special time together when you take your child out to do a much loved activity or go to a favorite place (as soon as you are getting enough sleep to stand up straight) so that it becomes a regular habit in your parenting repertoire. Focus on connection, engagement, listening, observation, and interaction while allowing your child to lead. For example, for infants and toddlers, one-on-one time should be spent down on the floor so that you are on your child's level, "joining him in his world and on his terms," as Dr. Stanley Greenspan says.

3. Overstimulation and overengaging. In an attempt to raise smart children, many parents give their kids too much stimulation too early, showering them with lots of "educational toys," DVDs, and music. One mother who attended one of my parenting lectures told me that she was playing Mozart literally twenty-four hours a day to stimulate her child's brain development! The poor kid never got a moment of peace and quiet! A lot of parents overdo it by playing with their kids way too much, surrounding them with too many people, and not giving them time to be by themselves. All this constant noise and well-intentioned stimulation are distracting and can drive a wedge between you and your child, preventing you from tuning into each other in a satisfying way.

4. Labels. Labels prevent us from fully seeing all the complexities and nuances of who our children really are. Good and bad, labels impose limitations, and the associations and value judgments attached to them can prove very difficult for children to break out of. Also, they prevent you from seeing characteristics that may contradict the label. For example, my toddler daughter Mendez is very vigilant. She really checks people out and gets to know them before she cozies up to them; as a result, she is an excellent judge of character. Another family might say she is "shy," but to give her that label would miss the strengths that are inherent in her choices. Worse, giving her that label might become self-fulfilling, creating a negative connotation that could be detrimental. Labels such as "fussy," "difficult," or "stubborn" prevent parents from accurately reading their children's cues and define the kids in a narrow, limiting, negative way. Even seemingly "good" labels can cause harm. The child who is always told how "smart" he is can become so afraid of making a mistake or saying the wrong thing that this seemingly "good" label becomes restricting.

5. Projection. Projection occurs when we transfer our own feelings onto someone else, causing us to overlook that person's experience. For example, Sarah's three-month-old daughter Elizabeth was having a difficult time settling down and became increasingly frustrated by her inability to calm down and fall asleep. Sarah was also getting frustrated and felt like a "bad mom." These feelings made her angry, but at the same time, she didn't feel it was okay to be angry with her beautiful baby girl, so she pushed those feelings away. When Sarah's husband asked her what was going on, she told him, "Elizabeth is angry at me because I am such a bad mom"—a statement that she truly believed. Projections like Sarah's prevent you from clearly seeing your children's needs and accurately reading their cues. If Sarah hadn't projected her own feelings onto Elizabeth, she would have been able to see and respond to what her daughter truly needed.

6. Anxiety and fear. Like so many other first-time parents, I really struggled with anxiety and fear—two powerful emotions that make it very hard to accurately read and tend to your child's cues. The most typical fears and anxieties in the first three years include being an inadequate parent, being separated from your child, dropping your baby, sudden infant death syndrome (SIDS), autism, choking hazards, and not being able to provide financially for your newly expanded family. The greatest antidote for these completely normal fears is to focus on the present and live in the moment with your child, rather than worrying about what might happen in the future. This allows you to focus on and better read your child's cues, so you can be a more responsive and confident parent.

7. Parent's own traumas. Parents who have had a difficult or abusive childhood can find it especially challenging to tune into their own children's needs

FROM THE EXPERTS . . .

Emotional Intelligence

In essence, Emotional Intelligence (EQ) is bringing intelligence to your emotional life by knowing who you are, what you're feeling, and how to identify and manage your emotions in relation to others. It is widely held that emotional intelligence is the key to success and happiness.

Because we now know the degree to which experience shapes the brain, we know how much parenting impacts a child's EQ. The first two decades of life are a critical window of opportunity to help children feel right, which in turn assists them in thinking clearly and behaving well.

The cornerstone of EQ is the ability to self-soothe and self-regulate. Parents can help—first by noticing and accepting their children's emotional experience and then by helping them label their feelings. You may first need to de-escalate your child's intense emotions by encouraging calming breaths, for instance. Then it's important to narrate what happened from his

without judgment or strong reactions. Resolving these traumas is particularly important in order to be an attentive and loving parent. A parent who has not resolved her own difficult past is likely to inflict trauma on her own children. If your childhood cries were met with violence, it is likely that you will treat your own child the way you were treated, instead of tuning into what he really needs. Even under these circumstances, children create attachments to their parents because they are dependent on them, but the attachment is confusing, disorganized, and ultimately unhealthy.

8. Life distractions. Life and its stresses can pull you in many directions, making it very difficult to put the day's difficulties aside in order to focus on your kids. Maybe you keep obsessing about that nasty comment your boss made, or you're worried about how you're going to pay the mortgage this month, or you can't shake the resentment you feel because your husband left his underwear on the floor. It is all too easy not to be present when you are with your child. But your focused, undistracted attention to your child is crucial for his development. Staying in the moment with him will help sensitize you to his cues.

9. Depression and postpartum depression. The stresses of giving birth, along with sleep deprivation and other pressures, leave women hormonally

---

point of view and express empathy with his situation. Your child learns from you that the full landscape of human emotions is acceptable, legitimate, and tolerable: you understand his feelings rather than seeking to "fix" them. Your reaction gives your child the respect he deserves and the time he needs to make sense of his emotions and integrate them into a healthy sense of identity. Your child feels safe, supported, and okay just as he is.

Mirroring children's experiences and feelings, without distortion, builds self-esteem and helps them deal with life's inevitable conflicts and disappointments. They learn self-acceptance, appropriate emotional expression, and feel competent to solve personal problems and to repair or enhance interpersonal relationships.

The good news is that your kids aren't the only ones who benefit. You learn EQ from teaching it. And, as you navigate life's hurts and disappointments together, your bond will become more loving and profound.

—Allison LaTona, MFT, BABYGROUP™ leader,
parenting consultant, and psychotherapist
www.allisonlatona.com

vulnerable to postpartum depression. Research shows that babies of depressed mothers have a less active left frontal brain (the part of the brain that specializes in the expression of positive emotions) and exhibit more withdrawal and depressive symptoms. These babies lack the normal left hemisphere predominance that other babies have, even when they appear to be quite happy. Statistically speaking, these children have a six times greater chance of being depressed when they grow up. These research findings really speak to the importance of treating depression, from its earliest signs, for both parent and child.

10. Difficulty accepting your child's negative emotions. It is easy to respond to your child when he is squealing with joy. But it is just as important to respond to his negative emotions. Your child needs your empathic responses to his anger, frustration, and resentments as much as, or even more than, to his happier emotions. Many parents have a difficult time knowing what to do when their children start to exhibit dark feelings with some regularity. At around nine months your child may become agitated when you take a toy away. He is old enough to know what he wants and can express it nonverbally, but he's not old enough to understand that objects continue to exist, even when they are removed from his sight. He needs to know that you accept the full range of his emotions and that you still love him and support him when he feels intense, angry feelings. It can be very effective to "narrate back" what you see. For example, you might say, "I know you really wanted to play with that toy some more, but Mommy had to take it. I can see you're angry and you really want the toy back." Sometimes just the experience of having his feelings reflected back to him can help a child feel understood and help him to calm himself, even before he is fully verbal.

When Parents Miss the Boat

Your baby comes into the world with a strong need for social interaction that must include empathic, attuned attention. In other words, he needs you to respond accurately to his feelings in order for his social brain to develop and organize in a healthy way. In short, the health and development of your baby's brain literally depends on the degree to which you are lovingly engaged with him. Neglect and abuse, especially during the formative first three years, can have lasting neurological and emotional effects. When you don't respond to your child's needs and feelings, he starts to believe that he cannot affect his own life and eventually learns to give up. The experience of feeling ineffectual creates what psychological experts call "learned helplessness," which ultimately leads to depression. Researchers have also proven that the combination of stress and helplessness creates high levels of cortisol and low levels of norepinephrine in the brain, making concentration more difficult, decreasing the ability to be emotionally flexible, and reducing the ability to experience pleasure.

When a child is repeatedly frightened by a parent (for example, by his or her substance abuse) or is abused himself, whether physically, emotionally, or verbally, it destroys his sense of security and fractures his relationship with his parent. In their book *Parenting from the Inside Out,* Dr. Daniel Siegel and Mary Hartzell accurately spell out the difficult scenario this creates: "There is no solution to the paradox that your parent is creating a state of disorientation or terror in you that drives you to seek comfort in the very source of your fear. The disorganizing experiences impair the child's ability to integrate the functions of the mind that enable him to regulate and cope with stress." In addition, research shows that abused children have trouble with social communication, academic reasoning tasks, emotional control, and impulse control and display a tendency toward violence. The effort of separating their emotions from all the pain they have suffered predisposes these children to disassociation. The push-pull created by the experience of loving and needing the very person who is the source of their pain creates confusion in the development of attachment and results in a disorganized attachment pattern.

Ten Reasons Why Reading Your Child's Cues Is So Important

1. Makes him feel safe.

2. Builds healthy self-esteem.

3. Teaches him to regulate his emotions.

4. Helps him learn to read cues in others.

5. Increases emotional intelligence.

6. Frees him for higher-order learning.

7. Facilitates social learning.

8. Maximizes his inborn potential.

9. Creates the foundation for positive relationships.

10. Makes you a valuable emotional coach for your child.

FROM THE EXPERTS . . .

Basic Safety and Security

Beginning life in a condition of total dependency, a child has no more basic requirement—as far as parental behavior is concerned—than that of safety and security. This entails the satisfaction of physiological needs, protection from the elements, and basic caretaking in all its obvious aspects. It entails the creation of an environment in which the child can feel nurtured and safe.

In this context the process of separation and individuation can unfold. A mind that can later learn to trust itself can begin to emerge. A person with a confident sense of boundaries can develop.

If the child is to learn to trust other human beings, and in effect, to find confidence that life is not malevolent, the foundation is laid at this level.

—Nathaniel Branden, PhD, the best-selling author of
The Six Pillars of Self-Esteem, How to Raise Your Self-Esteem, Honoring the Self, and more than twenty other books
www.nathanielbranden.com

Attachment 101

A secure attachment is evidence of a trusting relationship between you and your child that provides a foundation for healthy relationships in the future. While virtually all infants become attached to their parents, not all of them develop *secure* attachments. It is the consistent experience of having cues read and responded to in a loving manner that creates what attachment theorist Dr. John Bowlby refers to as a "secure base." This responsive, trusting relationship allows children to explore their environment because they know they can return to the loving arms of their parent. As children get older, they venture further away for longer periods of time. A very young child toddles away only to return to his mother's arms moments later, while an adolescent spends a weekend at a friend's house and later graduates from high school and ventures off to college. Each of these developmental steps is best accomplished from a secure, trusted base.

Developmental psychologist and attachment theorist Dr. Mary Salter Ainsworth developed the "Strange Situation," an assessment that gives a clear understanding of the three types of attachments babies can develop. She gathered mothers and their babies in private rooms and put them through the following steps:

1. Ainsworth made a brief introduction.
2. The baby was left alone in the room with the mother, free to explore and play with toys.
3. A stranger would enter the room.
4. The mother left the room, leaving the child with the stranger.
5. The mother returned and the stranger left the room.
6. The mother left the room, leaving the child completely alone.
7. The stranger came back in to comfort the child.
8. The mother returned.

Ainsworth focused her observation on the amount of exploration the children engaged in and their reactions to the departure and return of their mothers. Based on these observations, she categorized the children's attachment styles into one of three categories:

Ambivalent or insecure. These children were anxious about exploring and having contact with strangers, whether or not their mother was in the room. When she left, these children became very distressed and when she returned they were likely to hit or push her.

Avoidant. These children avoided or ignored their mother and showed little reaction when reunited with her. Children in this group ran away from their mother when she approached and failed to cling to her when they were picked up. They did not treat strangers much differently from their own mothers, and their range of emotions was poor, regardless of whether anyone else was in the room.

Secure. These children explored freely when their mother was there, engaged with strangers, were visibly upset when their mother left, and were happy to see her return. Generally, they did not engage with the stranger if their mother was not in the room.

> Dr. Jenn's
> ABCs of Attachment
>
> A = Be attuned and affectionate
>
> B = Build strong bonds
>
> C = Provide consistent care and be conscious of cues

All parents want their children to be securely attached. A secure attachment gives children a psychological advantage, helping them develop a sense of security and safety that is likely to translate into high self-esteem. So what can you do to achieve such attachment? Compared to the other parents, Ainsworth found a few differences in the mothering styles of women whose babies were securely attached. Those mothers

- were more responsive to their infant's signals. They were quicker to pick up their crying baby, held him longer, and appeared to get more pleasure out of the physical contact.
- scored better in scales of maternal behavior. They rated higher in sensitivity, acceptance, cooperation, and emotional accessibility.
- were more in tune with their children's feeding needs. These mothers fed their children promptly when they saw cues of hunger or else they held them off with gentle coaxing. They also allowed their babies to take more initiative during feeding.
- held their babies more tenderly. These mothers were more affectionate, were more careful, and responded accurately to their baby's cues indicating when the children wanted to be held and when they did not want contact.

Temperament and Fit: Parent and Child

Your personality style is your organizing principle. It propels you on your life path. It represents the orderly arrangement of all your attributes, thoughts, feelings, attitudes, behaviors, and coping mechanisms. It is the distinctive pattern of your psychological functioning—the way you think, feel, and behave—that makes you definitively you.

—JOHN M. OLDHAM AND LOIS B. MORRIS,
*The New Personality Self-Portrait:
Why You Think, Work, Love, and Act the Way You Do*

Behaviorists like B.F. Skinner believe that children are shaped by pure behavioral reward. For example, if you want your child to become a great baseball player, a behaviorist would encourage you to give him a reward, like a sticker or a "good boy!" every time he hits the ball, so he will want to play more and be motivated by the reward. Increasingly, however, researchers are discovering how much biology shapes temperament. Children begin to display their personality traits from birth. A parent who has an awareness of her child's temperament and personality can better read and understand his cues, provide the support he needs, and help him reach his full potential. Many parents make the mistake of fighting their child's temperament or making him feel guilty about who he is.

In their series of *Positive Discipline* books, authors Jane Nelsen, Cheryl Erwin, and Roslyn Ann Duffy touch upon nine temperaments. In getting to know your child, they recommend looking at the following areas:

1. **Activity level.** How active is your child? How much time does he spend being active versus inactive?

2. **Rhythmicity.** How predictable are your child's biological functions such as hunger, sleeping, and pooping?

3. **Approach or withdrawal.** How does your child react to a new situation? How does he respond to a new food, toy, person, or place?

4. **Adaptability.** How does your child adapt to a new situation over time? How long does it take him to adjust to change?

5. **Sensory threshold.** How sensitive to sensory input like touch, taste, sight, smell, and hearing is your child? Does he like noise and music? Is he drawn to lights and colors or does he turn away? Does he like new tastes and textures? Does he like to be touched and hugged?

6. **Quality of mood.** Does your child have an upbeat disposition? Is he a serious baby?

7. **Intensity of reactions.** Does your child have strong reactions? Is he quick to show emotion, positive or negative?

8. **Distractibility.** How much does outside stimulus interfere with your child's focus on a task like eating or playing?

9. **Persistence and attention span.** How willing is your child to pursue an activity in the face of obstacles? How long is he able to pursue an activity without interruption?

GOODNESS OF FIT

Parenting experts talk a lot about "goodness of fit," meaning your ability, as a parent, to understand and work with your child's temperament. No matter how much you love your child, your temperament and his may not mesh easily. This does not mean you are doomed—it just means you may have to work a little harder to understand him and his emotions. There is no such thing as a "bad" baby or child. While some temperaments may be easier for parents to work with, both parent and child can both grow together if you're patient and aware of your own issues and temperament.

For example, Devon's daughter Cynthia, nineteen months old, is easily distracted. While Devon loves to have music playing all the time and can multitask easily, she has had to reduce such distractions to make things easier for Cynthia. During dinnertime, Devon makes sure she turns off the music, keeps outside conversation to a minimum, and doesn't talk on the phone. This has helped Cynthia relax during mealtimes and as a result dinner takes twenty to thirty minutes instead of an hour or more.

DO YOU HAVE TO BE A PERFECT PARENT?

You don't have to be the perfect parent to do well by your child. What matters most is the consistency and general impression of love and acceptance your child gets from you. D.W. Winnicott, pediatrician and child psychiatrist, created the concept of the "good enough mother." According to Winnicott, the "good enough mother" adapts to her baby's needs and allows her child enough room to experience his own growing autonomy. Being a "good enough mother" means that you don't focus on a single, defining moment or obsess about being perfect, but you do read your child's cues often enough to make him feel safe. The good news is that parents get better and better at reading their child's cues. In a study of mothers' ability to read their infant's cues that examined this dynamic at three months, six months, and nine months, researchers found that at the start of the survey mothers failed to accurately read their child's cues up to 70 percent of the time, but, as the months passed and mothers became more experienced, they consistently became better and better at accurately reading their children's cues.

Frequently Asked Questions

Q *Can you spoil a child?*
A You cannot spoil a child with too much love or affection. You can, however, spoil a child by giving him too many *things* in place of attention, affection, and kindness. A while back, I was at an airport getting my shoes shined by a guy named Joe. When he found out I write parenting books, he asked me this question. He was worried that his mother-in-law was doing the wrong thing by picking up his infant son every time he cried. "I don't want him to become a spoiled sissy," he told me. Children don't get spoiled when you attend to their needs; on the contrary, responding to and caring for your children makes them feel more secure. Researchers Mary Ainsworth and Sylvia Bell found that babies whose cries were responded to more frequently cried less at the end of nine months than those who were responded to less frequently.

Q *Are babies manipulative?*
A No, they are not! Babies are constantly trying to get their needs met to the best of their abilities. This is normal and natural, not manipulative.

Q *How should I respond to all the intense and negative emotions my child is experiencing?*

A In the first few years of his life, your child's higher, more rational brain is so unfinished that his lower, more primitive, emotional brain is in charge. This explains a lot of his actions. At this stage, your child's emotions and impulses will drive many of his actions and overwhelm him frequently. He cannot help it. Keep this in mind when you see outbursts, screaming, and tantrums. Your child is not trying to be difficult; he just doesn't have the ability to be rational yet. Sometimes, even when he knows he is not allowed to do something, he is unable to stop himself because his primal brain is in charge.

It is important for parents to help children manage big emotional responses. In *The Science of Parenting,* Dr. Margot Sunderland writes, "When a child is not given enough help with his intense lower brain feelings and primitive impulses, his brain may not develop the pathways to enable him to manage stressful situations effectively." Children are particularly vulnerable to stress, and if they do not learn to manage these feelings early in life, they are left to face adulthood without the necessary tools.

From the beginning, your child needs to know that you can handle all of his many emotions, ranging from "good" to "bad." Reacting to a happy cooing baby is easy. The angry, heartfelt tantrums, protests, assertions of will, kicking, and hitting are much more challenging for parents to respond to. When you are able to empathize with your children, sharing in their emotional ups and downs, they grow up feeling understood. By narrating their experiences (i.e., saying what you see), you can help your children understand what they are experiencing. Narration lets them know that you understand what they are going through and gives them the words to express their emotions. Also, by staying with your children and remaining calm (when they are experiencing negative emotions), you are able to contain their feelings. Offering solutions is another way to help children calm down. For a very young child, a solution may be as simple and straightforward as a hug, a band-aid, or a pacifier, while an older child may be mature enough to come up with his own solution—with your help. It all comes down to four simple steps:

1. **Narration.** "I see you fell down. It looks like you tripped over this toy and hit your head."

2. **Empathy.** "Ow! That looked really painful. Let me take a look at your head."

3. **Containment.** "Daddy is right here. I don't blame you for crying. That was a big fall! It looks like it hurt, too."

4. **Solutions.** "Let's go get some ice for that bump. Would you like your pacifier or your teddy bear? Do you think a hug might help you feel better?"

When you help your child manage big feelings by using the four-step plan, you are stimulating the cells in his higher brain to start forming pathways that connect with those in his lower brain, allowing him, over time, to better control normal, but primitive impulses that come from his lower brain (such as rage, fear, and distress). This will ultimately enable him to think about and control overwhelming feelings.

Q What is the best way for me to get to know my child and tune in to his cues?

A Observe your child: while he lies in his crib, when he's playing with his toys, while you're holding him, when you're changing his diaper, any time he's in a safe place. But to really be a sensitive observer, you must get rid of all the distractions, such as the newspaper, the cell phone, television, music, and other conversations. You need to be fully engaged with your child and use all your senses as best as you can.

Make good use of other people who spend time with your child: a baby nurse or doula, a day-care worker, a nanny, friends, family members, and, yes, even your mother-in-law. As a parent, you need to put your ego aside and listen to everyone who sees your child from a different vantage point. All these people may have valuable insights to offer.

Here are some tips for observing your child:

- **Make sure to spend one-on-one time together.** This allows you to really focus your attention on getting to know your child better.

- **Do less and observe more.** This philosophy from Resources for Infant Educators (RIE) encourages children to do what they want to do while their parents are nearby for support. Parents interfere only if their child's safety is in jeopardy.

- **Be unobtrusive.** Don't direct your child's play. Too many parents direct their children's play by handing them a toy or shaking a rattle in front of their face. See what toys your child is drawn to and what really interests him. Also, watch him interact with his playmates without jumping in and interfering. You will learn a lot about your child's social development.

- **Provide a safe, baby-proof environment.** The freer your child is to explore on his own, the more you will learn from watching him.

- **Let your child solve his own problems whenever you can.** When Mendez was about five months old, I was sitting with her while she played with a ball that rolled out of her hands just out of her reach. My first instinct was to solve the problem for her.

After all, it was easy enough for me to give her the ball instead of watching her get frustrated. However, I held back and observed her to see what she would do while narrating what I saw (i.e., "I see the ball rolled out of your hands"). She slowly leaned toward the ball, reaching in a way she had never done before, and got the toy all by herself. This was a learning experience for both of us.

- **Don't assume.** Don't assume that all babies and children like the same things. Get to know *your* child's preferences.

Twenty Questions to Ask Yourself When Observing Your Child Playing with Others (18–36 months)

1. What does he do well?
2. What challenges him?
3. Which activities does he like or dislike?
4. What makes him laugh?
5. What frustrates him?
6. How does he express himself to others?
7. Is he physically expressive?
8. Is he able to empathize with others?
9. Does he engage with other kids or mostly participate in parallel play?
10. How does he handle conflict with other children?
11. Is he comfortable interacting with other adults?
12. How long is he able to play or work on a task?
13. How does he handle frustration?
14. How does he react to new situations?
15. How does he express anger?
16. How does he express excitement or enthusiasm?

17. Is he comfortable speaking to one other person?

18. Is he able to speak in a group?

19. Is he comfortable interacting with peers?

20. In what situations does he seek adult help?

Tick-Tock

Creating Security and Predictability

I was thrust into the deep end of the parenting pool when I gave birth to twins with *severe* colic and reflux. The schedules I created helped me to meet my daughters' needs and played the dual role of saving the little sanity I had left. They also allowed me to return emails, get work done while my kids napped, and even plan outings—when I wasn't too busy cleaning the vomit out of my hair.

I recognize that as a parent of twins I have a bias in favor of schedules. Parents with multiples tend to need organization and structure to make sure that all their children's needs are met. But as a therapist and a parenting expert, I have seen how beneficial schedules are to families who don't have more than one child.

Although some parents consider routines in child care a bad thing, I have seen significant evidence to the contrary. Routines provide the structure that children need to feel safe and secure, allowing them to flourish. Parents who have their children on a schedule have an easier time recognizing and responding accurately to their cues. This helps children feel understood and fosters self-esteem.

Structure is also the early foundation for discipline in young children. Toddlers and preschoolers love knowing what comes next in their world, and they do better in school when they have the experience of growing up with the structure and boundaries that schedules provide.

The Four Pillars of Security

Regardless of age, we all feel most secure when our world is predictable, manageable, and connected. For babies, a familiar face, the comfort of a good-night ritual, the smell of Mommy's skin, and the security of the child's crib combine to create a relaxed atmosphere. In the book *What Happened to My World?*, author Jim Greenman lists what he calls "The Four Pillars of Security," four factors that create trust and security in a child's life and emphasize how safe the world is:

- **People.** Security comes from familiar, trusted people who consistently meet our needs and understand us.
- **Place.** We find comfort in familiar order, sights, sounds, and smells.
- **Routine.** Familiar routines reassure and stabilize us, protecting us from the unknown.
- **Ritual.** Ritual helps us feel connected, teaches us what comes next, and creates positive associations.

A good schedule integrates all these elements into a regular routine that gives infants and toddlers the security they need.

THE NEW FLEXIBLE SCHEDULE

I have to admit that, when writing this book, I toyed with the idea of not using the word "schedule." It has such rigid and negative connotations that I worried parents would be turned off by the word or, even worse, use it to justify inflexible, strict, or insensitive responses to their child's cues. A schedule is a guideline that you use to bring order to your and your child's life. A good schedule actually helps to hone your ability to read and respond to your child's cues.

Actually, I'm a big believer in feeding on demand, but I believe that the best way to accomplish this goal is to create structure for your infant (or toddler) based on the experience of reading her cues and working with her rhythms, as soon as possible. In Alcoholics Anonymous they say you should never let yourself get too hungry, too tired, or too angry. The same applies to children. Please take the following recommendations to heart when you create a schedule for your own child:

1. Never deny food to a hungry baby.
2. Do not unnecessarily wake an infant who is in deep sleep.
3. Do not ignore a baby's cries.

The point of a schedule is to help a child be more comfortable and stable. Newborns come into this chaotic world yearning for a sense of security, and toddlers hunger for a sense of order and control. Schedules can provide that.

PRECIOUS **PLANNING**

Some parents who feed their infants on demand misinterpret cues, thinking that every cry is a hunger signal. An example of this happened recently while I was having lunch with my friend Mary. The moment we sat down at the table at the restaurant, her daughter, Emily, started crying. "I just fed her thirty minutes ago," Mary said, putting her nipple into her daughter's mouth; "how can she be hungry again?" Literally fifteen minutes later, Emily started to cry again, and, reflexively, Mary responded by feeding her another time. After three more rounds of this in less than an hour and a half, I suggested to Mary that maybe the restaurant was too stimulating for Emily and that perhaps we should move to a quieter place. As soon as we got out of the noisy eatery, Emily seemed quite calm and peaceful. The danger of not having a schedule is that it is all too easy to misinterpret cues and think that every cry is a bid for more food.

Schedules should be personalized to support your baby's needs, rhythms, and age. They should also support breastfeeding. Dr. Scott Cohen, pediatrician and author of *Eat, Sleep, Poop,* recommends "The Rule of Twos and Fours": for the first two to four months of life, your baby is likely to feed every two to four hours and will usually take two to four ounces of milk. Knowing this, and observing your child's hunger levels and patterns, you can start to gently guide her toward a regular schedule based on her needs.

From the start, you should keep track of when your baby seems hungry, tired, and alert. Jotting down a few notes in a log book will help you remember the details and observe patterns. Your baby's schedule should be built around her personal biological clock. In Appendix C you can check out schedules that have worked for other families, including my own. Pick and chose from these to create a schedule based on your child's particular personality and needs.

A good schedule is not rigid. It allows you to adjust to your child's changing needs while creating a structure that has the best possible chance of anticipating those needs. It should also give *you* the maximum amount of time to prepare in advance for various eventualities. For example, if you know your child is likely to eat lunch at noon, you can prepare a meal or a bottle or plan where you'd like to breast-feed in advance, making the experience that much more relaxed for everyone involved. The ideal schedule, like your child, is PRECIOUS:

> **P**redictable
> **R**esponsive
> **E**njoyable
> **C**onsistent
> **I**ntentional
> **O**rganized
> **U**ser-friendly
> **S**tructured

THREE DIFFERENT APPROACHES TO SCHEDULING

I call parents who take schedules to the extreme "rigid rulers." These folks live by the clock, frequently to their children's detriment. In their desire to provide much-needed structure, they tune out their children's cues and give priority to schedules over their children's needs. At the other end of the spectrum are parents whom I refer to as "cue controlled" because they are completely led by their children. These parents' intentions are good, but the lack of structure in their children's lives often makes it difficult, especially for young children, to regulate their rhythms. Parents in this group, like my friend Mary, also tend to assume that many non-food-related cues are a request for food. In the middle are the parents I call "PRECIOUS planners," those who have found a balance that both meets their children's needs and provides structure.

SCHEDULING STYLES

	Rigid Rulers	PRECIOUS Planners	Cue Controlled
The Approach	The clock determines when and how often the child is fed. Hunger cues are ignored.	A flexible schedule takes into account the child's needs; the clock acts as a guide to anticipate needs and create regularity, yet remains submissive to the child's cues.	The parents are completely guided by the child's cues, which are often open to misinterpretation. The result is inconsistent feeding and sleeping routines.
Who's in Charge	Parent	Parent and child work together to provide structure based on the child's needs.	Child
Ability to Plan	Extremely high	High	Very low
Sensitivity to Child's Cues	The child's cues are often ignored in order to stay on schedule.	Because the schedule is based on the child's rhythms, parents are able to anticipate needs and interpret different cries accurately.	Feeding times are determined by the child's cues, with the caveat that cries are easy to misinterpret without the benefit of some structure.

Continued on next page

SCHEDULING STYLES continued

	Rigid Rulers	PRECIOUS Planners	Cue Controlled
Feelings of Efficacy in Parents	Parents tend to feel frustrated by their baby's frequent crying, the result of making her wait for a feeding she needs at once. Parents may fail to develop the ability to read their baby's cues accurately because they become slaves to the clock.	Parents enjoy a high degree of self-efficacy, becoming increasingly confident in their ability to read their child's cues accurately, provide structure, and make plans to meet her needs.	Lack of structure can create anxiety in parents. Their inability to go out or plan an activity causes frustration. Also, the constant feedings and lack of sleep can leave parents exhausted and even reduce the mother's milk supply.

Eight More Reasons You Should Put Your Child on a Schedule

But believe it or not, no matter what the particular presenting issue— feeding problems, irregular sleep patterns, or misdiagnosed colic—a structured routine is often all it takes to solve the problem.

—Tracy Hogg, *Secrets of the Baby Whisperer*

In case I haven't convinced you yet, here are some more good reasons to start implementing a regular schedule as soon as your baby is old enough:

1. A schedule promotes safety, security, and trust. Babies don't like surprises. Bringing consistency and order to your infant's life is a calming gift that parents should provide for their children. When your child always enjoys an after-dinner cuddle and a book before bedtime, she grows to anticipate that experience and is soothed by the routine. She knows what is coming next and what is expected of her. This predictability promotes security and confirms her experience of the world as a predictable and trustworthy place. In *Positive Discipline: The First Three Years*, Jane Nelsen, Cheryl Erwin, and Roslyn Ann Duffy say, "By their rhythm and repetition, these events form patterns, helping little ones make sense of their days and nights. When a child can count on having her needs met and having life progress in predictable ways, she feels secure and learns to trust others and the world around her."

The same goes for toddlers. Toddlers demand order and predictability. Lack of structure is likely to result in a cranky and overwhelmed child. Providing order and predictability can greatly reduce the number of tantrums. Knowing when she will eat, sleep, and play is reassuring for a toddler. Make a practice of telling your child every day what is going to happen, what the plan is. At our house, we usually talk about what will happen that day when we are getting up and getting dressed in the morning. We talk about what day of the week it is, what activities we will be doing, what people my daughters will see, and anything out of the ordinary that will happen. I recommend doing this even before your child is verbal.

2. A schedule helps set your child's internal clock. A regular schedule for eating, sleeping, and activity helps regulate a child's circadian rhythm. According to Dr. Jodi Mindell, author of *Sleeping Through the Night,* "Since babies cannot tell time, they need us to set their internal time clocks throughout the day by their daily activities. They need to eat meals at basically the same time every day, and they need to go to bed at about the same time. By keeping your child's internal clock always consistent, she will fall asleep more easily and quickly."

Your baby's internal clock is regulated by the hypothalamus, a primitive area located deep in the brain that controls changes in hormone levels, appetite, blood pressure, and other basic functions. This biological clock actually runs about ten minutes slow compared to regular clock time. In other words, left to its own devices it would take twenty-four hours and ten minutes to complete a full twenty-four-hour cycle. The great news is that it gets reset every morning when the body wakes up. So if your child's schedule was off yesterday, she gets a fresh start today.

If your child's eating, sleeping, and activities are routinely disorganized, however, it can throw off her delicate biological clock and result in equally disorganized physiological rhythms. This means that she is likely to experience hunger and tiredness at unpredictable and inappropriate times of the day. Combined with poor sleep habits, this disorganization can prevent her body's rhythms from functioning in concert, as they are meant to work.

3. A schedule makes reading cues easier. It's all too easy to misinterpret your baby's cries if she's not on a schedule. This is especially true for first-time parents, who tend to be more anxious than veterans. Most experts estimate that babies cry an average of three to four hours a day. According to the Thomas Coram Research Unit, this crying usually peaks at four hours a day when babies are about six weeks old. The longer you hear your child cry without relief, the harder it becomes to figure out what she needs, due to your own feelings and anxieties. After surviving twins with colic and reflux, I can attest to this truth.

When a baby cries, most parents check to see if the diaper is dirty and if that is not the culprit, they offer food. Crying is a late signal of hunger. If your child is really crying from hunger, it means you may have missed more subtle cues along the way, such as chewing on a hand, making sucking motions, or whimpering. All too often a child who is not hungry, but needs the comfort of being held or the calming experience of sucking, will opt for a bottle or the breast. A parent whose child is on a schedule might look at the clock and say, "You usually eat at noon, but it's only 11:30. It looks like you're hungry a little earlier today," and choose to feed the child early. Or she might say, "No wonder you're crying! We're late for your nap," and put the child in her crib. You can see how having a schedule might make it easier to figure out your baby's cries.

There are many reasons why babies cry:

- Overstimulation
- Not wanting to do an activity (such as getting undressed or taking a bath)
- Stress
- Boredom
- Wet or dirty diaper
- Feeling too hot or too cold
- Tiredness
- Hunger
- Thirst
- Gas
- Colic
- Reflux
- Needing to be held
- Teething
- Feeling overwhelmed
- Pain (anything from diaper rash to a hair tightly wound around a little finger)
- Illness
- Developmental leap

The Beauty of the Log Book: Keeping Track

A good log book can help you keep track of feedings, pees and poops (especially helpful for a constipated baby), sleeping patterns, medications, triggers for fussiness, sensitivities or possible food allergies, baby's growth and weight gain, immunizations, and milestones. These books are particularly helpful when a child has multiple caregivers. They can help you know about your child's day and prevent potentially dangerous double dosing of medications. A log book can serve as a sweet keepsake for your child, too.

If your baby's crying is abnormally frequent, high-pitched, or accompanied by fever, rash, or any other sign of illness, you should call your pediatrician immediately.

4. A schedule prevents sleep problems. The earlier you create good sleep habits, the better off your child will be as she grows older. According to the American Academy of Pediatrics, a study of three-year-olds receiving treatment for sleep problems found that 84 percent of these kids had experienced sleep issues starting in infancy. Another study of college students with sleeping problems found similar results. According to Dr. Richard Ferber, author of *Solve Your Child's Sleep Problems,* "Children on uncontrolled schedules . . . can develop major sleep problems. Behavior problems may follow as well." New research is showing us that this may only be the tip of the iceberg.

Sleep problems, or lack of adequate sleep, have been linked to a host of problems in children such as poor attention span, inability to concentrate, reduced memory, learning issues, irritability, aggressive behavior, reduced coordination, tantrums, insomnia, and even obesity. A 2006 Australian study that examined the link between sleep duration and overweight in seven- to fifteen-year-olds found that children who sleep less than eight hours of sleep per night have a 310 percent higher rate of obesity than children who get about ten hours of sleep a night. It is believed that this overweight problem is due to changes in levels of several hormones including leptin, ghrelin, insulin, cortisol, and growth hormones that occur as a result of sleep deprivation. These hormonal changes may contribute to an energy imbalance that in turn leads to weight problems or even obesity.

In order to prevent future sleep problems, Jill Spivack and Jennifer Waldburger, renowned sleep experts and the authors of *The Sleepeasy Solution,* recommend providing what they call "good sleep nutrition." This means making sure your child gets good-quality sleep as well as the amount of sleep she needs. Sleep begets sleep and a child who develops good sleep habits early on is likely to maintain them for a lifetime.

5. A schedule promotes healthy growth. A consistent schedule sets up a pattern of optimal sleeping and eating habits that promote growth. According to Shirley Munro, a NICU specialist at UCLA Santa Monica Hospital, scheduled feedings allow for better control of feedings. She says this is especially important for newborns and premature babies because their stomachs are so tiny they can't hold a lot of food. Babies who are allowed to go too long without being fed can get over-hungry and then tend to overeat, which can lead to reflux problems. When a healthy baby is fed properly, she goes into a deep state of sleep, which promotes healthy weight gain and growth. If your newborn is not able to go into this deep sleep state but remains active and awake, she'll burn up a lot of extra calories, which prevents healthy growth.

Despite the old wives' tale that you should never wake a sleeping baby, Munro says there are times it is necessary to wake a newborn. A normal healthy newborn should wake from a deep sleep in response to hunger. But some babies, including those with jaundice, preemies, hypothermic babies, and near-term infants, may not wake themselves, even though it is time for a much-needed feeding. Munro recommends not letting a newborn sleep for more than four and a half hours at a time in order to make sure she gets all the nutrition she needs to grow. If your child is not waking for feeds or is having trouble feeding, you should consult with your pediatrician.

6. A schedule increases attention span and encourages learning. The implementation of a simple, predictable schedule that allows a child to anticipate upcoming activities allows her brain to focus on higher-order learning. For example, when she knows that dinner always comes after her bath, she doesn't have to worry if someone is going to feed her. This certainty frees her mind to learn the alphabet song you are singing while you bathe her.

We also know that children who have good sleep habits, which are best created through a consistent schedule, have better focus and learn better. Naps, in particular, have been shown to regulate attention span, which is vital for learning. Kids who nap have longer attention spans and are less fussy than those who don't. Young children have huge energy requirements, and one of the best ways to meet these needs is adequate sleep. Sleep provides a break from stimuli and allows children to recharge. This rest allows babies and children to absorb new information more efficiently. According to Dr. Marc Weissbluth, author of *Healthy Sleep Habits, Happy Child,* "A baby learns best in the quiet, alert state that follows right after a nap."

Contrary to popular belief, sleep does not become less important to cognitive skills as children get older. In a study by Dr. Avi Sadeh, fourth and sixth graders were randomly divided into two groups, one that got thirty minutes more sleep per night for three nights and the second that got thirty-one fewer minutes of sleep for three nights. The children's neurobiological functioning was then tested. The performance gap was enormous. Sadeh found that a "loss of one hour of sleep is equivalent to the loss of two years of cognitive maturation and development." In other words, a slightly sleepy second-grader will perform in class like a mere kindergartener. Because children's brains are a work-in-progress until early adulthood, and much of that work is done during sleeping hours, researchers came to the conclusion that this lost hour appears to have an exponential impact on children—even more so than it would for adults.

7. A schedule prepares your child for school. Structure at home helps children cope with structure in the world; this is especially applicable when children start school. Aiden's family didn't believe in schedules or routines. His parents were well-meaning, well-educated Berkeley graduates whose own parents had been too rigid with their schedules when they were growing up, so they went to the other extreme with their own child. Aiden had no particular bedtime, no wake-up time, and no specific times for meals or play. As a toddler, he would bang on the refrigerator to signal that he was hungry. At night he sometimes slept in his crib and sometimes in his parents' bed, not because they were a family that believed in the "family bed," but because his parents let Aiden make all the choices.

Preschool was very problematic for Aiden, who had never experienced structure. It was very difficult for him to follow his teacher's instructions, participate in classroom activities, and make transitions from one activity to another. Like many kids who grow up in unstructured environments, he had trouble following rules and recognizing that other children have needs too. For Aiden, being raised to have his every whim and wish met whenever he wanted led to huge social disadvantages at school.

Aiden's experience is typical of children who don't grow up with any schedule at home. Many preschools ask parents about their child's home schedule for this very reason. This information allows them to rule out children who they don't think will adapt to the structured expectations of a typical preschool day.

8. A schedule allows you to plan and take better care of yourself. Alison came to see me when her daughter Jaiden was five months old. Alison was a devoted mother who did not believe in schedules. Since the birth of her daughter, she had become extremely isolated and very depressed. She couldn't understand why. When I asked about her day-to-day life with her daughter, I discovered that Alison's life was totally unpredictable and, as a result, so was Jaiden's. Jaiden never slept, woke, ate, or played at the same time. Consequently her sleep quality was poor, and Alison had not had a good night's sleep in five months. Furthermore, Alison felt that she could not leave the house with the baby because she never knew when Jaiden would need to go home for a nap or meal. Alison had not gone out for a date with her husband or a night out with friends since her daughter had been born. In effect, Alison had become a slave to motherhood.

When Alison was able to work through her own resistance to scheduling and I was able to dispel some of her misconceptions about schedules, her life changed. Getting Jaiden on a schedule improved her sleep and therefore Alison's sleep as well; it improved the baby's eating habits; she was less fussy; and Alison's depression was alleviated, allowing her to get out of the house at planned intervals.

Dr. William Sears, considered the father of attachment parenting, says, "You will get more joy out of parenting if you create a routine that fits your baby rather than trying to make your baby fit the routine. Babies are creatures of habit, and the more predictable their day, the more restful the night is likely to be." Having a predictable schedule allows families to create better quality time together and gives parents the time to take care of more mundane needs, such as returning phone calls, taking a shower, or preparing a meal. As much as you love your kid, knowing that naptime is just an hour away can get you through those sixty minutes a lot easier. An established schedule also allows a nanny, babysitter, or grandparent to take care of your child, which in turn results in happier parents.

Big Changes

I confess I don't like change. It always seems that as soon as I get comfortable with a schedule and start to feel like I know how to handle things, my daughters pass some new developmental milestone that requires a change in routine. While some changes arise that may be totally unpredictable, here are a few predictable ones that you can look forward to. They are by no means the rule, since every child is different. Before you make any decisions about your child's schedule, consult with your pediatrician to make sure they are developmentally appropriate for your child.

PREDICTABLE MILESTONES FOR INFANTS THROUGH AGE FIVE

Age	Change
4 to 5 weeks or when baby shows signs of rolling over	Stop swaddling
4 to 5 weeks	Start using sleep sacks (a wearable blanket with or without sleeves)
3 to 6 months, depending on weight gain, appetite, and ability to sleep through the night without additional food	Stop the "dream feed" or nighttime feed
4 to 6 months	Start solid food
6 months, when child has full neck control or is able to get on all fours	Stop using sleep sacks
6 to 9 months	Switch from three naps to two naps
12 months	Switch from a bottle to a straw or sippy cup
14 to 18 months	Switch from two naps to one nap
18 months	Introduce the potty
3 to 3½ years	Move from a crib to a bed
3 to 4 years	Complete daytime toilet training
3 to 5 years old	Lose the last nap

FROM THE EXPERTS . . .

Multiples and Schedules

For first-time parents, taking care of multiples can seem particularly overwhelming. "Feeding on demand" makes it difficult for any parent to function in an organized way throughout the seemingly endless days and nights, but a schedule can take the stress out of day-to-day routines and give you the satisfaction of knowing what and when your babies' expectations are and if they're being met. In fact, scheduling children at any age allows you to know exactly when they need to be fed, changed, and bathed. (It also gives them some control, which means they're likely to be more cooperative and engaged.) Once you have a schedule in place you will be overcome by a sense of relief and happiness—and your babies will also automatically seem to understand that their needs will always be met.

—Sue Darrison,
twin expert and teacher at Babies First Class,
mother of six, including one set of twins
www.BabiesFirstClass.com

Five Myths about Schedules

People who shy away from schedules usually have a lot of misconceptions about them. When faced with the facts, however, most parents come around.

Myth #1: Schedules are rigid. Schedules should not be rigid. Routines should be structured around your child rather than the reverse. While some parents like to base their child's schedule on the clock, others base it on the order of activities. For example, Tracy Hogg, co-author of *Secrets of the Baby Whisperer*, recommends the following order of activities: eating, activity, sleeping, and then "you time." Some parents plan their baby's first nap two hours after waking, knowing that their infant cannot tolerate more than two hours of wakefulness without a nap. While order and predictability are important, so is the occasional opportunity to sleep in or stay at a birthday party a little later than planned.

Myth #2: You can make a child sleep. You cannot make your child sleep but you *can* "hold the frame." In other words, when you put your baby in her crib at the scheduled time, even if you don't expect her to sleep or she chooses not to, you are still providing her with the opportunity to rest and giving her the valuable experience of knowing what comes next.

On a different note, the time your child spends in the crib is also valuable because it gives her alone time and a chance to learn how to entertain herself, which is an inoculation against boredom, loneliness, and low self-esteem. The ability to play alone in a safe place becomes increasingly important, as she gets older, for both of you. A child who has had practice playing by herself since she was a baby will not need you or the television to entertain her while you make dinner. She will be content to sit in her crib "reading" or playing with toys.

Myth #3: You can make a child eat. Your job as a parent is to make nutritious, age-appropriate food available to your child, not to *make* her eat or control how much she eats. You cannot control how much your child weighs or what kind of body type she has. The more you try to get your child to gain or lose weight, the more likely your plans will backfire and the more likely she will develop a problem with food. You must make food available to your child when it is time to eat, or whenever she is hungry, and then let go of the outcome. (See Chapter 12 for more information about this.)

Myth #4: Babies don't need a schedule until they are six months old. The sooner your child is able to start developing a routine, the better off you will both be. When talking about starting infants on a schedule right away, Tracy Hogg says, "Their delicate systems do best when they eat, sleep, and play pretty much at the same time every day, and in the same order." Starting from birth, infants' hunger patterns are likely to become regular or inconsistent based on how consistent their day-to-day routines are. According to Gary Ezzo and Robert Bucknam in their book *On Becoming Baby Wise*, "The hunger mechanism (digestion and absorption) operates as if it has a metabolic memory reinforced by routine." Most experts, especially those who promote breastfeeding, recommend easing babies onto a schedule around the age of three to four months, but many parents, myself included, are able to follow their child's rhythms and fall into a regular schedule earlier than that.

Myth #5: If your baby is on a schedule, she will spend a lot of time crying. Babies who don't have their needs met, who are ignored, or who have colic or reflux cry a lot. Using the PRECIOUS Planner approach to scheduling (see page 53) does *not* mean ignoring your child's natural rhythms or letting her cry. On the contrary, the point of the plan is not only to meet your child's needs but to anticipate them before they arise.

Start from the Very Beginning: Sleep Learning 101

According to Spivack and Waldburger, sleep learning or sleep training is the act of teaching a child the skill of self-soothing so she can fall asleep or fall back to sleep for both daytime naps and nighttime sleeping.

Until your child is four months old and weighs fourteen pounds, her systems are too underdeveloped for sleep training, but after that point parents can do a lot to help their children, and themselves, get a good night's sleep. According to Waldburger, babies wake up to the world at this age and it is very common for sleep to be disrupted. What you can't really ask a baby to do before that developmental milestone, you now can, which means you can start to place your baby in the crib while she is awake so she can learn how to fall asleep on her own.

In the first four months or so, parents need to know two important sleep-training techniques. First, they need to establish a nighttime sleep ritual (see page 66 for more information about bedtime rituals). Second, parents have to help the baby learn the difference between daytime and nighttime sleep. During nighttime feedings, keep your voice low, feed your baby in semidarkness, and behave as if it were the middle of the night. During daytime feedings, allow louder noises, feed in full daylight, and behave as you normally would during daytime.

Even when a child is neurologically and developmentally mature enough for sleep training, many parents shy away from it because they are afraid that they will have to let their child "cry it out." It can be challenging for parents to find the balance between responding to their child's cues and teaching her how to self-soothe. During sleep training, a child generally cries for two reasons: (1) she doesn't yet know what to do to soothe herself, and (2) she is protesting the change. In order for her to learn the necessary skills to fall back to sleep on her own, she will have to do some crying.

Dr. Sears cautions parents, "With most of these baby-training regimens you run the risk of becoming desensitized to the cues of your infant, especially when it comes to letting your baby cry it out." But according to Spivack, sleep training is not an ongoing nonresponse to your child's cries; it is a time-limited, nondamaging tool to help parents teach their children to self-soothe. In the end, sleep training is good for the family, since it helps your child learn to sleep and self-soothe and gives you some much needed rest. After all, a well-rested parent is more patient and emotionally available to the child. In addition, Spivack says, "A child who isn't sleeping isn't developing properly physically, cognitively and emotionally. Once they start getting the right amount of sleep they start to thrive."

FROM THE EXPERTS . . .

Tips for Daylight Savings Time

Spring Ahead

1. Put your child to bed at his usual bedtime (e.g., 7:30 PM).
2. At midnight, turn all clocks one hour ahead (to 1 AM).

Dealing with morning wake time:

- If you'd like to capitalize on a later wake-up time, go ahead and let your child sleep in (e.g., to 7:30 AM). He should wake one hour later than normal (which will feel like 6:30 AM to him). If he's still napping, he will push his naps and bedtime one hour later as a result. This will result in a later sleep cycle.
- If you want to keep your child on his usual schedule, wake him at his normal wake-up time (e.g., 6:30 AM) and resume his normal schedule. He will lose an hour of sleep for the night, but within a few days, he'll adjust to the new schedule.

Fall Back

1. Put your child to bed at his usual bedtime (e.g., 7:30 PM).
2. At midnight, turn all clocks back one hour (to 11 PM).

Dealing with morning wake time:

- Your child will wake one hour EARLIER than usual in the morning. Get up with him (e.g., 5:30 AM!)

The keys to getting your child back on his old schedule:

- For a child who naps: Keep him awake until his NORMAL naptime.
- If your child does not nap any longer, keep him awake until his regular old bedtime for several nights—even if he's tired and cranky.

In three to four days, your child should adjust to the new time.

Until then, hang in there!

—Jill Spivack and Jennifer Waldburger,
founders of Sleepy Planet
and authors of *The Sleepeasy Solution.*
www.SleepyPlanet.com

SLEEP MILESTONES

Newborns. Infants generally need sixteen hours of sleep per day. The most important sleep lesson to teach your baby at this age is the difference between day and night. (The sooner your baby learns that night is for sleeping and daytime is for being active and awake, the sooner you'll get to sleep through the night!) The most typical obstacle parents face at this stage is that newborns rarely sleep for more than three or four hours at a time and do not stay awake for more than two hours at a time.

Three to six months. At this stage, infants typically need fourteen to fifteen hours of sleep a day, with nine to ten of those hours at night. According to Spivack and Waldburger, "your baby may start to resist a third nap and begin the transition from three naps to two." Your most important tasks at this stage are establishing predictable bedtimes and naptimes for your baby and creating bedtime rituals. The most typical obstacle you'll face is teaching your baby to fall asleep on her own. According to Mindell, "He needs to learn to fall asleep by himself, so that when he naturally awakens during the night (all babies wake 2 to 6 times per night) he can return to sleep on his own without your assistance."

Six to nine months. Babies at this age have similar sleeping needs and issues as they did in the previous stage. However, at this age many children develop separation anxiety and, as a result, may start waking up and having a difficult time falling back to sleep. Sleep disturbances often occur as your baby reaches major milestones in cognitive development. The excitement of learning new things may make it harder for your little one to sleep at this age.

Twelve to eighteen months. At this stage your baby typically needs fourteen hours of sleep—eleven hours of which are at night—and she may be ready to make the transition from two naps to one. It is not uncommon for your child to start resisting naptime or even bedtime toward the end of this period, due to developmental milestones such as walking.

Eighteen to twenty-four months. Toddlers at this age typically need eleven to twelve hours per night plus one nap of one to three hours each day. At this age children try to assert their independence and test limits. This combination can be difficult on

A Little Sun Can Go a Long Way

A study of healthy six- to twelve-week-old infants in the *Journal of Sleep Research* found that babies who slept well at night had been exposed to twice as much light between noon and 4 p.m. as the poor sleepers. It is believed that exposure to daylight encourages development of the biological clock, which regulates the secretion of melatonin, a chemical that tells the body when it is time to sleep.

parents. At bedtime, try to give your child choices you are comfortable with while maintaining boundaries. Allowing your child to pick between two acceptable choices gives her a feeling of control, but does not overwhelm her with too many options.

One of the greatest dangers for your child at this age is climbing out of her crib. If she shows signs of climbing out, lower the crib mattress or consider adding a crib tent if your pediatrician agrees that it is safe. Monitor her closely, and remove any crib toys that can be used as stepstools. Keep in mind that just because your child can get out of her crib doesn't mean she is ready for a bed. Most pediatric sleep experts recommend waiting until at least age three to transition from crib to bed.

Twenty-four to thirty-six months. At this age most children need eleven to fourteen hours of sleep, one to three hours of which are during the day. While some kids hold onto their afternoon nap as late as six years old, others start dropping it around age three. According to the National Sleep Foundation's Sleep in America poll, the percentage of children who still take one nap a day is as follows:

- 57 percent of three-year-olds
- 26 percent of four-year-olds
- 14 percent of five-year-olds
- 2 percent of six-year-olds

The greatest obstacle to quality sleep for your child at this age is her curiosity, active imagination, and desire to test limits. To help her transition to sleep time, it is particularly important to "hold the frame," or maintain the bedtime regardless of her resistance, and have a well-established nighttime ritual by this age.

CREATING A BEDTIME RITUAL

It is important to start a regular sleep-time ritual as early as possible—from the beginning, ideally, or at least in the first three months. The bedtime ritual should take fifteen to sixty minutes and will shift as your child gets older. The ritual consists of a series of predictable events that take place in the environment where your child sleeps, therefore signaling to her that it is time to go to sleep.

As children get older, they often have a hard time making the transition to bedtime. Toddlers typically have a hard time with bedtime for the following reasons:

- Bedtime involves separation.
- Toddlers don't want to slow their body down to sleep.
- A parent's bedtime commands make children feel controlled.
- Toddlers resist missing fun activities.
- They feel anxiety about being alone.

- They have imaginary fears (monsters, ghosts, etc.).
- They have difficulties with transitions.
- They fear relinquishing control and letting sleep take over.

The main goals for your nighttime ritual are to bring your child down from an alert, awake state to a calm state, make positive sleep associations, create feelings of connection, reduce anxiety, and create a sense of security and containment for her feelings of uncertainty. Structured bedtime rituals can foster feelings of connectedness that will make your child feel safe falling asleep.

In order to be effective, bedtime rituals must:

- be consistent and predictable
- be calming and not involve any physical activity, scary stories, or television
- last fifteen to sixty minutes
- end at the same time every night
- begin and end in the child's bedroom
- include transitions and gentle reminders
- be enjoyable

A good and consistent nighttime routine cues your child that it is time to go to sleep. Pick a combination of the following activities, based on your child's age and preferences, to create an effective nighttime ritual. Make sure to do the same activities in the same order every night.

Babies:
Giving a baby massage
Changing the diaper
Breast- or bottle-feeding

Toddlers:
Telling a story
Brushing teeth
Talking about the day
Looking at the stars through the window
Having a drink of water
Getting tucked in

All Ages:
Getting lots of cuddles
Taking a bath
Dimming lights
Listening to relaxing music
Putting on pajamas
Reading a book

Singing a soothing song
Saying a prayer
Giving good-night kisses

The nighttime, after-dinner ritual with my two-and-a-half-year-old twin daughters, Quincy and Mendez, takes place in their room and generally takes about forty-five minutes. Both children have already been bathed and are in pajamas at this point. First, each child gets to pick one book for me to read. I sit on the floor with both children in my lap and read the books. I then dim the lights and start the "nighty-night music" (*Golden Slumbers: A Father's Lullabye*). One of the girls—say, Quincy—settles down to cuddle with me in the rocking chair (we alternate who goes first each night); meanwhile, Mendez is usually sitting on the floor nearby "reading" a book. Cuddle time is uninterrupted time with Mom. I offer Quincy a drink of water and we talk about her day, what she will be doing tomorrow, and anything else she feels like talking about. Toward the end of the cuddle I give her a transition warning and a reminder: "Our cuddle is about to come to an end and soon you will be going to Grammy's lap for a cuddle" (or Papa's lap, depending on who is doing the ritual with me or if I am alone with them). Quincy then goes to the other lap for a cuddle and Mendez has her cuddle, water, and uninterrupted time with me. She is then transitioned to Papa or Grammy for cuddling. I then tuck both girls into their cribs and ask each of them what she'd like me to say on the two-way monitor. This part of the ritual, started after a bad bout of separation anxiety when Mendez and Quincy were around eighteen months old, serves as a nice reminder that Mommy is nearby. I then go to the monitor in my bedroom and repeat what they have asked me to say, remind them of their sleep plans (see page 70), and wish them good-night sprinkled with *I love you's*. When I do the nighttime ritual alone, the order stays the same. When the girls were too young to be on the floor by themselves and I was flying solo, the child who was not getting lap time had crib time with a few board books.

While this series of predictable events may sound rigid, it is really fun and enjoyable. There are no arguments about what comes next because everyone knows. Each of my children gets one-on-one time with me and with Dad or Grammy, which is extremely important. They get to exert their will by making choices, such as which book they want to read, and they get warnings prior to transitions, which makes them easier. Our nighttime ritual gives us, as parents, a truly delicious time to connect with our children. We all look forward to it.

TIPS FOR THE SCHEDULE-CHALLENGED

Ideally, you would, as Tracy Hogg says, "start as you mean to go on." But if you did not start with a schedule, it is never too late to begin following one. Start by adding structure to the beginning and the end of the day. Make sure to share the new plan with your child, even if she is preverbal. Do not make too many changes all at once. Start small and add one new ritual or event to your child's day every three to seven days, depending on how she reacts to the modifications and how big the new change is.

Here are a few suggestions to keep in mind as you develop your new schedule or refine the one you have. Some of these suggestions involve maintaining structure, while others are about sleep, because good sleep is the foundation on which the schedule is built.

1. Write down your schedule and keep it posted where you can see it, preferably in both the kitchen and your child's bedroom or bathroom. This also allows other caretakers to see it and helps keep everyone on track.

2. Keep a log book where you can make notes on your child's sleeping and eating habits so you can adjust the schedule as you notice your child's needs changing.

3. Keep wake-up time the same every day, within thirty minutes.

4. Bedtime and naptime should always be at the same time and in the same place every day.

5. To preserve good-quality nighttime sleep, don't let the last nap go past 4 p.m.

6. Keep the same schedule on weekends, even wake-up time.

7. In order to maintain consistency, maintain the schedule even in the face of protests. Be kind, gentle, and loving—but firm.

8. Avoid rocking a child to sleep, especially after the first six to twelve weeks. Lulling a child to sleep creates dependency and negative sleep associations (as opposed to beneficial nighttime rituals, which children participate in while they are still fully awake) before getting into their bed or crib.

9. At bedtime, offer only acceptable choices—for example, "Do you want to wear the red pajamas or the blue pajamas?"

10. Don't ask rhetorical questions (to which you don't really expect or want an answer), such as "Do you want to go to bed now?"

11. Put infants to bed when they're drowsy but awake so they can learn to fall asleep on their own.

12. Don't keep your child up late just because you've come home from work late; early bedtimes are crucial for quality sleep.

13. Keep your child's room between 68 and 72 degrees Fahrenheit for comfort, optimal sleep, and to reduce the risk of sudden infant death syndrome. For more information on SIDS, see Appendix D.

14. Tell your child what she'll be doing the next day so she knows what to expect.

THE PLAN

As soon as your child is verbal enough to have a conversation, you can start talking about a self-soothing plan and what he can do if he has trouble sleeping. As a parent, you have observed what has worked to help your child calm himself and what has not. The plan should include three things he can do on his own to soothe himself to sleep. Will, an eighteen-month-old toddler I worked with, had the following plan: pacifier, teddy bear, and blanket. Every night before bedtime, his mother would remind him to use his plan. They also talked about it throughout the day. If Will had any trouble sleeping in the middle of the night, his mother would remind him of the plan. These reminders had a dramatic impact on helping Will learn to self-soothe. Although there were times when he needed more than his plan could offer so his mom came in to help him, most of the time Will's plan enabled him to learn the skills he needed to bring himself back to sleep on his own.

Ten Things You Can Do to Get Better Organized

Planning and preparing in advance are the keys to being an organized parent. Here are some things you can do to make your life a little easier:

- Keep the schedule posted on the wall where you can see it.
- Make sure you have everything you need in the area where you breastfeed or pump, in advance.
- Keep diaper bags fully stocked with clean diapers, wipes, sunscreen, an extra change of clothes, nonperishable snacks, etc.
- Prepare meals and clean dishes and bottles while your child naps.
- If your child uses a bottle, sippy cup, or straw-cup for milk, pre-fill a day or two worth of drinks in advance.
- Set the table for breakfast the night before.
- Preset the coffeemaker if you drink coffee.
- Put children's next-day clothing out the night before, allowing older kids to help pick their clothes.
- Keep an ongoing shopping list so trips to the market are efficient.
- Buy frequently used items like diapers, diaper cream, shampoo, and sunscreen in bulk so you always have some on hand and get better prices.

Let Your Fingers Do the Walking

The Importance of Touch

The nurse brought little baby Catherine to her parents to hold for the last time. She was very sick. The doctors at Brigham and Women's Hospital in Boston had done everything they could to keep her alive, but her oxygen levels were dangerously low, causing her to have great difficulty breathing. She was in respiratory distress and was close to death. Hoping to soothe the parents' grief, one of the neonatal intensive care unit (NICU) nurses suggested that Edward and Marilyn Real hold their daughter against their skin. As they held their tiny baby girl, the monitors began to show dramatic changes—for the better. Taking turns holding Catherine for the next thirty-six hours straight, the Reals watched her condition gradually improve. Four months later she was able to go home and a month later she appeared on Good Morning America with her parents and nurse Marie Field, who spoke about the healing effects of touch, specifically what has become known as "kangaroo care." Edward Real said, "I believe if it hadn't been for the nurses letting us hold her, she wouldn't have made it."

It's All Over You!
The Significance of Skin

Your baby's body becomes sensitive to touch soon after conception, making skin sensitivity one of the earliest and most completely developed senses. This early development supports the theory—based on embryological law, the idea that the earlier a function develops, the more essential it is likely to be—that skin touch is vital to development. A child is born with 320 touch receptors per square inch, totaling about 5 million altogether. In fact, there are over 100 different types of receptors that allow your baby to respond to different types of touch, such as pain, pressure, temperature, and vibration. As Dr. Tiffany Field, director of The Touch Research Institute, aptly puts it, "because skin cannot shut its eyes or cover its ears, it is in a constant state of readiness to receive messages—it is always on." Your child's first experiences of the world, of himself, and of you come through this sense. In fact, further research by Dr. Ashley Montagu shows that your baby needs skin-to-skin contact in order for his nervous system to develop properly.

SKIN, IT'S NOT JUST NICE TO LOOK AT:
THE 8 BIGGEST PHYSICAL BENEFITS OF TOUCH

There are many ways you can provide positive touch for your baby: holding, hugging, stroking, rocking, breast-feeding, massage, and kangaroo care (KC) are just a few. For your baby, the benefits of your gentle touch are all-encompassing, dramatically improving his physical, emotional, and intellectual health. Here are eight physical benefits of touch, based on the most important findings of recent studies:

1. Smarter children. Eighty percent of your child's brain growth takes place during the first two years of life. Every time your baby is touched, that sensory input triggers the neurons in his brain to grow and branch out. In studies comparing animals deprived of touch to those that were not, the ones that were held and touched experienced an increase in gross brain mass, an increase in the number of synaptic junctions that connect neurons, and a higher ratio of cortical functioning.

In a study by Drs. Marshall Klaus and John Kennell in which mothers handled their babies, skin to skin, for an hour during the first two hours after birth and for five extra hours during the next three days, researchers found that a month later the mothers felt closer and more connected with their babies, and five years later their children scored higher on IQ and language tests. A study of preemies in the NICU found that those who were given additional strokes were found to be smarter when tested at age seven.

2. Healthier digestion. Because babies are born with poorly developed digestive systems, they frequently have digestive problems. Touch, and especially massage, can help. According to Dr. Field, when children are massaged, the pressure stimulates a branch of the cranial nerve, which, in turn, stimulates the gastrointestinal tract. In addition, massage stimulates the circulation of blood and lymphatic fluids, which help the body get rid of waste, release tension, and lower stress hormones. Massage also releases endorphins in the brain, giving the child a sense of well-being. Massage even helps relieve constipation because it encourages the necessary muscle contractions that push food down the esophagus, into the stomach, through the intestines, and out of the body.

FROM THE EXPERTS . . .

Bonding Tips for New Parents

The first hours after a baby is born are a critical time for the new mom, dad, and baby. Numerous hormonal, neurochemical, and physiologic changes take place in all three persons that set the stage for a lifetime of attachment for both parents and baby. A period of uninterrupted bonding should be allowed to take place in order to maximize these benefits:

- As soon as the baby is born, he should be placed directly on his mother's bare abdomen or chest.
- The mother (and father) should spend at least the first hour touching and gazing at their new baby.
- Allow the baby to suckle at the breast if he desires (but don't worry about whether or not baby accomplishes a vigorous feeding—this is just for bonding).
- The first hour or two after birth can be a very alert, wide-eyed time for a baby; spend as much time in eye-to-eye contact with baby as you can before he drifts off to sleep.

3. Improved weight gain. Massage can yield dramatic results. In a 1986 study of premature infants in the NICU at Jackson Memorial Hospital in Miami, researchers massaged the babies for three fifteen-minute periods each day for ten days with startling results. Compared to another group of babies, the infants who were massaged averaged a 47 percent greater weight gain per day, allowing them to leave the hospital six days sooner—and saving their parents an average of $3,000! In addition, the massaged babies were more active and alert, their motor skills were better, and they were more developmentally mature.

4. Improved immune system. Various studies have shown how important touch is to the health of children's immune systems. For example, in a study of babies whose mothers gave them back massages at ten weeks, there was a lower incidence of colds and diarrhea four months later. Other studies have shown the harsh flip side of the touch equation, where preschoolers who had been separated from their mothers—and consequently were touch deprived—experienced frequent illnesses, particularly constipation, diarrhea, and upper respiratory infections.

- Routine medical procedures, such as the vitamin K shot, eye ointment, needle sticks, weighing, and bathing should all be delayed until after the first feeding is accomplished (these can all wait at least several hours).
- The initial physical exam (usually performed by the labor and delivery nurse) should be done with baby right on mom's chest.
- For uncomplicated deliveries and healthy newborns, there is no reason for a baby to leave mom's presence during the recovery period.

The importance of the first hour of bonding is now recognized by the American Academy of Pediatrics (AAP). Its official written policy on how newborns should be cared for after birth includes many of the above tips (search "breastfeeding and the use of human milk" under the policy section of the AAP's website). Because many hospitals are behind the times and haven't adopted this AAP policy, parents-to-be should make sure their hospital is willing to abide by it. Who knows, you may be the catalyst for change at your local hospital.

—Dr. Bob Sears,
pediatrician and co-author of
The Baby Book and
HappyBaby: The Organic Guide to Baby's First 24 Months
www.askdrsears.com

5. Better sleep. Anyone who has ever had a massage before going to bed will tell you how much easier it is to fall asleep—and enjoy a *better quality* of sleep—afterward. It's no different for your children. Studies have shown that massage improves the quality of children's sleep. One dramatic study, in which nurses gently cradled the heads and stroked the abdomens of premature infants with respiratory distress syndrome, found that the babies had improved ratios of red blood cells, required less oxygen, needed fewer blood transfusions, and slept significantly better.

6. Enhanced muscle tone and coordination. Premature babies who receive as little as ten days of touch therapy display better body tone, head control, hand-mouth coordination, and alertness than babies who are not given the advantages of touch therapy. According to pediatrician Dr. Jay Gordon, "Massage stimulates and activates receptors in the skin, muscles, and joints, assisting your baby in learning to coordinate her muscular movements."

7. More developed sensory awareness. When children are born they don't have a strong sense of their bodies. Healthy touch, however, creates stimuli that encourage them to discover and become more aware and knowledgeable about their bodies in relation to the world around them.

8. Better ability to handle stress. You may wonder, "What does a baby have to be stressed about?" Believe it or not, being a baby is very stressful. Because they're so helpless and their resources so limited, it can be very frustrating for babies to get their needs met. It is even more trying for infants if their needs are not responded to. According to Sue Gerhardt, author of *Why Love Matters,* "When these needs are not met by others, the baby may become more aware of a sense of powerlessness and helplessness. Stress for babies may even have the quality of trauma."

How do you know if your baby is especially stressed? Experts identify six signs of baby stress:

- Heightened startle response
  (for example, reacting in fear to noises)
- Excessive fussing or complaining
- Continued crying, even after being held
- An arched back
- Increased breathing rate
- Shaking or twitching

Reducing your baby's stress is important because energy that is wasted on stress responses is energy your baby doesn't have available for other important functions like eating or learning.

Hands Off:
The Effects of Touch Deprivation

The most profound and heartbreaking documented examples of the need for touch took place in child-care institutions in Europe and the United States in the nineteenth and early twentieth centuries. Due to the lack of adequate child care and attempts to keep children germ-free, institutionalized children received very little hands-on care. Even though they were given proper food and medical care, many of them became sick. Many of these children cried for long periods of time, eventually became despondent and depressed, refused to eat, and ultimately died. This distressing phenomenon was so common that professionals gave it a number of different names, including marasmus, hospitalism, and "failure to thrive." In 1930, when Bellevue Hospital in New York City changed its policy to incorporate physical contact with children under hospital care, the mortality rate dropped from 30 percent to 10 percent.

THE INVISIBLE CAGE

Many of the modern conveniences that we find so helpful, such as strollers and portable car seats, actually reduce the amount of time we spend holding and touching our children. I am not advocating that we abolish these handy items: as a parent of twins I would have been lost without them, especially the first year. What I do recommend is that you use them less and use them more thoughtfully. I can't tell you the number of times I've seen parents leave kids in their car seats long after they've been removed from the car.

Take baby Sofia, for example. While riding with her parents to her grandparents' house for dinner, she falls asleep in her car seat. When they arrive, her parents remove Sofia, still in the car seat, from the car and sit her down near the dining room table where everyone is eating. When she wakes up, her parents rock the seat and dangle some toys in front of her to keep her entertained. After dinner they snap the car seat into the compatible stroller and take a walk outside. At the end of their visit, they put Sofia, still in her car seat, back in the car. Sofia has thus spent the entire time in her car seat. This means that, for four hours, she was largely deprived of touch, stimulation, and socialization.

Baby Henry, on the other hand, visits his grandparents under different circumstances. Henry, like Sofia, falls asleep in the car, but on arrival at his grandparents' house, his parents take him out of the car seat and put him in a sling, which allows him to continue sleeping against his dad's warm chest. When he wakes up, everyone takes turns holding him on their lap: grandpa reads him a story, grandma makes eye contact and talks to him. His mother puts a blanket on the floor, where he enjoys some "tummy time" and plays with his toys. Henry spends the entire time he's awake interacting and being stimulated by his parents and grandparents. His family's exertion of energy to entertain him results in a far more interesting trip for Henry as well as a boost in his brain development.

Instead of keeping your child cooped up in a car seat, try the following:

- Hold him.
- Sit him in your lap.
- Rock together in a chair.
- Carry him.
- Use a baby sling or carrier.
- Put a blanket on the floor and give him floor time or tummy time.
- Let him play with safe toys and books in his crib.

Reasons to Take Your Baby Out of the Car Seat

In 2003 the American Academy of Pediatrics suggested that infants "should spend minimal time in car seats (when not a passenger in a vehicle) or other seating that maintains supine positioning." Here are a few good reasons to follow the AAP's suggestion:

Flat-head syndrome (also called plagiocephaly). With the "back to sleep" campaign encouraging parents to put their children to sleep on their backs in order to reduce the risk of SIDS, doctors are seeing more and more children with what has been commonly called "flat-head syndrome," which occurs as a result of consistent pressure on a particular spot of the skull. Extended periods of time spent in car seats, strollers, swings, and other devices that put babies in a back-lying position contribute to this problem. According to experts, cranial distortion from the overuse of car seats and swings is more severe and complex than that caused by lying on the back on a mattress.

Eye gaze and sound orientation deprivation. Car-seat carriers tend to have high sides, nestling babies deep within the seat, as a safety feature. But this "cocooning" limits their ability to see or hear what is going on around them. A baby who hears a knock at the door may try to turn his head toward the sound, but he won't be able to if the sides of his car seat are too high.

Touch deprivation. When children are strapped into a plastic container, it is less likely their parents will touch them and connect with them.

Cervical spine alignment. According to Dr. Jeanne Ohm, executive coordinator of the International Pediatric Association, strollers and car seats force kids to tilt their heads to one side or the other, causing their upper cervical spine to go out of alignment.

Mom's aching back. A car seat usually weighs as much as your baby, and it can be awkward to carry without bumping it into your own body. New moms are particularly vulnerable to back injuries because of a hormone called relaxin, which keeps their joints loose for as long as nine months after giving birth.

A Good Rub-a-Dub-Dub:
The Emotional Benefits of Touch

The inadequately gentled animal . . .
is an emotionally unsatisfied creature.

—ASHLEY MONTAGU,
Touching: The Human Significance of the Skin

Physical, human contact—your gentle, positive touch—is a profound and essential element of your child's development and emotional health that communicates love, acceptance, worthiness, and safety. Physical touch has five main emotional benefits for your child:

1. Physical touch creates self-esteem. To a preverbal infant, touch is the language of love signaling that he is wanted, loved, accepted, and safe. This early message is crucial in the development of self-esteem. In addition, according to Dr. Field, "A child's first emotional bonds are built from physical contact, laying a foundation for further emotional and intellectual development." There is nothing quite as effective as touch for communicating a sense of love and belonging. Studies have shown that verbal reassurances, even when given from close proximity, do not provide nearly the same calming effect as physical touch and cuddling.

2. Physical touch helps children bond with caretakers. In 1958, a psychologist named Harry Harlow performed an experiment with rhesus macaque monkeys. He chose this species because they share roughly 94 percent of their genetic heritage with humans. When the monkeys were born, Harlow separated them from their mothers and gave them two choices of artificial surrogate "mothers." One was a soft, terrycloth-covered form with a lightbulb, which provided warmth. The second surrogate was made of wire with a milk-filled bottle attached to it. The baby monkeys spent only the time needed for feeding with the wire mother and clung for up to twenty-two hours a day to the cloth mother, which provided greater comfort. Harlow's discoveries fundamentally changed how we view the mother-child relationship. Prior to these experiments, experts believed that the act of feeding bonded children to their caregivers, but Harlow's research graphically proved that *touch,* not food, binds infants to their caregivers.

3. Physical touch teaches self-soothing. The ability to self-soothe acts as an inoculation against substance abuse, eating disorders, and all sorts of compulsive behaviors. The ability to calm yourself down and manage emotions is a crucial part of emotional intelligence. According to Joanne Bagshaw and Ilene Fox, authors of *Baby Massage for Dummies*, "The more frequently your baby experiences relaxation in his body, the easier it becomes for him to bring his body back into a relaxed state on his own." Remember the study in which the massaged infants gained 47 percent more weight than the control group? Those same babies were found to be better at calming themselves down, too. This makes sense biologically because positive maternal attention decreases the impact of stress on the brain and enhances the development of brain systems that support affect regulation, or the ability to regulate emotions.

4. Physical touch makes for better mothering. When you touch your newborn, your body releases a hormone called oxytocin, which helps you attach and bond with your baby. After you've given birth, oxytocin is also responsible for stimulating the uterus to contract; helping you to relax; and promoting the let-down reflex that moves milk into the breast, allowing your baby to receive milk when breastfeeding. It should come as no surprise that studies show that mothers who touch and massage their babies produce more milk.

In the Klaus and Kennell study, mothers who had skin-to-skin contact with their babies for an hour after birth and for five further hours during the next three days were significantly more engaged with their children compared with control-study moms who had less contact with their babies. In later interviews, researchers found that the engaged mothers

- soothed their infants more
- touched their babies and made more eye contact during feedings
- spent more time assisting doctors during the one-year examination
- asked their children more questions, thereby engaging them more
- gave fewer commands (such as "Put that down" or "Come over here") to their children two years later

5. Physical touch helps your baby learn to trust. Your baby is totally helpless and therefore completely dependent upon you to meet his needs. Developmental psychologist Erik Erikson believes that during the first eighteen months a child's primary task is to figure out if the world and his caregivers are trustworthy. Erikson calls this stage "trust versus mistrust." If your baby's needs (diaper changes, feeding, comforting, soothing touch, etc.) are consistently met, then he will come to believe that the world is a safe place. His sense of trust or mistrust is based on his sensory experiences of the world, which come, good or bad, is largely through his skin.

Everybody Needs a Hand: Two Types of Super-Touch

Everything that newborns and infants know about the universe they learn through their physical sensations.

—Dr. Reuven Bar-Levav

Parents touch their children during routine day-to-day care—changing a diaper, feeding, bathing—and gladly provide extra cuddles, hugs, kisses, and affection. But there is even more that moms and dads can do to give their children the maximum benefits of touch: "kangaroo care" and baby massage can easily be integrated into your daily routine and have benefits that are easy to see.

Kangaroo Care

When my twin daughters, Mendez and Quincy, were born premature, they weighed four and four-and-a-half pounds. They had trouble maintaining their body temperature, struggled to eat, and had a difficult time gaining weight. I had the great fortune to be introduced to kangaroo care by a very experienced NICU nurse, Shirley Munro of UCLA Santa Monica Hospital. Munro instructed my husband and me to place one baby on our bare chest and cover up with a warm, soft blanket. We did this for at least fifteen minutes each day for the first few months. As time went on, our girls grew bigger and stronger and we felt more and more attached to them.

This process, known as "kangaroo care" or "K-care," has been studied all over the world because of its effectiveness, especially for preemies. Parents who practice kangaroo care generally place their diaper-clad baby on their bare chest or stomach. Resting your baby's head on your chest allows her to hear and be soothed by your heartbeat, much as she did in utero.

Kangaroo care can have miraculous results, as we saw in Catherine Real's story. The technique appears to have originated in Bogotá, Colombia, in 1979, when neonatologists Dr. Edgar Rey and Dr. Hector Martinez found a way to take care of preemies despite the lack of reliable electrical power for incubators and other equipment. They not only found that skin-to-skin contact is the natural way of restoring an infant's vital signs and maintaining body temperature, but they also reduced the mortality rate in Bogotá from 70 percent to 30 percent.

Besides increasing the chances of survival for the babies in their care, Rey and Martinez found that this intervention was very comforting to both parent and child and was an excellent method of bonding. Since they began their kangaroo care regimen, many other hospitals and pediatricians all over the world have implemented similar programs. Studies consistently show that kangaroo care can

- help stabilize heart rates
- regulate breathing and improve oxygen dispersion throughout the body
- increase periods of alertness
- promote successful breastfeeding
- maximize weight gain
- improve sleep
- prevent infections
- reduce motor development delays
- decrease crying
- prevent stress from cold
- increase the likelihood of an early hospital discharge

During kangaroo care, an infant's systems are kept at a regular temperature, thanks to the mother's body. K-care researchers Drs. Susan Ludington-Hoe and Gene Anderson discovered what has been called "thermal synchrony," which occurs when mothers unconsciously regulate their infant's skin temperature by changing their own body temperature in response. In other words, when her baby starts to get cool, the skin temperature of the mother's breasts starts to rise in order to warm her child. The reverse is true, too. When her baby's temperature gets too high, the mother's temperature starts to cool, helping to keep her child's body at a level temperature. In a recent study, researchers found that just telling a mother that the baby in her arms was a little cold caused her breast temperature to rise, warming her child, and when the researchers told her that her baby was "warm enough now," her breast temperature plateaued, helping to keep her baby's temperature where it needed to be.

K-CARE ISN'T JUST FOR SICK BABIES

The advantages of kangaroo care are not just for preemies; children who are born at full term get just as much out of the experience. A comprehensive review of kangaroo care research led by Drs. Ludington-Hoe and Barbara Morrison, who examined five different types of kangaroo care, found that the benefits were universal. Compared to full-term babies who did not get K-care, many who did

- experienced earlier bonding
- had better sucking technique during breastfeeding

- experienced fewer infections
- kept a more consistent body temperature
- experienced less body temperature heat loss
- cried less frequently and have significantly shorter crying spells
- improved and increased their sleep
- showed better quality body movements
- interacted with their mothers more
- tolerated pain better
- had less colic
- had reduced rates of hypoglycemia
- did not lose any weight after leaving the hospital

Their mothers

- were more successful at breastfeeding
- showed more attachment behaviors
- experienced an increase in confidence
- were more affectionate with their babies

Kangaroo Care Tips

- Keep the room temperature at 70 to 72 degrees Fahrenheit.
- Stay away from air-conditioning vents, open doors, and drafts.
- Make sure you are healthy so you don't give your baby a cold or flu.
- Empty your bladder before starting.
- Don't start a K-care session on an empty stomach.
- Sit in a padded chair, preferably one that allows you to rock.
- Try using a footrest, which can make you more comfortable and maintain blood circulation in the legs.
- Wear comfortable clothing and make sure your shirt opens in the front.
- If you are lactating, wear breast pads, since you are likely to experience some letdown.
- Make sure your baby is wearing a clean diaper before beginning.
- Keep your infant warm with a soft blanket.
- Many infants are most comfortable during kangaroo care in a fetal position since it approximates their position in the womb.

Massage

Massage has been proved extremely beneficial for babies and children. Although proponents claim that massage can help your baby become smarter and relieve his constipation or gas, the real purpose of massage is to help you tune into your child and get to know him better. Joanne Bagshaw says it best in *Baby Massage for Dummies:* "Baby massage isn't just something that you do to your baby; it's a way of communicating through touch how much love you have for your little one."

You can't do this very well, however, if you're not fully focused on him. It is important to turn off the television (more on that in Chapter 10), put away the Blackberry, and concentrate completely on your child and his reactions to your touch. Ideally you want your child to be in what experts call a "quiet alert" state,

Medical Benefits of Baby Massage

While massage should never replace medical care for a child, it can ease many symptoms babies typically experience. Always consult your doctor to make sure massage is appropriate for your child. Proponents of massage claim that it can help relieve the following ailments:

Constipation	Colic
Eczema	Cradle cap
Asthma	Teething
Congestion	Dry skin
Gas	

a state of conscious attention, before beginning a massage. You'll know your baby is ready if he is interested in what you are doing, he is making eye contact with you, and he isn't fussy. No matter how young he is and though he may not understand what you're saying, make sure you ask your baby for permission before beginning. This shows your child respect and honors his personal boundaries. These early communications set the stage for the future.

Vimala McClure, founder of the International Association of Infant Massage and author of *Infant Massage,* recommends giving your child a special cue before starting every massage. A special cue could be as simple as rubbing some oil in your palms while saying, "It's time for your massage," which also has the added

benefit of verbally communicating to your child what is about to happen. A baby who is not receptive to massage will often throw his hands up, hiccup, flail his arms, or move his eyes around very quickly. If your child does not seem amenable to a massage, don't do it. Massage is meant to be a wonderfully pleasant time between parent and child, not a forced ordeal.

In the beginning, your baby may be able to tolerate only a couple of minutes of massage, which is normal. His tolerance level will build with experience as long as you watch his body language for clues and respond appropriately.

According to McClure, "A daily massage raises an infant's stimulation threshold. Babies who have difficulty handling stimulation gradually build tolerance. High-need babies begin to learn to regulate the manner in which they respond to stressful experiences, which reduces the level of tension they develop throughout the day."

Multiples and Touch

Meeting the needs of multiple children of the same age is particularly challenging. It is most difficult during the first year, when you are adjusting to parenthood and learning how to care for more than one child at the same time. Even though both (or more) of your children may be at the same stage of development and have the same needs at the same time, they deserve the focused, individual attention that singleton children receive. Because multiples tend to get touched, spoken to, and held less frequently than singleton children, it's essential to make a greater effort to tend to your kids' needs. Here are a few tips:

Try to have a one-to-one ratio of adults to children when giving a massage. If you do not have an available partner, grandparent, friend, or child-care provider to help give your children massages, work with one baby at a time. Don't jump back and forth between babies.

Use a sling whenever you can so you can keep your baby close to you, increasing the amount of holding and touching time your baby receives. Slings can free your hands to care for another child, and the close contact is comforting for both parent and child.

Feed your children individually. Hold each child individually, whether you are breast- or bottle-feeding. Food and love are inexorably linked, and that focused attention is vital for each child. The back-and-forth verbal and nonverbal exchanges that take place during feedings are essential to create feelings of connection, to help you learn to read your child's cues, and to give your child a sense of early communication.

Never "prop feed." Prop feeding, or using an object to prop up a bottle for your child to drink from, is a terrible idea. While it may seem like a great way to save time and free you to get other things done, it actually puts your child at high risk for choking. In addition, the disconnection between you and your child takes the joy out of feeding.

MASSAGE TIPS

- Check with your pediatrician before starting a massage regimen.

- Create a regular massage schedule. Babies love predictability.

- Keep the room between 75 and 80 degrees Fahrenheit. Babies lose heat from their bodies quickly.

- Wash your hands before and after the massage.

- Remove all rings and jewelry.

- Make sure your nails are trimmed so you don't scratch your baby.

- Use a gentle, but firm touch with long, slow, rhythmic pressure.

- Use oil specifically designed for infant massage or use a food-based oil, like olive oil. Studies show that infants who are massaged with oil show fewer stress behaviors than babies who are not massaged with oil.

- Be aware, if you are using oil, that your baby can get slippery. Pick him up in a towel so he doesn't slip out of your hands.

- Test any oil you intend to use on your child by putting it on a small patch of his skin in order to make sure he does not have a bad reaction.

- Play soothing music.

- Pay attention to your baby's cues.

- Don't use a fluttery, poking, or ticklish touch.

- Don't use essential oils because they are too concentrated and can be harmful for your baby if he swallows them.

- Don't use oils from nuts or seeds, even if you don't think your child is allergic to them.

- Don't use baby oils that are petroleum-based. They have possible human carcinogens and the long-term health effects are not yet known.

- Don't massage your baby if he has a fever, infectious disease, skin infection, rash, open wound, or bruise.

- Don't allow any distractions—turn off the television, phone, and computer.

- Don't massage immediately after your baby eats; wait one hour.

READY, SET, RUB!

Most infant massage instructors recommend starting massage on the first day of your baby's life in order to acclimate him to touch. According to Lynne Oyama, RN, a certified infant massage instructor, starting a massage routine should be "organic," but the most important thing is to be in tune with your child's cues. Some babies love a bedtime massage, while others find it too stimulating. That's why it's important to experiment with massages at different times of the day to see what works for your child. Once you have figured out what is best, establish a ritual. Oyama notes that kids love predictability; they feel secure if you let them know what's going to happen. It is ideal to begin massaging from an early age but it is never too late to begin. Once your child is about six months old and becomes more mobile, it'll become hard for him to sit still during a massage, although he may still enjoy a naptime massage. If you can keep up this calming routine, even as your baby becomes more active, he may still be interested when he's a toddler and ask on his own for a massage.

The Tiniest of Massage Clients: Your Preemie

Because premature babies' systems are so underdeveloped, your preemie may not be able to initially handle massage. It is especially important to be sensitive to your preemie's cues, including keeping him clothed during massage if you think he might be vulnerable to losing body heat if he's not fully dressed. To improve your chances of a successful massage, keep the lights dim and the room quiet to avoid overstimulation. Use downward strokes, moving toward your baby's feet, a technique that is less stimulating than many other strokes, and start by massaging, or even just holding, individual parts of his body (legs, toes, or fingers).

If your baby has received a heel stick (a common method for drawing blood that uses a needle prick in an infant's foot), keep in mind that this area can remain sensitive long after the bruises have faded. The value of touch for preemies was shown in a study of premature babies who had blood drawn via a heel prick. Those who received skin-to-skin contact while being held by their mothers for fifteen minutes before the procedure cried less than those in the control group who were swaddled in incubators before the procedure. When researchers rated the infant's pain by measuring heartbeat, oxygen saturation, and facial expression thirty seconds, sixty seconds, and two minutes after the procedure, they found that by the two-minute point, the babies held by their mothers were only in half as much pain as those in the incubators.

TRICKS OF THE TRADE: TECHNIQUES

Now that you know the benefits of massage, it is time to start massaging! Put a large clean blanket on the floor, preferably on a soft surface, in your baby's room to start. At the beginning of every massage, rub warm oil on your hands in front of your child and ask him for permission to begin. Remember to be very gentle as you massage your baby. For an easy start, I recommend five basic techniques:

1. Swedish Milking. Sometimes it is easiest to start with a leg massage since babies are less defensive about this area of the body and are used to exploring the world with their arms and legs.

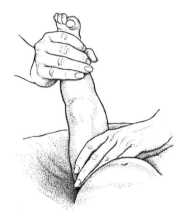

Support your child's left ankle with your left hand. With your right hand, use a smooth downward "milking" stroke to massage his leg from ankle to hip. Switch hands and massage the other side of his leg.

2. Back Strokes. Although babies don't have enough muscle development to get "knots" in their muscles, as adults do, it is very common for infants and their parents to have identical tension spots. Therefore, this is one of my favorites.

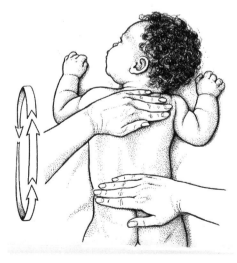

Place one hand horizontally across the top of your baby's back, just below his neck, and gently, but firmly, glide it toward his buttocks. Lift your hand just before you get there and place your other hand in the starting position. Then stroke downward with that hand, just as you did with the first. Repeat these strokes several times.

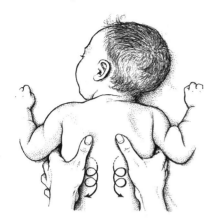

Put your hands on either side of your baby's back with your thumbs on his spine just below the neck. Make small circular movements with your thumbs, moving them down his back, stopping just before his bottom. Make sure your thumbs are on either side of his spine, not on the spine itself.

3. Pruning the Branches. Starting massage with your child's extremities can be a great way to introduce techniques to babies. Be aware, however, that, according to Oyama, the arms are often the hardest to massage because they are so mobile. Rubbing the fingers first can relax the arm.

4. Tummy Like an Open Book. Keep in mind that the abdomen is a particularly sensitive and vulnerable part of the body for most babies, especially preemies. If your preemie has stomach tubes or other invasive work in this area, you may want to skip this one.

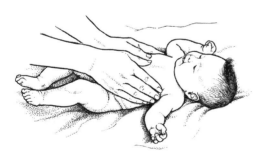

Put both hands together at the center of your child's chest and stroke in an outward motion toward the sides, as if you were flattening the pages of a book. Keep your hands on your child as you move them down, around, and back to your starting point in a heart-shaped motion. The pressure comes from the

Ten Signs Your Baby Is Overstimulated by Massage

Any one of these cues may be a sign that it is time to put down the massage oil because your baby is overstimulated:

1. He is not making eye contact with you, closing his eyes or turning away.
2. He fusses, whines, cries, or tries to squirm away.
3. He grimaces.
4. His face reddens or pales.
5. He arches his back.
6. He stiffens his arms and splays his fingers.
7. He tenses his body.
8. He gets the hiccups.
9. He sticks out his tongue.
10. He yawns or falls asleep.

starting position on your child's chest, while the rest of the motion serves just to keep your hands in contact with his body. Remember to be gentle.

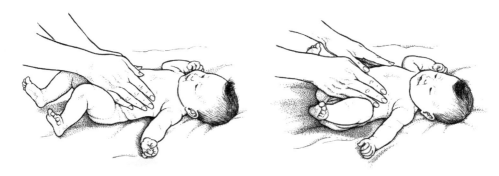

5. Happy Faces Technique. Some babies love a facial massage from the very beginning, while others never take to it. For most babies it's an acquired taste. Be sensitive to your baby's reaction when you begin a facial massage, and be especially careful around his "soft spot."

Cup your hands around your baby's head with your forefingers on his hairline. Then stroke your hands simultaneously backward over the crown of his head.

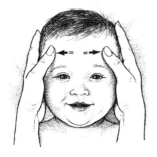

Put your thumbs in the middle of your baby's forehead directly above the bridge of his nose. Stroke each thumb outward in a straight line to the sides of his face. Repeat all the way down the forehead as if you were drawing a series of lines.

Put your thumbs on either side of the bridge of your baby's nose, near the nostril, and simultaneously sweep both thumbs outward toward the bottom of his ears.

More Than Chitchat

Promoting Language Development

Despite an IQ in the genius range, my friend David did not utter his first words until the age of three. When I asked his mother why it took so long for such a bright kid to speak, she said, "I figured there was no point in talking to him since he couldn't understand me anyway." David's early childhood experience and subsequent late speech development suggest the importance of verbal communication with infants and young children. His early years read like a chapter on "what not to do" for early language acquisition.

Twin studies show that language development is as much as 50 percent genetic, yet researchers say that the single biggest determinant in a child's language acquisition is exposure. You are your child's most important language teacher, and you don't need flash cards, computer programs, special classes, or educational videos to help your child thrive, even if you want to give her an extra edge. Her advantage will come from everyday language-filled interactions with you and other loving people in her life. In this chapter, I will provide tons of tips that boost language development. But, please note, they all come from meaningful interactions with real people. When children are immersed in language from the start, they tend to use it early and efficiently. To create an enriched environment for your child, aim for both quantity and quality.

Quantity

It has been shown that the sheer number of words spoken to a child is directly proportionate to the size of her vocabulary. However, this applies only to direct conversations you have with your child. The words she overhears from television, videos, radio, or other conversations do not count.

In an epic study of language, researchers Betty Hart and Todd Risley spent two and a half years recording, transcribing, and analyzing the words spoken at home by forty-two families from three different socioeconomic groups. This study generated what scholars believe to be the most comprehensive data on how differing language environments influence language outcome. The results were shocking.

Hart and Risley found that vocabulary differed sharply by class. By the age of three, children of "professional" families had an average vocabulary of 1,116 words, children of "working-class" families averaged 749 words, and children of "welfare" families had vocabularies that averaged 525 words. When Hart and Risley probed a little further, they found that the reason for these disparities lay in language exposure. The average professional parents used 2,153 words per hour, the working-class parents averaged 1,251 words per hour, and the welfare parents averaged 616 words per hour. Over the course of a year, this means that the welfare child was exposed to 3 million words, the working-class child to 6 million, and the professional child to 11 million. By the end of the study, the spoken vocabularies of the three-year-olds from professional families were even larger than those recorded for the *parents* in the welfare families.

These environmental influences have long-term consequences. According to Dr. Lise Eliot, author of *What's Going On in There?,* "Speech is without a doubt the most important form of stimulation a baby receives. When parents talk to their babies, they are activating hearing, social, emotional, and linguistic centers of the brain all at once, but their influence on language development is especially profound." A study of mice exposed to an enriched environment found that they had more brain cells than mice that were raised under less intellectually stimulating conditions. The incoming stream of sights, smells, noises, touch, and, most importantly, language and eye contact—which make for connection and stimulation—literally makes the brain take shape. The act of learning language actually modifies the linguistic brain.

Some language experts recommend that parents aim to use 30,000 words per day with their child. Thirty thousand words per day is equal to about twenty-one words per minute, which is equivalent to reading *The Cat in the Hat* eighteen times per day. According to Professor Judy Montgomery of Chapman University in California, most parents overestimate how much they speak to their children. If you can afford it, a language analysis program like the LENA™ system, an audio recognition system that your child can wear in her clothing, will actually count the number of words that are spoken directly to your infant or child. While you don't need a fancy system to determine how many words you are speaking directly to your child each day, a device like LENA™ can help you figure out what your child's exposure to language is and give you the chance to improve and keep track of her progress—if you find it to be deficient.

Quality

Regardless of social class or education, how well parents speak to their children varies widely. Exposure is not enough; the way you speak to your child will have a tremendous impact on her language development. Parents who speak too quickly, jumble their words together ("doesbabywantsomemilk?"), or do not focus on their child in a meaningful way that allows her to learn will miss opportunities.

Exposure to diverse vocabulary also makes a difference. In the Hart Risley study, 86 to 98 percent of the words recorded in each child's vocabulary consisted of words recorded in their parent's vocabularies. By the age of three, these children were talking and using many words that were similar to their parent's averages. By this age, the amount of talk, vocabulary growth, and style of interaction were already well established.

When Hart and Risley looked at the quality of the interactions, specifically the "feedback tone," they found that hearing a lot of prohibitions and discouragements ("Don't do that," "Stop it," "No!") has a negative impact on a child's IQ, while hearing affirmations and complex sentences ("Wow! You put the milk on the table," "If you want to hit something you can hit this pillow") has a positive effect on IQ. At thirteen to eighteen months, 80 percent of the feedback from the professional parents in the study was affirmative and about 50 percent of the working-class parents' feedback was positive, but almost 80 percent of the welfare parents' feedback to their children was negative. By the age of three, all the children's feedback tone mirrored what they had received. In other words, if the children received 80 percent negative feedback, by age three their own tone with their parents and family was negative 80 percent of the time.

Use Your Words, Mommy!

Long before children utter their first words, they start to understand words spoken around them. Studies have shown that infants as young as four months can recognize their own name. It is believed that there is a five-month lag time between when a child can understand words and when she is actually able to say them. It takes a lot of skill and ability to form those first words and retrieve them from the brain's neurological files. If you have ever taken a foreign language class, you probably had the experience of recognizing words before you could understand them. Then, you probably went through a period when you could understand the teacher, but were not yet able to recall and pronounce the words you wanted to say. It is believed that this experience is similar for infants who are learning language.

In a study conducted by the McArthur Foundation, researchers examined babies' ability to understand versus their ability to speak. The study, in which children were compared to test norms, was so comprehensive that it has come to be used as an assessment tool by many professionals. The researchers found that at ten months of age babies can understand forty words, which is pretty amazing since the average child won't be able to say forty words for another six months!

FROM THE EXPERTS . . .

Your Child's Best Language Teacher

Technology abounds in our society and many people, including parents, seem to embrace it wholeheartedly. It is not surprising, then, that marketers are encouraging parents to use technology products to help their children develop language skills. Parents, don't be fooled! As recent news reports have shown, there is no scientific evidence that babies or toddlers need or benefit from listening to television or computer programs that claim to teach language skills. Remember, parents, YOU are the best language teachers for your child. When you talk to your child about what she is doing or what she is looking at, when you read short stories or engage your child in rhyming games, when you hear your child babble and pretend it is a real language and expand on that idea, YOU are providing the strongest language-learning tool your child needs. Your baby needs to hear how and why and when words are used. Because of the language you and other significant others use with your baby, he will start down that wonderful road of language learning.

—Kenn Apel, PhD, CCC-SLP, professor,
Florida State University School of Communication Science and Disorders,
and co-author of *Beyond Baby Talk: From Sounds to Sentences—
A Parent's Complete Guide to Language Development*
http://roll.cci.fsu.edu/

BEYOND GOO-GOO GA-GA

Children spend the first year of life training and preparing for the utterance of their first word. The average child premieres her first word at the age of one year, but the range of "normal" is quite wide: some children start as early as nine months and others wait until they are a full two years old. Some of these children are simply late talkers, but for others, this is a sign of a serious language problem. (See pages 114–116 for more information.)

We often take for granted what goes into the evolution of a child's first word. The level of intellect, energy, and tenacity it requires is so miraculous, it's a wonder that any child makes the leap at all! Using "cat" as an example, let's look at what it takes to form that first amazing word. Your child must do all of the following:

1. She has to understand that the word is a symbol that represents the object—in this case, an animal.
2. She has to develop what experts call "naming insight," which means that she has to recognize that all objects have a name.
3. She has to notice the word among all the other words she hears all day.
4. She has to figure out where the word begins and ends when Mommy asks Daddy, "Didyoufeedthecattoday?" (easier said than done).
5. She has to be able to find sentences within the streams of words she hears.
6. She has to figure out what the word means. Does the word "cat" apply only to the family cat? Does it apply to all four-legged creatures?
7. She has to figure out the proper tongue and mouth placement to speak the word.
8. She needs to understand the cause and effect: "If I say 'cat,' Mommy brings me the cat that I want to pet."

Children generally learn to communicate for two reasons: to comment on their environment and to make a request. It is with those reasons in mind that babies choose their first word. A number of factors will help your baby choose her first word:

- **Environment.** For a child growing up in New York City, "taxi," as opposed to "rooster," is more likely to be in her early vocabulary. Kids are influenced by the words they hear most often.
- **Word type.** Most first words tend to be nouns because they are so concrete. But some babies start with social words like "bye-bye" or "hello."

- **Word sound.** Babies tend to pick words that have sounds in them that they have already mastered. "Mama" and "Dada" are popular first words, which makes sense since "m" and "d" are early sounds children are able to master.
- **Usefulness.** On the same "Mama" "Dada" note, children tend to pick words that are useful to them. Knowing how to get your parent's attention is very motivating.
- **Style.** When it comes to language expression (and life), some children are more cautious than others and more likely to choose a word that contains sounds they have mastered and are comfortable with. They are also likely to gravitate toward words that describe people and objects. More risk-taking babies don't wait to pronounce the word perfectly and are more likely to use all different types of words.

Interestingly, research shows that in the early stages of language acquisition, children are not able to talk and express emotion at the same time. A study by Lois Bloom found that two to eight seconds before a young child says a word, her face takes on a "sober" expression. Researchers concluded that speaking takes tremendous cognitive energy in the beginning, and a child cannot spend energy on both emotion and cognition at the same time until she becomes very comfortable with expressing words.

Many parents wonder if children who say their first words earlier than the average are actually smarter than other kids. But experts say that for children who are in the "normal range" there is no correlation between the age at which a child's first word is spoken and her later IQ score. That said, earlier speech does seem to have advantages for children. According to Dr. Eliot, "Earlier talkers are obviously better able to communicate their needs, initiate interactions with others, and understand what's going on around them. So an earlier start at language seemingly can't help but accelerate all aspects of a child's emotional, social, and cognitive development."

Open Windows

Critical periods, also known as critical windows, are periods of time when the development or learning of a certain skill is most easily accomplished. When this stage is over, acquiring the skill is difficult or even impossible. For example, several critical periods are important for the development of normal vision. A child's eye has to have the experience of seeing in order for her brain to become properly wired for vision. Studies of animals deprived of sight during critical periods showed that they experienced permanent damage to both the structure and function of the visual cortex, preventing them from ever developing full sight. According to Dr. Eliot, "language, like vision and most other brain functions, is bound by a critical period, an early phase in which a child must experience language, or else its special hardware won't wire up right." It is the combination of sounds, meaning, and grammar that molds and develops the large language network required for speech.

Children are like language sponges. Some experts, such as Steven Pinker, author of *The Language Instinct,* believe that language is completely instinctual—"a biological adaptation to communicate information." Like spiders that come into the world knowing how to spin a web without needing to be formally taught by their spider mommies, children, according to Pinker, come into the world with a language instinct. Prior to 1980, deaf children in Nicaragua were extremely isolated because there were no schools for the deaf and no official sign language in the country. In 1980 a school called Villa Libertad was opened to provide deaf children with spoken language and lip-reading instruction. Signing was prohibited in classrooms and discouraged elsewhere. In their desire to communicate, the school's children developed a sign language of their own, complete with grammar and structure. This invented language is now known as Idioma de Señas de Nicaragua. The point is that the instinct and the desire for language and communication are immense.

Beware of Ear Infections!

In addition to being able to hear language modeled, hearing one's own vocalizations is essential for language development. While it may seem obvious, making sure that your child can hear is crucial. Most parents will take their child to the pediatrician when they suspect illness or an ear infection, but many fail to return to the doctor for a follow-up to make sure that the ear is clear of fluid after an ear infection. Fluid can remain in the ear for fourteen to thirty days after an ear infection resolves, possibly causing re-infections. Long-term fluid in the ears has the potential to harm language development.

Here are the signs that could indicate an ear infection:

- Fever
- Runny nose
- Fussiness or irritability
- Trouble sleeping
- Reduced appetite
- Discharge from the ear
- Ear pain

If you suspect your child has an ear infection, treat it like any other potential illness and call your pediatrician right away.

We know that children's brains are most capable of acquiring language, especially the rules of grammar, during the first six to seven years of life, with the first three years being especially important. There is another sharp decline again after puberty. As parents, we must take advantage of this optimal time for language acquisition.

FIFTEEN SIMPLE THINGS PARENTS CAN DO TO PROMOTE LANGUAGE DEVELOPMENT

Providing your child with an enriched language environment does not require a lot of money or special equipment, but it does take conscious effort. Giving your child lots of opportunities to communicate and be heard is one of the greatest gifts you can give.

1. Look for opportunities to talk. In the early years you have three particularly useful occasions to engage with your infant. The first is when your child gazes at you or an object. The second is when your child gestures (i.e., points, reaches, or shows you an object). The third is vocalization or cooing. All three of these attempts at communication are great opportunities to open up conversation with your child.

2. Use lots of repetition. While repetition may be boring for you, it is fascinating to your baby. In very young children, it actually reinforces neural pathways that link sound and meaning in your child's brain. Repetition also gives her the chance to search her memory for the concept you are presenting and ultimately to confirm it in her mind. By the time your child is a year old, she will have most of the necessary speech sounds she needs in her repertoire, but she does not yet speak well because she doesn't know where those sounds belong. Repetition is the key to helping her master this task.

3. Let your child lead. A study in the *Journal of Speech and Hearing Research* found that "facilitative parents" who followed their children's lead and gave them opportunities to communicate were able to assist in their language development far more than parents with a "directive style," in which they chose the play objects and subjects to talk about and overanticipated their children's needs.

Talking about your child's interests, rather than what interests you, is far more beneficial for her language development. Children's attention spans are so short, especially in the early months and years, that it is much easier for her to focus and learn when you are talking about what interests *her*.

4. Take turns talking. Taking turns talking accomplishes a few things. It shows respect toward your child and teaches her the give-and-take of conversation.

This should begin from day one, long before your child has words. Even if she is just gurgling or babbling, she should be treated like an active participant in the conversation. This reciprocal experience also gives her the opportunity to practice speaking.

5. Always respond to your child's attempts to communicate. When your baby is preverbal, you should respond to her sounds and babbles by talking back and acknowledging her attempts at communication ("You really like the teddy bear!"). When she is first learning to speak and throwing out one-word observations and demands, elaborate on her observations ("Yes, that is a dog! He sure is big, and look at his blue eyes!"). As your child starts to put words together, help her form sentences without blatantly correcting her ("Did you say you want to go outside and play? Let's do that!").

You are your child's greatest source of validation when it comes to language. How you respond to her attempts to communicate will determine how comfortable she is when attempting to speak and connect. When you honor these attempts, no matter how imperfect they may be, you are teaching her that she is safe and therefore encouraging her to take more verbal risks.

6. Make eye contact. It is very helpful for your child to see your face when you're communicating. Besides allowing her to connect with you, this enables her to see the way you use your mouth to form words and sounds. The positive feedback she receives in the way of facial expressions, head nods, and smiles encourages further communication.

Face-to-face contact also helps toddlers better understand what you are saying. It can be especially valuable to kneel, sit, or bend down when you speak to your toddler. We have made a habit of doing that in our home. One day I was sitting on the floor and found myself eye to eye with one of my toddler daughters, who was leaning over to make eye contact with me as she spoke. As she did this, I noticed how important and special I felt; it wasn't the content of what she was saying that made me feel that way, but simply that she took the care and energy to look me in the eye. It is that feeling of significance and love that gives children the confidence to use language.

7. Use "Motherese." You know that silly, animated, high-pitched, singsong way parents often talk to their babies? Language researchers call it Motherese, Parentese (the PC version), or Child-Directed Speech (CDS), and it actually helps children develop language in the early years. Before our daughters were born, my husband and I swore we wouldn't use it. But like a moth to a flame, I found myself sometimes compelled to speak in Motherese to my daughters. This way of speaking has been observed across many different cultures and countries, and babies just love it.

Besides the research-confirmed fact that babies actually show more interest in people speaking Motherese, studies show that infants exposed to this type of speech have greater vocabulary and better grammatical accuracy. There are a number of reasons why Motherese is believed to be beneficial:

- It gets your child's attention because the tone, inflection, and attention that accompany it say, "This talk is for you."
- The slow-paced speech is easy for your child to follow, given that babies process auditory information twice as slowly as adults.
- It reveals your emotions as you speak, helping your child connect and increasing her interest in what you're saying.
- It tends to be loud and direct, which helps your infant separate what you're saying from other background sounds; this is particularly helpful since an infant's hearing is much less sensitive than an adult's.
- The pitch falls within the frequency range that your baby is most sensitive to.
- Your exaggerated pronunciations help your baby discern sounds and words.

Experts recommend reducing this type of talk when your child is somewhere between eighteen months and two-and-a half years of age.

8. Provide opportunity for communication. Start encouraging communication by creating situations in which your child needs to communicate with you to get her needs met. Instead of anticipating her needs, give her room to ask for what she wants, even before she is verbal. If she finishes her bananas and you think she is going to want more, instead of automatically putting more on her plate, wait for her to point, sign, grunt, or ask for more (depending on her age and level of communication), or simply ask, "Would you like more bananas?" You should never withhold food or force your child to ask for it; instead, give her the opportunity to ask for what she wants.

Always look for these chances to encourage communication. For example:

- Your child is enjoying watching you blow bubbles. Pause a moment and wait for her to signal or ask for more instead of just continuing to blow the bubbles.
- After taking her out of the tub, give her choices such as "Do you want the green towel or the yellow towel?" instead of just wrapping her up.
- If you're playing a game of bouncy horse, bouncing your child on your knee, stop and wait for a request for more before starting another round of play.

9. Take advantage of your captive audience. Use daily care rituals—diaper changes, feeding, bathing, dressing and undressing, naps, and bedtime—to connect and communicate with your child. By simply narrating what you are doing and commenting on her actions and curiosities, you will be speaking 30,000 words a day in no time!

10. Use sign language. Many parents think that if they teach their child to use sign language she will not be motivated to speak, when, in fact, the opposite is true. "Signs and gestures enhance your baby's ability to communicate and motivate her to begin to speak," says Dr. Robert Owens and Leah Feldon, authors of *Help Your Baby Talk.* Studies have shown that when compared to nonsigning children, children without hearing impairments who learn to sign have better recognition of letters and sounds, larger vocabularies, more advanced communication skills, and higher reading levels. Signing is such an important tool that I have devoted an entire chapter to it. (See Chapter 6.)

11. Be a language role model. Babies learn how to speak by imitating what they hear; thus you are the greatest "language role model" your children have. Make your children's job, to learn language, as easy as possible by doing the following:

- Use small words that your child could feasibly learn.
- Speak slowly so she can hear all the sounds that make up a word.
- Pause between words so she can identify word boundaries.
- Use words appropriately so your child doesn't learn poor word usage.

12. Read to your child. Reading provides a great opportunity for language stimulation. It is engaging and can set the stage for a lifelong love of books. It is never too early to start! By eight months of age, babies can recognize specific words up to two weeks after hearing them read in a storybook. In addition, studies of two-year-olds who were frequently read to, starting at an early age, found that those children had more advanced language skills than children who were read to less frequently. This topic, too, is so important that it has its own chapter. (See Chapter 8.)

13. Borrow some techniques from speech pathologists. While the techniques listed in the table below were developed for children who are having trouble learning language, they are beneficial for children at any point in their language development. They will also help you increase the number of words spoken per day, hopefully getting you near that 30,000-word goal. When using any of these methods, avoid seeming to correct your child's language.

TIPS FOR ENCOURAGING LANGUAGE

Technique	Description	Example
Modeling	Model the correct word your child is trying to say without correcting her.	Child: Baba! (pointing to bottle). Dad: Would you like your *bottle?*
Self-talk	Describe what you are doing, thinking, feeling, seeing, or hearing.	"Now I am putting your dirty clothes into the hamper. I want to make sure they are clean for the next time you want to wear them."
Parallel talk	Describe what your child is doing.	"Shayla is putting away her toys."
Expansion	Develop a child's utterance into a complete sentence, expanding on it without changing the order of the words or intended meaning.	Child: Mommy eat. Mom: Yes, Mommy is eating lunch with Ashley.
Recasting	Create a statement or question based upon the child's statement while also adding new information *or* sharing correct pronunciation.	Child: You shirt is lellow! Dad: Yes, my shirt is yellow!
Extension	Add information to a topic your child has initiated without necessarily modeling a complete sentence.	Child: Airplane! Mom: Big airplane high in the sky!

14. Take language stimulation trips. In his book *Talking from Infancy,* William Fowler suggests taking children on what he refers to as "language stimulation trips." Expensive? Not really. You don't have to take your child to the Champs-Elysées for a beneficial language trip. You can simply take her for a walk around the house and talk about what you see, labeling the different things you find. If you feel adventurous, walk her around the neighborhood or drive someplace interesting, like the beach. Make sure you pay close attention to what interests your child and use language that is appropriate to her age and level of language development. Early on, you can carry her, but as she becomes more mobile, you can encourage her to crawl or walk so you get a more accurate sense of where she wants to go and what interests her. You can even make a game of it by asking questions like "Where is your chair?" or "Do you see something blue?" Make sure the trip doesn't come off as if you are drilling her. Keep it light and fun.

15. Focus on the process, not the outcome. There is a huge variation in what is considered developmentally "normal." Ultimately, you cannot control when your child reaches a developmental milestone; all you can do is create the optimal environment to make that happen. In many twelve-step programs they say, "Do the footwork and then turn it over." In other words, make sure you have done everything you can to support your child and then let go of the outcome. Dr. Jill Stamm and Paula Spencer said it best in their book *Bright from the Start:* "Instead of focusing on what a child does or does not do (that is largely out of your control), . . . focus on what YOU, as the caregiver, can actually do to promote language development and communication with your child."

What in the World Are You Talking About?

Intelligibility is the proportion of a child's speech that a listener can understand. When children first learn to speak, understanding their efforts can be difficult for non-family members. It takes a level of mastery and vocal coordination for a child to be able to speak clearly. Here's what you can expect.

A TIMEFRAME FOR YOUR CHILD'S INTELLIGIBILITY

Child's Age	Percentage of Speech That Can Be Understood by Parents	Percentage of Speech That Can Be Understood by Strangers
18 months	95%	25%
2 years old	98%	50%
3 years old	100%	75%
4 years old	100%	100%

How to Avoid the Eight Biggest Mistakes Parents Make

Parents, even those with the best intentions, sometimes make mistakes out of an overwhelming desire to expedite their child's language development or because they're misinformed. Many parents simply push too hard, an effort that almost always backfires. No one was in a bigger rush to get her children talking than I was. As a therapist, my whole life revolves around verbal expression and understanding people's psyches through words. I couldn't wait for my children to be able to tell me what was going on in those minds of theirs so we could talk.

1. Talk with your baby, not at her. Start having "conversations" when your child is still preverbal. Respond to her coos and cries and don't talk over her responses to your words. Allowing this type of conversational template to develop sets the stage for later communication, encourages her to be an active participant, and helps her learn the social rules of communication. It also teaches her that you are interested in what she has to say, which will encourage her to communicate with you all the more.

Most people are not great listeners; indeed, many parents talk *at* their children instead of *with* them. As a matter of fact, researchers have found that many parents miss their children's first words. This is easy enough to do when first words are often mispronunciations. When you pause to listen to your baby's babbles, you may actually hear that "ba" means "bottle." When you hear those first words and encourage your child to keep saying them, you are truly promoting language development.

When You Have No Clue What Your Child Is Saying

No matter how articulate your child is, there are times when you just aren't sure what she is saying. Sometimes, to avoid upsetting their child, parents will pretend they understand by saying things like "Uh-huh," "Oh," or "That's nice." Pretending to understand your child won't fool her and is disrespectful. She is trying to tell you something that is important to her. Take the time to help her communicate, thus sending the message that you care what she has to say and encouraging her to communicate more. Try one of these suggestions:

- Ask her to repeat what she has said.
- Tell her that you don't understand what she is saying but you really want to know.
- Take her by the hand and ask her to show you.
- Repeat back to her the words you do understand.
- Ask questions such as "Are you talking about this toy?" or "You said something about an apple. Do you want to have one?"

2. Don't correct your child. Correcting children's speech does not improve their language; on the contrary, it inhibits it. This occurs for a number of reasons: (1) correction quashes your child's enthusiasm and her attempts to connect with you; (2) your baby doesn't understand exactly which part of her verbiage you are correcting; and (3) she is resistant to altering her communication to suit an adult's model.

Have you ever had the experience of enthusiastically talking to a know-it-all friend, or maybe to an adult when you were a child, and getting corrected mid-sentence? It completely takes the wind out of your sails and makes you feel like not talking at all. That is the last thing you want your child to feel. The good news is that, for the most part, your child will eventually correct her mispronunciations and grammatical errors herself. The best thing you can do to encourage correct grammar and pronunciation is to use the "Tips for Encouraging Language" on page 103 and to both consistently and frequently model correct speech to your child.

3. Avoid questions and commands. Avoid asking too many direct questions such as "How do you say . . . ?," "What is this?," and "What's the word for . . . ?" This approach can be intimidating and puts a lot of pressure on your child to perform. Cognitively speaking, questions are difficult for children to process. In general, "what" and "where" questions tend to be easier for young children than "when," "how," and "why" questions.

Avoid withholding things your child wants until she says a word or sentence. In other words, don't do the following:

> **Baby:** Uh, uh (reaching for the ball).
> **Dad:** Say ball (holding the ball out of her reach).
> **Baby:** Uh (getting frustrated).
> **Dad:** If you want the ball, say ball (still holding the ball out of baby's reach).
> **Baby:** Weh, weh (now she is frustrated and crying).

Trust that, as long as you are providing plenty of quality language, your child will learn to speak.

4. Don't use baby talk. Don't use cutesy baby talk. Your job is to model correct speech. You don't have to be formal—and it's important to have fun—but using baby talk can give your child misinformation about language. Keep in mind that "baby talk" is different from "Motherese." Unlike baby talk, Motherese doesn't reinforce incorrect speech. For example, if a child says "I want my milkey!" a parent speaking baby talk would say, "Here is your milkey!" whereas a parent speaking Motherese would say, "You want your milk." She might say it slowly or be especially animated about saying it, but she would use the correct word.

5. Know when to shut up. Shortly after telling a friend of mine about the Hart Risley study (see page 93), which found that the number of words spoken to a child has a direct impact on future language and IQ scores, I spent an afternoon with her and her toddler son at the park. From the moment we met until the time we left the park, my anxious friend never stopped speaking. "Tree! This is a tree! Trees have leaves! Look at the leaves! They are green! Look at the squirrel! Squirrels eat nuts! Sometimes we eat nuts! Nuts are crunchy!" She seemed to be trying to squeeze the recommended 30,000 words a day into one hour. By the time we left the park I had a headache and her son had barely spoken a word—paradoxically the opposite result from the one she intended. Fortunately, my friend was open to my feedback and quickly changed her approach. But her mistake is common and one that well-meaning parents often make.

6. Don't anticipate your child's needs. Good moms and dads are psychics who become adept at anticipating their child's needs (or at least many of them) without exchanging words. When your child gets into her crib, you hand her a pacifier before she can ask. When she finishes her cereal, you, unprompted, pour more into her bowl, knowing that she's still hungry. But if you always anticipate your child's needs and don't give her a chance to use words to get what she wants, you are teaching her that she doesn't need to use language to get her needs met. This can discourage her from trying to use language and therefore slow down her language learning.

7. Turn off the television and don't fall for "educational" DVDs. Television is so harmful to your child's development during the first three years of life that I have devoted an entire chapter of this book to addressing the issue (see Chapter 10). Even though the American Academy of Pediatrics strongly recommends that no child under the age of two watch any television, a study by the Kaiser Family Foundation found that on a typical day, 61 percent of babies one year and younger watch television, and a study in *Pediatrics* reported that 29 percent of children under the age of four have a television in their room.

Television is a medium that encourages passivity and completely lacks the interactive communication that is necessary to develop language. When children view videos, they are passive recipients of information and are not truly engaged. Television talks at children and does not comment on the child's topic of interest, which we know is the best way to spark language learning. A study by Dr. Dimitri Christakis, published in *Pediatrics,* revealed that, for every hour of television watched by two groups of children—ages one and three—each child faced a 10 percent increased risk of having attention problems by age seven.

Many parents do not realize that so-called educational videos pose the same risks as television-viewing. Parents who are fans of DVDs like Baby Einstein and Brainy Baby received an extremely rude awakening when a study in the *Journal of*

Pediatrics revealed that for every hour per day that babies eight to sixteen months old were shown "infantainment," they knew six to eight *fewer* words than other children. An even more recent study of one- and two-year-olds printed in the *Archives of Pediatrics & Adolescent Medicine* found that after six weeks of watching *Baby Wordsmith,* a DVD from the Baby Einstein series, tests of language skills revealed that children who watched the video a few times a week did not fare any better than those who did not watch it at all. But when researchers asked parents about their children's viewing prior to the study, they found that the earlier a child started watching these types of DVDs, the smaller her vocabulary was.

According to Dr. Susan Linn, the co-founder of the Campaign for a Commercial-Free Childhood (CCFC), "Not only is there no evidence that baby videos do any of the things the baby video industry claims they do, but these media may actually be undermining the development of the very skills they claim to foster." Thanks to the hard work of the CCFC, in 2009 Baby Einstein, a subsidiary of Walt Disney Company, agreed to offer refunds to consumers who purchased Baby Einstein videos due to the false claims made on the DVD packaging and website.

8. Don't settle for low-quality childcare. A study of early childhood care by the National Institute of Child Health and Human Development found that children in high-quality day-care environments have larger vocabularies and more complex language skills than those in lower-quality care. Given that 70 percent of American women with children under the age of three are in the workforce, finding quality child care is a challenge that most of us have to face at some point. Whether you are hiring a nanny or using a child-care facility, there are four things—after the obvious issues of safety—you should look for in a child-care situation that can make a big difference in your child's language skills (for more information about child care, see Appendix A):

- Make sure the provider is loving, attentive, and responsive to your child's needs. Responsiveness provides your child with the confidence to communicate.
- Make sure that your child receives consistent care from one person who can bond with and get to know her. The feeling of safety that your child enjoys from this level of care actually frees up her brain to do the complex work of language acquisition.
- Ideally your child's caregiver should have an understanding of child development. Studies have shown that this can make a big difference in language acquisition.
- The more educated your caregiver is, the better. Children whose care providers have high levels of education score better on language tests.

The Curse of the Sippy Cup

Somewhere between the bottle and the glass lies the sippy cup. Hoping to avoid spills, parents have been using sippy cups for over fifty years. But according to speech pathologists, the use of sippy cups can create difficulties with articulation and cause the development of a lisp. The continual suckle-swallow activity required by the typical sippy cup forces the tongue to lie flat or move in a back and forth motion. Drinking from a cup requires a child's cheeks and lips to suck in the liquid while the tongue squeezes, lifts, and sends the liquid down the child's throat, a process that develops the mouth muscles used in speech. Most speech therapists recommend the use of straw-cups or recessed-lid drinking cups.

The ABCs of Talking by Ages and Stages

Children learn to speak by following a series of fairly predictable stages of language learning and landmarks. There is a wide range of what is considered "normal," but there are certain milestones, in a certain order, that parents can anticipate. Research shows that 60 percent of children will fall into the broad range of "normal" development, while 30 percent will fall outside that range and another 10 percent will be "abnormally late," indicating a significant developmental problem. Generally speaking, the range of "normal" takes into account word production, not comprehension. Delayed word comprehension is a significant factor in evaluating a language delay.

It never hurts to have a professional pediatric speech pathologist evaluate your child if you have any concerns. Waiting too long to get an assessment can cause your child to miss important neurological and developmental windows of opportunity that are vital to her development and growth and can make catching up much harder.

BIRTH TO SIX MONTHS

In the beginning, your infant's first sounds will be unintentional. Because she does not yet realize that she has the ability to influence you or get her needs met through communication, most of her sounds will merely be responses to her body. But very shortly after birth she will start to realize that her sounds have an impact, and she will use them to communicate with you.

The first exciting milestone typical of this stage is the "social smile." This reciprocal gesture occurs in response to something someone has done to get your child's attention, like smiling, making a face, or chatting with her. This milestone, which usually occurs at four to six weeks, is a sign that her brain is developing properly: she is able to see short distances, make sense of an object, and produce her own smile in return. This is one of the first steps toward early communication and greatly enhances bonding.

Somewhere around two months of age your baby will begin to babble. This vocal play is an attempt to learn how to use her mouth, tongue, and throat to create sound—the infant equivalent of rehearsing for a speech. Interestingly, babies in all parts of the world, though exposed to different types of language, coo in the same way at the same age, even those who are deaf. There is a direct correlation between the amount of babbling your child does and the amount of attention you pay to it. Parents who respond and encourage these vocalizations will hear more of them and, in turn, will help build their child's language skills.

Between the ages of three and six months, your baby should be able to identify the location of a sound by turning her head toward that sound. She should also be able to vocalize excitement or displeasure and to babble, using speech-like sounds.

Here are some other milestones to look forward to at this age:

- Your baby becomes quiet or smiles when spoken to.
- She recognizes your voice.
- She uses different cries to signify different needs.
- She moves her eyes in the direction of sounds.
- She follows the direction of your eyes when you look from her to an object.
- She vocalizes pleasure and displeasure.

SIX TO TWELVE MONTHS

When it comes to communication, the two most exciting things that occur at this age are "variegated babble" and gesturing. Both of these milestones signify cognitive developmental leaps that bring babies close to speech.

Between six and nine months, babies usually begin imitating speech patterns and their babbling begins to have both long and short groups of sounds. These combinations of vowels and consonants, which sound like a string of babbled sentences that actually have the intonations and inflections of regular adult sentences, are referred to by linguists as "variegated babble." At times, when I used to listen to my daughters chatting away on the baby monitor, it really seemed that they were deep in real conversation with themselves or each other. At this point in development, if you were to put two babies from different countries in the same room, the inflections in their babble would be specific enough to allow you to figure out which countries they come from.

Between nine and twelve months, babies are usually able to shake their heads "no," wave "good-bye," point to objects they desire, and reach for things. Sometimes these gestures are combined with grunting noises. Your baby's facility with pointing and gesturing makes this an ideal time to start using sign language. (See Chapter 6 for more information.) At this age she is able to initiate communication with you and get your attention. Until now, most of her communication has been a response to her feelings of boredom, frustration, anger, etc., or a response to you. But now she's developing the ability to decide, on her own, that something interests her, and she can express her desire to share it with you by pointing, squealing, and gesturing. This is a huge developmental leap for your baby because it shows that she has a basic understanding of cause and effect and even an ability to think ahead.

Here are some other milestones to look forward to at this age:

- Your baby listens when spoken to.
- She enjoys social games like peek-a-boo.
- She recognizes words for common items.
- She responds to simple questions or directions like "Come here" or "Do you want more?"
- She may even use a couple of basic words.

TWELVE TO EIGHTEEN MONTHS

Twelve months is the average age when all the cumulative skills that have been learned so far erupt in the long-awaited first word, with some "normal" children saying it as early as ten months and as late as eighteen months. During the first few months of talking, vocabulary grows slowly. By twelve months the average child will understand fifty words, but she won't be able to say fifty until she's about twenty-four months old. At this age she still struggles with pronunciation and only immediate family members may be able to understand what she is saying. I felt like an interpreter when I went out with my kids at this age. Toward the end of this six-month period, when your child starts to repeat two-word phrases like "All done," they may come out as one word. My friend Leslie's adorable daughter, Goldie, would flutter her hands at the end of a meal and say, "All-dee!"

Here are some other milestones to look forward to at this age:

- Your baby points to body parts or pictures in a book when named.
- She follows simple commands.
- She shakes her head "no" and pushes away undesirable objects.
- She uses single-word speech.
- She uses ritual words like "Hi" and "Bye."

EIGHTEEN TO TWENTY-FOUR MONTHS

This is the age of vocabulary explosion, when it starts to get really exciting! Once your child has mastered fifty words, which usually happens between eighteen and twenty-four months, she has a huge growth spurt in word use. Early on she may have mastered eight to eleven new words every month, but during the last half of the second year, the rate may be as high as nine new words a day—sixty-three new words each week! This vocabulary explosion represents a spurt in brain development as well, paving the way for two-word phrases.

One of the many reasons why vocabulary bursts occur at this time is that children are now developmentally equipped to read social cues. This new skill allows them to pick up on even the most subtle clues to word learning after only one exposure. For example, little Nicole hears Dad ask Mom where the milk is. When Mom answers "It's on the counter" and Nicole sees Dad pick it up off the counter, she comes to the conclusion that *the counter* is that flat surface in the kitchen near the sink, even though this is the first time she has ever heard the word. Language specialists refer to this ability—knowing where and when to apply a newly heard word after hearing it only once—as fast mapping. It is *the* key to dramatic language growth at this age. Studies also show that children who have not had this vocabulary spurt were unable to fast-map, since it appears that this skill develops right before or during the word spurt.

Here are some other milestones to look forward to at this age:

- Your baby makes two-word combinations.
- She asks simple questions such as "What's that?"
- She follows more complex commands.

TWO TO THREE YEARS

This is the age of the grammar spurt, when your child makes the jump from two-word phrases to full-blown speech. There is no three-word phase. By the time a child is thirty to thirty-six months of age, her average sentence is six words long—"embedded sentences"—that combine two sentences with more than one idea. For example, a child at this age might say, "I want to play with that toy but I cannot find it," which contains "I want to play with that toy" and "I cannot find it." Each of these sentences can stand on its own. By this age, most children are considered fluent in their native language.

This is also the age of the question. Now that your child has mastered "What," "Who," and "When," you will likely hear her ask a lot more questions starting with "Can I," "Why," and even "How."

Here are some other milestones to look forward to at this age:

- Your child makes two-part requests ("Please, open the refrigerator and get me an apple").

- She uses multiword sentences and engages in short dialogues.
- She provides descriptive details.
- She starts to use articles such as "a" and "the."
- She adds word endings to verbs like "play*ing*" and "jump*ed*."
- She talks when playing alone.
- Her speech is understood by familiar listeners most of the time.
- She expresses emotion verbally.

Three Common Reasons for Speech Delays

In the area of language development, there is a lot of variation that is considered developmentally "normal." However, there are certain factors that can make a minor language delay more likely.

GENDER

Generally speaking, girls are more verbal than boys. This difference in ability starts in utero. A study of fetuses in the second trimester found that girls moved their mouths significantly more than boys. This early practice appears to prepare them for speaking, as demonstrated by the fact that girls tend to start speaking a month or two earlier than boys. Girls articulate better than boys and use longer, more complex sentences, more varied grammar, more abstract speech, and bigger vocabularies. Boys generally catch up by the time they are four or five years old, but some never do. Perhaps the reason, as research has shown, is that mothers tend to use more complex sentences and discuss more abstract concepts, like feelings, with girls than with boys, or, as indicated by those second trimester findings, perhaps it is just in the wiring. Some biological researchers postulate that, because girls mature earlier than boys, the area of the brain that controls language becomes specialized sooner, giving girls a biological advantage.

BIRTH ORDER

First-born children also do better in developing vocabulary skills during their second year of life than do later-born siblings. They are also more likely to reach the fifty-word milestone and two-word phrasing sooner than their later-born siblings. Some studies have found that language skills are weaker with each increase in numerical birth order. It is believed that this is due to decreasing one-on-one verbal interactions between parent and child as the family grows. For a child to maximally benefit from language exposure, language needs to be addressed directly to her and, ideally, should be about something she is interested in. This becomes increasingly difficult with each new sibling. First-born children get undivided, specialized attention from their parents, whereas later-born siblings receive diluted attention.

MULTIPLES

Twins tend to acquire language more slowly than singletons because the parents of twins are often overwhelmed, short on time, and have less verbal interaction with their children than parents of single babies. An Australian study that measured the length of communication between mothers and their children found that mothers of single children averaged two-minute interactions while mothers of twins averaged only ninety seconds per child. Children need to hear the speech patterns and language usage of adults as a model in order to learn to communicate in that language. Also, because mom's talk is divided between two listeners, twins receive half the individual language attention. For higher-order multiples, you can divide by the number of children to get an idea of how watered down language attention is at home.

Another reason why twins and multiples acquire language more slowly than singletons has to do with their weight and development at birth. It has been estimated that 60 percent of twins, more than 90 percent of triplets, and 100 percent of quadruplets and higher-order multiples are born premature. Prematurity and low birth weights are associated with early developmental delays. In twins, these delays are usually offset by a subsequent tendency among preemie twins to grow and develop faster than other babies. Studies show that any developmental or intellectual gaps that may exist between singletons and multiples tend to be closed by the age of six.

The most common explanation, however, why twins learn to speak their primary language slower than other children is that twins tend to learn language skills from each other. Because they spend so much time together, they tend to model language for each other, which means that they pick up each other's mispronunciations and poor grammar. This often accounts for what many people call the "secret twin language," which experts refer to as idioglossia or autonomous language. It is estimated that 40 percent of all twins use this type of communication with each other. While outsiders may view this as a secret language, it is really just a form of shared baby talk, the result of modeling incorrect language to each other. Most twins outgrow this language by the age of four.

Houston, We Have a Problem

Speech and language disorders are the number one developmental impairment in children under the age of five. Often, when children do not develop speech skills properly or in accordance with what is considered normal, parents start to suspect that something is wrong, but are told by well-meaning friends not to worry. These parents are often lulled into a false sense of relief when they learn that Albert Einstein didn't start speaking until he was three years old or they hear stories about other "late talkers" who now speak just fine. The problem with waiting to get professional assessment and treatment is that your child can miss an important critical window, making treatment much more difficult.

In *The Late Talker: What to Do If Your Child Isn't Talking Yet*, authors Marilyn Agin, Lisa Geng, and Malcolm Nicholl differentiate between a delay and a disorder. They define a delay as "a maturational lag in development," after which a child catches up to her peers naturally and without any intervention. A disorder, on the other hand, "is a significant (severe) delay with a disruption in the normal sequence of development that's a stark contrast to his or her typically developing peers." This child is not able to catch up without some sort of professional intervention.

If your child is not achieving the developmental milestones mentioned previously, there could be a problem. However, it is important for parents to understand that there is a fairly wide window in which children develop, acquire language and speaking skills, and still fall within the "normal" range. How do you know if your child is okay? Agin, Geng, and Nicholl point out eight likely predictors of speech disorders:

1. Toddlers produce limited consonants and make frequent errors in vowel and consonant pronunciation.
2. Children have poor verbal repertoires and frequently use simple words (e.g., "want," "go," "got").
3. Two-year-olds use only four or five consonants and a limited number of words.
4. Toddlers don't imitate.
5. A toddler's play seems developmentally immature.
6. Children don't use any gestures.
7. Preschool children prefer to initiate conversations with adults instead of peers.
8. Preschool children have behavior problems.

Above all, as a parent, you need to trust your instincts. If you think there is something wrong with your child's speech development, you lose nothing by getting a professional evaluation. On the other hand, if there is a problem, your child may lose valuable time if you wait too long.

STUTTERING

True stuttering affects only 5 percent of children, according to Patricia McAleer Hamaguchi, and it is very unusual in toddlers. Stuttering is often accompanied by secondary behaviors such as

- physical movements, such as putting a hand to the mouth or patting the leg, in an attempt to get the words out
- increased facial movements, such as excessive blinking, indicating the child is struggling to speak
- consistent insertion of unnecessary words such as "um," "like," "so," or "ah"
- word substitution, especially when the chosen word is less appropriate

While about 4 percent of children will experience stuttering for as long as six months, many will recover by late childhood; only about 25 percent of those affected will develop severe, chronic stuttering. If you think that your child may be stuttering, early intervention is key. There is no harm in getting your child evaluated, while there can be real harm in waiting: you can miss an important window of opportunity to deal with your child's stuttering when it is most treatable. Even toddlers who stutter can learn strategies that will reduce its effect.

If you're looking for qualified help, the first person to consult is your child's pediatrician. Pediatricians can be a very helpful resource for both information and referrals. However, most parents will ultimately want to meet with a pediatric speech pathologist as well. Another useful resource is the Stuttering Foundation at www.stutteringhelp.org. You should meet and interview different pathologists to make sure that the one you choose is a good fit with your child in terms of approach, philosophy, and personality. Good speech therapy should be fun for a child.

Is My Toddler Stuttering?

Between the ages of thirty months and five years, many children start having trouble speaking fluently. The technical term that many speech experts use for this development is "language issue dysfluency" or "nonfluency," which typically occurs when your child is experiencing a big developmental leap in language skills. What happens? Her thoughts are happening faster than her ability to recall the proper words, so she gets stuck on one word or syllable and repeats it over and over until she is able to complete the sentence.
This repetition can sound a lot like stuttering and cause panic in an already anxious parent.

Unlike stuttering, where a child typically gets stuck on the first sound in the word ("d-d-d-d-dog") or opens her mouth to speak and nothing comes out, children with nonfluency will often pause as if they are searching for the word or repeat the first word ("the-the-the dog was at the park") or first syllable ("The wa-wa-water is cold"). This condition can be exacerbated by exhaustion, excitement, or just being upset.

Talk to the Hand

Sign Language

When I first started using sign language with my infant daughters, I wondered if they would pick it up. For months and months I signed and nothing happened. Then, one day, Mendez looked up from her high chair and made the sign MILK. I felt like Anne Sullivan in *The Miracle Worker* when Helen Keller signed WATER for the first time. Suddenly, my daughter had the ability to communicate what she wanted!

Using sign language to communicate with hearing children has been practiced since the late 1980s, but didn't become popular in the United States until 2005, when the grandson in the movie *Meet the Fockers* signed that he was hungry, tired, and needed a diaper change. Suddenly, signing went from a tool used exclusively by the hearing impaired and eccentric, type-A parents for their hearing kids to a socially accepted and viable way to bridge the communication gap between parents and their preverbal infants.

Because babies develop the fine muscles in their hands long before they develop the necessary oral coordination and muscle control required for speech, signing is a practical way to help infants communicate. Many infants start by using symbolic gestures, such as waving good-bye, on their own. As mentioned in Chapter 5, children's receptive language (ability to understand words) develops much faster than their ability to speak. The youngest of children have wants, needs, and thoughts they want to express but no ability to make them understood. That is where sign language comes in.

Why You Should Let Your Fingers Do the Talking

There are many reasons why parents choose to start signing with their hearing infants. Many of these reasons are well researched, some are more controversial, and a few are anecdotal. One thing I can tell you, not just as a parenting expert, but as a mom who chose to sign with her family: it was an overwhelmingly positive experience that I am very happy I took the time to do.

1. Sign language helps children acquire speech earlier and increases vocabulary. Signing helps provide a strong foundation for language. We know that using language begets more language skills, and study after study shows that sign language helps in this linguistic process. Children are generally able to use signs much earlier and more efficiently than words because words are much more difficult to create. At the point when one of my daughters was able to say fourteen spoken words, she was able to sign triple that number. Being able to triple her vocabulary so early in the communication process made communicating her needs much easier for both of us. Signs also enabled her to transmit abstract concepts such as "thirsty," "hungry," "help," or "hurt," which helped me better meet her needs.

In a study headed by Linda Acredolo and Susan Goodwyn for the National Institutes of Health, 140 families with eleven-month-old babies were divided into three groups. One group of families was taught sign language, the second was told to make a special effort to speak to their children more often than they normally would, and the third was a control group. Researchers found the following:

- At twenty-four months the signing babies had the vocabulary of a twenty-seven- or twenty-eight-month-old child.
- At twenty-four months the signing babies used significantly longer sentences.
- At thirty-six months the signing children spoke at the level of a forty-seven-month-old child.

The average nonsigning child at twelve months will have two or three words and at eighteen months he is likely to have ten to fifty spoken words. According to child development researchers and educators Drs. Michelle Anthony and Reyna Lindert, the signing children they studied averaged twenty-five signs and sixteen spoken words at twelve months and 70 sign and 105 words at eighteen months. That dramatic disparity makes a world of difference when a child is trying to get his needs met, which is one of the top reasons that young children get frustrated.

2. Signing reduces frustration. Reduced frustration is not just a benefit for the child; it's a boon for the parents as well. Nothing makes parents feel more competent than being able to help their children and meet their needs. Let me share an example of two families. The Jones family and the Smith family met each other in a Mommy & Me class when their children were a year old. The Joneses chose not to introduce their daughter Olivia to sign language, while the Smiths opted to teach sign language to their son Max.

At two o'clock one morning, Amy Jones was awakened by a terrible cry. She ran into Olivia's room to see what was wrong with her. She checked Olivia's diaper but it was dry. She felt the baby's head but detected no sign of a fever. Since Olivia had eaten a short while ago, Amy reasoned that she couldn't be hungry and she didn't want any water. At a loss about how to console her child, Amy spent most of the night holding Olivia to her chest and pacing the floor. Few things are worse than finding yourself, exhausted and holding a screaming child in your arms in the middle of the night, unable to console her or find out what's wrong.

Unbeknownst to Amy, her friend Jamie Smith was awakened at the same time on the same night to very similar cries. After she went through the same checklist, however, her son Max told her what was wrong with his hands. He put two index fingers together in front of his mouth, indicating that his teeth hurt. Just like Olivia, he was teething. Jamie gave him medicine for his pain and they both went back to sleep.

Giving a child a way to express his needs and feelings greatly reduces frustration. One of the biggest reasons children have tantrums, especially during what has become known as the "terrible twos," is their inability to clearly express their needs. At that age kids have strong ideas of what they want but their spoken language ability has usually not caught up. Having a way to communicate can greatly reduce the number of tantrums a child has.

3. Signing is correlated with increased IQ scores. In a follow-up to the National Institutes of Health study, also by Acredolo and Goodwyn, it was found that signing children scored an average of twelve points higher on IQ tests than their nonsigning counterparts when they were eight years old. The signing children had an average IQ score of 114 compared with the nonsigning children, who averaged 102. One reason for these results may be that spoken or hearing-related (aural) information is stored in the left hemisphere of the brain, while visual information is stored in the right hemisphere. Children who sign use both sides of the brain, thereby increasing brain function. In addition, some experts speculate that learning sign language in the first three years is particularly beneficial because it stimulates the brain at a time when significant brain growth takes place, adding skills when the brain is at the height of plasticity (the ability to change as a result of an activity or experience). Acredolo reports that many years later the signing children in the test group achieved higher than average scores on their SATs.

4. Signing advances reading and vocabulary skills. Dr. Marilyn Daniels, author of *Dancing with Words: Signing for Hearing Children's Literacy,* is considered the most prolific researcher in the use of sign language with hearing children. Daniels has designed numerous studies that have repeatedly shown that sign language can be used to improve hearing children's vocabulary, reading ability, and spelling proficiency. Daniels repeatedly found that children taught American Sign Language (ASL) had higher reading levels than those with no ASL instruction. Additionally,

- A study of hearing kindergarten students receiving ASL instruction found that they made statistically significant gains in their understanding of vocabulary and tested higher than nonsigning students in reading tests.

- In a study of fourteen signing children who were given the Peabody Picture Vocabulary Test, signing kids scored approximately 10 percent higher than control group nonsigners in vocabulary.

- A study of sixty underprivileged kids whose kindergarten teachers signed words and phrases and used letter signing as they introduced letters of the alphabet found that children exposed to signing scored fifteen points higher on the Peabody Picture Vocabulary test. This result is particularly significant because, according to Daniels, "every word in a child's vocabulary acts as the currency for learning more words."

Adding finger spelling (which uses the ASL finger alphabet to indicate specific letters or spell out words) to the signing process can help children gain interest in letters and sounds, which, as the basis for reading, will help them start earlier, as well. I always found that using finger spelling with my young children made them laugh and promoted their desire to learn the alphabet. As a result, I believe that signing was one of the major factors that led to their very early interest in spelling and reading.

5. Signing increases brain development. Learning sign language from infancy seems to activate a part of the right brain that is devoted to visual-spatial processing more fully than it does when signing is learned later in life. A study using magnetic resonance imaging (MRI) of twenty-seven hearing adults who learned sign language during early childhood, sixteen of whom started at birth, found that the group who learned to use sign language starting in infancy use a region of the brain that those who learn to sign later in life can't access. Only those who learn nonspoken languages from birth seem to develop the full potential of this brain area.

Effective signing helps a child learn a word more easily because he sees the sign for the word, hears the word, and has the physical sensation of making the sign. This multisensory experience stimulates the brain in multiple places. It also helps children with different learning styles. Children may be auditory, visual, or kinesthetic learners—what author Cheri Fullers refers to as "talkers, watchers, or doers"—and get the greatest learning benefits by experiencing the word used in all three ways.

6. Signing gives you insight into your child's thinking and helps you meet his needs. Signing gives you an early glimpse into your child's mind. In his book *Sign with Your Baby,* Dr. Joseph Garcia tells a story about when his eleven-month-old son Damian signed AIRPLANE to initiate a conversation about an airplane they

FROM THE EXPERTS . . .

Opening Doors to Communication

Babies crawl before they walk, and sign before they talk. It is as natural as waving goodbye or pointing. Babies want to communicate; they just need us to expand their vocabulary beyond waving "bye-bye" and pointing.

This has been my war cry since 1998, when I realized my then fourteen-month-old daughter Leah was deaf. I became a sign language ambassador. First, out of necessity—I wanted a world that could communicate with Leah. Then, out of passion—I could have never imagined the power of a few signs to alter so many lives. Not just babies, but elementary age children, as well as children with special needs. Since the release of the first Signing Time! video in 2002, I have had the profound privilege of meeting families whose lives have been enriched and even transformed by sign language.

Stacey Warnick approached me after a seminar and shared that her one-year-old son's constant signs expressing an unquenchable thirst, "MORE-MILK-PLEASE," helped lead to the early diagnosis of diabetes, a diagnosis that typically would not have occurred without a medical emergency.

Kelly Chambliss called the Two Little Hands Productions office in tears to share that she had just "met" her three-year-old son, Jacob, who had autism. She explained that she just "met" him because he could finally express his wants through the signs he learned from Signing Time!

had seen overhead earlier that day. Because he knew how to sign, Damian was able to tell his father that he was thinking about the airplane and wanted to talk about it. Signing allowed him to initiate a conversation on his own.

7. Signing allows for discreet communication. I am in a Mommy & Me class when I smell that poopy smell. I can see from the wiggling noses in the room that I am not the only mother noticing that someone needs a diaper change. From across the room my fourteen-month-old daughter makes eye contact with me. Inquisitively I sign to her POOP? to which she signs, NO, PEE and continues to play while the pooping offender is located.

As children get older, many families choose to keep at least a few signs for this very reason. They can be especially helpful during toilet training with toddlers and preschoolers, who often need to be reminded to make a trip to the bathroom but consider it the ultimate offense to be asked in front of their friends.

Kei Malone told me how her four-year-old son William, who has Down syndrome, amazed his teachers and medical team not only with his extensive signing vocabulary, but with his ability to read and spell those words.

I watched with awe as my five-month-old nephew signed MILK.

Every day I hear or read inspiring stories about the end of tantrums, babies reading and spelling, amazing connection and communication, and the miraculous stories of children with special needs blossoming beyond their perceived limitations and breaking through their communication challenges. I've seen my own daughter Leah read and spell by age two, and communicating with a sign vocabulary that far surpassed her hearing peers. My daughter Lucy was born with spina bifida and cerebral palsy. Lucy's doctors warned that she would be diagnosed as mentally retarded and assumed she would never communicate through spoken words or signs. Lucy's first communications came at the age of two, and they came through her deaf sister's language . . . sign language.

I don't care how old you are. We all want to be understood! It is no different for a baby or child. It's funny, after being immersed in sign language for all these years I am still amazed that something so simple, and so fun, can literally transform the experience of being a child . . . and a parent.

—Rachel Coleman, creator of the series Signing Time!
www.SigningTime.com

A simple sign can get the job done. Signing can also be helpful when reminding a child in front of others to say "please" or "thank you." And it can have useful applications for parents, too; my husband and I have used signs at restaurants or work functions when we've needed to communicate something discreet like "I forgot my wallet" or "We should pick up the check" and, of course, "I am bored—let's go home."

8. Signing improves family dynamics and connection. The ability to communicate at a young age allows a baby to participate in family dynamics and make his own contributions to a conversation. This experience of being seen, heard, and understood at an early age is a huge boost to self-esteem. It sends a message to your child that he is worth understanding and paying attention to. In my work with signing families, I have noticed that parents tend to pay closer attention to their child in order to catch any signs he makes. This attentiveness can help you read your child's cues and increase the parent-child bond.

Signing siblings have the opportunity to "teach" sign to newer members of the family. Being in a position of power and authority can ease a little bit of sibling rivalry and help an older sibling feel valuable at a time when children often feel jealous and replaced.

9. Sign can be used as a bridge to other languages. Signing can facilitate multiple-language learning, too. When my daughters, about fourteen months old, started teaching their Chinese instructor signs, it became a connector between the two languages. As I watched them sign, I also found it easier to learn words in Mandarin because I was seeing a visual reminder as I learned the word. Signing can also bridge the gaps between adopted children and their parents who don't speak the same language, which is very common in international adoptions.

When they first start learning language, children generally choose only one word for a given object. But as they get older, bilingual children develop "metalinguistic awareness"—an understanding that different languages use different labels for the same object. According to linguist Linda Easton-Waller, "By giving infants the same visual symbol (sign) for both 'leche' and 'milk,' you make the job of connecting the object with the meanings of both words MUCH easier for babies." When a baby hears "leche," paired with the sign, and then also hears "milk," paired with the same sign, the visual indication that they mean the same thing makes it easier for him to understand that both words represent the same thing.

10. Signing opens the door to another culture. When I was nine years old I saw the play *Children of a Lesser God*, a love story that takes place in a school for the hearing impaired. The way the characters communicated powerful emotions using sign language inspired me to buy a sign language dictionary and teach myself to sign. I was so taken by the beauty of this unique form of communication that I studied signs daily. I will never forget the day I walked into a store and was able to sign with a teenage hearing-impaired sales clerk. It was an amazing feeling, as a child, to be able to communicate in another language and bond with a person that I might not otherwise have been able to connect with. Our conversation seemed to please him too. Teaching your child to sign has the potential to open doors to another world, culture, and group of people that he might never get to know otherwise. Given that there are 28 million deaf and hard-of-hearing people in the United States, that opens a lot of doors. "Just creating more awareness for the deaf community is good," says Reeba Lynn, a literacy outreach manager in San Mateo, California, whose seventeen-year-old daughter is deaf. Lynn's nine-month-old son signed "cold" for the first time after watching his older sister sign. All of Lynn's three children are now fluent in ASL.

First Signs of Readiness

Most experts recommend introducing sign language to children at the age of six or seven months. Before this age, most children aren't capable of remembering a sign, much less making an association between the sign and a word or action. However, every child is different, and your child may be ready a little earlier or a little later than six months. Here are some indications that your child may be ready to start signing:

- He points to objects he wants.
- He waves "hello" or "good-bye."
- He is able to sit up unassisted.
- He looks at your face intently when you speak.
- He shows interest in things you do with your hands.
- He has a good pincer grasp (the coordination to sign).
- You are able to keep his attention for five to ten seconds.

Many parents who start signing earlier than six months are getting amazing results, and while some experts still recommend waiting for the signs of readiness mentioned above, others are now suggesting that parents begin using two or three signs from the start. There are even some reports of infants who receive early exposure to sign language and start signing at four and five months without the parents doing anything more than simply signing to their child over the course of the day.

Start at the Very Beginning ...

Most signing experts recommend starting with three signs that will help your child communicate something that is important to him, like MILK, MORE, and EAT. I recommend increasing three signs to six and twelve as soon as you have mastered each set of three and your baby has some familiarity with them. Sticking to only three signs will limit the number of contexts in which you can sign to your child, and increasing beyond twelve signs may overwhelm him.

NEED SIGNS

Need signs reflect things your baby is likely to request—for example, SLEEP, PACIFIER, BLANKET, HUNGRY, THIRSTY, BED.

Milk
Open and close fist as if milking a cow.

Eat
Tap fingertips on lips a few times.

More
Repeatedly tap fingertips of hands together.

All done
Shake open palms in front of body a few times.

HIGH-INTEREST SIGNS

These signs refer to things that are really exciting to your child—BICYCLE, TELEPHONE, DOG, CAT, FLOWER, BIRD, AIRPLANE, BALL, PLAY, SWING.

Father
Place thumb tip of open hand
against center of forehead.

Mother
Place thumb tip of open hand
against center of chin.

PARENT INTEREST SIGNS

These signs communicate basic needs, requests, and manners that can make everyone's lives easier—TOILET, PEE, HURT, CAREFUL, GENTLE, SHARE, STOP, GO.

Diaper Change
Place closed hands wrist to
wrist with right hand on top,
then left hand.

Bath
Move closed hands up and
down against chest as if
scrubbing.

Please
Run flat hand over heart in
circular motion.

Thank you
Touch fingertips of flat hand
to lips, then move hand
down with palm facing up.

You should sign immediately before, during, and after performing the action related to the sign. Before feeding your child, you might say, "It's time for some milk" (signing MILK). While he is feeding, "It looks like you are enjoying your milk" (signing MILK). When he is done, "You finished your milk" (signing MILK). Make sure that you sign just below your child's sight line, and always sign and speak at the same time.

In Dr. Joseph Garcia's *Sign with Your Baby,* he recommends taking advantage of three different types of gazes to teach a sign:

- **Expressive gaze:** when your baby has a want or need and is looking to you with that "I want something" expression.
- **Chance mutual gaze:** when you and your baby just happen to look at each other at the same time for no particular reason.
- **Pointed gaze:** when you and your child look at the same thing and then look at each other.

Each of those moments is an opportunity to introduce a sign.

OTHER TEACHABLE MOMENTS

Children are particularly receptive to learning signs during meals, while taking baths, when they are getting dressed, at bedtime, when you are reading to them, and during diaper changes. Signing MORE before giving your child more food, for example, helps make the connection between the sign and getting more of what he wants. Showing him the sign for DIAPER CHANGE can help him understand what is going to happen next and, possibly, make future potty training easier if he is able to tell you when he needs a diaper change.

When your baby first starts to sign, the signs may not be as obvious as you expect because it takes a while for children to develop the fine motor skills required to make easily discernible signs. For example, the first time my daughter Quincy signed MORE, I thought she was just clapping her hands. Then it hit me that she was signing, and I was able to give her another helping of what she was asking for. She was thrilled!

While it is never too late to start signing with your baby, it is especially helpful if you start before the toddler years. Around the age of eighteen months, children tend to get easily frustrated and have tantrums because their ability to tolerate frustration is low and their need to express themselves is high. Children who know how to sign tend to have fewer meltdowns as a result.

BE YOUR OWN ANNIE SULLIVAN

It is important to make signing fun and never force it on your child. You are best off incorporating it into your day-to-day activities. I recommend keeping a book with signs in an accessible place. We always keep a few signing books in baskets in the kitchen, the kids' bathroom, and their bedroom. In addition, my husband and I especially enjoy the Signing Time! series of books, flashcards, CDs, and DVDs that teach signs through repetition and music. While I do not recommend watching DVDs with kids prior to the age of three (see Chapter 10), I do recommend enjoying them yourself and using them to increase your signing vocabulary. We love Signing Time! so much that we attended a concert with our kids. It was an amazing, moving, and inspiring experience for the whole family that we never would have had if we didn't have an interest in sign language.

Signing classes are also a great way to learn new signs, meet other signing families, and take your child's communication to the next level. My daughters and I had the great fortune to attend a signing class taught by Etel Leit, who runs the Los Angeles-based signing program SignShine. By the time I took the class I had already been signing with my kids for almost a year, and, in all honesty, I was skeptical about whether the class would be any more beneficial than what I was already doing at home. What I found was that it took my kids' (as well as my own) signing to the next level. The combination of being in a room with other signing children, exposure to new signs, the use of music with signing, and a truly great teacher created a dramatic increase in my daughters' signing vocabulary, understanding, and interest. After attending only a couple of classes, my daughters started asking me how to sign new words, and I found Mendez "reading" books to herself by signing the words.

Ten Reasons You Should Use ASL Instead of "Baby Sign"

Most children who are exposed to "baby sign language" are exposed to one of three variations: American Sign Language (ASL), an established language used by deaf Americans; baby-modified sign language, a variation of ASL used by some parents to teach their children to sign depending on their level of coordination and motor skills; and home signs, invented by parents or children themselves and usually resembling the words or actions they symbolize.

ASL is by far the best option for children for a number of reasons.

1. It is an established language; therefore, there is no reason to invent one for your baby.
2. If you forget a sign, you can always look it up in a book, whereas made-up signs may be done a little differently each time based on your memory of what you did the last time. Writing down each sign that you make up, so you don't forget it, is extremely time-consuming.
3. ASL can improve your child's fine motor skills. Dumbing down a sign to make it easier for a baby is the equivalent of always calling water "wa-wa" because your child has trouble pronouncing the correct word. Teaching him the correct word gives him the opportunity to develop real skills.
4. ASL includes finger spelling (a finger alphabet used to indicate

specific letters or spell out words), a useful skill that can increase spelling and reading abilities.

5. With ASL there are tons of resources at your fingertips, so to speak. You can easily find instruction books, children's books, websites, dictionaries, classes, games, posters, and more.

6. Using ASL allows other caregivers, teachers, and relatives to learn how to communicate with your child. A child who uses made-up signs will be confused and frustrated when other people don't understand him.

7. A unified language like ASL allows your child to sign with his peers and to participate in signing classes.

My Two Favorite Sign Language Dictionaries

Sure, you can look up words online for free, but it's handy to have a dictionary available. These are my favorites:

The Gallaudet Dictionary of American Sign Language (Gallaudet University Press)

Talking with Your Hands, Listening with Your Eyes (Square One Publishers*)*

8. You and your child can communicate with the deaf. Creating made-up signs eliminates the foundation for learning ASL later in life.

9. Research shows that hearing infants actually prefer ASL over invented sign language.

10. When parents use ASL, they are able to more clearly assess their child's fine motor skill development and enjoy his progress.

Give That Baby a Hand: Twenty-Six Tips for Big Fingers

Signing is a great experience for the whole family. The small commitment of time and minimal expense involved can make for a much more peaceful home for everybody. Here are some things you can do to optimize your family's signing experience.

1. Babies learn from repetition. The more you sign, the quicker you will get results.

2. Always use the same signs for the same words.

3. Always say the word as you sign.

4. Sign close to your face and make lots of eye contact.

5. Exaggerate the sign in order to make it clear for beginners.

6. Continue modeling the correct sign even if your child does it incorrectly.

7. Continue to use the signs your child has mastered as you add new ones.

8. Recognize your child's attempts at signs.

9. Always respond to signed or spoken invitations by your child.

10. Sign things and objects that your child is experiencing in the present.

11. Follow your child's lead by paying attention to what he wants to learn, as opposed to what you want to teach him.

12. Learn signs you think your child might be interested in.

13. Give your child positive reinforcement by signing back, commenting on his signs, or giving him what he has requested whenever appropriate.

14. Capture your baby's interest by using vivid facial expressions that mirror what you are signing. If you sign SAD, let your face express the meaning of the word.

15. Use sign language when you read to your child by signing key words.

16. If you don't know what your child is saying, ask him to "tell me with your hands."

17. Make signing fun.

18. Be patient with your child's progress.

19. Create opportunities for signing in your day-to-day life with your child.

20. Sign in many different places, not just at home.

21. Keep a sign language dictionary in the house so you can look up words as you need them.

22. Use more than one sign in a sentence as your child's signing gets more advanced.

23. Keep in mind that the more signs your child knows, the easier it is for him to learn more.

24. Keep in mind that experiencing new developmental leaps, teething, or illness can temporarily affect signing and communication.

25. Get the whole family signing.

26. Make sure you teach all caregivers your child's newest signs.

The Five Biggest Myths about Teaching Signing to Babies

There are many misconceptions and myths about teaching sign language to babies. Most of them are based on misinformation or a lack of interaction with signing families. Here are a few of the most common ones.

1. Sign language will delay spoken language. Because sign encourages early communication, increases vocabulary, reduces frustration, and expands expressive language, most speech experts are in favor of introducing sign to babies. According to Dr. Marilyn Agin, Lisa Geng, and Malcolm Nicholl, authors of *The Late Talker,* "Research indicates that signing is a stepping stone—and a very important one—on the way to speech. As the child's ability to vocalize increases,

FROM THE EXPERTS . . .

Why Sign When He Is Already Speaking?

Some signing families acknowledge that they cut back on signing as their children become more verbal and have a wider range of expressive words. "Baby Sign Language" is misinterpreted as just that, signing for babies, but the benefits of signing with children don't end when speech begins. More and more early childhood education experts and parents are agreeing that ASL promotes academic and social development in hearing preschoolers and elementary-age children when it is used as a complement to spoken language:

Cognitive Stimulation. Children who know how to sign

* Have larger vocabularies
* Are better spellers
* Are able to retain information more effectively
* Improve their reading skills
* Have enhanced fine motor coordination for writing skills

Emotional Stimulation. Children who know how to sign

* Express emotions more productively
* Interact better with peers

signing falls by the way side. The signs are not an alternative to speech, but a method of helping the child *discover* speech."

2. Signing is expensive and time-consuming. Signing does not take a lot of time or cost a bundle. The amount of time you devote to signing and the degree to which you integrate it into your family's life is completely up to you. Granted, the more you do, the more likely you are to see results. I have seen families who use only three signs benefit from the experience. As far as the financial commitment goes, it can be as little as the cost of one paperback book. Compiling a signing library, using DVDs, or taking a class can be a lot of fun and will enhance your signing vocabulary, but they are not mandatory, especially when there are so many helpful resources online.

3. Signing is something only type-A parents who are trying to raise a genius baby would do. I think Dr. Alan Greene said it best: "teaching your baby

---

- ✦ Embrace cultural sensitivities
- ✦ Gain confidence and self-esteem
- ✦ Use manners effectively

Marilyn Daniels, PhD, discovered that signing promotes brain development by stimulating both the right and left sides of the brain. She has found that signing expands kindergarteners' receptive and expressive English vocabularies and raises their reading level. For example, when a child uses ABC finger spelling she is making physical, visual, tactile, and kinesthetic connections.

When older children are signing they make eye contact, use body language, and facial expression. They can more sensitively read other people's emotions and stay connected. This is the foundation of emotional growth, a tool that is missing in the age of computers and social media.

Continue signing to your child even if she stops. The magic is to offer different opportunities to sign, and which are more complex than a baby's world: feelings, colors, manners, concepts (i.e., opposites and adjectives), and even as a "secret language."

Signing adds a new, fun dimension to a child's educational experiences. And when learning is fun, kids learn better and retain knowledge longer.

—Etel Leit, MS, signing with babies and children expert, and founder and owner of SignShine
National: www.SignShine.com · International: www.BabySignShine.com

---

sign language is not about power-parenting, it's another loving way to interact." Signing can potentially increase your child's IQ, vocabulary, and reading ability, but the most important thing about it is that it opens the door to communication for your child much earlier than it would happen otherwise, allowing you and your child to get closer. This ability to communicate with your child sooner is a gift that can reduce tears and frustration for both parent and child. Who wouldn't want that?

4. ASL is too complicated for babies. Whenever I speak to my toddlers, Mendez and Quincy, I use real words so I can provide an accurate model, even though I know they are not yet able to reproduce the sounds I'm making. As children get more speaking experience, they refine their speech and become more capable of accurately pronouncing words. It is a bad idea to invent words to take the place of complex words your child can't pronounce yet. If he can't say the word "preschool," you wouldn't teach him to call it "baba" because it's easier. You would just continue to model the correct word until he is able to say it. Similarly, there is no reason to make up your own hand signs because the ASL versions are more sophisticated. You can trust that your child's motor skills will catch up.

5. You have to learn a whole new language. You don't have to learn a complete language in order to begin signing with your child. You only have to know the signs that are valuable to you and your baby. Ideally you should be at least one step ahead of your child, although many adults learn the signs along *with* their children. You will be amazed how quickly you increase your own signing vocabulary just by looking up each of the signs as you become curious or your child asks for them. My husband, parents, and close friends thought learning ASL was a lot of fun.

Frequently Asked Questions about Signing

Q *Can all babies sign?*
A All able-bodied babies are capable of signing. As a matter of fact, gestures are natural to a baby's development, and even babies who are not exposed to sign will start to gesture (point to something they want, wave, etc.) between six and nine months of age. According to Diane Ryan, founder of KinderSign and the author of *The Complete Idiot's Guide to Baby Sign Language,* "The degree of signing success a baby achieves is in direct proportion to the level of dedication and enthusiasm of his parents!"

Q *When can I expect my baby to start signing?*

A There are many variables that affect how soon a child starts signing:

Health and development. Where your child is in his development has a significant effect on his learning process. Decreases in signing (or new word acquisition) are very common before reaching developmental milestones (crawling, standing, walking, first word) or when a child is ill or teething.

Mood and temperament. Some kids just can't wait to express themselves and embrace signing immediately, whereas others can be a little slower to warm up. Children are less likely to sign when they are overly tired or cranky.

Commitment and consistency. The more you sign, the sooner your baby will start signing back. Also, the more reinforcement he gets from other members of the family and friends, the faster he will develop his own signing vocabulary.

WHEN TO START SIGNING

Age of child when first exposed to sign	When the child is likely to start signing	Developmental notes
3–6 months old	3–6 months later	While some experts recommend starting to sign when a child is 6 or 7 months old, many children who grow up in a signing home make their first signs between 6 and 9 months of age.
6–9 months old	2 months later	A baby's memory skills are increasing dramatically at this age. He is likely to start to sit up by himself, which increases the likelihood of a first sign.
8–10 months old	6–8 weeks later	Because your child's fine motor skills improve so much during this stage, he is likely to start signing.
10–12 months old	2–3 weeks later	At this age your child is better able to focus, will gesture naturally, can better coordinate his movements, and understands that signs and words are symbolic for objects and behaviors.
12–18 months old	2 days–2 weeks later	Take advantage of your child's natural inclination to imitate at this age. Children exposed to signing at this stage of development often catch on very quickly.

Q *Should I make my baby look at me when I sign?*

A You should never force a child to look at you. Forcing your child's face in your direction is not going to make him more interested in signing, and it certainly won't make it fun, two things that are mandatory for your child to become a signer. If he is actually looking away, as opposed to just looking at something else that has caught his eye, it may mean that he is overwhelmed or overstimulated. Make sure that you are not overwhelming him by trying to teach him too many new signs or by being too "in his face." Give him a little space.

Make sure you take advantage of optimal signing times when you have his attention. Be aware of the three types of gazes (see page 128) in order to take advantage of your child's focus. Also, use caretaking times, like meals, baths, dressing, bedtime, and diaper changes, when your child is often looking at you or another caregiver, to communicate using signs. Signs can also make these times more fun. Keep in mind, as Etel Leit often reminds parents, "Your baby may be paying attention even when you think that she is not!" Do not give up on signing just because you think you've lost your audience. There are probably signs percolating in that baby brain.

Five Signing "No-No's"

Never show disappointment.

Don't get frustrated with your child's signing abilities.

Don't ask your child to perform for others.

Don't sign out of context.

Don't compare your child to other signing children.

Q *What should I do if my child mixes up signs or makes up his own?*

A Make sure to be really positive and responsive but handle it the same way you would if he said a word incorrectly. If, when reaching for his shoe, he makes up his own sign for SHOE or instead signs SOCK, try saying something like, "I see you want your shoe" (while signing SHOE) or "Do you want your shoe or your sock?" (while signing SHOE and SOCK). This acknowledges what he wants and teaches him the correct sign without blatantly correcting him.

Q *Should I teach my child to sign letters?*

A While I wouldn't recommend starting finger spelling sign language before a child is six months old, it is helpful to teach kids letters as they get older. Understanding letters only makes learning new signs easier. For example, the sign for TOILET, which involves pivoting the wrist back and forth with a closed fist while sticking the thumb out between the index and third finger, makes a lot more sense when you know that the hand positioning stands for the letter "T." Kids love to learn the alphabet and how to fingerspell their first name. My daughters used to giggle with glee when I signed the alphabet song. When Quincy was only a year and a half, she would hold up her hands and try to sign all the letters herself. This kind of early, fun introduction to letters can facilitate reading development in the future.

Q *Are signing videos a good idea?*

A Along with the American Academy of Pediatrics, I recommend no screen time (no television, DVDs, or movies) before age two. I encourage parents to wait until the age of three whenever possible. When children view videos they are passive recipients of information and are not truly engaged. Children learn sign (and spoken) language best from being meaningfully engaged in conversation with real people, not passively watching a screen. That said, if you insist on showing your child a video, the Signing Time! series would be at the top of my list of recommendations. This was the first DVD my own children watched, after turning three.

Q *Is it possible to use sign with your child when you work outside of the home?*

A Absolutely! The key is open communication with care providers. So let whoever takes care of your child know that you are using sign language at home. Make sure to give or loan them a sign language dictionary and keep them apprised of new signs your child has learned. My daughters' nanny and I learned signs together and taught each other new words as we learned them. I know one working mom who gave her son's day-care providers a free sign language lesson once a month. This got the providers excited about signing and reassured the mother that they knew her son's most frequently used signs.

It's All Fun and Games

Using signs to play and connect with your child can be a lot of fun and keeps kids excited about signing. Here are a few games you can play with children of different ages and skill levels.

Bubbles
For: Infants
Supplies: Nontoxic bubbles

Blow bubbles for your child while signing BUBBLES. Very young children will often sign MORE or BUBBLES when you stop. Give your child the opportunity to ask for more. You can also teach him a song about bubbles or make up one of your own.

The Good-Night Walk
For: Babies six months and up
Supplies: None

Incorporate a "good-night walk" into your nighttime ritual: just as in Margaret Wise Brown and Clement Hurd's classic book *Good Night Moon*, you and your child say and sign GOOD-NIGHT to the people and things he cares about: Mommy, Daddy, dog, cat, teddy bear, sister, brother, moon, stars, friends, grandparents. He may even choose to KISS them good-night. Try to keep the good-nights in the same order every evening so your child can anticipate what is coming and focus on the signs. If someone he wants to say good-night to is not present, you can always use a photo.

Reading Books
For: Your child—as soon as you start reading together
Supplies: Books

Sign key words in the book you are reading. You can use signs with any kind of book. There are also many wonderful children's books that integrate signing into the story.

Where Is?
For: Babies six months and up
Supplies: A sheer scarf and items that fit under the scarf. Do not use anything that can fit through a standard toilet paper roll because it might be a potential choking hazard.

Place the scarf over the object when your child isn't looking and ask, "WHERE is the BALL?" while signing key words. Use various objects that capture your child's interest.

Pick Me Up!
Fun Songs for Learning Signs
For: Babies seven months and up
Supplies: *Pick Me Up!* CD and book

Pick Me Up teaches songs and signs.

Photo Game
For: Babies nine months and up
Supplies: Photos of family and friends (maybe a few pets too)

Favorite Sign and Sing Books

Baa Baa, Black Sheep: Sign & Singalong

Head and Shoulder, Knees and Toes: Sign & Singalong

Itsy Bitsy Spider: Sign & Singalong

Teddy Bear, Teddy Bear! Sign & Singalong

Pick Me Up! Fun Songs for Learning Signs by Sign2Me

Pull out a photo and say who it is while signing, e.g., GRAMMY. With older kids you can lay out the photos and then ask "WHERE is GRAMMY?"

Mama's Purse
For: Babies nine months and up
Supplies: An empty handbag containing items that your baby has shown interest in and that you know how to sign—a cell phone, for example, or a ball, a photo of Dad, a pacifier, a banana.

Allow your child to pull items from the bag while you ask and sign, "WHAT is in MOMMY'S purse?" Name and sign all the items as he pulls them out. With older children, you can sign items while your child finds them in the bag.

Card Games
For: Babies nine months and up (depending on which game you play)
Supplies: Flashcards with pictures

There are many fun games you can play with flash cards (my favorite is the DK My First card series), but the most important thing is *never* use flash cards to drill your child or pressure him to learn. However, I have to admit one of my daughters used to quiz me! She would point to the cards and say "dat dat?" ("What's that?") over and over. Make sure you keep it light and fun.

- You can sign WHERE IS and then sign something you see on a card and let your baby find it.
- Tell a story using signs along with the cards to create visual images.
- Use the cards to ask questions like "Do you see a BROWN ANIMAL?" (Answer: HORSE) or "Which is the DOG's BABY?" (Answer: PUPPY).

Hot/Cold
For: Children fourteen months and up
Supplies: Warm and cold objects, making sure that none are dangerously hot or choking hazards. Small teddy bears are a good way to start this game. Prior to playing, put one teddy bear in the dryer and one in the freezer. Bring them to your child to see and touch, showing him the sign for HOT when you touch the hot bear and COLD when you touch the cold one. You can then move on to any other safe objects, like ice cubes or a warm (not hot) heating pad, that demonstrate the hot/cold concept.

Foodie Picnic
For: Children eighteen months and up
Supplies: Wooden or plastic food

Have a pretend picnic. Put out a blanket with toy food, using it as an opportunity to practice signs: "Can you GIVE me an APPLE?" "Do you WANT a CARROT?" "I am EATING a SANDWICH," and so on.

Hide and Seek
For: Children eighteen months and older
Supplies: Safe objects

Hide an object, say and sign, "WHERE IS the SHOE?," and let your child find it. Keep signing all the names of the different objects you are hiding for your child.

I Spy
For: Children two years and up
Supplies: None

Look around the room and tell your child something you see by saying "I spy ..." and signing the item while letting him find it.

Stop and Go
For: Children two-and-a-half years and up
Supplies: None

Explain to your child that when you sign STOP he has to stop, and when you sign GO he can go. Run around together, dance, and play until you say and sign STOP. Wait a minute and sign GO. This is a useful skill for your child to have when you are out together.

How Am I Feeling?
For: Children two-and-a-half years and older
Supplies: Pictures from a book like *Baby Faces* or cutouts of people's faces from magazines

This is a great way to practice signs that identify feelings, as well as learning how to read people's faces (a crucial component of emotional intelligence). Pull out a picture and ask your child how he thinks the person in the photo is feeling. When he identifies the feeling, make the sign as you say the word.

The Alphabet Song
For: Your child, as soon as he shows interest when you move your fingers—as long as you don't expect your child to be able to fingerspell.
Supplies: None

Sing and sign the alphabet song.

Signing Bingo
For: Children three and older
Supplies: Signing Bingo by Garlic Press

Play bingo with cards that show signs instead of numbers.

Babies without Borders

Foreign Language

*Promoting bilingualism is one of the best things
a parent can do for his or her 21st-century child.*

—STEVEN PARKER, *7 Steps to Raising a Bilingual Child*

About nine months after my daughters were born, I read a book called *The Bilingual Edge: Why, When, and How to Teach Your Child a Second Language* and was so inspired by it that I began to read extensively about the benefits of teaching children another language. As a result of my research, I decided to introduce my daughters to Mandarin Chinese and Spanish. I know it sounds like a very type-A thing to do, but bear with me while I explain how rewarding it can be to share a foreign language with your child.

I admit I have a love of languages. To me, the sound of a new language is like a secret code giving me a window into someone else's culture, experience, and psyche. When I was about ten years old, I developed a friendship with Julia, a Spanish-speaking friend, who spoke almost no English. In order to communicate with her, I learned Spanish, and soon Julia became a close friend of mine. When I was fourteen, I competed in a sport called rhythmic gymnastics and attended an international competition with Mexico's national rhythmic gymnastics team. None of the members spoke English and they had no interpreters with them. Thanks to Julia, I was fluent enough in Spanish to act as their interpreter.

This chance opened up an amazing new world of culture, friendship, and experience to me. I enjoyed it so much that I started studying French, and, after years of listening to my Russian gymnastics coach scream at me in Russian, I decided to add Russian to my repertoire.

By the time I was an adult, however, I spoke only one language. While some of my Spanish skills remained, I was nowhere near fluent anymore; I never completely took to French; and after I retired from gymnastics and stopped hearing Russian regularly, I started to lose that language, too. Unlike some of the families described in this chapter, everyone in my home is a native English speaker. My husband, who also has a love of languages, spoke Hebrew, Italian, Spanish, and French at various points in his life, but is no longer fluent in any of them. After reviewing the literature, we were both convinced that we wanted to raise our children to be bilingual—or trilingual—despite our limited language skills. In this chapter I will tell you about the choices we've made and how you can raise your child to be bilingual or multilingual, whatever your circumstances.

Beneficios, Bienfaits, Вы́года, and More Benefits

What really sold me on bringing second language learning into our home were all the neurological, psychological, and social advantages for children, which study after study have shown to be dramatic.

While some of the findings may apply only to children who develop a high level of proficiency in a second language, children who are not as fluent benefit tremendously as well. In a study of English-speaking children who learned just a little Italian, it was found that they had a greater understanding of words and more enhanced reading skills than their monolingual peers. The researchers concluded that children gain cognitive and academic benefits from even just a little exposure to a second language, which I found to be very encouraging!

Here are ten more benefits of second language acquisition:

1. Higher IQs. Bilingual children develop a more flexible brain system. In a landmark study, Canadian French-English bilingual fourth graders were compared to monolingual children on intelligence tests. Bilinguals scored significantly higher than monolinguals on most measures of verbal and nonverbal intelligence. The researchers came to the conclusion that bilinguals outperform their monolingual peers because second language acquisition provides them with more mental flexibility and stronger concept formation skills.

2. Increased focus. Bilinguals consistently score better than monolinguals on tests that require them to focus on one or two aspects of a task while blocking out attention to another. The ability to ignore conflicting or extraneous information is crucial to developing focused attention. Researchers found that the more misleading the material to be ignored, the greater the bilingual advantage. This held true in tests of perception, as well as verbal tests of selective attention.

3. Increased creativity. Divergent thinking—the ability to come up with different solutions—is considered a key element in creativity. In tests where subjects were asked to think of more uses for typical objects—a paperclip, brick, or cardboard box, for example—bilinguals were able to come up with significantly more possible solutions than the monolinguals. When put through a science inquiry test, bilinguals were able to generate three times more high-quality hypotheses for solving science problems.

4. Better thinking ability. Study after study shows enhanced thought processes in multilingual children. Studies of four- to nine-year-old South African children, who were fluent in both English and Afrikaans, showed them to be two to three years ahead of their monolingual peers in semantic development. In a study of five- to eight-year-old children in the United States and Israel, researchers challenged the kids to complete multiple patterns of organization with three levels of pegs on a pegboard. Monolinguals and bilinguals performed the reorganization equally well, but the bilinguals' descriptions were more analytical and systematic than the monolinguals'. They were also better able to keep track of how the pegs were related, refer to multiple dimensions, seek out rules behind patterns, and use rules to organize their understanding of pattern changes.

5. Heightened language awareness. "Language is a code and once you have this code presented to you, you have a template," explains Angelika Putintseva, director of WorldSpeak, a language school for children in Los Angeles. An understanding of this code makes it easier for children to comprehend that there are many different words in many different languages for one object. This kind of abstract thinking makes it easier to conceptualize new languages.

Bilingual children score better in word association tests. Try it yourself. What's the first word you think of when I say "dog"? Children usually respond with a word like "bark," as if they were completing a sentence, whereas adults tend to give more abstract relationship responses like "cat." The more childlike "sentence match" responses are typical of children between the ages of five and eight, whereas the more abstract, adult "dictionary matches" show an ability to think about the words separate from the sentences in which they usually appear. A study of bilingual children found that they gave "dictionary match" responses much sooner than did monolingual children.

Another skill that multilingual children demonstrate is "phonemic awareness," or the awareness of how sounds, syllables, and units work within words. This linguistic awareness is the foundation for learning to read and write. It also helps children learn a third, fourth, or even fifth language more easily.

6. Improved math ability. Bilingual children are able to grasp rules and process information more easily, which gives them a head start in problem solving. It appears that these skills translate to mathematical ability. A study of multilingual children in secondary school in Brussels found that they outperformed their monolingual peers in problem-solving and fraction exercises. A fascinating study of the effects of foreign language study on reading and math skills found that after one term of weekly ninety-minute language study with an experimental group that received ninety minutes' less math instruction per week, the language study group still outperformed the control group in math.

7. Earlier skills in reading and writing. In a study of bilingual and monolingual emergent readers, children were shown pictures of two objects (for example, a dog and a cat). The tester told the child, "This card has the word 'dog' written on it and I am going to put it here" and placed it under the picture of the dog. The experimenter then created a scuffle between two stuffed animals, causing the card with the word on it to end up under the wrong picture. The tester then asked the child to identify what was written on the card. Only 38 percent of the monolingual children gave the correct answer, whereas 82 percent of the bilingual kids gave the correct answer. The four-year-old bilinguals even tested ahead of the five-year-old monolinguals, revealing a significant reading advantage to bilingual children.

A University of Florida study of reading skills looked at 960 elementary-school children in three categories: 1) monolingual; 2) English-Spanish bilinguals in English-only schools; and 3) English-Spanish bilinguals in dual-language schools. Understandably there was no difference in kindergarteners, since children are generally not expected to know how to read at that age. By second grade, however, the bilinguals showed an advantage. Three years later, as fifth graders, the dual-study children not only did better in Spanish reading, which would be expected, but they scored better in English reading as well.

8. Increased cultural sensitivity. Languages provide a window into the soul of another culture and provide insight into that culture's way of thinking. Three cultural issues are especially significant. First there is the obvious: when a child learns to speak another language, she is able to develop friendships and relationships with people of different cultures, allowing her to get to know those cultures.

The second issue is "linguistic relativity," the idea that language determines how you think about and perceive the world and that learning to speak a different language helps form a different conception of the world based on those linguistic differences. For example, the expression "to give birth" in Spanish is "dar a luz," which literally means to "to give to light" or "into the light." To understand the Spanish phrasing is to understand the philosophical idea that giving birth is both a physical and spiritual act in that culture.

The third concept is what linguists call "communicative competence," the intuitive understanding that you speak to different people in different ways, mainly in different languages. This illustrates a sensitivity to both language and identity that generally develops very early in bilingual children, often as young as two years of age. Recently, one of my daughters walked up to a Spanish-speaking person and began speaking Spanish to him. Interestingly, she had not heard me speak to this person in Spanish prior to this encounter. Language truly shapes the way we view the world: according to Dr. Barbara Zurer Pearson, author of *Raising a Bilingual Child,* "Bilinguals have already broken out of the confines of the single worldview of each of their languages and have shown themselves to be more flexible, divergent thinkers and superior problem solvers. If we had just one language and one worldview on earth, the lack of cultural diversity would reduce our margin of adaptability to changing conditions, which is the hallmark of survival of the fittest."

9. Higher earning power. According to a team of political researchers at the University of Miami who studied the earning potential of bilinguals and monolinguals, bilinguals have an advantage in lifetime earnings. Speaking a second language gives a business person international reach; understanding other cultures allows her to appeal to different audiences, and an ability to communicate in that language expands her professional opportunities. If your child is able to master another language, there will always be job opportunities available to her.

10. Prevention of Alzheimer's disease. Speaking more than one language appears to have lifelong benefits for your cognitive well-being. A Canadian study that examined the effects of bilingualism on dementia found that speaking a second language throughout one's life can delay dementia by four years, compared to people who speak only one language. It found that the average age of onset of dementia symptoms in the monolingual group was 71.4 years, while in the bilingual group it was 75.5 years. According to Dr. Morris Freedman, a member of the research team and an authority on cognitive impairments due to diseases like Alzheimer's, "There are no pharmacological interventions that are this dramatic."

Bilingualism: The Home Version

Figuring out how to integrate a second language into your home life can be challenging if you've been speaking only one language until now. Even if you speak a "second" language, starting is often the hardest part. According to a report by Dr. Pearson, it takes parents who decide to use a different language at home four to six weeks to adjust. For those of you, like me, who are not native speakers of a second language, keep in mind that while hearing a native accent is ideal, children can learn language from imperfect speakers as well. Giving them the exposure they need to hear can be challenging, but if you follow these tips, your child will be speaking another language before you know it!

1. Create meaningful interactions in the language. According to Drs. Kendall King and Alison Mackey, authors of *The Bilingual Edge,* "The truly critical factor is rich, dynamic, and meaningful interaction with speakers of those languages (and this can come in many different forms)." Engaging your child in the language is the key:

- Address her directly, making sure you engage her in that language in interesting conversation.
- Speak to your child at her developmental level: for example, use Motherese in the second language when your child is a baby and use the appropriate level of the second language with your toddler, depending on where she is developmentally.
- Do your best to aim for quantity of language over quality, especially in the beginning. For your child, sheer exposure is key to picking up a second language.

- Make sure to use the second language when you are being affectionate and sharing loving moments together. When you go into your child's bedroom in the middle of the night, try soothing her in the other language to create positive, reassuring associations.

2. Keep it fun! Keep second language conversation and learning light and fun. Try to create positive associations for your child. Talk about your child's favorite subjects in the second language. Follow her lead in figuring out what interests her at any given moment. Bringing a second language to play helps your child *own* it. In particular, dramatic play in another language requires children to use and be exposed to more language without even noticing it. Make sure you also use a second language while playing games, doing arts and crafts, singing, and just being silly together.

3. Read . . . a lot! The most powerful language-learning tool is a book. Researchers have found that the size of a child's vocabulary in their first language, what linguists call "L1," is directly related to how often they are read to in that language. In 2002, Dr. Janet Patterson set out to see if the same is true of children who use a second language by examining the vocabularies of sixty four-year-olds learning Spanish and English. She found that the size of their vocabulary in each language was directly related to how often they were read to in that language. Here is the shocker—the frequency with which children were read to in a foreign language had more of an impact than even the total exposure they had to that language. According to Dr. Patterson's results, reading may be a bigger vocabulary booster than conversation.

I started reading board books in Spanish to my girls when they were very young and I found that reading in Spanish brought back my Spanish language skills. I even learned the Spanish for words like "pacifier," "crib," "slippers," and "peek-a-boo"—words that I certainly had had no reason to use when I was at my most fluent.

4. Make it a cultural experience. Have fun with the culture. Introduce age-appropriate music, food, toys, and games. This type of layered cultural experience makes it more likely a child will have positive associations. If the language is the native language of one of the parents, this can create an early sense of pride and identity while also enhancing family connections and traditions. Research shows that children who have a strong sense of identity and connection with their culture do better in school and have stronger self-esteem.

5. Encourage your child to chat. Encourage your child to speak the second language. When she does, make sure you give a positive, supportive response. Ask questions in the language and encourage your child to do the same. Try to engage her by narrating in your target language (e.g., "I see you pointing to the teddy bear. You seem to want it"). Make sure you use the techniques of modeling, self-talk, parallel talk, expansion, recasting, and extension that were described on page 103.

A Short Biography of a Linguist

Charles Berlitz, the grandson of Maximilian Berlitz, founder of the famous Berlitz language schools, spoke thirty-two languages. On the orders of his father, every relative and servant was ordered to speak to Charles in a different language. His father spoke to him in German, his grandfather in Russian, his nanny in Spanish. For many years he thought every human being spoke a unique language and couldn't understand why he didn't have his own language.

Six Approaches to Bilingualism

Most mixed-language families struggle to find a balance between the two languages that the parents speak.Usually the goal is to be equally fluent in both languages. But according to Dr. Naomi Steiner, author of 7 *Steps to Raising a Bilingual Child,* "it is rare for bilingual children (or adults, for that matter) to exhibit equal proficiency in both languages." "Balanced bilinguals," as language experts call them, are unusual. Most bilinguals have a dominant language, even if they have grown up in a home where two languages were always spoken.

Figuring out the right approach for your family—if there are no native speakers of the target language in the house—can be challenging. Different approaches work for different families, so I recommend experimenting in your own home, keeping in mind that you may need to change strategies over time.

APPROACHES TO MULTILINGUALISM

Name	Description of Approach	Pros	Cons
One-Parent-One-Language (OPOL)	One parent always speaks one language to the child and the other parent always speaks the other language to the child.	Considered the gold standard of maximum language input from both languages. • Simple, easy to remember • Consistent • Clear boundaries • Child gets maximum language exposure in both languages • Naturally leads to child responding in the language in which she has been addressed	• Can result in passive bilingualism (the ability to understand a language without speaking it) • Can get complicated when child is outside the home with nonspeakers of the parent's language • Child may start to resist the minority (second) language
One-Caregiver-One-Language (OCOL)	One caregiver (nanny, babysitter, grandparent, friend, or relative) always speaks the target language.	• Naturally creates meaningful engagement in language • Child motivated to learn in order to get needs met • High level of language exposure depending on frequency	• If child knows that caregiver speaks the dominant (first) language (usually English), she may resist speaking the target language • A parent who does not speak the target language may get jealous
Minority language at Home (ML@H)	Family supports the minority language by using only that language at home.	• High language exposure • Leads to fluency • High level of emotional reinforcement since both parents speak the language • Not complicated	• Young child who is not exposed to the culture's dominant language can have difficulty adjusting to school or day-care in the dominant language • If one parent is not completely fluent, communication may be difficult

Name	Description of Approach	Pros	Cons
Time and Place Strategy or Mixed Language Strategy (T&P or MLS)	The family uses a specific language in predetermined situations, places, activities, or rituals; e.g., speaking only French at dinnertime, speaking only German at grandparents' house, speaking only Spanish when playing soccer with a Spanish-speaking team, watching only Korean-language television stations	• Provides regular language exposure • Can make those chosen language activities special • Can be easier for a nonfluent speaker in the home	• Boundaries can become blurry • Difficult to redirect a child to speak a certain language unless she is motivated • Dependent on child's motivation and positive self-identification as language speaker • Bias toward majority language
Trilingual Strategy (Tri)	The family speaks three languages; e.g., Mom speaks Spanish to child, Dad speaks French to child, parents speak to each other in English (the language in which they "met" and developed their relationship)	• Child is exposed to three languages • Makes the family internationally mobile	• Requires two parents who are willing to use a third language to communicate • Using a less familiar language can lead to misunderstanding • Can be difficult to get equal exposure to all three languages
Non-Native Strategy or Artificial Strategy (NNS or AS)	Two native speakers of the dominant language create regular situations that provide language exposure; e.g., • Hiring a language tutor • Creating a language playgroup • Planning family vacations around language exposure • Moving to another country	• Creates a good starting foundation for future language learning • The created situation can be fun and add diversity to a child's schedule • A good way for non-foreign-language-speaking parents to support a foreign language they might not otherwise be able to provide	• The acquisition of a second language depends on exposure and consistency of use • Parents must make sure that interactions in the language are meaningful in order to create motivation for the child to speak in that language • It can be challenging to reinforce the second language

FROM THE EXPERTS . . .

"But Which Language?"

The issue of "which language" is one of the most important early questions that parents need to address. Language choice is easier for some parents than others. For example, some parents are bilingual and already know they want their child to be able to communicate in their heritage language. Others don't speak a second language themselves, but know they want to give their child an important opportunity that they didn't have. It's helpful for parents to understand that knowledge of any two (or more) languages is an asset for children in many different ways, both cognitive and social. What's important in choosing a language is that you are able to *stick with it* over time. This is because most of the benefits of bilingualism come with knowing a second language well. So prior to investing time, energy, and effort into language learning, parents need to consider:

—*The personal:* What language skills do the parents and extended family have? How much time can these individuals spend interacting with your child? Are most of the adults on board about the importance of consistently using a second language with your child?

—*The local:* What opportunities are there in the neighborhood and community to learn and use the language? What options are there for bilingual babysitters and play-dates? Bilingual schools or day camps and weekend or summer language learning classes? Bilingual playgroups?

—*The global:* What opportunities exist to use the language later on in life? Which languages are on the rise? In demand? Are these trends likely to continue?

New parents should consider their own feelings carefully and do as much investigation as possible. While there is no one-size-fits-all answer out there for families choosing a second language, there is, no doubt, a best answer for you and your child.

—Kendall King, PhD and Alison Mackey, PhD, authors of *The Bilingual Edge* and professors, respectively, at the University of Minnesota and Georgetown University

The Kids, the Myths, the Language

Myths about second language learning are abundant. Because you are likely to encounter them from well-meaning friends and relatives and even doctors and teachers, I want to make sure to address these myths and arm you with the latest information to dispel them.

Myth #1: Learning another language will cause your child to have a speech delay. Although there is a huge variation in the ages at which children begin to speak, vocalization of the first word usually occurs between ten and eighteen months. When a child is bilingual, there is a tendency to blame the use of a second language if she is on the later side of the articulation spectrum (fifteen to eighteen months). According to Drs. King and Mackey, however, "there is no scientific evidence to show that hearing two, three, or more languages leads to delays or disorders in language acquisition." In addition, it is important to keep in mind that, statistically speaking, 5 to 10 percent of all children experience some language impairment whether or not they are bilingual. Bilingualism does not cause language delays.

Environment is key to language acquisition. A two-year-old boy named Alex provides an example. Alex grew up in a home where no one read to him, the television was on most of the time, and much of the language input he received was in the form of mandates ("Put your toys away," "Stop playing with your food," "Don't touch that!"). Although he was addressed in Russian by his mother and English by his father, the environment was not conducive for him to speak or learn language. Even if he was able to get the quantity of language input he needed, the quality of language was terrible: it wasn't engaging or on his level and, as a result, Alex was very behind his peers in the dominant language. To an untrained teacher, seeing him at day care, it might have looked as if bilingualism was causing a problem when in fact it was his environment that was at fault.

What about total vocabulary? According to Dr. Steiner, "Research shows that if you consider *total* vocabulary from both languages, a bilingual child usually knows the same number of words as her monolingual peers. Any small discrepancies wane over time, and typically disappear by kindergarten. After that, a bilingual child may actually end up with *greater* word comprehension than a monolingual child."

Myth #2: Your child is using two languages in one sentence. You must be confusing her by teaching her another language. Language mixing, which linguists refer to as code switching, is a normal part of bilingual development. This type of language mixing generally occurs between sentences or within sentences. Believe it or not, this practice has been linked to greater language proficiency as well as higher scores on intelligence tests. It takes a certain level of mastery and language understanding to code mix. Lexical code switching occurs when a person replaces a word in one language with its equivalent in another: for example, "Quiero ir a la book store" (I want to go to the book store) instead of "Quiero ir a la librería." Grammatical code switching occurs when a speaker starts a sentence in one language and finishes in another: for example, "Quiero ir a la casa de Grammy and Grampy's to play" (I want to go to Grammy and Grampy's house to play).

There are a few common reasons why a child tends to code switch:

1. There is a gap in the child's vocabulary in the language she is speaking.
2. She recognizes that the term in the language she is speaking is not quite the equivalent of the term in the other language.
3. She is responding to an emotional trigger, which is a word or grammatical element that facilitates a switch from one language to another.
4. She associates the activity or thing she is talking about with the other language so she switches to that language.
5. People around her are code mixing so she thinks it is the norm.

Language mixing is not the result of confusion. In her book 7 *Steps to Raising a Bilingual Child,* Dr. Steiner tells a story about a little girl who said, "Je veux aller (I want to go) swimming now." When her mother asked if she was confused about the languages she was speaking, the girl responded, "Even if I don't know the word in French, I still want to go swimming."

Is it okay for your child to code switch and what should you do when she does it? You never want to criticize your child's language or discourage her from speaking, but at the same time you do not want to encourage this habit. Here are five tips for handling language switching:

1. Don't switch languages in your child's presence. You are your child's best role model.
2. Don't correct or criticize when she mixes languages.
3. Be positive when she uses full sentences in the target language.
4. Repeat the sentence in the target language using only words from the language without calling attention to it ("So you are asking if you can have your doll?").
5. Pause to see if she catches herself and naturally switches into the target language.

Myth #3: TV, DVDs, and talking books and toys are a good way to teach your child a language. Millions of dollars are spent on marketing DVDs and television programs in an attempt to convince parents that these methods successfully foster second-language development, but manufacturers' claims about these products couldn't be further from the truth. As mentioned previously, the Baby Einstein company was pressured to completely redesign its website, refrain from making educational claims about its DVDs and videos, and give refunds to consumers as a result of a Federal Trade Commission complaint filed by the Campaign for a Commercial-Free Childhood. A study in the *Journal of Pediatrics* revealed that for every hour per day that babies eight to sixteen months old were shown "infantainment," such as *Brainy Baby* or *Baby Einstein,* they knew six to eight fewer words than other children. It is fair to assume that this finding translates to foreign languages as well.

While studies show that as little as one hour of interaction in the target language can help a child hear small distinctions in the sound system of a language, that interaction must come from a real human being. A study by Dr. Daniel Anderson that compared children's ability to learn and follow instructions from viewing a live demonstration versus a video of the same demonstration reported that children learn substantially less from watching a video. Another study that specifically examined whether or not babies learn foreign language from audiovisual or audio-only recordings of the language found that this type of experience was completely useless for language learning. In this study, researchers divided their nine-month-old subjects into three groups. One group was exposed to native Mandarin Chinese speakers in twelve laboratory sessions. The second group heard English only for twelve sessions. The third group was exposed to the same Mandarin speakers and materials but only through audiovisual and audio recordings. The conclusion was that exposure to Mandarin through audiovisual and audio-only materials had absolutely no effect, whereas the children exposed to live Mandarin showed phonetic learning.

While "talking books" might seem like a great idea, especially for the non-native-speaking parent who hopes to increase a child's exposure to the language, studies have shown them to be ineffective as well. In a study of mothers using talking books with their children, it was found that while the quantity of talk was not that much different from books that were read by moms to their children, the quality of the talk was dramatically different. Researchers in the study found that most of the talk from parent to child was devoted to behavior management such as "Don't touch that," "Let it go," and so on, while the children whose parents read to them regularly from books benefited from much richer conversations and vocabulary.

When it comes to electronic toys, once again, they are not as useful for teaching children a second language as direct interaction with a person. A two-year government-funded study by the University of Stirling in Scotland found that educational electronic toys have no discernible benefit for children. The only way electronic toys are helpful is if a person uses them to do all the interacting. For example, one of the few electronic toys my kids have is a Language Littles doll called Ling, who spouts phrases in Mandarin Chinese when you press her hand. My kids enjoy playing with Ling, but neither I nor they have any expectation of learning any Chinese from her unless I (or someone who speaks Chinese better than I do) use Ling as a catalyst to start conversations about or in Chinese.

Myth #4: Only bilingual parents can teach their child a language. You do not have to be completely bilingual yourself in order for your child to acquire a second language. Many parents who are not fluent or do not speak a second language at all choose to bring in a nanny, au pair, or language teacher, whereas some just use the target language to the best of their ability. While native speakers have a clear advantage in teaching their children their language, it is possible for a monolingual parent to create a strong foundation. Many nonfluent speakers worry that if they speak the language to their child, she will pick up bad habits, poor pronunciation, or bad grammar. But, according to Dr. Pearson, "As long as you have the desire to do it, and have reasonable fluency in the language, in most cases the extra opportunity you provide for your children to practice the language outweighs the potential inconvenience of their picking up your errors." If you make an effort to expose your child to the language in other places, she is likely to hear native accents and fluency and learn from that as well.

At a play center I was attending with one of my daughters, I met Emily, a British woman who spoke only Spanish to her two-year-old daughter. Although clearly she was not a native speaker, her Spanish was quite good: her daughter not only understood every word but responded in Spanish as well. I was impressed. When I asked Emily about the use of Spanish in her home, she told me that both she and her husband were English, but she had spent a lot of time in Spain during her teenage years and wanted to make sure her daughter knew Spanish because Emily had such a love for it. Personally, I always find stories like this one to be inspirational.

If you are monolingual and want your child to grow up speaking and under-standing a second language, there are many things you can do. While the task is certainly more challenging than it would be for a native speaker, monolingual parents *can* help their children learn another language. Here are some tips:

1. Keep bilingual dictionaries in the house and be quick to look up words that you do not know so you can increase your (and your child's) vocabulary.
2. Consult with native speakers when you have language questions.
3. Plan family excursions to local places where the language is spoken.
4. Plan family vacations around language exposure.
5. Learn from children's materials—songs, rhymes, stories, picture books, and so on.
6. Seek out resources such as language schools and language camps for your children.

When it comes to developing fluency, "20 percent" seems to be the magic number. In a study of kids who were being raised to be bilingual, researchers looked at three types of families: those with two parents who were both bilingual in Spanish and English, those with one parent who was proficient in Spanish, and those whose nanny or babysitter was the only source of Spanish. The children who were exposed to a second language for as little as 20 percent (one-fifth) of their waking hours were able to develop a productive vocabulary. Kids who were less exposed to a second language were hesitant to speak it at all. Later in this chapter you will learn how to perform a language audit of your own home to see how many hours of the target language your child is being exposed to and make your own language plan.

Myth #5: If your child is having a language problem in one or both languages, you should stick to one language. Sara brought her two-year-old son Max to his pediatrician, who was not knowledgeable about bilingual learning, for his annual visit. When Max used two languages in a sentence (a normal part of bilingual development), the pediatrician recommended that Sara stop speaking her native French to Max because he was getting "mixed up." Before throwing out her native tongue, Sara wisely consulted a speech pathologist whose specialty was bilingualism. Fortunately for Sara and Max, the pathologist recognized that mixed language was normal and encouraged Sara to continue both French and English in the home. Max, now six years old, is completely fluent in both languages and doesn't mix them up at all.

"We can now safely say that there is no scientific evidence to support the idea that giving up one language necessarily promotes the development of another," says Dr. Steiner. "A child who stops speaking Spanish or Russian, for instance, will not become a better English speaker simply because he focuses his attention on one language." We do know, however, that if a second language is learned but not used, the brain loses its ability to recall words and grammatical structure, thus preventing that person from being able to speak that language on command. There is so much to lose! Therefore it is especially important to get the opinion of an expert who is familiar with second language learning if you are advised to give up a second language in the home.

What if a child has a true language impairment? According to Dr. Fred Genesee, co-author of *Dual Language Development and Disorders,* most bilingual children with language impairments express those impairments in both languages. Every language has its own areas of vulnerability, so an impairment will be expressed in a different manner in the child's primary language and in a second language. Because 5 to 10 percent of children are diagnosed with a language disorder, it is important to work with a speech pathologist who is familiar with dual language learning. Also, make sure to rule out hearing problems, which are one of the most common causes of language difficulties for young children.

FROM THE EXPERTS...

Choose a Foreign Language Program

There are many benefits to learning a second language for young children, but how does one go about evaluating a program?

Here are some criteria:

1. Native speaking teachers—the teachers should be able to speak comfortably and naturally. Ideally the teacher would also have a background in second language acquisition and early child development.

2. 100% use of the native language—a program that is 100% in the target language provides the best environment for developing listening comprehension. Children ages 0–3 do not need translation.

Keeping the Window to Language Open

Children are born as citizens of the world. In other words, an infant's brain is wired to learn any language to which she is exposed. If a baby is born in Norway, she will learn to speak Norwegian like a native, and if the same baby were born in Italy, she would speak Italian with the same accent as a native. All children are born with the ability to hear the subtle differences between different sounds, even those of languages to which they are not exposed regularly. Somewhere between the age of six and twelve months, a baby's brain begins to focus on the primary language to which she is exposed. The neural pathways in the brain begin to consolidate and specialize, causing her to lose the ability to hear the sounds of languages she does not regularly hear. This is often called a "critical window" or a "sensitive period." A window doesn't just slam shut, preventing your child from learning a language. It's more like a gradual decline.

Adult Japanese speakers, for example, who do not speak a second language are not able to hear the difference between "l" and "r" sounds, as used in "lake" and "rake." However, studies have found that Japanese infants are born with the ability to hear the tonal differences between those two sounds but lose the ability to hear them over time because of disuse. In short, babies are wired to hear the subtle differences of the sounds that are used around them every day.

If you are interested in teaching your young child a second language, but

3. Human interaction using a variety of methods—The teacher might use songs, physical movement, building things, and acting in dramatic play to touch upon the multiple ways in which children learn.

4. Theme- or story-based programs—programs that are built around themes or stories provide context that enables children to comprehend more easily. It is much easier to remember a storyline than an isolated list of animals or colors.

5. A fun, developmentally appropriate, and stress-free environment— Finally, a class should be enjoyable, geared to the age group so that it may be of interest to them and allow them to learn at their own pace without pressure to perform. This lowers anxiety and allows more input to be received, thus facilitating language acquisition.

—Sharon Huang, founder and director of Bilingual Buds, a Mandarin immersion program for children www.bilingualbuds.com

she is already long past ten months old, do not despair. While earlier is best, the next "window" doesn't close until your child is about the age of six, after which it becomes progressively more difficult to acquire a second language and native nuances and accents become more difficult or impossible to acquire. According to a *Parent's Press* article titled "Earlier Is Better," from birth until puberty the brain literally formats itself to perform various specialized functions, such as language acquisition and use, based upon the input it gets from the world it experiences. Neural networks gradually form and will function more and more efficiently as they are used. If a second language is part of that input, networks for understanding and using it will grow richer. Therefore, early exposure to a second language actually causes more connections to grow in a child's brain, allowing for easier learning in both the second and, surprisingly, the first language as well. This process, while continuing at different rates throughout a person's life, is especially active in the first six years.

Grammar seems to have a particularly specific window, however. A study of grammar use by immigrants found that the age of arrival in this country was the biggest determinant of the quality of the grammar used, even more so than motivation, attitude, number of years of training, or number of years in the United States. Those who had immigrated by the age of seven tested (spoke) like native speakers. Performance declined based on the immigrants' age at arrival, with the youngest scoring the best and the oldest scoring the worst. Those who came to the United States after age seventeen performed the worst.

Another window of opportunity for easy language acquisition shuts around puberty, due to a process in the brain that disposes of connections it no longer uses, making it more difficult to recognize unfamiliar sounds that may be used in another language. In addition, once they hit puberty, teens tend to be less willing to take risks for fear of looking foolish. Learning a new language requires a person to make mistakes often and out loud.

Learning Your ABCs and αβγ's

While second-language learning is relatively easy for children, given that their brains are hardwired for the task, experts believe that the younger an infant is exposed to language and begins the learning process, the easier it will be for her to pick up the language. Children go through typical stages when learning a second language through immersion, whether at home or in a new country. These stages are described by educational psychologist Dr. Patton Tabors:

STAGES OF LEARNING A FOREIGN LANGUAGE

Stage	Name	Description
Stage 1	Testing	The child tries using her first language only to discover that it is not effective in a new atmosphere.
Stage 2	The Silent Period	The child does not speak much, so it may appear, mistakenly, as if nothing linguistic is happening. In fact, this is a very active learning time when the child is listening to and learning sounds, sound combinations, word boundaries, grammar, vocabulary, and appropriate word usage.
Stage 3	Formula Usage	The child learns and uses a few ready-made phrases and formulas, which she uses as much as possible. This stage is a stepping-stone.
Stage 4	Productive Use	The child starts to use the new language productively, as opposed to speaking it perfectly. This is the point in the learning process when she is communicating in the language effectively.

Many factors affect the way a child acquires a language. One important factor frequently cited in language learning is "phonological working memory," which is a person's ability to remember what she has heard for short periods of time.

The higher she scores in this ability, the easier she'll find it to learn languages. Another factor frequently referenced is what King and Mackey refer to as "fluency learners" versus "precision learners." Fluency learners are people who tend to speak in quick phrases because they are willing to take language risks, even if it results in less precise pronunciation and grammar. Precision learners, on the other hand, focus on perfecting sounds and syllables and are likely to resist the use of a word that is difficult for them to pronounce.

Different children have different learning styles and preferences. Some children learn best using visual approaches; others favor auditory or kinesthetic learning. There is no right or wrong when it comes to learning styles, but understanding your child's learning style can help you make language learning, not to mention communicating in the future, easier and more fun for the whole family. It can also help you, in your learning experience, to get a sense of your own learning style.

THREE LEARNING STYLES

Learning Style	Description	Best Approaches for Language Learning
Visual	Visual learners prefer to see language and do best with visual input: pictures, colors, and the written word (for older kids).	• Looking at picture books • Reading • Using photographs to learn words and tell stories • Showing how things are put together
Auditory	Auditory learners tend to prefer hearing language and do best with auditory input like music or spoken words.	• Listening to stories • Hearing songs • Singing • Following verbal directions • Talking
Kinesthetic	Kinesthetic learners prefer to experience language using activity, movement, and touch.	• Touch-and-feel books • Arts and crafts (finger painting, coloring, etc.) • Dance and movement related to language • Field trips to language-rich environments

LANGUAGE GOALS

In order to figure out the best approach for your family, you need to be clear about your goals. Karen, who lives in Los Angeles, was hoping her daughter Jillian would be able to understand enough Spanish to be able to have a cursory conversation with their Spanish-speaking neighbors. Marina wanted her daughter Alexandra to be able to speak and understand enough Russian to feel comfortable at family events where Russian is spoken exclusively. Nicole wanted her son John to be able to speak enough French so that he might go to school in Switzerland when he was older. Language comprehension takes place on a continuum that spans a lifetime. Because one skill generally builds on another, the learning curve looks something like this:

Understanding   Speaking   Reading   Writing

It is important to examine your goals to see if they are realistic. I would love my daughters to be completely fluent in Chinese and Spanish, but given the amount of language input they receive and what my family's limitations are, I know this is probably not a realistic goal. Dr. Steiner notes that "it is very important to match your bilingual goal with the amount of time and effort your child can devote to the second language." Keep in mind that your goals may change over time.

PLANS AND AUDITS

Now that you have figured out your goals, it is time to create an action plan. Keep in mind the following suggestions:

1. Take baby steps. Small, attainable goals are more likely to help you stay motivated.
2. Make the use of the language a priority for your family and make sure your child is aware that it is.
3. Make sure that you include your partner in your linguistic goals.
4. Support and encourage your partner to learn the target language, even if it is not his first language.
5. Figure out which parent will speak a second language and when it will be spoken.
6. Be consistent. Creating language rituals and patterns makes it easier to stick to your plan.

7. Seek out secondary language support like a Korean-speaking babysitter, a French music class, or visits with Arabic-speaking relatives.

8. Be ready to reevaluate your plans and change your approach based on changes in your child's life (e.g., starting preschool, changes in child care, developmental leaps).

9. Don't beat yourself up for what you did in the past. Use this knowledge to move forward.

10. Keep it fun. Give your child plenty of reasons to want to use the minority language.

In order to make changes, you need to know where you stand first, and in order to do that I recommend doing a language audit. A language audit provides you with a bird's-eye view of the language exposure your child is getting on a weekly basis. It is a particularly valuable assessment because your perceptions don't always line up with the reality of what you are doing. In making this record of language use, it will be helpful to note the difference between interactive and passive uses of the language. Active interactions occur between people and usually require skills such as listening, talking, and moving. Active interactions include talking, having a playdate, going to a music class, attending a playgroup, reading books with a caregiver, playing a game, and taking a bath. Passive interactions are those that involve passive listening, such as attending a puppet show, attending a story hour, listening to a CD, and watching television. Interactive language experiences are the most valuable. Sitting your child in front of the television so she can watch *Dora the Explorer* in Spanish is passive, and for a child under the age of two, it can actually be detrimental (the American Academy of Pediatrics recommends no TV before age two). While many passive activities, like listening to music or attending a show, can be beneficial, it is the active ones that are most valuable, since meaningful interactions lead to language fluency.

While creating your language goals and filling out your audit, it is important to keep in mind that the best way to get your child to use a language is to provide fun, meaningful interactions in the target language. Any attempt to make rigid language rules or force the language on your child will backfire and she will resist the target language.

The following is a blank audit that covers a typical week. If your child does not have a regular schedule, use her activities from the previous week as a sample (unless you were on vacation or there were other unusual circumstances). To fill out the audit, make a note of the activity and language used, and check either the "Interactive" or "Passive" box.

LANGUAGE AUDIT

Time	Monday	Tuesday	Wednesday
6 a.m.	Activity: Language: ☐ Interactive ☐ Passive	Activity: Language: ☐ Interactive ☐ Passive	Activity: Language: ☐ Interactive ☐ Passive
7 a.m.	Activity: Language: ☐ Interactive ☐ Passive	Activity: Language: ☐ Interactive ☐ Passive	Activity: Language: ☐ Interactive ☐ Passive
8 a.m.	Activity: Language: ☐ Interactive ☐ Passive	Activity: Language: ☐ Interactive ☐ Passive	Activity: Language: ☐ Interactive ☐ Passive
9 a.m.	Activity: Language: ☐ Interactive ☐ Passive	Activity: Language: ☐ Interactive ☐ Passive	Activity: Language: ☐ Interactive ☐ Passive
10 a.m.	Activity: Language: ☐ Interactive ☐ Passive	Activity: Language: ☐ Interactive ☐ Passive	Activity: Language: ☐ Interactive ☐ Passive

Thursday	Friday	Saturday	Sunday
Activity: Language: ☐ Interactive ☐ Passive	Activity: Language: ☐ Interactive ☐ Passive	Activity: Language: ☐ Interactive ☐ Passive	Activity: Language: ☐ Interactive ☐ Passive
Activity: Language: ☐ Interactive ☐ Passive	Activity: Language: ☐ Interactive ☐ Passive	Activity: Language: ☐ Interactive ☐ Passive	Activity: Language: ☐ Interactive ☐ Passive
Activity: Language: ☐ Interactive ☐ Passive	Activity: Language: ☐ Interactive ☐ Passive	Activity: Language: ☐ Interactive ☐ Passive	Activity: Language: ☐ Interactive ☐ Passive
Activity: Language: ☐ Interactive ☐ Passive	Activity: Language: ☐ Interactive ☐ Passive	Activity: Language: ☐ Interactive ☐ Passive	Activity: Language: ☐ Interactive ☐ Passive
Activity: Language: ☐ Interactive ☐ Passive	Activity: Language: ☐ Interactive ☐ Passive	Activity: Language: ☐ Interactive ☐ Passive	Activity: Language: ☐ Interactive ☐ Passive

Time	Monday	Tuesday	Wednesday
11 a.m.	Activity: Language: ☐ Interactive ☐ Passive	Activity: Language: ☐ Interactive ☐ Passive	Activity: Language: ☐ Interactive ☐ Passive
noon	Activity: Language: ☐ Interactive ☐ Passive	Activity: Language: ☐ Interactive ☐ Passive	Activity: Language: ☐ Interactive ☐ Passive
1 p.m.	Activity: Language: ☐ Interactive ☐ Passive	Activity: Language: ☐ Interactive ☐ Passive	Activity: Language: ☐ Interactive ☐ Passive
2 p.m.	Activity: Language: ☐ Interactive ☐ Passive	Activity: Language: ☐ Interactive ☐ Passive	Activity: Language: ☐ Interactive ☐ Passive
3 p.m.	Activity: Language: ☐ Interactive ☐ Passive	Activity: Language: ☐ Interactive ☐ Passive	Activity: Language: ☐ Interactive ☐ Passive

Thursday	Friday	Saturday	Sunday
Activity: Language: ☐ Interactive ☐ Passive	Activity: Language: ☐ Interactive ☐ Passive	Activity: Language: ☐ Interactive ☐ Passive	Activity: Language: ☐ Interactive ☐ Passive
Activity: Language: ☐ Interactive ☐ Passive	Activity: Language: ☐ Interactive ☐ Passive	Activity: Language: ☐ Interactive ☐ Passive	Activity: Language: ☐ Interactive ☐ Passive
Activity: Language: ☐ Interactive ☐ Passive	Activity: Language: ☐ Interactive ☐ Passive	Activity: Language: ☐ Interactive ☐ Passive	Activity: Language: ☐ Interactive ☐ Passive
Activity: Language: ☐ Interactive ☐ Passive	Activity: Language: ☐ Interactive ☐ Passive	Activity: Language: ☐ Interactive ☐ Passive	Activity: Language: ☐ Interactive ☐ Passive
Activity: Language: ☐ Interactive ☐ Passive	Activity: Language: ☐ Interactive ☐ Passive	Activity: Language: ☐ Interactive ☐ Passive	Activity: Language: ☐ Interactive ☐ Passive

Time	Monday	Tuesday	Wednesday
4 p.m.	Activity: Language: ☐ Interactive ☐ Passive	Activity: Language: ☐ Interactive ☐ Passive	Activity: Language: ☐ Interactive ☐ Passive
5 p.m.	Activity: Language: ☐ Interactive ☐ Passive	Activity: Language: ☐ Interactive ☐ Passive	Activity: Language: ☐ Interactive ☐ Passive
6 p.m.	Activity: Language: ☐ Interactive ☐ Passive	Activity: Language: ☐ Interactive ☐ Passive	Activity: Language: ☐ Interactive ☐ Passive
7 p.m.	Activity: Language: ☐ Interactive ☐ Passive	Activity: Language: ☐ Interactive ☐ Passive	Activity: Language: ☐ Interactive ☐ Passive
8 p.m.	Activity: Language: ☐ Interactive ☐ Passive	Activity: Language: ☐ Interactive ☐ Passive	Activity: Language: ☐ Interactive ☐ Passive

Thursday	Friday	Saturday	Sunday
Activity: Language: ☐ Interactive ☐ Passive	Activity: Language: ☐ Interactive ☐ Passive	Activity: Language: ☐ Interactive ☐ Passive	Activity: Language: ☐ Interactive ☐ Passive
Activity: Language: ☐ Interactive ☐ Passive	Activity: Language: ☐ Interactive ☐ Passive	Activity: Language: ☐ Interactive ☐ Passive	Activity: Language: ☐ Interactive ☐ Passive
Activity: Language: ☐ Interactive ☐ Passive	Activity: Language: ☐ Interactive ☐ Passive	Activity: Language: ☐ Interactive ☐ Passive	Activity: Language: ☐ Interactive ☐ Passive
Activity: Language: ☐ Interactive ☐ Passive	Activity: Language: ☐ Interactive ☐ Passive	Activity: Language: ☐ Interactive ☐ Passive	Activity: Language: ☐ Interactive ☐ Passive
Activity: Language: ☐ Interactive ☐ Passive	Activity: Language: ☐ Interactive ☐ Passive	Activity: Language: ☐ Interactive ☐ Passive	Activity: Language: ☐ Interactive ☐ Passive

AUDIT SUMMARY

Language				
Active				
Passive				
Total hours awake:	Total hours:	Total hours:	Total hours:	Total hours:

Here is the language audit summary for my daughters:

Language	Spanish	Chinese
Active	7.3 hours	2 hours
Passive	0	0
Total hours awake: 70	Total hours: 7.3	Total hours: 2

In doing this language audit, I discovered the following: since my two-and-a-half-year-olds sleep approximately twelve hours each night and have a two-hour nap every day, they are awake seventy hours in one week. When I keep to my current language plan (and I am nowhere near perfect), my daughters get approximately seven hours and twenty minutes of Spanish exposure, which is approximately 10 percent exposure. All of this interaction is active: they read books, take a music class, and talk with their grandmother and me almost every night (she supports their language development by taking Spanish classes). They are exposed to two hours of Chinese each week, all of which comes from their class. I chose not to count their music exposure, of which they get an hour each day in either language, because it is very passive and somewhat inconsistent. I also did not count the reinforcement we do on a daily basis with what little Chinese my husband and I have acquired. While we use Chinese words daily, we are not yet fluent enough to speak in sentences or have conversations—unless you count "Hello. How are you?" "I am fine." We are also planning some immersion vacations in the future.

Now that you have done your own language audit, you can see the strengths and weaknesses of your program. The next step is to make new goals. I suggest three small, manageable goals. For example, I have set these three new goals:

- Currently, I read two books a day to my kids in Spanish. My new goal is to read three books a day in Spanish.
- I would like to increase my kids' passive language exposure through more music at a time when they are likely to listen. We play a few CDs, both in Spanish and Chinese, that they like so much that they sing along with them. Since neither child actually sleeps during

naptime any more (they are on the verge of giving up the nap) and often play and "read" in their cribs, my new goal is to play one of their favorite Chinese or Spanish music CDs instead of the orchestral or symphonic music we currently play.

• I would like to make a commitment to speak Spanish more at dinnertime, even when my mother does not join us. My husband's Spanish is pretty good and he is a strong supporter of our language goals and always up for a new challenge.

Before you write out your new goals, think about what has been working and what has not. Make sure your new goals are realistic. Building on successes makes it more likely you will accomplish your new goals.

Goal #1: _____

Goal #2: _____

Goal #3: _____

Eight Target Language Reading Tips

1. **Start with simple board books at your child's level.** If you are not a native speaker, you can use these books to gauge your own language growth.

2. **Choose books with lots of interesting pictures.** The more interested your child is in the images, the more likely she is to pay attention to the words you are reading.

3. **Find books that reflect your child's interests.** If she likes garbage trucks, get books in the language about garbage trucks. If she likes bicycles, get books about bicycles.

4. **Talk about the book in the language as you read.** Occasionally stop and share your observations in the language (e.g., "That is a blue flower. I have never seen a blue flower").

5. **Get books that your child is already familiar with in the second language.** Books by authors like Todd Parr, Sandra Boynton, Eric Carle, Margaret Wise Brown, and even Dr. Seuss all have been translated into multiple languages.

6. **Make reading a connected positive experience.** Curl up with your child and a book, create a reading ritual that you can share, and have fun book

time together. Make sure you do not try to teach as you read; just have fun enjoying the pictures, words, and language.

7. **Let your child pick the book.** Give your child a basket of books in the target language and let her pick which one she wants to read.

8. **Keep the language books in an accessible, child-friendly place.** Children who have constant access to books develop the habit of turning to them for entertainment.

Getting to 20 Percent

So you've assessed your child's language exposure and maybe you're coming up short of 20 percent—or maybe you're just exposing her to less of the target language than you had hoped. Here are twenty ways you can up the language ante and increase your child's exposure to a second language. They're relatively inexpensive—or even free—and can be a lot of fun.

1. Narrate what you are doing in the language.
2. Think out loud in the language.
3. Make playing music in that language a regular part of your child's life.
4. Start a playgroup in the target language.
5. Create special one-on-one time in the target language.
6. Have specific games that you play only in that language.
7. Find a music class in the target language.
8. When you call home to speak to your child, try speaking in the language.
9. Find a story hour in your target language at the local library or bookstore.
10. Purchase children's books in your target language.
11. Host theme nights in the language at home, where you speak only that language, eat food from the culture, and listen to music in that language.
12. Plan time with friends and family who speak the target language and encourage them to use only that language with your child.
13. Bring in a language teacher, making sure that the teacher knows how to work with young children and will keep the lessons light and fun.
14. Replace your regular babysitter with one who speaks the target language.
15. Hire a nanny or au pair who speaks the target language.

16. Send your child to a bilingual school or day care. If that is not possible, send your child to a school with a foreign language program, or help your child's school create one (currently, 31 percent of public elementary schools in the United States have language programs).

17. For your older children, try a weekend or "heritage" school, which teaches language and culture that connect children to the country where the language is spoken.

18. Plan your next family vacation around language exposure.

19. Try a family language camp, a camp for adults and children that focuses on language learning and often provides a total emersion experience.

20. Buy talking toys in the target language, keeping in mind that *you* are still the catalyst for language learning—not the dolls or toys.

MOTIVATION AND RESISTANCE

The degree of success you have raising your child to be bilingual will be directly related to your own family's definition of bilingualism and to your conviction that pursuing that level of language proficiency is the right thing to do.

—Dr. Naomi Steiner, *7 Steps to Raising a Bilingual Child*

Having a positive attitude toward the acquisition of a second (or third) language is vital. Knowing that you can influence your child's language practices gives you the opportunity to create reasons for her to want to use the language and fun opportunities for exposure, which are all important in maintaining motivation. But even if you do everything "right," you will still meet resistance at some point, most likely after both the emergence of will (eighteen months) and the understanding that different people speak different languages (between two and three years of age). Usually, a child's resistance to a language activity, like taking a class or being read to in that language, will pass in time, but sometimes it will take a little bit of change (a new teacher, new music, or new activities) to get past the hurdles.

One of the toughest forms of resistance is a child's refusal to speak the target language. There are many ways to respond:

- Act like you don't understand a language other than the target language. Make sure to let your child know the new plan (to speak and respond only to the target language) in advance so she is aware of your expectations and can anticipate your response.

- Question what your child said using both languages (for example, "Did you say 'quiero una mansana'?")
- Code switch with the child (for example, "You want a galleta [cookie]?")
- Repeat the child's statement in the target language.
- Ask the child for clarification in the target language.
- Just continue to speak in the target language without addressing the issue.
- Use "I" statements as Dr. Pearson suggests, like "I feel so good when you answer me in my language."
- Try reverse psychology (this can be a gamble depending on your child's personality) and tell her that she is not allowed to speak the language. I am not a fan of this tactic but I hear it can work.
- Make the language seem special by emphasizing how grown-up it is to speak another language.
- Dangle the vacation carrot (only if you are really planning a trip) and let your child know that you are going somewhere where people speak only this language and you want her to be able to understand what is going on during the trip.

Whatever you decide to do, you are likely to be very pleased with the results of bringing a new language into your home. I wish you the best of luck on your language journey.

Baby Got Book

Reading

The single most important activity for building knowledge required
for eventual success in reading is reading aloud to children.

—BECOMING A NATION OF READERS:
The Report of the Commission on Reading

Before becoming a parent, many of us fantasize about sitting in a cozy rocking chair, a child in our arms, sharing a good book. Perhaps the book is a classic from our own childhood, like *Goodnight Moon, The Cat in the Hat,* or *The Little Engine That Could.* In the fantasy you are totally connected with your child, who gazes adoringly at you as you read. Tender moments like this can be a reality, especially if you start reading to your child from the beginning.

Reading is a wonderful way to bond with your child. The shared experience and focused attention connect parent and child, strengthening the attachment for both. Reading is a particularly great way for dads to bond with their children, especially in the early months when breastfeeding can make a father feel irrelevant. While Mom may be the only one with the equipment to feed baby's belly, Daddy can still feed baby's brain through reading.

Six Immediate Benefits of Reading

Reading does much more than help you bond with your child. As a matter of fact, reading aloud to young children is so crucial that the American Academy of

Pediatrics recommends that "doctors prescribe reading activities along with other advice given to parents at regular check-ups." As you will see in this chapter, the benefits are significant:

1. The Pleasure Principle: Enjoying Books Each time you read to your child, you are conditioning his brain to make an association between reading and pleasure. The close proximity between parent and child, the shared experience, the attention, and the joy of a story and its illustrations all get processed as pleasure. We all seek out what we enjoy the most. If your child makes these early associations, he is more likely to be a reader later in life. If you start reading to him while he's an infant, you will see the early fruits of your accomplishment when he toddles up to you completely on his own, hands you a book, and asks you to read it to him.

If your child is exposed to books from the start, you will also find that he has the ability to sit with a book and "read" on his own, even before he can read the words. This will enable him to entertain himself for long periods of time, giving you the freedom to do other things. My own toddlers have such a love of books that they will sit quietly while I'm cooking in the kitchen. I have never had to turn on the television to entertain my children so that I can complete a task. They have always been happy to entertain themselves on the kitchen floor or in their cribs with a book—or a stack of them. I believe this is largely due to the way we have used books in our home. You too can have the same experience if you follow my recommendations.

2. Yada, Yada, Yada: Increased Vocabulary Want to know a quick, cheap way to increase your child's vocabulary? Believe it or not, just reading three picture books each week has been shown to increase vocabulary by 15 to 40 percent, a rate that continues to keep pace over time. As far as I am concerned, three times a week is minimal; I recommend that parents read at least three books each day. Most young children's books are short, so it will take you only a few minutes to read your child a board book like *Brown Bear, Brown Bear, What Do You See?* or a storybook like *The Snail and the Whale.* It doesn't have to be *War and Peace* but it does need to be interesting and engaging.

In terms of sophistication, there are three types of words. First, there is the "basic lexicon," the 5,000 words most commonly used in everyday language. Typically, 83 percent of the words a child hears in conversation come from 1,000 of the most frequently used words. The next tier, "less frequently used words," is composed of the next most commonly used 5,000 words. Together these 10,000 words form what researchers Dr. Donald Hayes and Margaret Ahrens refer to as the "common lexicon." Any words not in this group of 10,000 are called "rare words."

Ultimately, the greatest measure of our vocabulary is our knowledge of those "rare words," and the best way to acquire them is by reading books. Typically, when we speak to children under the age of five, we use only nine rare words per thousand words, while preschool books use sixteen, and the average children's book uses more than thirty per thousand. Anyone who thinks that television is a good source of vocabulary may be surprised to hear that 95 percent of all the words used on television are drawn from the basic lexicon group—in other words, the simplest 5,000.

3. What Did You Say Your Name Was? Better Attention Span and Memory
The ability to pay attention and the ability to remember facts are interconnected. If you are not able to pay attention, there is no way you will remember. Because babies' brains are wired to search for meaning, patterns, and information, they have the ability to concentrate. It is important to nurture that ability with reading, which requires a focused state of mind, rather than expose your child to television's quick, scattered, and schizophrenic images and sound bites.

Reading is the most powerful tool parents have to increase a child's attention span and memory. Give your child the best chance to develop that focus by creating a calm, quiet reading environment. Turn off the music and the TV (in Chapter 10 you will learn why it shouldn't be on in the first place) so there is no competition for your child's attention. Allow him to enjoy the sound and inflection of your voice as you read, while you enjoy the pleasure of your joint attention on a book.

That "joint attention" is a valuable tool for your child. In a study of seven- to nine-month-old infants, researchers introduced an unknown object to the children and gave it a nonsense name. In the first scenario, the researcher and child shared a joint visual gaze while the object was labeled, while in the second scenario the researcher looked away while labeling the object. The children were able to correctly identify and locate the objects they had been introduced to with *shared joint attention* but had a difficult time identifying the objects that were introduced without joint attention. Reading out loud with your child is an organic and enjoyable way to develop this skill. The sooner you start this process, the sooner your child will begin to build these mental muscles.

4. Hear Ye, Hear Ye: Better Listeners
Children who are read to are actually better listeners, and what parent doesn't want a child who is a good listener? A study of 150,000 fourth graders revealed that those who were read to often at home scored thirty points higher in listening comprehension.

When your child starts school, the two biggest advantages you can give him are a large vocabulary and strong listening skills. Because most of the instruction children receive in the first four years of life is oral, children with these strengths tend to enjoy the process and achieve much more than their peers. Having the words to know what someone is saying to you allows you to understand, and having the ability to understand allows you to grasp the content of what is being said.

The link between listening and vocabulary is undeniable. In Jim Trelease's groundbreaking book *The Read-Aloud Handbook,* he describes how words go from comprehension vocabulary to speaking vocabulary. "Inside the ear, these words collect in a reservoir called the listening vocabulary. Eventually, if you pour enough words into it, the reservoir starts to overflow—pouring words into the speaking vocabulary."

5. School Days: Reading and Writing Skills Reading begets readers. Early on, children who have been read to since birth become familiar with the way a book works: they understanding that print is for reading, what is "right side up," where the book begins and ends, the order of reading a page (top to bottom), what to do at the end of a line and what to do at the end of a page. Children who are read to regularly become aware of words, letters, numbers, and sentences and, on a more complex level, become familiar with literary devices such as alliteration ("In the great green room there was a telephone") and rhyming ("There were three little bears sitting on chairs"), rare words, complex sentences, descriptive language, and story conventions ("once upon a time"). All these elements create better readers. According to the Early Childhood Longitudinal Study, children who are read to at least three times a week by a family member are almost twice as likely to score in the top 25 percent in reading.

In the first three years, it may be difficult for you to imagine your baby writing, much less breezing through English class in high school, but the more you read to your child, the more likely he is to become a great reader. According to a study published in the *Review of Applied Linguistics,* students who read more had less "writing apprehension," or fear of writing, because of their exceptional grasp on written language.

6. Taking a Magic Carpet Ride: Creativity and Imagination Reading opens up a world of creativity and imagination that nurtures a child's ability to think outside the box. Hearing books read aloud paves the way to creating his own images. Children who are exposed to great narratives grow up with a passion for stories and become great storytellers themselves.

We know that older students who are big readers are more creative than their peers. A study of high school students found that the most creative students read significantly more than their peers; these students reported that they read over fifty books a year. Great writers are great readers. The National Assessment of Educational Progress Writing Report Card revealed that the highest-scoring writers were not those who wrote the most but those who read the most recreationally and had the most printed materials at home.

Dr. Jenn's Top Twelve Favorite Books for the First Three Years

After reading hundreds of children's books and even writing one myself, I compiled this list of my favorites for the first three years, many of which are available as board books. I tend to like books that are creative, quirky, a bit sophisticated, and don't involve television or cartoon characters.

1. *Bear on a Bike* by Stella Blackstone and Debbie Harter

2. *Rockin' Babies* by Dr. Jenn Berman and Cynthia Weil

3. *Mi Amor Por Ti/ My Love for You* by Susan L. Roth

4. *C Is for Coco* by Sloane Tanen and Stefan Hagen

5. *Snowmen at Night* by Caralyn Buehner and Mark Buehner

6. *The Peace Book* by Todd Parr

7. *The Snail and the Whale* by Julia Donaldson and Axel Scheffler

8. *Iggy Peck, Architect* by Andrea Beaty and David Roberts

9. *Smash! Mash! There Goes the Trash!* by Barbara Odanaka and Will Hillenbrandt

10. *Bats at the Library* by Brian Lies

11. *Michael Recycle Meets Litterbug Doug* by Ellie Bethel and Alexandra Colombo

12. *Wild About Books* by Judy Sierra and Marc Brown

From Once Upon a Time to Happily Ever After

You can never start reading to your child too soon. As crazy as this may sound, I recommend reading to your child in utero. In a study by Drs. Anthony DeCasper and Melanie Spence, pregnant mothers were asked to read the Dr. Seuss book *The Cat in the Hat* to their babies in utero starting at thirty-two and thirty-seven weeks of gestation. The researchers then tested the babies at thirty-eight weeks gestation and again shortly after birth, measuring heart rates and sucking patterns. They found that the babies preferred the familiar passage to unfamiliar ones read by the same voice. If your family is using a surrogate, I recommend sending her recordings of your favorite children's books so that your baby can hear your voice while he is still in utero. I believe this will not only help the bonding process but pave the way to a great love of books as well.

Even if you did not start reading to your child while he was in the womb, it is never too late. Many parents don't think of reading to their children until they are toddlers or even preschoolers. I encourage you to start right away; if not in utero, then at least as soon as your child is born. Make sure to pack a few books in your hospital bag for after the birth. According to Trelease, "If a child is old enough to talk to, she's old enough to read to." Just as you would speak, using words your infant does not yet understand, you should read to your infant before he knows how to speak. This way your child will come into consciousness associating reading with love and pleasure.

Many parents stop reading aloud to their children as soon as they are able to read for themselves. This is a mistake! I encourage you to continue to read aloud as long as possible to your child. One of my happiest childhood memories is my mother reading *The Secret Garden* by Frances Hodgson Burnett. She read the same copy of the book to me that her own mother had read to her, the same one that I will one day read to my daughters. I was about seven years old at the time and even though the book is recommended for nine- to twelve-year-olds, I loved it. Children are able to listen on a different and more advanced reading level than they are able to read. It isn't until about the eighth grade that they are able to listen and read on the same level. Because of that, I recommend that parents take age recommendations with a grain of salt, focusing more on what they think their child will enjoy hearing and what the parent enjoys reading.

Creating a Print-Rich Environment

It is up to you to create an enthusiastic reader. Studies show that children who come from what researchers call a "print-rich environment" consistently score better in writing, reading, and math skills than children who come from a "print-poor environment." Print, in this case, relates to a wide variety of materials, including books, magazines, newspapers, and even comic books. When researchers examined twenty-one kindergarten classes to see who displayed high interest in reading and who showed low interest, it became clear that the home environment and parents' reading habits were crucial factors. The difference between home environments, activities, and choices between the high-interest readers and the low-interest readers was dramatic, as shown in this table:

Home Environment	High-Interest Group	Low-Interest Group
Mothers read for leisure	78%	28%
Fathers read for leisure	60%	16%
Average number of books in the home	80	32
Percentage of children who reported being taken to the library	98%	7%
Child owns a library card	38%	3%
Child is read to daily	76%	2%

Book ownership is another significant factor in reading enthusiasm and achievement. According to Trelease, children need to own their own books that they can put their name in and don't have to share with siblings. He also believes that as they get older kids should be able to mark up books by writing in the margins and

FROM THE EXPERTS . . .

Fostering Independent Reading As Your Child Gets Older

People who lose the ability to make choices become disempowered. This is true for adults and it is true for young readers. When every book a child reads is chosen for her—by parents or teachers—she will lose self-motivation to read and interest in reading. Children should choose their own reading material most of the time, but they need exposure to a book flood in order to determine which books they like and learn how to choose their own. You can support your child by:

Introducing authors and books through read-alouds. Select books by prolific authors or the first book in a series and read them with your child. When your child enjoys the read-aloud, locate another book or two by the same author, follow a series together, or read another book in the same genre. Develop reading fans and you will develop readers.

highlighting and earmarking pages. This allows them to learn new words, come back to passages that intrigue them, and make the reading experience their own.

Creating a print-rich environment in the home doesn't have to cost you a fortune. Thanks to local libraries, used bookstores (bricks and mortar as well as online), and book-swapping clubs, developing a home library for your child can be a reasonable undertaking. Looking at unused copies of *Goodnight Moon* as an example—the board book edition costs $9, the paperback $7, and the hardback $12, which means that if you have three fewer venti lattes, you can buy your kid a book to have for life.

You should never force books on your child—instead, make reading such a fun and available part of your family culture that a book is hard to turn down. The old saying "you can lead a horse to water but you can't make it drink" is applicable here. The key is providing access to the water, in this case the books. If you make books accessible to your child, provide good reading role models, and make reading aloud a regular habit, your child will grow to love books.

One of the greatest tools for creating a print-rich environment for your child is book baskets. A book basket doesn't have to be an actual basket; it can be a soft container of some sort that your child can reach into to get books. I love the cloth

Creating frequent opportunities for children to preview, share, and select books. Children need to become comfortable with books and feel growing proficiency in choosing books for themselves. Take children to the library or bookstore and discuss books that you might read. Talk about books that you read as a child and explain what you enjoyed about these books.

Increasing children's access to books by building a home library. The more books children own, the more they read, and the more comfortable they feel choosing books away from home. Visit e-bay, garage sales, book swaps, and library sales to locate low-cost books for your child. Give books as presents for holidays and birthdays, and encourage relatives to do the same. Purchase gift cards for bookstores and invite your child to choose a new book.

Above all, validate your child's book choices even when you wish he would choose others. We often complain that children do not read, and bemoan their less than high-brow choices when they do choose their own books. It is OK for your child to read comics, read the same book over and over, or prefer fantasy books. After all, adult readers have strong preferences in what they choose to read, too!

—Donalyn Miller, language arts teacher and author of
The Book Whisperer: Awakening the Inner Reader in Every Child

boxes that many people give with gifts. You should always keep book baskets on the floor where your child can reach them. We keep ours in my kids' rooms, our bedroom (we have a "Mama book box" and a "Papa book box"), the kitchen, bathrooms, and even the car. Every Friday we rotate the books so we have some variety. If my kids are particularly attached to a specific title, that book can stick around another week or longer.

I also recommend keeping books with you wherever you go. They can be particularly helpful any place you are likely to have to wait, such as the supermarket, doctor's office, restaurant, airplane, or bus. It is easy enough to throw a couple of small board books into a diaper bag or, better yet, always keep a few in there to have on hand.

Dr. Jenn's Top Twelve Favorite Classic Books for the First Three Years

Every family needs to have some children's classics in their collection. Some of these are tried-and-true books, while others are more contemporary. Most are also available as board books.

1. *Swimmy* by Leo Lionni
2. *The Carrot Seed* by Ruth Krauss and Crockett Johnson
3. *Goodnight Moon* by Margaret Wise Brown and Clement Hurd
4. *Brown Bear, Brown Bear, What Do You See?* by Bill Martin Jr. and Eric Carle
5. *The Cat in the Hat* by Dr. Seuss
6. *The Kissing Hand* by Audrey Penn
7. *The Very Hungry Caterpillar* by Eric Carle
8. *Blue Hat, Green Hat* by Sandra Boynton
9. *The Runaway Bunny* by Margaret Wise Brown and Clement Hurd
10. *Make Way for Ducklings* by Robert McCloskey
11. *The Little Engine That Could* by Watty Piper, George Hauman, and Doris Hauman
12. *Harold and the Purple Crayon* by Crockett Johnson

Stacking the Shelves: Creating a Well-Rounded Home Library

A well-rounded home library does not happen overnight. Getting the right books for your child is a learning experience filled with trial and error. Most children's home libraries start out with a few books that were received as shower gifts or hand-me downs from other family members. I recommend that parents start collecting baby books and children's books as soon as they start thinking about having a family. Most babies start out with board books because they are virtually indestructible and can be bitten, chewed, and thrown out of a crib without tearing a page. I encourage you to think outside of the proverbial (book) box and consider alternative reading materials for your baby like magazines, comic strips, and homemade books. But make sure if you are reading these less traditional reading materials that they stay in your hands, not your baby's, in order to avoid choking hazards or potentially toxic material.

Studies show that the best readers read from the widest variety of texts. There is no reason not to start that habit early. Furthermore, it raises your chance of finding material that your child connects with. The more he is exposed to, the more likely he is to find his first "ah-ha" book . . . the one that makes him realize how truly wonderful reading is and gets him addicted to the process. I like to hook them when they're young. There are a number of things to keep in mind when picking books for your child:

Start with cloth books and board books. These books can be thrown in the laundry or wiped clean, which makes them particularly baby-friendly. The pages are also easy for little fingers to turn. Because they are made for babies, you can usually let your child take them to bed.

Babies love to see other babies. Babies are mesmerized by the sight of other children's faces. Close-up photos are especially exciting to them. Make sure to buy books with babies of all different races and ethnicities so your child can see people who look like him as well as people who are different.

Always screen books before reading them to your child. Make sure that there isn't anything that you find objectionable in the book. In preparing my girls for the death of our very old cat Tai Chi, I started getting books that talked about death and the loss of a pet. I was shocked when I read a Berenstain Bears book in which the parents initially lie about the death of a goldfish and then replace it with a new one without telling their child. This is not the kind of message I want to send to my kids!

Don't stick to typical gender stereotypes. Many parents only think to get truck books for their sons and ballet books for their daughters. Present everything to your child so you can see what really interests him or her. My daughters love books about trucks, bugs, and sports because they have always seen them. They also love books about more typically feminine things as well.

Be skeptical of recommended age levels for books. As I mentioned earlier, suggested reading levels are usually a reflection of how old the child "should" be in order to read the book on his own, as opposed to when he is ready to *listen* to (and understand) it. Kids, especially toddlers and preschoolers, listen at a much older level than they can read. Infants care more about the sound of your voice than the content. One of the dads in my practice regularly reads the sports section to his infant daughter, who giggles with glee at the sound of his voice.

Get imaginative and innovative about book selections. It wasn't until I started getting creative about our reading selections that things really got interesting for all of us at our house. When I moved past the typical classic animal, counting, and ABC books and started looking for babies' and children's books about historical figures, the environment, different professions, and cities around the world, our reading became an exciting, entertaining, learning experience for all of us.

Use books for bibliotherapy. When your child or family is going through a difficult time or a big transition, like moving into a new house, potty training, starting preschool, or going through a divorce, use books to ease the transition. When our cat died, my kids and I appreciated books like *I'll Always Love You Forever, Jasper's Day, When a Pet Dies*, and *The Tenth Good Thing About Barney*. These books helped explain complex ideas, opened conversation, and gave us words for our grief.

When you find an author that you and your child like, check out what else she or he has written. If you like the writer's style, you will probably enjoy other books written by the same person. The same goes for publishers. Many offer series of books, like DK's Touch and Feel series, which offers a great tactile experience for kids.

Follow your child's interests. During the board book years when my kids became obsessed with snowmen, I got them *Snowmen at Night, That's Not My Snowman*, and *How to Build a Snowman*. When they got curious about bicycles, I got them *Let's Ride Bikes* and *Bear on a Bike*. Following Quincy and Mendez's interests allowed us to discover wonderful authors like Stella Blackstone and Caralyn Buehner, whom we may never have otherwise encountered.

Because I am such a voracious consumer of children's books, along with my kids, I am often asked about my favorites in different categories. Here are a few of our favorites in each category for ages zero through three. I tend to like books that are a little quirky or unusual and I have a soft spot for rhyming books. In developing your own diverse library, you may find it helpful to keep the following categories in mind so that your child gets to read different types of reading materials on diverse topics. I hope these books get you and your family passionate about books too!

MORE BOOK FAVORITES FOR KIDS UP TO AGE THREE, GROUPED BY CATEGORY

Type or Theme of Reading Material	Book, Author, and Illustrator *All book lists in this chapter are arranged by age order, youngest to oldest.

Cloth books	Touch and Feel Cloth Book Series
	  (*Fluffy Chick and Friends, Fuzzy Bee and Friends,*
	    Squishy Turtle and Friends, and others)
	  by Roger Priddy
	Little Green Books (*Little Panda and Little Monkey*)
	  by Kimberly Ainsworth and Michelle Berg
	My First Taggies Book Series (*Sweet Dreams, I Love You,*
	  and others) by Kaori Watanabe

Babies	*Baby Faces* by DK Publishing *Global Babies* by Global Fund for Children *Good Night, Baby!* by Mike Good

Animals	*Touch & Feel Animals* (boxed set) by DK Publishing
	My First Animal Book by DK Publishing
	What Do You Say? by Mandy Stanley
	Animal Friends: A Global Celebration of Children and Animals
	  by Maya Ajmera, John D. Ivanko, and Global Fund
	  for Children
	Click, Clack, Moo: Cows That Type by Doreen Cronin and
	  Betsy Lewin

ABC	*ABC: A Child's First Alphabet Book* by Alison Jay
	B Is for Bulldozer: A Construction ABC by June Sobel and
	  Melissa Iwai
	26 Big Things Small Hands Can Do by Coleen Paratore and
	  Mike Reed
	Alligators All Around by Maurice Sendak
	ABC, NYC: A Book About Seeing New York City by
	  Joanne Dugan and Pamela Hovland

Counting	*My First Number Board Book* by DK Publishing *1-2-3: A Child's First Counting Book* by Alison Jay *One Was Johnny: A Counting Book* by Maurice Sendak *My Grammy Went to Market: A Round-the-World Counting* *Rhyme* by Stella Blackstone and Christopher Corr

Colors	*My First Colors Board Book* by DK Publishing *Seek and Find: Counting Colors* by Roger Priddy *Colors of China* by Iris Siao and Ken Lay
Touch and Feel	Touch and Feel Series (*Baby Animals, Wild Animals, Farm,* and many more) by DK Publishing *That's Not My . . . (Puppy, Monkey, Teddy, Kitten, Bunny,* and many more) by Fiona Watt and Rachel Wells Funny Faces Series (*Charlie Monkey, Millie Cow,* and others) by Roger Priddy
Wordless (or very few words)	*Hug* by Jez Alborough *Pancakes for Breakfast* by Tomie dePaola *A Boy, a Dog, and a Frog* by Mercer Mayer
Rhyming	*The Snail and the Whale* by Julia Donaldson and Axel Scheffler *Iggy Peck, Architect* by Andrea Beaty and David Roberts *Smash! Mash! There Goes the Trash!* by Barbara Odanaka and Will Hillenbrandt
Poetry	*Welcome, Baby! Baby Rhymes for Baby Times* and *Good for You! Toddler Rhymes for Toddler Times* by Stephanie Calmenson and Melissa Sweet *More Pocket Poems* by Bobbi Katz and Deborah Zemke *Button Up! Wrinkled Rhymes* by Alice Schertle and Petra Mathers *Falling Down the Page: A Book of List Poems* by Georgia Heard
Mother Goose	*Mary Engelbreit's Silly Mother Goose by* Mary Engelbreit *Mother Goose's Storytime Nursery Rhymes* by Axel Scheffler *Clare Beaton's Mother Goose Remembers* (with sing-along CD) by Clare Beaton *The Neighborhood Mother Goose* by Nina Crews *Mary Had a Little Jam and Other Silly Rhymes* by Bruce Lansky and Stephen Carpenter
Find the . . .	*Where's the Cat?* by Stella Blackstone and Debbie Harter *Seek and Find: Can You Find Me?* by Roger Priddy I Spy Series (*Little Letters, Little Numbers,* and more) by Jean Marzollo and Walter Wick
Pop-up	*Animal Popposites: A Pop-Up Book of Opposites* by Matthew Reinhart *ABC3D* by Marion Bataille *Cookie Count: A Tasty Pop-Up* by Robert Sabuda *The Movable Mother Goose* (Mother Goose Pop-Up) by Robert Sabuda

Lift-the-flap	*Dear Zoo* by Rod Campbell
	Peekaboo Series (*Bedtime, Farm Time, Play Time*, and more)
	    by DK Publishing
	Excuse Me! A Little Book of Manners and *I Can Share* by
	    Karen Katz

Cut-outs	*Peek-A-Who?* by Nina Laden *Lemons Are Not Red* by Laura Vaccaro Seeger *The Very Hungry Caterpillar* by Eric Carle *Wheels on the Bus Go Round and Round* by Annie Kubler *Joseph Had a Little Overcoat* by Simms Taback

Art	Touch the Art Series (*Brush Mona Lisa's Hair, Feed Matisse's
	    Fish*, and others) by Julie Appel and Amy Guglielmo
	Mini Masters Series (*A Picnic with Monet, Dancing with
	    Degas,* and others) by Julie Merberg and Suzanne Bober
	Bob Raczka's Art Adventures Series (*3-D ABC: A Sculptural
	    Alphabet, Art Is . . .*, and others) by Bob Raczka
	I Spy Series *(I Spy: An Alphabet in Art, I Spy Colors in Art,*
	    and others) by Lucy Micklethwait

Coloring books	*My Giant Sticker Animal Coloring Book* by Priddy Books *My Giant Sticker Coloring Book* by Priddy Books
Comic books	*Supercat* by Kate McMullan and Pascal Lemaitre *Otto's Orange Day* by Frank Cammuso and Jay Lynch *The Furry News: How to Make a Newspaper* by Loreen Leedy

Magazines	*Babybug* (age 0–3), *Ladybug* (ages 2–7), *Click* (ages 3–7)
	    at www.cricket.com
	Wild Animal Baby (ages 1–4) and *Your Big Backyard* (ages
	    3–7) by National Wildlife Federation at www.nwf.org
	High Five (ages 2–6) by Highlights at www.highlights.com
	Little Kids National Geographic (ages 3–6) at
	    www.nationalgeographic.com

Cities and destinations	Good Night Our World Series (includes U.S. and international
	    cities) by Adam Gamble and Cooper Kelly
	101 Board Books (includes all major cities, major
	    universities, and some historical figures) by Brad M.
	    Epstein
	This Is . . . Series (New York, Paris, London, Britain, and
	    many other cities and countries) by Miroslav Sasek

Historical figures	*The Story of Martin Luther King Jr.* by Johney Ray Moore
	    and Amy Wummer
	The Story of Rosa Parks by Patricia Pingry and Steven Walker
	*Wilma Unlimited: How Wilma Rudolph Became the World's
	    Fastest Woman* by Kathleen Krull and David Diaz

Nondenominational holidays	New Year's: *Happy New Year Corduroy* by Don Freeman and Lisa McCue Valentine's Day: *The Ballad of Valentine* by Alison Jackson and Tricia Tusa Presidents' Day: *Celebrating Presidents' Day: What Is a President?* by Kimberly Jordano, Trisha Callella-Jones, Joel Kupperstein, and Tammie Lyon Presidents' Day: *Presidents' Day* by Anne Rockwell and Lizzy Rockwell Memorial Day: *Memorial Day Surprise* by Theresa Martin Golding and Alexandra Artigas Flag Day: *F Is for Flag* by Wendy Cheyette Lewison and Barbara Duke Independence Day: *The Story of America's Birthday* by Patricia A. Pingry and Stacy Venturi-Pickett Independence Day: *L Is for Liberty* by Wendy Cheyette Lewison and Laura Freeman Hines Labor Day: *Labor Day* (Rookie Read-About Holidays) by Carmen Bredeson Halloween: *Ghoulish Gang: A Halloween Touch & Feel Book* by Jill McDonald Thanksgiving: *'Twas the Night Before Thanksgiving* by Dav Pilkey
Environment	*Eco Babies Wear Green* by Michelle Sinclair Colman and Nathalie Dion *I'm Not Too Little to Help the Earth* by W.Y. Taylor and Natalia Vasquez *The Earth and I* by Frank Asch *10 Things I Can Do to Help My World* by Melanie Walsh *The Lorax* by Dr. Seuss *Michael Recycle and Michael Recycle Meets Litterbug Doug* by Ellie Bethel and Alexandra Colombo *Winston of Churchill: One Bear's Battle Against Global Warming* by Jean Davies Okimoto and Jeremiah Trammell
Potty training	*A Potty for Me! A Lift-the-Flap Instruction Manual* by Karen Katz *Big Girls Use the Potty!* and *Big Boys Use the Potty!* by Andrea Pinnington *My Big Girl Potty* and *My Big Boy Potty* by Joanna Cole and Maxie Chambliss
Big bed	*Your Own Big Bed* by Rita Bergstein and Susan Kathleen Hartung *Sophie's Big Bed* by Tina Burke *My Own Big Bed* by Anna Grossnickle Hines and Mary Watson

Starting preschool	*D.W.'s Guide to Preschool* by Marc Brown *What to Expect at Preschool* by Heidi Murkoff and Laura Rader
Day care	*Going to Day Care* (Mister Rogers' Neighborhood) by Fred Rogers *When Mommy and Daddy Go to Work* by Joanna Cole and Maxie Chambliss *Adam's Daycare* by Julie Ovenell-Carter and Ruth Ohi *Benjamin Comes Back/Benjamin Regresa* by Amy Brandt and Janice Lee Porter
Coping with separation	*The Kissing Hand* by Audrey Penn *Mommy in My Pocket* by Carol Hunt Senderak and Hiroe Nakata *Mama Always Comes Home* by Karma Wilson and Brooke Dyer *You Go Away* by Dorothy Corey and Diane Paterson *I Love You All Day Long* by Francesca Rusackas and Priscilla Burris *Oh My Baby, Little One* by Kathi Appelt and Jane Dyer
Parents' travel	*When Mommy Travels* and *When Daddy Travels* by Harriet Ziefert and Emily Bolam *My Mom Travels a Lot* by Caroline Feller Bauer and Nancy Winslow Parker *Home to Me, Home to You* by Jennifer A. Ericsson and Ashley Wolff *I'll See You When the Moon Is Full* by Jim Fowler and Susi Gregg Fowler *Daddy, Will You Miss Me?* by Wendy McCormick and Jennifer Eachus Sometimes I Work in . . . Series (Atlanta/Chicago/Fort Lauderdale/New York) by Tom Daly and Stefán Kjartansson
Body movement	Baby Board Book Series (*I'm a Little Tea Pot, Head, Shoulders, Knees and Toes*, and others) by Anne Kubler *Little Yoga: A Toddler's First Book of Yoga* and *Sleepy Little Yoga: A Toddler's Sleepy Book of Yoga* by Rebecca Whitford and Martina Selway *Pat-a-Cake* by Joanne Cole, Stephanie Calmenson and Alan Tiegreen *Mommy Draw Stars on My Tummy: Rhymes, Songs and Touch-Play Activities to Stay Connected* by Martine Goeneveld
Puppet books	Finger Puppet Book Series (includes *Little Snowman, Little Bee, Little Kitten*, and others) by Chronicle Books *In My Pond* by Sara Gillingham and Lorena Siminovich Finger Puppet Storybook Series by Alex Toys and Jill McDonald

Song-CD-book combination	*Puff, the Magic Dragon* by Peter Yarrow, Lenny Lipton, and Eric Puybaret *Goodnight, My Angel: A Lullabye* by Billy Joel and Yvonne Gilbert *Whole World* by Christopher Corr and Fred Penner *Sunshine on My Shoulders* by John Denver and Christopher Canyon
Storybook with CD	*Dewey Doo-it Series* (Includes *Dewey Doo-it Builds a House, Dewey Doo-it Feeds a Friend, and others*) by Brahm Wenfer and Alan Green *Yellow Umbrella* by Dong Il Sheen and Jae-Soo Liu *On the Day You Were Born* by Debra Frasier
Personalized books	*My Very Own Name* by Maia Haag and Mark Mille at www.iseeme.com *Eco the Eagle Series* by Barry Peacock, Michael Suter, and Gabby Redford at www.wildfirepublishing.com
Books with CDs sold separately	*Really Rosie* CD by Carole King and Nutshell Library (includes *Alligators All Around, Chicken Soup with Rice, One Was Johnny,* and *Pierre* by Maurice Sendak) *The Cat in the Hat and Other Dr. Seuss Favorites; Green Eggs and Ham and Other Servings of Dr. Seuss* by Listening Library; Dr. Seuss books sold independently
Reference	DK First Reference Series (*First Atlas, First Human Body Encyclopedia, First Animal Encyclopedia, First Encyclopedia,* and others) by DK Publishing *My First Dictionary: 1,000 Words, Pictures, and Definitions* by Betty Root *Stanley: The Great Book of Everything* by Andrew Griffin
Helping others	*The Peace Book* by Todd Parr *Little Bear's Little Boat* by Eve Bunting and Nancy Carpenter *Heartprints* by P.K. Hallinan *Because of You* by B.G. Hennessy and Hiroe Nakata
Manners	*Excuse Me! A Little Book of Manners* by Karen Katz Best Behavior Series (*Hands Are Not for Hitting, Teeth Are Not for Biting,* and more) by Free Spirit Publishing *Manners Are Important* by Todd Snow and Carrie Hartman *It's a Spoon, Not a Shovel* by Caralyn Buehner and Mark Buehner

Reading ABCs: The Tips of the Trade

Ideally you want reading to be a fun, connected, loving, and educational experience for your child. Books can create curiosity and interest as well as a love of literacy, even in the earliest of years. In order for your child to get the most out of the reading experience, here are a few tips:

1. Hold and cuddle your child while you read. Creating an atmosphere of affection, love, and intimacy around books will build positive associations that last a lifetime. What your child wants most is time and attention from you. Let books be the catalyst.

2. Give the book a proper introduction. The first time you read a book to your young child, make sure you spend a little time with it before starting to read. Talk about who wrote it, who did the illustrations, what the book might be about, and even what made you pick this book for your child.

3. Give positive feedback and encouragement. When you observe your baby quietly gazing at books, you can comment that you see how much she is enjoying her book or make a correlation with a parent (e.g., "It looks like you love books as much as your Daddy!"). You want your child to know that reading is a valued and esteemed activity in your home.

4. Invite participation. Let him touch the book, hold it, turn the pages, point to things, chew the pages of board books, and ask questions. Make sure he can see the pictures when you read to him and stop to answer any questions he has during the reading. Engage him by allowing him to finish sentences ("Llama llama red pajama reads a story with his…?"). This method works especially well with rhyming books. Let him have fun by supplying sound effects or even acting out parts of the text. My daughters once did the cutest impromptu performance of Robert McCloskey's *Make Way for Ducklings* that included directing traffic like a police officer and waddling around with their noses in the air like proud ducklings.

5. Create some mama drama (or papa drama). Get expressive when reading. Use the full range of your voice, speaking fast or slow, loud or soft, deep- or high-pitched depending on the characters, dialogue, and action in the text. Make sure to use facial expressions that reflect how the characters feel. But make sure you are not over expressive or patronizing to your child.

6. Don't require strict attention. A child who does not appear to be paying attention is often taking in more than you think. Let your infant nurse, suck on a teether, or play with a toy while you read if he cannot sit still. Allow your older child to sit on the floor with some crayons and paper while you read, if he has a difficult time staying still and likes to color. Whatever keeps him in the room and makes it a pleasurable experience works.

7. Create a reading team. Make sure everyone who comes into contact with your child supports the reading experience—and encourage them to add to it. The other night my mother-in-law, who lives 3,000 miles away, read a good-night story on the phone to my daughters. How cool is that? It is especially important that any child-care providers or day-care personnel support your reading goals. Make sure that the people who take care of your child when you are not there are reading to him as well.

8. Keep in mind that repetition supports memory and helps assimilate emotional experiences. It may be crazy-making to read *The Runaway Bunny* for the tenth time in one sitting, but that is how a child's brain creates useful neural pathways that help him learn the words, patterns, and story. Also, hearing an emotionally laden story, or one about a character who is going through something your child is experiencing, helps him work through complex emotions.

9. Always point to the words as you read them. This subtle tool allows you to map the spoken language for your child. By simply following the text with your finger, you take nothing away from the reading experience for your child and add so much! Doing this initially allows him to see the way that the English language is used in book form: we read a page from top to bottom, we pause at the end of a sentence, we turn pages from right to left, and so on. As time goes on, this pointing helps your child make the correlation between the printed and spoken word in a completely organic way. According to Timothy D. Kailing, author of *Native Reading,* this correlation develops naturally: "children do not need to be taught this relationship, it will just be a natural and obvious part of their world; they will simply absorb it. Rather than being a complicated new skill they have to struggle with later in childhood, reading is simply a natural extension of language as they have always known it."

Keep pointing to words and following the text with your finger, even if your child does not appear to be paying attention. Keep in mind you are *not* trying to teach reading. You are just creating an environment that will provide information for your child and prepare him for the moment when he is ready to learn to read. Never point out what you are doing, make a big deal about it, or quiz your children about words you are pointing to.

According to Trelease, the visual receptors in the brain outnumber the auditory receptors 30 to 1, so the odds of retaining a word in our memory are thirty times greater if we see the word than if we just hear it. Pointing helps make the visual and auditory connection for kids so they can start making the connection between letters and sounds. I wish I had started doing this earlier, since I noticed an almost immediate response from my daughters when I started using this method. Suddenly they started pointing to the words themselves, asking questions, pointing out letters, and wanting to "read" to me.

10. Create reading rituals and goals. Many reading experts recommend a goal of reading to your child thirty minutes a day. Personally, I find it easier to set a minimum number of books to read each day. I aim for a minimum of six but almost always go into the double digits. Given that most board books are only about twenty pages long, this doesn't take long. But it does establish great reading habits early on.

Make sure that you create daily reading rituals. Pretty much from the moment my daughters could sit in a high chair, we started reading two books at the end of each meal. As soon as they were old enough to let me know which books they preferred, each of them was encouraged to choose a book for us to read. My girls get to pick a book at bedtime too. These reading rituals have become a regular part of our routine.

11. Constantly make correlations between the written and spoken language. Make sure your child is exposed to letters and words often and early. You can do this by naturally incorporating them into play. (See pages 200–207 for more information). According to Kailing, "By doing this simple thing, children learn that these symbols are an important and meaningful part of their world. With this foundation it becomes perfectly natural for your child to be interested in the symbols of written language." Your purpose here isn't to try to teach or push this information on your child—you simply want to make letter and word play a fun part of his life. Simple activities like playing with letter magnets and letter sponges in the bathtub, using letter cookie cutters when you bake, and pointing out words and letters in your day-to-day life are all good ways to make those correlations.

12. Use the tricks of the read-aloud trade. There are several techniques that make reading a fun, dynamic, interactive, and, yes, educational experience. You can see which models feel most natural for you and your child. Feel free to borrow from all of them or skip them altogether. As long as you and your child are having fun, you are doing it right. Try these three:

- **Reading with explanation** is a vocabulary-focused method in which the reader gives brief explanations of unknown words by either using synonyms for the new word or pointing to a picture on the page. In a study of eight-year-old children who were read the same story three times in seven days, the group that used this method experienced almost a 40 percent gain in vocabulary, whereas the control group gained less than 2 percent.

- **Dialogic reading is an interactive reading technique.** While it is ideal for children who have at least fifty words in their vocabulary, it can be used with preverbal children as well. When using this method with a preverbal child, the parent responds in the child's place. There are reports of dialogic reading accelerating two-year-old children's language development by as much as nine months.

Dialogic reading involves three different methods:

1. Asking "what" questions and then restating your child's response. *Example:* "What's this?" . . . "Yes, that is a rabbit!"

2. Expanding on what your child has stated. Keep your expansions short and make sure you build on what your child has said. *Example:* "Yes, that is a rabbit. It is a big pink rabbit!"

3. Asking open-ended questions. Once your child is advanced enough to get passed the "what" questions, try asking open-ended questions.
   Example:"What else do you see?" "What would happen if the rabbit jumped up that hill?" or "What do you think about the way the rabbit helped the boy?"

- **Active engagement** is a reading technique that borrows from dialogic reading techniques, engaging the child as an active listener. Active engagement involves four steps:

  1. Pause periodically and ask open-ended questions.
  2. Expand on the child's answer.
  3. Suggest alternative possibilities.
  4. Pose progressively more challenging questions.

A group of parents of preschoolers received one-hour training in this method and then spent a month reading eight times a week with their children before coming back to have their children tested. The children, who averaged two-and-a-half years old, improved 8.5 months in verbal expression. In other words, the two-and-a-half-year-olds tested at the level of 38.5-month-old children and scored six months ahead of the expected level of vocabulary for 24-month-old children!

Ten Reasons to Slam a Book Shut (or Choose Not to Buy It!)

1. **Child characters exhibiting mean, destructive, or dangerous behavior.** I don't want to teach my children to misbehave.

2. **Scary ideas or images (like monsters).** Unless a child is struggling with specific fears and you can find a book that uses scary ideas or images to address those issues appropriately, it is better to keep away from anxiety-provoking images.

3. **Parent characters scolding or lying to a child.** I prefer books in which parents and children have a mutually respectful relationship.

4. **Princess themes.** I have an anti-princess bias because I don't like the message these books send to children about priorities, entitlement, materialism, and being rescued.

5. **Commercial characters.** I do my best to avoid books that feature commercialized characters because they are often used to lure children into becoming young consumers, eager to buy the dolls, foods, and DVDs associated with the characters.

6. **Product placement.** I don't like books made by cereal, candy, cracker, or even raisin companies because they manipulate kids into becoming consumers of their products—for example, by teaching them to count while they play with or eat those products.

7. **Gender stereotypes.** Avoid books that have hyperfeminine images and messages about girls or hypermasculine images and messages about boys. When children read books that portray these images, they are more likely to be limited by gender stereotypes.

8. **Child characters who get hurt.** Avoid books where children get hurt or injured since this is a subject that can be very scary for young kids.

9. **Parent characters who die or abandon the child.** We all loved *Bambi*, but I have seen too many kids become traumatized by stories in which a parent dies or abandons them.

10. **Characters using words to threaten.** I recently came close to buying a book that sounded great until I read a review that said that the child in the book tells his mother, "I am going to kill you if you lose my toy." Who needs to put ideas like that into a child's head?

Teach Your Children Well

Parents should read to preschool children and informally teach them about reading and writing. Reading to children, discussing stories and experiences with them, and, with a light touch, helping them learn letters and words are practices that are constantly associated with eventual success in reading.

—Becoming a Nation of Readers:
The Report of the Commission on Reading

The seeds of academic success can be directly traced back to the home. Quite simply, children whose parents take the time to read to them as well as introduce letters, words, and sounds will do better in school. Much of how well a child will do academically depends on how much he has learned before he gets to school.

While you might expect school to help your child catch up if he lacks certain skills, the reverse is generally true. Studies show that children enter kindergarten at different levels. The most advanced (kids in the seventy-fifth percentile) are about a year ahead of the most delayed (kids in the twenty-fifth percentile) and, as time goes on, that gap only widens. According to Dr. Andrew Biemiller, author of *Language and Reading Success,* "the gap between children with advanced language and children with restricted language grows wider during the elementary years." By third grade the advanced child's comprehension is generally one year ahead of grade average, and the delayed child is one year behind.

How Bedtime Reading Actually Changes Your Physiology

A study examining why bedtime reading is so pleasurable monitored the physiological responses of readers compared to activities like relaxing with closed eyes, listening to white noise, doing mental arithmetic, and performing visualizations. The study revealed that the readers were more stimulated, initially, than they were when relaxing with their eyes closed, but shortly afterward, as they continued to read, they became even more relaxed than they had been when their eyes were shut. This finding suggests how effective reading can be to help your child wind down before bedtime.

In order for children to do well, they must be aware of three basic concepts before entering preschool:

- **Print awareness.** Words are for reading and pictures are for observing. Different sounds make up words and combinations of words make up sentences that convey meaning.

- **Alphabet awareness.** Letters have unique shapes and sounds. When combined, they make words.

- **Phonic awareness.** Words are made up of different sounds that are represented by letters. These letters can be isolated to make individual sounds. When combined, they make words.

Understand that, in using the term "awareness," I do not mean mastery. These are very abstract concepts, but they are ones your child will naturally start to know if you read aloud to him every day.

Freeze!
Step Away from the Chalk!

What we teach children to love and desire
will always outweigh what we make them learn.

—Jim Trelease, *The Read-Aloud Handbook*

Under no circumstances should you do any *formal* teaching of your infant or toddler at home. While this may seem like a contradiction to what you've just read, it is not. Sitting and drilling your child with flash cards or quizzing him about words on the page is a quick way to turn reading and learning into a stressful, high-pressure, repellent chore. Pressure is the opposite of what works.

Focus on the process instead, not the outcome. Make reading enjoyable and your child will want to do it. It is that simple. You cannot control when your child recognizes a letter or reads his first word, but it is up to you to make words and letters fun. According to Helen Coronato, a teacher, librarian, and author of *The Complete Idiot's Guide to Reading with Your Child,* "when we encourage reading through routines, rituals, games, and guidance, then mastering the skill of reading becomes a byproduct of reading enjoyment."

I'M LOOKING AT THE MOM IN THE MIRROR

Every night when I press the "play" button on the CD player in my daughters' room to put on the nighttime music, I place my left hand on the side of the boom box to adjust the volume controls. I thought this was a subtle—and an unnoticed—movement until one of my daughter's was old enough and tall enough to start doing it herself. From the first time she pressed the "play" button, she put her left hand on the side of the player, not knowing why exactly, but mimicking my gesture nonetheless. This example really shows how closely our children observe our behavior, imitate our actions, and re-create our habits. Reading is no different.

Our actions say more than our words. We are our children's greatest role models. In the early years, we model the pleasure of reading in two ways. The first is by reading aloud with our children, therefore making it a priority. Second, we let our children see us reading. Sometimes when I go into my children's room to sit with them while they play, I bring a book. My husband always reads the newspaper at the breakfast table and shares the pictures with our daughters. He even gives them the comic section so they can have their own newspaper experience of looking at the pictures and the words, even though they are not old enough to be able to read the words on their own. It is particularly important that children see both parents reading so they don't associate reading with only one parent or one gender. Remember, you don't have to sit and read in front of your child for hours at a time. Let them see you read when you put them down for a nap, watch them play in a safe place, or even sit down on the toilet (we all have to use the bathroom at some point!). The biggest thing that takes parents (and kids) away from reading, however, is the television. Turn it off. You are a far better role model when you are reading than when you are watching TV. I know that old habits are hard to break, but if a confirmed TV addict like me can do it, so can you.

Thirty-Six Activities
That Will Make Kids of All Ages Love Lit

Keeping your children excited about reading is easier than you would imagine. Keep it fun and interesting by always seeking out engaging books with eye-catching artwork and compelling stories (for older children). Your enthusiasm goes a long way, and the enjoyment of reading is something you can model for your kids.

It does not take much effort to make reading not just a daily habit in your home, but a special activity that everyone looks forward to. In our house we have a special bookshelf where we keep unique and delicate books (like pop-ups) and books from my own and my husband's childhood. The shelf is just beyond the reach of our girls. Sharing these books, which have particular sentimental value for us, with Quincy and Mendez makes the experience of reading them that much more significant for all of us.

Let your child keep the light on in his room so he can "read" books a little longer. Once he's older and you give him a bed lamp, Trelease recommends saying something like this: "We think you are now old enough to stay up later at night, like Mommy and Daddy do, so we bought you this lamp so you can stay up and read if you want. If you don't want to read, that is okay too. We'll just turn off the light at the usual time." This makes reading time very special.

Give books to your child as birthday presents and, sometimes, for no reason at all. Make books appear out of nowhere. The other day, I felt like a magician when Mendez pointed to a picture of a book she wanted and asked me if I would buy it for her. Having guessed that she would like that particular book, I had already bought it and was holding onto it, waiting for the perfect moment to make it appear!

Taking your child to the library is another experience that encourages a love of books. In a study of children from print-poor environments, parents reported that 96 percent of the children became more interested in reading after a single visit to the library, and 94 percent spent more time with books after one visit.

Encourage your child to get to know the librarian. My friend Andrea shares a book obsession with me. She has wisely befriended Rachael, her local librarian, who helps her screen books before purchasing them for her kids' collection at home. Andrea often brings her children to the library and her son, Brandon, has developed such a great relationship with Rachael that he cried when she wasn't at the library one day. That is one book-loving boy! I can see his brilliant future now!

Here are some activities, games, and toys that you can use to foster a love of books. They apply to different ages and stages of development, so make sure that you match activity and age levels appropriately.

1. Display the first letter of your child's name prominently in his room. This creates early interest in reading. Mendez has a big "M" over her crib and Quincy has a big "Q." Not surprisingly, the first letter Mendez learned was "M" and the first letter Quincy learned was "Q." (We got our big letters from Craft-Cuts.com.)

2. Choose a "Letter of the Day." When kids are first learning the alphabet, a great way to avoid overwhelming them is to pick a Letter of the Day. Plan a fun activity to do with a letter every day. Challenge yourself to get creative and keep the focus on the fun.

3. Play peek-a-boo or hide-and-seek with letters. Instead of hiding a toy or your own face, hide letters. Cover a sponge or magnetic letter, or one you wrote on an index card, with a scarf and ask, "Where's the A?" "There it is! Peek-a-boo A!" Or show your child a letter and then hide it someplace in the room (where he can find it) and ask, "Where is the Q?"

4. Point out print and familiar or recurring words. Point out the letters on a stop sign and other street signs while you're waiting at a red light. Read the letters on a friend's T-shirt. The more aware your child is of the print all around him, the more eager he will be to understand the words.

5. Make bath time word time. Read to your child in the bath or let him play with bath books that are made for the water. Check out sponge alphabet letters that can be used in the bathtub for letter play.

6. Make a family scrapbook with pictures and words. I made one using *Baby's My First Photo Album of Family & Friends* by Genius Baby, which is nice and soft. I just slipped in photos and used a label maker to add names. The family photos served as a helpful transitional object to leave in a crib. Sometimes I would go into my girls' room in the morning to find the book open to a page with my picture.

7. Personalize an ABC book for your child. For young kids who still need indestructible books, you can make one at home on your computer. You can glue words, photographs, and pictures cut from magazines onto paper, which you can then laminate and bind with inexpensive coil to hold the pages together as a book. I made mine at Kinko's, but you can do the lamination at home with self-adhesive lamination sheets and then bring it to a Kinko's-type store to bind it. For older kids you can easily make a book on a photo-sharing website like Kodak or Snapfish.

8. Tell stories. This is a wonderful way for children to learn about narrative, creativity, and storytelling. Make up a story of your own; share a story from your own childhood or one about a grandparent or great-grandparent. You can use stories to help your child work through an issue, get to know you better, or learn about a deceased member of the family. My husband tells my children the most creative stories about two recurring characters that are thinly disguised versions of Quincy and Mendez. In these stories, the two characters treat each other with kindness, learn to use the toilet, and have all kinds of interesting adventures.

9. Have a reading playdate. Ask other parents to bring their children over to your house or meet at a library or park with three of their favorite books. Get in a circle together and read. This tends to work best with very young kids, before they are mobile, and older kids who can sit still. Reading playdates can have themes, too, on whatever subjects appeal most to the kids. Sharing with other families is a terrific way to discover new books.

10. Attend a storybook hour. Most local libraries and bookstores have free story readings when professional storytellers, authors, or librarians read to children. These wonderful readers make books come alive and really grab kids' attention.

11. Keep a book journal or chart. Write down all the books you read with your child. When he is a little older, he will love to look back and remember all the books he read with you. Also, older kids feel a sense of accomplishment as they add titles to the list. One mom I know keeps a poster on the back of the door to her kid's room where they write down each book they read. This super-crafty mom also makes stickers showing the covers of the books to add to the poster.

12. Visit a bookstore as an activity. Most bookstores have a children's section with a reading corner and kid-sized tables and chairs. Regular visits to these special places help your children learn to love books and allow you to see what types of books they are drawn to when they're surrounded by a variety of titles.

13. Let your child "buy" books. Let your child pick his own books sometimes by showing him pictures of the covers on line or reading books at the bookstore and letting him choose.

14. Read books about bookworms, word lovers, and authors. I admit my bias here. I am an author and both my parents are writers. My great-aunt, Toni Mendez, a literary agent, was a significant influence on me. So I come from a family that has the utmost appreciation for the written word. That said, reading books about people who have a literary passion is a fun way to get your child excited about books. Here's a list of book-lover books:

About books and reading:

Bats at the Library by Brian Lies

Book! by Kristine O'Connell George

Book! Book! Book! by Deborah Bruss and Tiphanie Beeke

Born to Read by Judy Sierra and Marc Brown

Our Library by Eve Bunting and Maggie Smith

Read Anything Good Lately? by Susan Allen and Jane Lindaman

Reading Makes You Feel Good by Todd Parr

Wild About Books by Judy Sierra and Marc Brown

About words:

Big Words for Little People by Jamie Lee Curtis and Laura Cornell

Cassie's Word Quilt by Faith Ringgold

Max's Words by Kate Banks and Boris Kulikov

About writers:

The Boy Who Loved Words by Roni Schotter and Giselle Potter

What Do Authors Do? by Eileen Christelow

Written Anything Good Lately? by Susan Allen, Jane Lindman, and Vicky Enright

15. Help your child connect with favorite authors. Make authors come alive by visiting their websites, reading about them, and even celebrating their birthdays. I think it is important that children realize that books don't just appear by magic but are written and illustrated by actual people. We recently used self-adhesive lamination sheets to make a picture of one of our favorite authors, Todd Parr, with his dog, along with his name and some of his illustrations, and placed it on a board in the kids' room.

16. Frame a book. Make a color copy of your child's favorite book cover and frame it in his room. This is an inexpensive way to decorate a room and send a message that books are important.

17. Listen to an audio book. You can buy a CD (or check out one from the library) or download an MP3 of your favorite children's books. The sound effects, professional readings, and accompanying music can add a whole new dimension to reading with your child. This is also an enjoyable and helpful activity when using the point-while-you-read method, which actually takes some getting used to. Audio stories are also a nice option for car rides, especially if your child can look at the book while he listens.

18. Make your own audio book for your child. Record yourself reading your child's favorite book so he can listen to your voice whenever he wants. Hearing you read can help him connect with literature, and the sound of your voice can ease the separation when you have a night out.

19. Read a book with suggested activities built into it. This is so much fun for kids—and parents! Nancy Elizabeth Wallace has a wonderful series for older kids, including *The Kindness Quilt, Recycle Every Day!, Shells! Shells! Shells!, Leaves! Leaves! Leaves!,* and *Seeds! Seeds! Seeds!* In fact, *Seeds! Seeds! Seeds!* was so inspiring that my kids grew a lavender plant from seeds and toasted squash seeds, which we all enjoyed eating.

20. Try a book-based field trip. Read a book about a topic and then make a visit to a related place. For example, depending on your child's age, you might read one of the following books about fish (listed from the youngest to the oldest reading level) and then visit an aquarium or pet store that sells fish.

> *Five Fish!* by Fiona Macmillan, Amanda Wood, and Emma Dodd
> *The Ocean Alphabet* by Jerry Pallotta and Frank Mazzola Jr.
> *One Fish, Two Fish, Red Fish, Blue Fish* by Dr. Seuss
> *Swimmy* by Leo Lionni
> *Into the A, B, Sea: An Ocean Alphabet Book*
>   by Deborah Lee Rose and Steve Jenkins

21. Create a three-dimensional learning experience. For example, if your child likes bugs, get an ant farm (they're available at toy stores or online) and read books about ants:

> *Hey, Little Ant* by Phillip M. Hoose, Hannah Hoose, and Debbie Tilley
> *I Saw an Ant in a Parking Lot* by Joshua Prince and Macky Pamintuan
> *The Life and Times of the Ant* by Charles Micucci

You can even download and sing ant-related songs:

> "High Hopes" by Jimmy Van Heusen and Sammy Cahn
> "Ants Go Marching!" (Anonymous)
> "I'm an Ant" by Jennifer Fixman

And, if your child eats nut butters, you can eat "ants on a log" (a halved banana spread with peanut or almond butter and dotted with raisins, placed as if they were ants on a log).

22. Play with letter dice. Letter dice (like the ones used in the game Boggle) are an entertaining way to play with letters. Roll a handful with your child and let him look for the first letter of his name. Practice putting together his favorite three-letter words. See how high you can stack the dice and name the letters before the pile falls over. Montessori Alphabet Dice are particularly easy for this use because they are simple wooden dice with small and capital letters clearly written in black. Just keep in mind that children should not be left alone with any small toys that can be a choking hazard.

23. Play with letter tiles. Have fun using letters tiles to find and match favorite letters in an alphabet book or to spell your child's name. Because they are so small, you can keep a bag of tiles in your diaper bag or purse to use when you are standing on line and your child is bored. Bananagrams actually comes with a banana-shaped carrying case that zips up.

24. Let your child be the author. When your child is old enough to string sentences together, let him dictate a story or whatever is on his mind. You can write his story in a book format and he can draw the pictures—or you can illustrate the book yourself. Make sure you give the book a title and credit the author and illustrator on the cover!

25. Discuss the newspaper. Share appropriate stories (in child-friendly abbreviated form, of course) or pictures with your child. Ask him if he can find an object ("Can you find the car?") or show him something important to you ("This man is playing baseball. He plays for my favorite team . . ."). Let your child look at pictures and notice words in the comic section. Familiarizing your child with the newspaper makes it more likely he will look to the printed word as a source for news when he is older.

26. Send your child a postcard. Everyone loves to get mail, especially children. Keep it simple and colorful. I bought sign language stamps that show words and letters with ASL signs that my almost-preschoolers can understand even though they can't yet read.

27. Write letters or emails together. Let your child help you compose letters to relatives or friends who live out of town—on paper, ideally, but typing emails works too. This can be especially fun for young relatives who enjoy getting mail. Another idea is to write a fan letter to your child's favorite author or illustrator. Too many kids become focused on meaningless celebrities, even at a young age, so this is a way to show your child how much you value words and creativity. There are some really unique books about sending letters that you can share:

> *A Letter to Amy* by Ezra Jack Keats
> *Dear Mr. Blueberry* by Simon James
> *Dear Annie* by Judith Caseley

The Jolly Postman: Or Other People's Letters
    by Alan Ahlberg and Janet Ahlberg

Or try books that explain how mail works:

Delivering Your Mail: A Book About Mail Carriers
    by Ann Owen and Eric Thomas
A Day with a Mail Carrier by Jan Lottke
The Post Office Book: Mail and How It Moves by Gail Gibbons

28. Look it up! Make a point of looking up answers to questions, even when your kids are very young. We keep a basket of reference books, many of which are child-friendly, in a book basket in our kitchen, since that seems to be where most of the questions come up. In this basket we keep a Spanish-English dictionary, a sign language dictionary, a children's English dictionary, an encyclopedia of the human body, an atlas, a guide to outer space, a dinosaur book, and a few other reference books. But you don't need to limit yourself to books; if you are deciding what to wear for the day, you can look up the weather in the newspaper..

29. Play with alphabet puzzles. Lots of companies make wooden puzzles that allow a child to place a letter into the matching letter-shaped space. Some have clues to help your child figure out where pieces go. I am a big fan of Melissa & Doug alphabet puzzles for kids. This company also sells a "See & Spell" puzzle that shows a picture of an object (car, bus, fish, etc.) and has letter-shaped spaces where each letter belongs.

30. Check out a magnetic alphabet maze. I am not sure who liked this toy more—my kids or me! This permanently sealed hardwood maze has colorful balloons for each letter of the alphabet, plus twenty-six corresponding letter magnets. Kids use the attached magnetic wand to guide each letter into place. This is useful for learning colors and letters and mastering fine motor skills. The one we have is called Magnetic Alphabet Maze and can be found at Lakeshore Learning at www.lakeshorelearning.com.

31. Use refrigerator magnets. Use letter and word magnets and give your children a set of their own to play with, too. Make sure you keep refrigerator magnets at child level and leave simple messages where everyone can see them. (Always supervise this activity, since these small magnets can be a choking hazard for young children.)

32. Cook a book. Read a book that mentions food and then cook that item. For example, read Laura Numeroff and Felicia Bond's *If You Give a Pig a Pancake* while you whip up a batch of pancakes. According to Esmé Raji Codell, author of *How to Get Your Child to Love Reading*, "Sampling foods that coincide with the text is a great way to involve children in literature and bring books to life." There are also a few "kid lit"-based cookbooks that offer recipes corresponding to storylines or characters in specific books (keep in mind that some of the recipes are healthier than others):

> *Once Upon a Recipe* by Karen Greene
> *The Fairy Tale Cookbook: Fun Recipes for Families to Create and Eat Together* by Sandre Moore
> *Fairy Tale Feasts: A Literary Cookbook for Young Readers and Eaters* by Jane Yolen
> *Recipes for Reading* by Gwynne Spencer
> *Green Eggs and Ham Cookbook* by Dr. Seuss

33. Go to a book fair. Book fairs are a fun way to learn about new books, enjoy readings, and meet authors. Most towns and cities have local book fairs and many schools sponsor them as well. One company, Scholastic, helps bring book fairs to local schools (www.Scholastic.com/bookfairs/). Plan your next family vacation around a big book fair like the Los Angeles Times Festival of Books, which has child-oriented readings and events.

34. Start a book club. Book clubs are a social way to nurture a lifelong love of reading by giving kids the chance to share their reading experience with other children. Book clubs are generally best for kids five years and older. You can check out two great books about forming books clubs:

> *The Kid's Book Club Book,* by Judy Gelman and Vicky Levy Krupp
> *The Mother-Daughter Book Club: How Ten Busy Mothers and Daughters Came Together to Talk, Laugh, and Learn Through Their Love of Reading,* rev. ed., by Shireen Dodson

35. Create a book nook or build a reading fort. Put a cozy child-sized armchair or beanbag chair in a well lighted area and keep an assortment of books nearby. I especially love seeing my kids curl up with a book in their book nook at their grandparents' house.

To make a reading fort, pitch a tent or drape blankets over a couple of chairs in your kid's room to create a tent. Grab a fun book and have story time with your child in this new cozy spot. At nighttime you can turn off the lights and pull out a flashlight to read; just make sure none of the books are scary.

36. Encourage your children to do their own storytelling. Encourage your children to tell stories, whether using puppets, acting out stories they already know, or using their own words to tell a story based on illustrations from a familiar picture book. Anything that uses their newly emerging creativity is fantastic.

Ten Reading Don'ts

Reading together is one of the most wonderful experiences parents can share with their children. In order to keep it positive, remember the following:

1. Don't correct your child.

2. Don't criticize your child.

3. Don't answer the phone during story time.

4. Don't tell a child who is pretending to read that he isn't.

5. Don't use reading as a punishment.

6. Don't threaten to take away reading time or books.

7. Don't continue reading a book that your child doesn't like.

8. Don't punish a child for tearing a page
   (but do let him help you repair it).

9. Don't get angry with your child for getting a book messy.

10. Don't make books compete with television by asking questions like "Do you want to read or watch TV?"

Most of all, keep reading exciting and fun.

A Different Kind
of Toy Story

The Importance of Play

At a playgroup at a friend's house, three-month-old Ben lies on his back while his mother blows bubbles for him. He does his best to follow with his eyes the different sized bubbles floating all around him. He squeals with glee each time he touches one.

Seven-month-old Amy lies in her crib at home sucking her big toe. She examines it up close and decides to try the other foot.

One-year-old Trevor walks past his Mommy and Me classmates to the toy kitchen. He opens and closes the cabinets while his classmate, Daniel, plays with the refrigerator. They hardly seem to notice each other because they are so engrossed in their own activity.

At the park, twenty-month-old Jason is being pushed in the swing by his father. "More! More! More!" he tells his dad, laughing with glee.

At a day-care center, two-year-old Charlotte stacks blocks, building them higher and higher until they are almost as tall as she is and they collapse to the ground. She starts all over again.

Two-and-a-half-year-old Jack stands at the easel in his art class, picking a color. He dips his brush in the purple paint, splashing it on his clothes in the process. He strokes the brush across the white paper, beginning his masterpiece.

At preschool, three-year-old Jasmine puts on the doctor's coat. "This shot is going to hurt but then you will feel much better," she tells Duncan, her patient and classmate, as she pushes the plastic syringe against his arm.

All the children in the above scenarios are playing in their own way at their own level. The kids are indoors, outdoors, playing with peers, parents, or friends. At home, in classes, at the park, in day care, and at school, they are all learning. Play teaches children about themselves, their world, and the people around them. It helps children master new skills and perfect old ones.

In the hope of creating a smart child, many parents discount the importance of play. But play is crucial to developing minds. Studies show that play increases IQ and promotes problem solving, creativity, learning, attention span, language development, self-regulation, social skills, the ability to work through difficult life events, and much more.

But play is disappearing. It is being devoured by television, "learning toys," structured classes, flash cards, and "edutainment" DVDs for kids. Parents are being scared into spending hundreds—and in some cases thousands—of dollars on so-called educational toys so their children won't lose out on some imagined intellectual edge. Other parents park their children in front of the television for hours every day, because they don't know any better or need some time to themselves. All these activities eat away at the playtime that is so necessary for child development. According to Kathy Hirsh-Pasek, Roberta Michnick Golinkoff, and Diane E. Eyer, authors of *Einstein Never Used Flashcards,* play is "the very fuel of every intellectual activity that our children engage in."

It has been estimated that children have lost twelve hours of free time per week in the last two decades, and it gets worse as kids get older. According to a recent report titled *Crisis in the Kindergarten: Why Children Need Play in School*, kindergartners in the major cities now spend about three hours a day on reading, math instruction, and test preparation but less than thirty minutes a day in free play.

The irony is that this attempt to expedite children's learning does more harm than good. In the article "Playtime in Peril," author Lea Winerman points out that, "Parents and educators are ignoring decades of evidence that young children learn best through active, exploratory play (sometimes guided by an adult) rather than through direct, lecture-style classroom instruction, flash cards and push-button computer learning toys that can push them to memorize facts that they're not cognitively ready to understand."

The Perks of Play: Developmental Benefits

Play is crucial for child development on every level. Play, starting in babyhood, is inexorably linked to learning, socialization, and development. Here are ten of the most important developmental benefits of play:

1. Play teaches problem solving. Researchers put a desirable toy in a clear box and told four- and five-year-olds to get the toy out of the box without moving out of their chairs or leaning toward the box. The only way a child could get to the toy was to connect two long sticks and use them to "rake in" the box. One group of kids was allowed to play with the sticks and some toys for ten minutes, while a second group was shown how to solve the problem using the sticks, but were not allowed to play before being told to get the prize out of the box, and a third group did not get either opportunity. The children who were allowed to play did much better than either of the other two groups. They worked more eagerly and persistently and demonstrated better problem-solving abilities. The conclusion that the researchers came to was that play is a learning experience that teaches problem-solving skills.

2. Play helps social development. Play helps children learn important social skills like taking turns, collaboration, following rules, empathy, self-regulation, and impulse control. Play helps children learn the rules of social interaction, which, in turn, helps them in all their relationships. Children who play well together are able to work well together, and these skills translate into good social skills as they mature into adults.

Around the age of three, sociodramatic play increases. Children weave together make-believe stories, develop characters, and create social rules in their play. This development demonstrates a dramatic cognitive and social leap. In an extensive study of make-believe play, Drs. Wendy Haight and Peggy Miller found that 68 to 75 percent of make-believe play is social in nature. In fact, these early interactions build the foundation for future social relationships and exert external pressure on children to act in socially desirable ways, pushing them to the next level of socialization where they have an understanding of social rules and manners. The child who throws a baby doll at her friend while playing house breaks the rhythm of the game, and in all likelihood her friend will not ask to her play house again. It is during these moments of imaginary play that children are forced to rise above their natural desires. As prominent child development expert Dr. Lev Vygotsky writes, "In play, a child is always above his average age, above his daily behavior; in play, it is as though he were a head taller than himself."

3. Play helps develop impulse control. It has often been said that play is the work of children and, indeed, it is more work than it looks like. Free play, in particular, is not so "free": it is all about self-control and following social rules, which requires tremendous impulse control. According to Dr. Vygotsky, children repeatedly face conflicts between the rules of make-believe situations and what they would do if they could act impulsively, and they usually decide in favor of the rules.

According to Dr. Laura E. Berk, author of *Awakening Children's Minds*, free play strengthens children's *internal* capacity to become civilized and socially responsible and, furthermore, exerts powerful *external* pressure on them to act in socially desirable ways. In a two-year study of play that examined three- and four-year-olds, it was found that children who engaged in complex sociodramatic play showed greater improvements in social responsibility over a five- to six-month period. This was particularly noticeable in children who were reported to be "highly impulsive" by their parents. The good news is that the children who have the greatest need to curb their impulsiveness benefit the most from play.

4. Play makes kids smarter. Play is the foundation of intellectual exploration. It provides children with a template that teaches them how to learn. Play and toys are the primary methods by which children learn and acquire many basic skills. According to researchers at the University of Illinois, the brain's activity increases by 25 percent during play. Another study at Baylor University revealed that the brain mass of children who did not play in the first five years of life was 20 to 30 percent less than that of children who had played during those formative years. A different study that focused on preschoolers found that children who spend time in sociodramatic play are more advanced in their intellectual development than their peers and are judged more socially competent by their teachers than children who do not spend as much time playing.

5. Play improves concentration, attention span, and memory. Attention and concentration are learned skills, and play is one of the most natural and enjoyable ways for a child to begin developing these skills. We have all seen a child so lost in play that she doesn't even hear when you call her name. This focus is essentially the same skill a child needs years later to write a term paper, listen to a lecture, or perform a piano concerto. A study of children's play patterns reveals how attention and focus change over time. One- to two-year-olds' attention is dictated by the physical properties of a toy, which causes them to lose interest and switch toys relatively quickly, but once they are old enough to have play goals that require effort—like stacking blocks—their attention span changes as well. The more complex the play goals, the more they display focused, effortful attention and the more such attention increases over time.

Children remember things that are presented to them in a play context much better than they do when they're asked to memorize information that is presented to them without a context. In a study in which children were asked to memorize a list of toys, one group of children had the opportunity to play with the toys and the second group was asked only to memorize the list. The children who played with the toys first memorized the list effortlessly, whereas the non-play group did not do nearly as well.

6. Play aids in physical development. Play helps children develop coordination, fine motor skills, gross motor skills, and muscle strength; it also prevents obesity. Sensorimotor play—play that uses both the senses and the muscles—allows an infant or toddler to discover her own body and its abilities. Preschool children develop this awareness through both small-muscle activity, like getting both hands to work together, and large-muscle activity, such as walking, running, and climbing. The sensorimotor play of preschool children helps them understand and control the use of their bodies. This mastery of the physical body also promotes self-esteem. The feeling of accomplishment is obvious the first time a child crawls across a room, bangs on a drum, or kicks a ball.

It has been estimated that 32 percent of American children are obese. For many of these kids, lack of play is largely to blame. Many children now live a sedentary lifestyle that starts in infancy. Studies show that the more television children watch, the heavier they tend to be. In fact, the American Academy of Pediatrics suggests that children under the age of two should not be allowed to watch any television or videos at all. TV habits, which have their roots early in life, tend to persist. Two-year-olds who are heavy TV watchers are two-and-a-half times more likely to become excessive television viewers by the age of six. Every hour your child spends in front of the television is an hour she is not playing, moving, or experiencing real life.

Activity leads to more activity. The first five years of life are crucial in developing healthy habits. Children who are used to being physical and spending free time playing grow up to be physically active adults. Kids who grow up in front of the television and become overweight are less likely to find enjoyment in physical activity, creating a vicious cycle.

7. Play helps children master new skills and understand the way things work. Have you ever noticed how children do things over and over again? Eden, eighteen months old, climbs up the baby slide and slides down over and over again, while two-and-a-half-year-old Cayden kicks the ball again and again. They are both working on the same thing: mastery. Children master new skills through repetitive play, and once they have conquered that skill they take it to the next level. Once a child has learned to walk, she will try to run. Once she has learned to stack the blocks, she will start to build more complex structures. Play gives children skills to build on.

Exploring, manipulating, touching, dropping, sorting, and exploring all give children the ability to make inferences about how things work. This process starts early. In a study of this phenomenon, researchers gave toy horns that made a noise when the bulb was squeezed to 9- to 16-month-old babies. They allowed the children to play with the toy horns and then took them away, replacing them with other horns of different colors and sizes that worked the same way. What they found was that all the babies made what the researchers called an "inductive inference"; in other words, they were able to make assumptions about the new toys based on their experiences with the previous toys. All the babies squeezed the bulb on the horns right away.

8. Play helps develop mathematical thinking. When children play with blocks, trains, Legos, dress-up clothes, puzzles, or almost any other toy, they are playing directly with mathematics without even knowing it. Because play teaches children about the relationships between things, it actually helps them develop the type of reasoning that aids in mathematical performance. According to Professor Ranald Jarrell, an expert in the development of mathematical thinking, "Experimental research on play shows a strong relationship between play, the growth of mathematical understanding, and improved mathematical performance...Without play...children's powers of mathematical reasoning would be seriously underdeveloped."

Board games are a fun way for older children to learn mathematical concepts without any formal teaching. In a study of preschoolers, the children were given the opportunity to play with one of two board games that were similar in format to the commercial board game Chutes and Ladders, except the one used in the study was based on numbers rather than colors. The researchers found that just one hour of playing the numerical board game greatly improved the children's ability to identify numbers, count, make number comparisons, and identify where a number exists on a number line.

A kindergartner's mathematical knowledge predicts her math achievement test scores in elementary, middle, and even high school, just as her ability to read, as a kindergartner, is a reliable indicator of her academic success later on. Studies show that the relationship between early and later mathematical ability is twice as strong as that between early and late reading achievement.

9. Play promotes language development and literacy. Play, especially dramatic play, requires children to use and be exposed to language. In a study of four-year-olds who frequently engaged in sociodramatic play, researchers found that when compared to a non-sociodramatic playgroup, these children exhibited an increase in the total number of words used, the length of their sentences, and the complexity of their speech.

One reason why kids' verbal skills and vocabulary increase with dramatic play is that children often correct each other's errors, directly or through modeling, when they play together. When Ella and Maggie play house, and Maggie's baby doll says, "I want baba!" Ella corrects her, saying, "You're supposed to say 'I want my bottle.'" In another corner of the room, Sabastien and Nicole are playing "work." When Nicole introduces Sabastien to a new colleague, she tells him, "You should say, 'Nice to meet you.'" Learning has taken place.

It is therefore no surprise that play has a positive effect on literacy. In one study, kids who spent fifty to sixty minutes of a two-and-a-half hour program participating in sociodramatic play scored higher in literacy skills than children who did not participate in the program. Some experts believe that the experience of using symbolism in play helps children apply the concept that letters and words act as symbols for sounds and language, which helps them understand reading concepts.

10. Play promotes strong neural pathways and lots of brain cells. Each time a child engages in a play activity such as stacking blocks, the synapses between brain cells are activated, and over time the level of a chemical needed to make those connections decreases, making it easier to perform the task. According to Dr. Jill Stamm and Paula Spencer, authors of *Bright from the Start*, that "repetitive activity results in patterned neural activity that changes the brain." This creates an enjoyable learning experience that links play to pleasure, making children return to play over and over again. What constitutes play changes over time; for the infant it is a game of peek-a-boo, for the toddler it may be playing with trains, for the preschooler it could be a game of dress-up, and for Mom it might be a game of Scrabble. According to Stamm and Spencer, the biology of play stays the same regardless of age: "When something feels good, the accompanying chemical response makes our brain cells want to experience those positive feelings again."

Creating an enriched play environment can really benefit children and doesn't have to cost a fortune. In a study in which rats were given a stimulating play atmosphere that included lots of climbing tubes, running wheels, and social interaction, the rats grew an extra 50,000 brain cells in each side of the hippocampus (the area of the brain responsible for memory and learning) after only two months. This study suggests the importance of having play materials available for your child. They don't have to be expensive, they don't have to be new, and they should not be electronic (see page 231 for more information). Simple, inexpensive toys like measuring cups, cardboard boxes, open-weave scarves, homemade sock puppets, balls, musical instruments,

Why Blocks Rock!

A study printed in the *Archives of Pediatrics & Adolescent Medicine* found that playing with blocks may improve language development. The study participants were 175 families with children between the ages of eighteen and thirty months. Half of the families received a free set of building blocks and a booklet about ways for toddlers to play with the blocks, whereas the other families did not get the free building blocks. At the end of the six-month study, the parents completed a questionnaire in which they rated their child's language skills. The language skills of the children who got the free building blocks at the beginning of the study were rated 15% higher.

Want some cool blocks of your own? Check out Uncle Goose blocks, which come in fourteen languages, including English, sign language, and Braille. The company also sells theme blocks that include nursery rhymes, bugs, and presidents. The blocks are made in America with lightweight wood and nontoxic inks. (For more information on Uncle Goose, go to www.lindenwoodinc.com.)

crayons, and paper help create an enriched play environment. In a study of 130 children, researchers found that the availability of play materials was one of the most consistent predictors of intelligence.

Coping in the Sandbox: The Emotional Benefits of Play

In addition to providing developmental benefits, play promotes children's emotional and social growth, giving them valuable opportunities:

1. Play allows children to experiment with being the boss. Throughout their day kids are told what to do: "It's time to take a nap," "Don't throw your carrots on the floor," "It's time to put your pee in the potty," "Now we are going to the doctor." During play, children get to experience what it feels like to be in charge and gain a sense of mastery. They get to pretend to be the Mommy, the Daddy, the doctor—the person in control. They get to have the experience of putting the baby down for a nap or giving the shot, which helps them assimilate the experience of being helpless and gives them a sense of what it feels like to be powerful and competent. Furthermore, they can repeat these experiences over and over again as much as they want.

2. Play allows children to assimilate emotional experiences. Pretend play, in particular, helps children integrate emotional experiences they need to work through. It allows them to express the things that they may not be sophisticated enough to talk about with adults. As much as we try, we cannot completely protect our children from pain, suffering, and loss. Even if your child never experiences a trauma, the separation created by naptime, a mean child on the playground, or an unexpected trip to the emergency room leaves plenty for children to work through in play. Play allows children to create meaning from challenging experiences and conquer adversity. Shortly after 9/11, quite a few children in my practice saw the footage of airplanes crashing into the World Trade Center towers on the news. Traumatized by the footage, many of them flew their toy airplanes into their own miniature buildings over and over again for months after the event. Some parents might be frightened of this type of play, but it is completely healthy and normal. This is the way children assimilate information.

3. Play reduces stress. "What stress?" you may wonder. Sure your child gets to take naps, eats snacks, and play for most of the day, but childhood is stressful. It involves learning social rules, controlling impulses, doing what adults say, coping with separations, and mastering new skills. Play can reduce stress and anxiety. Researchers found that children who played more on their first day of preschool had much less anxiety about the transition. In another study, children were divided into three groups. They were all shown a stressful movie scene. One group was allowed to play before watching, one was allowed to play after watching, and the third was not allowed to play at all. The two groups that were allowed to play showed less stress and anxiety compared with the "no play" group.

4. Play allows children to voice difficult feelings. Powerful feelings, especially negative ones like anger, jealousy, and fear, can be overwhelming for children. Play provides a voice and a healthy outlet for the expression of those negative and overwhelming feelings. It is important for parents to give children the room to explore those difficult feelings. Two-and-a-half-year-old Jamie was not happy about the arrival of her baby brother, Hank. While playing, she repeatedly put her baby doll in the trash, saying, "Bye-bye Hank!" to her mother. A less insightful mom might have said, "We don't put babies in the trash!" or "You don't really hate Hank!" but instead Jamie's mother said, "I see that you really don't want to share me with Hank." Giving Jamie the room to act out her anger in play reduces the likelihood of her acting it out in real life.

5. Play allows children to develop private speech. Private speech is language spoken to oneself for communication, self-guidance, and self-regulation of behavior. This self-talk is particularly significant from age two through age five and accounts for 20 to 60 percent of preschoolers' utterances. It has been found that the more children interact with adults, the more they internalize their messages, which become part of their private speech. Experts believe that the use of private speech signifies that children are taking over the support provided by others and using it to guide and control their own thinking and behavior. Children who use private speech have been found to perform better on challenging tasks. A study of preschoolers found that those who were judged by their teachers to be good at regulating emotion used more private speech than their less emotionally regulated classmates.

6. Play helps children experience flow. Psychologist Mihaly Csikszentmihalyi coined the term "flow" to describe the experience of total concentration on, or complete absorption in, the activity at hand. During flow a person loses all sense of time, is completely unselfconscious, and is totally absorbed in the activity to the extent that she loses all sense of self. This utterly focused, enjoyable state lets the participant *be* completely in the moment. Children experience this state of mind during play, allowing stresses, anxieties, and concerns to drift away.

Too Much and Not Enough

Two of the biggest issues for kids today are at the opposite ends of the spectrum and might seem to be a contradiction: too many toys and not enough play.

Experts believe that lack of play can lead to depression, hostility, and aggressive behavior in children. Among other things, kids need downtime to:

- decompress
- assimilate new things they have learned
- renew their energy
- master new skills
- gravitate toward activities they enjoy
- have quiet time
- be creative
- work through the day's experiences

Because depriving children of play would be unethical, the only studies that have been done on the subject have used animals. When rats with damage to the frontal lobe (the part of the brain that has been linked to attention and self-control) were allowed to play, some of the damage spontaneously repaired itself. Rats that were not allowed to play, on the other hand, experienced serious delays in the brain's development.

While a wide *variety* of toys is crucial to children's development, children do not need to have hundreds of toys. Now that toys are mass-marketed and often inexpensive, there is a tendency to buy and give too many to children. Toys that used to be given for special occasions—birthdays and holidays—are now provided year-round regardless of how little or how much money one has to spend. This abundance makes the toys themselves less special and prevents children from forming attachments with their playthings. According to Dr. David Elkind, author of *The Power of Play*, "the sheer number of toys owned by contemporary children weakens the power of playthings to engage children in dramatic thinking. Abundance, like familiarity, breeds contempt."

Because of this overabundance, the current generation of children has a tendency not to value toys in the same way previous generations did. Today's kids, overwhelmed and overstimulated, often go from toy to toy without completely exploring any of them. As Elkind points out, these toys are used for amusement and distraction and not imaginative inspiration. It is not until a child has spent time with one particular toy that she can "weave it into a story tapestry of her own invention."

In many visits to children for in-home consultations (as well as in the homes of my own children's playmates), I've found rooms that look more like toy stores than bedrooms and living rooms that parents have given over to their children's mounds of toys. Well-meaning parents are under more pressure than ever to buy stuff, especially those so-called educational toys, for their kids. Many parents worry that their children will be at a disadvantage if they don't purchase the latest microchipped toy that claims to teach very young kids Swahili and promises to get them to put their clothes in the hamper. But I believe, as Elkind does, that huge disadvantages come with excess: overabundance creates a consumer mentality, lessens the value of any given toy, and impairs creativity.

Parents feel tremendous pressure to buy what Elkind refers to as "fad toys"—spin-offs of movies and television shows that often become a means of social acceptance for children, create a falsely elevated self-esteem, and can be used against other children whose parents are either less able or less interested in purchasing such items. These toys are nothing but schemes to promote a brand and create loyal consumers from birth. Advertisers now spend an estimated $12 billion each year marketing products to kids in order to create what the business calls "cradle-to-grave consumers." It can be a challenge to find diapers, toothbrushes, and even underwear for children that don't have a commercialized character on them. These items, along with toys, are where consumerism begins for children today. Buying those commercialized toys is not personally engaging for the child; their purpose is solely to promote the brand, not the development of the individual child.

The ABCs and 1-2-3s of Play

In order for a child to be ready and available for play, she must experience certain things first. In *The Roots and Fruits of Pretending*, Dr. Marilyn Segal says that the following three things provide the foundation for meaningful play:

1. a secure attachment
2. a developmentally appropriate environment
3. nurturing, interactive adults

These three things—which all parents, regardless of income or education, have the ability to provide—create the motive, opportunity, and safety necessary for a child to fully engage in play.

If "play is the work of children," how do you know if a child is working or playing? Researchers Catherine Garvey and Kenneth Rubin define the five elements of play this way:

1. It must be pleasurable and enjoyable. Quite simply put, play should be fun.
2. It should not have any extrinsic goals. It should be done simply for the sake of fun, not to gain specific skills.
3. It must be spontaneous and voluntary. It must be freely chosen by the player. In a study in which a kindergarten teacher assigned her students a play activity, the students thought it was work; when they initiated the same activity themselves, however, they described it as play.
4. It must involve active engagement. The player has to be actively involved, not passively watching on the sidelines.

5. It contains a level of make-believe. The child is pretending or working with objects or materials in a nonliteral way—for example, building a sand castle.

As children mature, their social play changes and develops. Babies start out engaging in *solitary play*—for example, watching a mobile or playing with a toy truck. This stage of play begins in infancy and extends through toddlerhood. Next children *parallel play,* playing side by side and occasionally noticing each other, but not always. This is particularly evident during the toddler years. Then comes associative play, starting in toddlerhood and extending through preschool age, when children play side by side and occasionally incorporate aspects of their playmate's play. This is followed by *cooperative play,* when children work and play together to create an activity or make a product. This advanced stage of play generally begins in the preschool years. Children don't complete one stage and then start another. They keep adding on. For example, a child who is able to play cooperatively may choose to play alone or experience parallel play.

The Floor...Get Down on It

Playing on the floor with your child, from infancy through the toddler years, is especially important. Being on the floor literally puts you on your child's level and allows you to see the world from her perspective, read her facial and body cues more easily, and, just as important, show her that you care. One time, when I was sitting on the floor with my then-toddler-daughters, one of them came over to me, bent down (she was finally taller than me when I was sitting and she was standing), and looked me in the eye to ask me a question. The care she took to bend down and make eye contact with me made me feel important and even nurtured by her. Providing that same experience for a child is a great gift.

There are two types of floor time that are particularly important to integrate into your child's experience.

TUMMY TIME

Since the implementation of the national "Back to Sleep" campaign in 1994, which recommends that parents put their infants to sleep on their backs, the number of deaths from sudden infant death syndrome (SIDS) has been reduced by more than 40 percent. However, there are side effects of back sleeping: weak neck muscles, delayed motor skills, and plagiocephaly (flat head syndrome). In order to prevent these and related problems, parents need to give their children "tummy time."

During tummy time, you place your baby on her tummy to give her the chance to lift her head in order to develop the neck muscles she'll need to use for rolling, crawling, and standing. If you have very hard floors, you can use those padded, solid, square mats that fit together (don't bother with the alphabet mats in which the letters come out; they are cute but will drive you crazy when your baby starts taking out the letters or when they come apart every time you put them away). Donna Holloran, child development expert and founder of the popular Los Angeles based Mommy & Me class BABYGROUP™, recommends the following steps in order to make tummy time a respectful experience for your infant:

1. Lay your baby on her back. When a child is placed directly on the floor face first, it can be overwhelming and unpleasant to see the floor "coming at" her.
2. Tell her, "I'm going to roll you over onto your tummy."
3. Place one hand on your baby's bottom and one hand on her stomach for support as you roll her gently (without lifting her from the floor), first onto her side and then down onto her tummy. Carefully support her arms, making sure they don't get trapped under her body.
4. Be encouraging yet sensitive to her cues. Many babies struggle or grunt while trying to master the skill of lifting their heads up off the floor. Always make sure that your baby is able to lift her head enough to be able to breathe freely.
5. When you are done, let her know what is going to happen next (before you do anything) by saying something along the lines of: "I'm going to roll you onto your back now and we'll have more tummy time again later."

Tummy time is important for infants because it helps them to

- develop both fine and gross motor skills
- practice reaching, pivoting, and scooting—all precursors to crawling
- strengthen the upper body
- prevent "flat head syndrome"
- improve hand use

When your child actually gets to the exciting milestone of crawling, according to Stamm and Spencer, the act of coordinating movement on the right side and the left side of the body activates fibers in the corpus callosum, a structure of the brain that connects the right and left cerebral hemispheres. The better developed these fibers are and the better connected the two hemispheres, the faster the communication will be between the two sides of the brain.

Experts recommend that babies spend at least five minutes a day doing tummy time for every hour they are awake. At first, your baby may protest, out of discomfort and frustration at learning this new and challenging skill, but the sooner you start, the sooner she'll get used to it. There are also a number of other effective ways to do tummy time, especially as your baby's neck muscles get stronger:

- Lie on your back with the baby on her tummy just below your chest. Talk with her or sing. Eventually she will try to pick up her head to see you or even scoot closer.
- Put your tiny infant's chest-down on your forearm, like a football, while holding her securely; this position will allow her to pick up her head and look around.
- Put an unbreakable infant mirror in front of her while she is on the floor to give her motivation to look up.
- Holding onto your baby securely, drape her, tummy down, over a slightly deflated beach ball, stack of pillows, nursing pillow, or rolled-up towel while rocking her gently back and forth.
- While she is on her forearms, dim the lights and shine a flashlight onto the floor in front of her while encouraging her to lift her head and follow the light with her eyes.

FLOOR TIME

Most of a small child's play life takes place on the floor, where she feels most comfortable and stable (and of course this is where her toys live). Getting down on the floor gets you close to her level, creates a sense of equity, and engages her. It is easy for her to talk to you, make eye contact, and play with you when you are there with her. Dr. Stanley I. Greenspan, legendary child psychiatrist and author of *Building Healthy Minds,* says that all children need play time on the floor, with meaningful adults, where they are allowed to be in charge. He recommends that parents impose only two limits: no hurting people and no breaking toys.

Letting your child be the leader during floor time provides these important benefits:

- You get to know your child.
- She learns to engage with others.
- You both enjoy open communication.
- You both enjoy increased closeness.
- She can explore feelings through play.
- She gains an increased sense of confidence.
- She gains an experience of mastery.

Children—especially those two years old and up—spend a lot of their day being bossed around and told what to do. Floor time, when kids are in charge, can give them a sense of power and—sometimes—make them less likely to act out and test limits.

During floor time, let your child be the boss and follow her interests. Even an eight-month-old wants to be in charge of her own play. If your infant is clapping her hands, join her in the clapping. If your toddler is playing with blocks, join the action. If she is painting a picture, follow her suggestions in order to create pictures together. The key is to allow her to lead the play.

Ain't No Mountain High Enough: Raising the Level of Play

Research repeatedly shows that when adults engage in play with children, it raises their level of play. Experts refer to this as scaffolding, because it provides a framework for children to build upon, helping their play become more complex more quickly. Several studies have revealed that when one- to three-year-old children play with their mothers, they engage in twice as much imaginative play. They also engage in much more complex sequences, the themes are more varied, and the activity lasts longer. For example, a child playing alone might just put her baby doll to bed, but when playing with an adult, she might choose to brush the doll's teeth, read her a book, sing a song, and give her a good-night kiss.

When you join your child in play, let her lead; be a sensitive play partner by taking her cues about how much she wants you to be involved. Playing with your child does not mean directing the play. As a matter of fact, a study of mothers playing with their fifteen- to twenty-four-month-old children found that the moms who repeatedly asked questions, gave a lot of directions, and initiated new activities that were unrelated to the child's current play elicited an immature response from their children, exemplified by their merely mouthing, touching, or looking at the toys. The children of mothers who were sensitive play partners, took turns, and were mutually engaged in play had higher levels of pretend play.

Dr. Sue Jenner, author of *The Parent-Child Game,* has repeatedly found that "difficult," poorly behaved children do not participate in enough child-led play with their parents. She reports that when the parents of these children are taught how to let their child lead, the children stop their challenging behavior. According to Dr. Margot Sunderland, author of *The Science of Parenting,* child-led play activates opioids in the brain, which reduce stress, and also sends a message to the child that her ideas are valuable and that she can impact her environment, which in turn, increases self-esteem. On the other hand, when parents dominate their child's play, it can reduce dopamine levels in the brain and activate stress chemicals that trigger a rage response. Parent-dominated play restricts a child's freedom and sends the message that there is a right and a wrong way to play. Worse yet, it damages the emotional connection between parent and child, making it more likely that the child will either lose interest in playing or shut down emotionally to comply with the parent.

CHILD-LED PLAY

Parents' Approach	Example
Ask to join the play.	"What would you like me to do?"
Describe what your child is doing.	"I see you're putting the giraffe in the car."
Use effective praise (see Chapter 1).	"You piled the blocks so high!"
Use noninvasive touch.	Gently putting a hand on your child's back for a second to connect and show affection.
Build on your child's creative play.	"Is the giraffe washing his hair in the bathtub?"

ADULT-DOMINATED PLAY

Parents' Approach	Example
Give instructions.	"Now put the red block over here."
Make corrections.	"Giraffes don't go in bathtubs."
Give commands.	"Do it like this."
Give criticisms	"Don't be so messy."
Instruct and give lessons.	"You drew it wrong; cars have four wheels, not three. Draw another wheel."
Use negative touch.	Grabbing a child's wrist while saying, "Don't get paint on the table."
Interrupt.	Talking over your child.

Parents should always focus on process over product, making the play the focus over the completed art project or lessons learned. This type of sensitive interaction helps children develop both verbally and socially, fostering abilities that will help them communicate and cooperate with their peers later in life.

All Work and No Variety in Play Makes Jack a Dull Boy

As children get older, they need more well-rounded play. I see too many parents whose children only take structured classes or only play at the park, for example. It is also easy to let your child play with the same playmates every time (especially if there is an available sibling) or simply play by herself. But children need variety and balance in their play, a need that becomes more important as they get older.

These days, the most common mistake parents make is to sign their kids up for too many structured classes—some kids take classes seven days a week! Classes can be wonderful, but too much structure doesn't allow a child the breathing time she needs. On the other end of the spectrum, if a child is eighteen months old and has not already taken a class, I recommend enrolling in one so she can benefit from group socialization, new experiences, and a little bit of structure to lay the groundwork so preschool will not be as jolting. There are so many Mommy & Me groups, music classes, and gym-based classes for toddlers out there. Children can participate in these classes with their parents or other caregivers.

Here are a few types of play that children should have the opportunity to experience, although I'm not suggesting that your child should do *all* these activities every day or even every week. My point is merely that it's good for kids to try all different kinds of play. Also, keep in mind that not all types of play are appropriate for all ages; for example, you can't expect your six-month-old to participate in sociodramatic play.

- Free play
- Structured play (a class, for example)
- Solitary play
- One-on-one play with a friend
- Group play
- Indoor play
- Outdoor play
- Tactile play (play involving appropriate touch like "This Little Piggy")
- Physical play (riding a tricycle, throwing a ball, etc.)

FROM THE EXPERTS . . .

Sharing

To a toddler, the whole world, and everything in it, is "MINE!" Toddlers take what they want; they show it to you; and if they give it to you, they usually want it right back. This is how a toddler practices giving and taking, and learns to hold on tight. It's how a toddler learns that what she gives away she'll get back—or maybe not. It's how a toddler learns about now, and a moment in the future. A toddler needs a lot of practice with this. She also needs patience from her parents while she grasps and practices the concept of SHARING and TAKING TURNS! This takes time . . . a lot of time.

Sit in a room filled with toddlers and their parents, and within just a few minutes, you'll hear a parent bellow, "Share!" and children yelling, "MINE!" What can a parent do? Stay close by and offer suggestions if your toddler is struggling over a toy: "Jack, it looks look Mollie wants a turn when you are finished!" "Mollie, can you tell Jack, 'take a turn.'" "Jack, can you help Mollie find another truck?" "Mollie, I can help you wait for your turn." And, sometimes, it's just helpful to let them yell "MINE!" "MINE!" as long as no one is getting hurt. Most of the time these verbal struggles end up with the children running off to play side by side, or with one another. And, when it doesn't, parents can be there to offer comfort. And, this all takes time . . . a lot of time.

Parents: Stay calm and focused. Talk to your child, offer choices, and provide support and encouragement. Most of all, share something of your own: "I will share my drink with you." "Can I have a sip of your drink . . . we are sharing a drink!" "It's my turn, and then it will be your turn . . . we are taking turns . . . we are sharing!" Think about what you want to teach your child to learn about sharing. Again, this takes time. But isn't that true of everything that's good?

—Donna Holloran, founder of BABYGROUP™
and creator of the DVDs

Babygroup: 0–6 Months—Surviving and Thriving During Your Baby's First 6 Months!
Babygroup: 6–12 Months—Surviving and Thriving During Your Baby's Second 6 Months!
www.babygroup.ME

Dr. Jenn's Toy Hit List

"Active toys make for passive children."

—CHARLOTTE TO MIRANDA,
while picking toys for Miranda's baby shower registry, SEX AND THE CITY

Charlotte was onto something. The more a toy does for a child, the less the child needs to do. We want our children to engage with their toys because that is how they learn and grow, not by passively pushing a button. It is not the toy, but the way a child interacts with it that determines if the toy is a success. Good toys contribute to the interactive process, encourage imagination, and promote exploration. Bad toys encourage a child to be a passive recipient of what the toy does, limit creative possibilities, promote aggressive behavior, send negative messages, and even prevent proper physical development. Here are a few toys on my hit list that should definitely sleep with the fishes:

1. Walkers. Walkers are particularly dangerous. In 1999, an estimated 8,800 children younger than fifteen months were treated in hospital emergency departments in the United States for injuries associated with infant walkers; there may be as many as ten times more injuries that are treated in pediatricians' offices or do not require medical attention. Thirty-four deaths caused by infant walkers were reported from 1973 through 1998. According to parent reports, as many as 40 percent of infants who use walkers experience a related injury. The most common serious—and in some cases fatal—injuries are broken limbs and concussions from rolling down the stairs; drowning, when a child falls into a pool or bathtub in a walker; burns—for example, from stoves—because walkers allow children to reach high enough to touch a burner; and poisoning, because, once again, walkers make it easy for a child to reach cleaning fluids and other hazards they wouldn't normally be able to reach. As a result, the American Medical Association has tried to ban walkers.

Because babies can get around in walkers, the urge to move across the floor is satisfied and they are less motivated to try to crawl, creep, or scoot, all of which are important for developing strength and coordination. These contraptions can also inhibit walking. In a study of 109 infants, where half of the group had never used a walker, a third used the newest-style walkers, which have large trays that block an infant's view of her feet, and the remainder used older-style walkers, which allowed the infant to grab objects and see her feet as the moved, it was found that the children who used the newest-style walkers sat upright, crawled, and walked later than infants who had never used a walker. Doctors and physical therapists warn that walkers can delay walking because they foster bad posture and weakened back and stomach muscles.

2. Exersaucers. These contraptions allow very small children to sit in an upright position before their muscles are ready. As a result, babies hyperextend their backs and push their stomachs out and forward when they use exersaucers, which causes swayback. Much like the newer walkers, exersaucers prevent children from seeing their feet; according to Dr. Suzanne Dixon, a pediatric developmental-behavioral health specialist, "this lack of visual feedback hinders kids' learning from their own movements." The other problem with exersaucers is that they trap children in one position and limit their play choices (which should be numerous and varied) to merely pushing buttons, an unsatisfactory play experience that gives small children very little stimulation. While the use of exersaucers may seem freeing to parents, it greatly limits children's ability to learn valuable skills. According to Dr. Peter Gorski, director of developmental research at Massachusetts General Hospital, walkers and exersaucers are selfish props: "Children learn very actively, so inhibiting their activity to some extent inhibits their learning abilities."

3. Jumpers. These devices have a seat that is suspended by cables that attach to a doorway, enabling a child to jump up and down. Parents have to be very careful that a child using a jumper does not hit her head against the doorway because it is very difficult for a child to control the motion of her body when it is strapped into one of these toys. In the book *Pediatric Physical Therapy,* Emilie J. Aubert notes that even limited use of jumpers may lead to problems with the hips and ankles. Other physical therapists report that jumpers cause a baby to push off the ground using her toes, which promotes the overuse and shortening of calf muscles, which can lead to toe walking and severe muscle tightness in later years.

4. Construction toy kits. There is a new trend in the toy market. More and more toy companies are making construction toys that provide pictures and instructions, along with a photograph, of how the toy is "supposed" to be built. The implication is that there is a right and a wrong way to build from blocks or Legos or whatever the building material happens to be. The problem here is that kids are robbed of the creative process. In effect, the manufacturers' approach to these toys promotes rigid thinking instead of giving children leeway to come up with their own creative ideas. According to Dr. Susan Linn, author of *The Case for Make Believe,* "If children are, from birth, provided mostly with kits and electronic or media-based toys they won't have a chance to learn how to enjoy or even approach challenges that call for imagination, experimentation, inventiveness, or creative problem solving."

5. Electronic toys, especially "learning toys." More and more top-selling toys on the market—at least 75 percent of them, according to some experts—have electronic components. These toys are active and teach children to be reactive or, worse yet, passive. They teach kids to let the toy lead them in their play; they prevent kids from using their own imaginations or truly learning about the interactive process of play, which teaches problem solving and spontaneity. Sitting and pushing a button over and over again, even if that button is emblazoned with a letter or a number, doesn't teach kids anything. Children learn the alphabet from meaningful interactions with adults who are excited about using the ABCs, not from pushing a button.

The multibillion-dollar educational toy industry is less interested in what promotes child development and more interested in profits. It sells toys that claim to teach isolated facts to children as soon as they are old enough to push a button, but completely overlook the fact that a child's own interests and interactions are what create self-direction and learning. These marketers sell false hope to anxious parents who want to make sure their child is keeping up with the button-presser next door. These toys teach children to look for guidance and answers from computers, not from experience or even from people. But we know that the greatest teachers are those who are insightful observers of their students. This is a basic tenet of adult instruction, but it is paramount in teaching babies, whose behavior is our most helpful cue to their interests and talents, given their limited communication abilities.

Dolls with programmed electronic responses deprive a child of the opportunity to give the doll her own voice, an essential ingredient in the creative process. Every preprogrammed response negates a child's vision of who she had hoped that doll would become. In my observation, once a child hears that a doll has a preprogrammed persona, it is unlikely that she will give it any properties of her own. Young children tend to be rule followers in this way, because they don't want to be "wrong" in their play.

Children tend to get bored with electronic and "learning" toys as soon as they've figured them out. Kids then want another toy. This constant need for new toys hinders children from developing an attention span (not to mention promoting consumerism). As a result, a shortened attention span can make more traditional play seem boring to a child who is overstimulated by electronic toys. In an article in *Child Magazine* called "Hi-Tech Toys: How Are They Really Affecting Your Child," it was noted that experts fear that these "smart" toys may actually be dumbing down our children's play, stunting their intellectual growth, stifling creativity, shortening their attention span, and undermining their relationships.

6. Commercialized toys. When you buy your child a toy or doll modeled on a well-known, commercialized character, the brand dictates the play, not the child. The doll takes on the attributes that Nickelodeon or Disney wants it to, not the ones your child dreams up. When your child plays with a doll like Elmo Live, which speaks, moves, tells stories, sings songs, plays games, and acts like he is getting tickled, your child is deprived of the chance to make the doll do activities that she makes up herself. On the other hand, if your child doesn't know that the doll is named Elmo and is unfamiliar with its given attributes, she is free to teach the doll to dance on her own terms and invent her own play scenarios.

Children who play with commercialized toys, especially those that are modeled on television characters, bypass their own creative impulses and invariably stick to the same prescribed plots and personalities that the original creators gave the toy. At the same time, the children become "friends" with the commercialized characters, who then become familiar, safe, and even comforting, thus creating loyalty to the brand—often before kids are even old enough to sit up unattended. With each character toy we buy for our children, we further indoctrinate them into the consumer culture, training them to value consumption. The big corporations are counting on us to hand over our children so they can be trained to become insatiable consumers.

Questions to Ask before a Playdate

Playdates allow kids unstructured time in which to play with other kids, develop social skills, and get exposed to new ways of playing. Before a playdate at your house, ask your child if there are any toys she does not want to share so they can be put out of sight in order to avoid conflicts. Ask your guests if they have any food or pet allergies; discuss in advance whether you plan to eat together. During your child's first three years, you probably won't be dropping her off for a playdate elsewhere, except perhaps at a very close relative's house, but as you move closer to that big milestone you should get ready to ask your hosts some uncomfortable questions in order to protect your child.

1. Is there a swimming pool at the house? If so, is it gated, netted, or alarmed?

2. Are there any guns in the house? If so, how and where are they stored?

3. Are there any cleaning solutions or medications kept where children could potentially reach them?

4. What other adults will be in the house at the time of the playdate (this includes a repair person, plumber, etc.)?

5. What activities will the children be doing? Clarify that you do not want your child watching television, playing video games, or spending time on the

computer during playdates. You should also make sure the playdate host is not planning to take your child someplace you don't want her to go.

6. Who will be monitoring the kids?

These questions can be extremely difficult to ask, but there is nothing more important than keeping your child safe.

Ten Questions to Ask Before You Buy Another Toy

Even for adults, both bricks-and-mortar and online toy stores can be very seductive, especially since so many new toys are inexpensive, available (literally 24/7, if you buy online), and beautifully packaged. Advertisers are clearly marketing to both parents and kids. It's also clear that they saturate the market and overhype some toys, while many great toys never get the publicity they deserve. Before you buy yet another toy, ask yourself a few questions:

1. *How does this toy balance my child's toy collection?* If your child has a dozen baby dolls, she may be better off getting a ball or a truck she likes instead.

2. *How long can I expect this toy to last?* Always look for durable, well-made toys.

3. *Is this toy safe and age-appropriate?* Keep in mind that the age suggestions on toys are usually based on safety issues like choking hazards, not on a child's intelligence. Make sure toys have been safety-tested. Products that contain the mark of an independent, third-party product safety and certification organization, such as Underwriters Laboratories (UL), have been tested for safety. Make sure that any toy you buy does not have components that could present a choking or strangulation hazard or contain toxic materials.

4. *What message is this toy sending my child?* If you buy your daughter a purse that comes with a wallet and plastic credit card, you may be teaching her more about becoming a little consumer than about what it's like to be a grown woman.

5. *What activities will this toy inspire?* A box of wooden fruit might inspire your child to count or to pretend to shop at the supermarket and make dinner for the family, while a toy water gun is likely to inspire aggressive behavior and start fights with siblings.

6. *How long is this toy likely to keep my child busy?* You should aim for toys that are likely to engage your child for more than a few moments, allowing her to increase her attention span.

What does this toy teach my child about gender roles? If you buy the toy kitchen for your daughter and the trucks for your son, you send a message about gender roles. Let your son play with kitchens, baby dolls, and strollers; let your daughter play with trucks and cars and throw a ball. These opportunities create more well-rounded kids.

8. *What will my child learn from this toy?* Your child doesn't have to learn something academic from every toy, but all children learn bits and pieces about how the world works from their toys. For example, when children bang on pots and pans, they learn how they can affect things and how to make different kinds of sounds.

9. *Is this a social toy or a solitary toy?* Either one is fine but you do want to have a balance of the two. Understanding how your child uses her toys, whether she likes to play with a particular toy alone or interactively with a friend, can make for better playdates and will help you to have easier interactions with your child.

10. *Is this toy fun?* While it is always nice if a toy is fun for you—because it will inspire greater connection between you and your child—it is more important that your child enjoys it!

Great Websites for Toys

Ape to Zebra, www.Ape2Zebra.com

Back to Basics Toys,
   www.BacktobasicsToys.com

Beyond Play, www.beyondplay.com

Dr. Toy, www.DrToy.com

eBeanstalk, www.eBeanstalk.com

Environments, www.eichild.com

Lakeshore Learning,
   www.LakeshoreLearning.com

Maple Landmark,
   www.maplelandmark.com

Melissa & Doug,
   www.melissaanddoug.com

Mookla, www.Mookla.com

Nova Natural,
   www.novanatural.com

Nuno Organics,
   www.nunoorganic.com

Oompa Toys, www.Oompa.com

Plan Toys, www.PlanToys.com

The Little Seed,
   www.TheLittleSeed.com

Uncle Goose,
   www.lindenwoodinc.com

Wooden Wagon,
   www.WoodenWagon.com

Just Tell Me What Toys I Should Get!

Play is to early childhood what gas is to a car.

—Drs. Kathy Hirsh-Pasek, Roberta Michnick Golinkoff, & Diane Eyer,
*Einstein Never Used Flash Cards: How Our Children Really Learn—
and Why They Need to Play More and Memorize Less*

I am a firm believer that children don't need tons of toys, especially when so many of the store-bought variety are no better than home versions, like sock puppets, pots and pans, Tupperware—or, just as likely, the box that the expensive toy came in. Nevertheless, parents constantly ask me which toys they should get for their kids. The chart below should give you a sense of what is going on with your children at different ages and stages and which toys might be age-appropriate for their mental and emotional development. I am not suggesting that you buy all the toys mentioned below, even if you can afford to. My intention is to give you a preview of what your child might enjoy, depending on where she is developmentally. You should always check the safety of any toy you buy and never leave your child alone with a toy that she could choke on or hurt herself with. Even a simple stuffed animal can have plastic eyes or a nose that could become a choking hazard. As you can probably guess, I consider books the best toys money can buy.

DR. JENN'S RECOMMENDED TOYS AND GAMES
FROM BIRTH TO AGE THREE

Age	Your Child's Significant Developments	Toys
Birth to three months	• Starts to learn to visually track objects • Newborn can see only eight to fourteen inches in front of her face • Most babies are attracted to faces • High-contrast patterns are easiest for babies to see	• Baby mirrors • Bubbles • Activity mats with hanging toys • Small soft balls • Baby Whoozits • Links • Play mats • Rattles • Mobiles • Sock and wrist rattles

Age	Your Child's Significant Developments	Toys
Three to six months	• Able to grasp objects • Likes to pick things up • Learns to sit up • Puts everything in her mouth • Often starts to push up on hands and knees at around five months • New teeth start to break through and teething begins	• Mobiles • Skwishes • Winkels • Oballs • Small maracas • Open-weave scarves • Finger puppets • Soft stuffed animals • Squeaky toys • Teething rings • Links • Household items like plastic bowls and wooden spoons • Wooden blocks and soft blocks • Baby-friendly toy cars
Six to nine months	• Starts to understand object permanence, the idea that things exist even when the baby cannot see them • Begins feeling separation anxiety • Develops a pincer grasp • Starts to crawl	• Small balls • Peek-a-boo balls • Plush trucks • Four-wheeled push toys • Crinkle toys • Animal or people figurines • Fabric tunnels
Nine to twelve months	• Able to bang objects together • Very mobile: creeps, crawls, walks with the aid of furniture • Interested in using objects as tools • Enjoys interactive games with adults • Increased problem-solving skills	• Stacking and sorting toys • Nesting toys (cups) • Toy food • Sandbox toys (bucket, shovel, etc.) • Extra-large Lego-type building blocks • Shape-sorting toys • Balls that can bounce • Toy telephones • Soft baby dolls
Twelve to eighteen months	• Stronger fine motor skills • Learning cause and effect • Very active and mobile	• Blocks • Puppets • Sorting toys • Push toys

Age	Your Child's Significant Developments	Toys
Twelve to eighteen months *Continued*	• Has better hand coordination and is able to hold a crayon, paintbrush, or writing utensil well enough to scribble • Stranger anxiety often peaks around fifteen months	• Pull toys • Hammering toys • Large wooden peg puzzles • Bug box for observing insects • Wagon • Music toys • Sandbox • Finger paints • Nontoxic crayons and paper • Toy tool bench • Toy kitchen • Toy animal and people figurines (nonchokable) • Dolls with removable dresses and accessories • Ball pit (small ones are available for home use) • Padded rocking horse for toddlers
Eighteen to twenty-four months	• Able to recognize herself in the mirror and in photos • Asserts her will (get ready for power struggles!) • Able to imitate grown-up behavior • Has more refined fine motor skills • Asserts independence (expect to hear lots of "I can do it myself!")	• Toy versions of grown-up objects: phones, purses, wallets, keys, etc. • Unbreakable tea sets • Dolls, strollers, bottles • Doctor's kits, tool kits • Tricycle • Nontoxic crayons and markers, paper, glue sticks • Stickers • Water or sand table • Bead mazes • Trains • Cars • Nontoxic play dough • Sit n' Spin or Spin Around • Etch-a-Sketch® or Doodle Pro™ • Large magnet letters • Letter trains • Potty training dolls

Age	Your Child's Significant Developments	Toys
Two to three years (and up)	• Develops symbolic play, or using objects in a way that is different from the intended purpose of the object • Is very verbal • Faces many conflicts due to her new-found abilities and is frustrated when she needs help • Improved memory skills • Knows many colors and letters and can count to ten • Can get dressed and brush her own teeth by age three • Can walk run, jump, and balance on one leg • Imaginary play gets much more complex • Has lots of tantrums • Is "ritualistic," i.e., likes things to be put in the same place in the same way	• Tricycle • Dress-up clothes • Matching games • Doll house and dolls • Toy gardening set • Ant farm • Arts and crafts supplies • Train sets • Kids basketball hoop and ball • Kid-size brooms, dust pans, and vacuum cleaners • More advanced puzzles • Basic board games like Candyland and Concentration (age three and up) • Easels • Bean bags • Lacing beads (large size) • Small, child-friendly tent for a clubhouse • Kaleidoscopes • Child-friendly magnifying glasses • Sidewalk chalk • Stickers • Pipe cleaners • Stamps and nontoxic ink • Eye Spy Bags® • Magna Tiles ®

Thinking Outside the Box

Screen Time

In the interest of full disclosure, there are a few things I need to admit. The first is that, prior to the birth of my children, I was a bit of a television addict. I know that is a lot like being "sort of pregnant," but I don't think I realized how out of hand I had let my TV viewing become. I would wake up, turn on the news, catch the morning shows, and leave the TV on until I walked out the door. I even found myself listening to television in the car on my way to the office thanks to satellite radio. When I arrived back at home, I would grab the remote again and watch shows for hours. By and large, the television was on from the moment I woke up until the moment I went to sleep, except when I was seeing clients or writing. When my husband and I moved into our house, he suggested that we not put a television in the bedroom. I was horrified at the notion, but willing to consider it, until I found a beautiful armoire for our bedroom, in which our old television fit perfectly. In retrospect, my husband's suggestion was right on for many reasons, but having become accustomed to having a TV in my bedroom, I was not ready to make such a dramatic move.

This leads me to confession number two: I grew up with a television in my bedroom. Apparently, when I was a very young child, I developed the habit of rising at 5:30 in the morning and waking my poor parents, hoping they were ready to play. In a moment of desperation my otherwise highly insightful mother thought that putting a TV in my room might buy my parents a few hours of desperately needed sleep.

In this chapter I will tell you why this was a bad move and why allowing your child to have a television in his bedroom is exponentially more destructive today than it was during my childhood.

I have always considered myself fairly liberal about exposing children to media. That was until the fall of 2004, when my editor at *Los Angeles Family Magazine* asked me to write my "Dr. Jenn" column about children and television. As I researched the subject, I was shocked by what I discovered. World-renowned pediatrician and child-care expert Dr. Benjamin Spock writes, "Of all the media, television has the most pervasive influence on children," and modern-day pediatric guru Dr. T. Berry Brazelton refers to media as "the biggest competitor for our children's hearts and minds." While these positions may sound extreme, these experts are not being dramatic.

What I have learned since writing that original article, and subsequently perusing volumes of research, led me to the decision not to expose my children to *any* TV, computer, or video time *at all* (not even in the background) during the first three years of their lives. Needless to say, as a result, my husband and I have dramatically changed our own viewing habits. I hope that, after you read this chapter, you will make the same choice for your children. In fact, it may be one of the best things you can do to directly impact your child's physical, social, mental, and emotional development.

Despite my strong views on television, it has been a challenge for my husband and me to stick to our decision. We are constantly tested by friends and relatives and often face logistical difficulties if a television is on wherever we happen to be, but we've managed to make it work. There were plenty of times, though, when we both recognized how easy it would have been to put our kids in front of the tube—especially when they were screaming infants struggling with severe reflux and colic; when I needed to get work done (like writing this book!); at the end of the day, when I was exhausted and my daughters had dropped their last nap; when I was alone with them and needed to make dinner; when they got sick; and when I was just jonesing for some TV entertainment. Despite all those tempting reasons, I am proud to say that I never once turned on the TV. I felt so strongly about what I'd learned from my research that I was able to keep my commitment to my family and myself. This chapter will tell you why it is a worthy endeavor and how you can do it too.

Educational, My Tushy!

Despite the American Academy of Pediatrics' highly publicized recommendation that children under the age of two watch no television, many parents still choose to turn on the TV for their infants and toddlers. It has been reported that, by the age of three months, 40 percent of babies are regular viewers of DVDs, videos, or TV; by the time they are two years old, almost 90 percent of all kids in the United States are spending two to three hours each day in front of the screen. The most recent Nielsen numbers revealed that television usage by children has reached an eight-year high with children ages two to five watching an average of more than thirty-two hours each week—more than four and a half hours a day. And 51 percent of families leave the television on most or all of the time, even when no one is watching, effectively making television a constant background noise for those children.

Often, the parents of very young children are seduced into buying what have become known as "edutainment" or "infantainment" DVDs, like the Baby Einstein and Brainy Baby series. The DVDs claim to "give your child a learning advantage," "help develop cognitive skills and spatial reasoning," "foster the development of your toddler's speech and language," and my favorite, "create dedicated neurons in the auditory cortex, resulting in greater brain capacity." Perhaps it is this slick marketing material or maybe it's peer pressure from other parents, who have bought into the genre's false claims, or anxiety that their baby won't get the same "advantage," that convinces tired parents, desperate to believe anything that will allow them to get a break long enough to take a shower, to buy the stuff.

In August 2007, fans of these best-selling DVDs received a rude awakening when the *Journal of Pediatrics* released a damning study indicating that, for every hour per day that babies eight to sixteen months old were shown infantainment DVDs, they knew six to eight fewer words than other children. According to Dr. Dimitri Christakis, one of the study's researchers and also the coauthor of *The Elephant in the Living Room,* "children whose parents read to them or told them stories had larger vocabularies." Experts have long known that children benefit most from meaningful interaction with adults. When children view videos, they are passive recipients of information and are not truly engaged. Parents who want their children to have large vocabularies and to excel in their studies are best served by engaging their children regularly through reading and speaking with them.

TV's quick scene-changes (every four seconds), disconnected images, and incoherent subject matter are confusing to young children who can't follow the content and don't have the cognitive skills to create a narrative for the images. According to Christakis, "For them, it isn't a day at the farm at all; it's just a series of stimuli coming at them full throttle. They will sit in front of the 30-minute feature not because they are interested in the content but because they are biologically programmed not to look away."

On May 1, 2006, the advocacy group Campaign for a Commercial-Free Childhood (CCFC) filed a formal complaint with the U.S. Federal Trade Commission accusing the makers of Baby Einstein and Brainy Baby, two of the leading producers of videos for infants and toddlers, of "false and deceptive marketing." As a result, Baby Einstein (a subsidiary of the Walt Disney Company) has completely redesigned its website; it is no longer making educational claims about its DVDs or videos, and it has offered refunds to customers who purchased the videos. According to Dr. Susan Linn, the cofounder of CCFC, "Not only is there no evidence that baby videos do any of the things the baby video industry claims they do, but these media may actually be undermining the development of the very skills they claim to foster."

What gets baby's neurons all lit up are real-life experiences: the feel of grass under his feet, the sound of Mommy's voice, cold finger paint on his hands, and the smell of the family dog after a swim. Babies need to touch, smell, hear, and see to learn. There are no shortcuts. Allowing infants to watch images on a screen will create lifelong viewing habits. The American Academy of Pediatrics found that TV habits, which have their roots early in life, tend to persist. Two-year-olds who are heavy TV watchers are two and a half times more likely to become excessive television viewers by the age of six. According to Linn, "By targeting babies, media companies are marketing not just programs and characters but lifelong habits, values, and behaviors."

How TV Pushes Your Kid's Buttons: Fourteen Viewing Risks for Children

1. Attention deficit disorder. In a study of 1,354 children published in *Pediatrics* in April 2004, it was found that for every hour of television watched per day, at age one and age three, children had almost a 10 percent higher chance of developing attention problems that could be diagnosed as attention deficit hyperactive disorder (ADHD) by age seven. A toddler watching two hours a day would be approximately 20 percent more likely to have attention problems, and a baby watching three hours of infant television daily would have nearly a 30 percent higher chance of having attention problems in school. The researchers hypothesize that exposing a baby to the quick-changing images of modern television may overstimulate his developing brain, causing permanent changes in the developing neural pathways.

A more recent study, also published in *Pediatrics,* examined the long-term effects of the childhood viewing habits of 1,037 kids. The study was based on parents' and teachers' reports, as well as children's self-examinations, of attention problems at age thirteen and fifteen. What the researchers found was that childhood viewing was associated with attention problems in adolescence, even after other conditions and circumstances that might be influencers, such as gender, attention problems in childhood, cognitive abilities, and socioeconomic status, had been ruled out. The researchers concluded not only that television viewing might contribute to the development of attention problems, but that "the effects may be long lasting" as well.

Interactions in the real world teach children how to focus—unlike television, which robs kids of the opportunity to practice how to concentrate. A child, held captive by the screen, has no control over the constantly changing images, a model that actually "rewards" the distracted child with even more stimulating new images. The point is that parents who are able to follow their children's interests and language are best able to assist their child's learning. Television does the opposite; watching television does not follow a child's interest and is completely out of his control.

2. Autism. In a controversial study titled "Does Television Cause Autism?" Cornell University researchers discovered what appears to be a statistically significant relationship between autism rates and television watching by children under the age of 3. In examining the rates of autism, they found that as cable television became common in California and Pennsylvania, beginning around 1980, childhood autism rose more in the areas that had cable TV than in the areas that did not. They also found that the more time toddlers spent in front of the television (based on assumptions related to rain, snow, and television subscription rates), the more likely they were to exhibit symptoms of autism disorders.

While autism is believed to be biologically based, the study points to a significant correlation between rising autism rates and more frequent television viewing. According to researcher Dr. Michael Waldman, "We are not saying we have found the cause of autism, we're saying we have found a critical piece of evidence." Because autism rates are increasing broadly across the country as well as in every income and ethnic group, it seems logical to conclude that the trigger is something that children are exposed to across the board. Or, perhaps, for a child who is particularly vulnerable to autism for whatever reasons, television may be a factor in exacerbating symptoms. In my opinion, it is worth avoiding television exposure in the early, more vulnerable, years until more definitive research is available. Some DVDs are believed to help children who are "on the spectrum," but, because much of this information is anecdotal, I believe it is still best to reserve television viewing for your children until after the age of three.

3. Asthma. Children who watch more than two hours per day of television are twice as likely to develop asthma as those who watch less, according to a British study of over 3,000 children who were monitored from birth through age eleven and a half. "Breathing patterns associated with sedentary behavior could lead to developmental changes in the lungs," explains Dr. Andrea Sherriff, one of the researchers from the study. Greg Smith, chief executive officer of The Asthma Foundation in New South Wales, says the current generation of children has become captive to "the screen." He further encourages parents to keep their children active from an early age and recommends that parents of asthmatic children work with their pediatrician to help their kids develop an active lifestyle.

4. High blood pressure. In a study of inactivity and blood pressure published in the *Archives of Pediatric and Adolescent Medicine,* researchers who studied 111 children ages 3 to 8 and found that of all the forms of inactivity they examined, television-viewing was the worst. It was linked to significantly higher blood pressure in children — the more TV kids watched, the higher their blood pressure — and this held true regardless of whether a child was heavy or at a healthy weight. Kids watching from 90 to 330 minutes of television each day had blood-pressure readings (both systolic and diastolic) that were five to seven points higher than those of children watching less than half an hour of television a day. According to Dr. Joey Eisenmann, a kinesiologist at Michigan State University and one of the study's co-authors, "These results show that sedentary behavior, and more specifically television-viewing, is related to blood pressure independent of body fat or obesity level." In previous studies involving the same group of children, whom he and the other scientists have been studying for four years, about 20% of the children had developed prehypertension or hypertension.

5. Poor sleep. In a study of over 2,000 children under the age of three, researchers found that the number of hours that babies watched television was associated with irregular nap and bedtime schedules, which, as parents know, lead to poor quality sleep. Another study of over 500 children found that the more television a child viewed, the more likely he was to resist going to bed, to have difficulty falling asleep and trouble staying asleep, to be afraid to sleep, and to wake up

FROM THE EXPERTS . . .

The Other Screen: Kids and Computers

Many parents have been sold on the claim that computers help toddlers and even infants learn language and math skills. There's no evidence to support such claims. On the contrary, many child development experts believe that excessive computer use can stunt physical and social development during the critical early years.

Human beings, and especially young children, learn best through physical experience, by literally touching the world around them, manipulating it, making it their own. Neurologist Frank Wilson explains in his book *The Hand* how a huge part of the human brain is linked to the hand. Children experience hands-on kinds of learning most deeply.

The computer limits hands-on learning and real play. The content may seem educational, but moving and clicking a mouse or poking a screen is

during the night. The sleep problems created by TV viewing in childhood often persist throughout adolescence and into adulthood. This troubling reality was confirmed by study results that showed that watching three or more hours of television per day during childhood more than doubled the chances of a child having sleep problems in adulthood.

The lack of sleep associated with TV viewing has been linked to a number of health problems. Screen time lowers the body's level of the hormone melatonin, which develops the immune system, regulates circadian rhythm and sleep cycles, controls hormone levels, and helps learning and memory, among many other important bodily functions. It is even believed that a lowered melatonin level may be one of the factors contributing to the early onset of puberty in girls as young as eight and nine. Furthermore, scientists at the University of Florence in Italy found that when children were deprived of television, computers, and video games, their melatonin production increased by an average of 30 percent.

6. Poor eyesight. Mom wasn't wrong when she said, "Stop staring at the TV or it will hurt your eyes." The long periods of fixed attention required by viewers are now believed to be a significant cause of an increase in myopia, which in extreme cases can lead to blindness. A review of forty studies, printed in the *American Journal of Human Genetics,* ruled out genetics and pointed to lifestyle factors,

a far cry from the grasping, stroking, reaching, digging, running, balancing, throwing, catching, and yes, even tasting, through which young children learn about the world around them. Compared with the real world, the computer is a pale and lifeless teacher. Robust play stimulates the mind, strengthens the body, and develops social skills and emotional maturity. Too many toddlers are growing up today deprived of this kind of play.

While computers teach young children little of value, they do convey deep lessons. They teach children to pay less attention to people—parents and peers—and more attention to machines. They alter a child's social development. Today many business managers complain that their young employees do not have the "soft skills" that are essential for working with others. They can communicate through the medium of the machine but they lack face-to-face social skills. We have made a cold screen the child's first teacher, and the lifelong lessons are profound, though unintended.

—Joan Almon and Ed Miller, co-founders, Alliance for Childhood,
and authors of *Crisis in the Kindergarten: Why Children Need to Play in School*
www.allianceforchildhood.org

specifically television, as the cause for the dramatic increases in shortsighted-ness. Researchers found that countries where children watched more television had higher rates of myopia. In Singapore, for example, 80 percent of eighteen-year-old men recruited for the army are shortsighted, compared with only 25 percent just thirty years ago.

Many eye specialists believe that television and video games are responsible for damaging children's visual development and are a major cause of impairing children's reading and learning abilities. These visual problems are believed to make it more difficult for kids to read books and carry out tasks as simple as adjusting their eyes as they look from the desk to the blackboard.

Parents should limit TV and computer usage, especially in children under the age of six, whose sight is still developing. According to Professor Andrea Thau, speaking for the American Optometric Association, children need appro-priate visual stimulation for sight to develop normally. Dr. Keith Holland, a leading specialist in children's eye problems, and his team have examined the eyes of 12,500 children in the past decade and report a dramatic increase in problems linked to screen exposure. According to Dr. Holland, "Humans are not designed to look at a flat screen for long periods and this is especially the case for children or infants, whose vision is developing, and we believe visual skills are being damaged." Holland further reports that he is seeing a growing number of ten-year-olds with the eye-focusing skills equivalent to a person of fifty, and teenagers with the immature eye movements of a three-year-old child. Caroline Hurst, chair of the British Association of Behavioral Optometrists, concludes, "Staring at a two-dimensional screen instead of going outside to play in the three-dimensional world gives children a non-functioning distorted visual system."

Children who have trouble focusing their eyes on a book or a blackboard are unlikely to succeed in school. As a matter of fact, one study performed by Holland and his team found that eighteen of twenty-one children expelled from school had undiagnosed sight problems.

7. Academic problems. The American Academy of Child and Adolescent Psy-chiatry states that children who watch a lot of television are likely to have lower grades in school and read fewer books. The American Academy of Pediatrics, which adamantly states that children should not watch *any* screen until after the first two years, still recommends no more than ten hours of TV per week after the age of two. This recommendation is based on research that examined the rela-tionship between TV viewing and learning in a group of over 87,000 children in four countries. Researchers found that ten is the magic number of TV-watching hours per week at which academic scores started to decline for school age kids

We know that children in homes where the TV is on all the time are less likely to be able to read by the age of six and that children who have televisions in their bedrooms have the worst scores on school achievement tests. Aric Sigman, author of *Remotely Controlled,* hypothesizes that "along with television viewing displacing educational and play activities, it is suspected this harm may be due to the visual and auditory output from the television actually damaging the child's rapidly developing brain."

A study by Drs. Dimitri Christakis and Fredrick Zimmerman—which examined the effects of television viewing on reading and math outcomes at age six and also looked at children younger than three and between the ages of three and five—found that children who watched television before the age of three had worse scores on tests of reading and math ability at age six. The children who watched little or no television had the best scores in reading and math, regardless of their viewing habits from age three to five. The magnitude of the impact of TV viewing on kids under the age of three is comparable to the effects of a mother's low IQ on her child. The dramatic results of this study led Drs. Christakis and Zimmerman to recommend that parents not allow their children to watch any television prior to the age of three.

8. Depression. A child's early years create the habits and set the tone for his television use in the future. While it may be hard to imagine your young child as a teenager, a recent study about teens, television, and depression is worth paying attention to. This study of over 4,000 teenagers found that those who watched TV were more likely to report symptoms of depression, with the rate increasing 8 percent with every additional hour of TV viewing. That's a pretty significant increase, especially since researchers excluded teenagers who reported symptoms of depression at the beginning of the study, which also revealed that most teenagers watch three to four hours of TV a day. Dr. Margot Sunderland, author of *The Science of Parenting,* believes that sitting in front of the television creates lower levels of dopamine in the brain, resulting in a lack of motivation, drive, and creative thinking. She says, "It is hard to activate a drive for life in adulthood if it has not been awakened in childhood."

One of the things that creates self-esteem is the experience of mastery. The sense of accomplishment a child gets when he works hard to do something—roll over for the first time, throw a ball, or complete a puzzle—creates a sense of self-efficacy. Television is antithetical to experience of mastery. There is no "aha" experience in television. There is no sense that you can make a difference or effect change when you sit passively in front of the set. This dynamic contributes to depression as well.

9. Displaced activities. "Suppose there wasn't any TV—what do you think your child would do with the time now spent watching TV?" This insightful question was actually asked of a large group of mothers in 1972, long before children were sitting in front of the television for four and a half hours a day—or more than six and a half hours if you include DVDs and video games. The results, which were published in the surgeon general's *Report on Television and Social Behavior,* revealed that 90 percent of mothers answered that their child would be *playing* in one way or another if he were not watching TV. (See Chapter 9 for information about why play is so crucial to child development.)

It is simple math. There are only so many hours in the day and the hours spent in front of the television cannot go to other pursuits. A 2006 study called "Time Well Spent? Relating Use to Children's Free-Time Activities" found that television watching is displacing three other activities for the average child: it reduces time spent with parents and siblings as well time spent partaking in creative play. This was especially significant for children under the age of five. For older children, ages seven through twelve, it also reduced time doing homework.

10. Drop in creativity. Once upon a time there was a town in British Columbia that could not get TV reception because it was situated in a remote valley. In 1973 the town elders convinced the Canadian Broadcasting Corporation to install a transmitter just for them. Fortunately for curious types like us, Tannis MacBeth Williams, a professor of sociology at the University of British Columbia in Vancouver, heard about the installation and decided to investigate the effects of television by studying the town before and after TV arrived. It is extremely rare for a researcher to have the opportunity to examine such a large number of subjects who have never been touched by the golden box. Williams arrived at the place she code-named "Notel" with her research staff and tested the adults and children in their last moments of pre-television purity to see how they scored in creativity, among other things. She returned two years later to retest everyone and compare the results.

Prior to the introduction of television, the Notel children tested significantly higher in creativity than children in other towns. Researchers used a test called Alternate Uses, where kids are given five objects (a magazine, a knife, a shoe, a button, and a key) and asked to write down all the different uses they can think of for them. There's no time limit. The researchers tested grades four and seven both times and grades six and nine in Phase Two (as part of the longitudinal study). Interestingly, there was little correlation between IQ and creativity. The researchers also looked at creativity through the lens of "original ideas" as opposed to sheer number of ideas. Still, the drop in creativity scores in those two years—nearly 40 percent—was dramatic.

In the book *Baby Read Aloud Basics,* authors Caroline Blakemore and Barbara Weston Ramirez note that "as teachers, we see a number of children who cannot pretend; these children often have less vocabulary and have watched too much television. Imagination allows us to imagine our future and plan what we will do with our lives." I hear their sentiments echoed whenever I speak to educators and child therapists. In her book *The Case for Make Believe,* author and child play expert Dr. Susan Linn describes a similar scenario. "The children I see at the day-care center often begin our sessions by picking up animals or little people figures and reenacting the exact same cartoon violence so popular on television, bringing nothing of their unique experience to their play."

In an English study of creative writing, a group of more than 400 children between the ages of ten and twelve were asked to write short stories about a "face at the window." Many children just copied plot lines straight from television. The researchers concluded, "the ubiquity and ease of access to television and videos perhaps robs today's children of the need to pursue their own thoughts and devise their own occupations, distracting them from inner processes and constantly demanding responses to external agendas, and suggests that this may have implications for the development of imaginative capacity." This does not bode well for our children's future or, ironically, for the creative future of television writers.

11. Aggression and violence. In a Joint Statement on the Impact of Entertainment Violence on Children from the Congressional Public Health Summit, six of America's most prominent medical groups (American Academy of Pediatrics, American Academy of Child and Adolescent Psychiatry, American Psychological Association, American Medical Association, American Academy of Family Physicians, and American Psychiatric Association) stated that after thirty years of research, it was determined that "viewing entertainment violence can lead to increases in aggressive attitudes, values and behavior, particularly in children." The medical groups determined four ways that viewing violence on television is likely to affect children. According to this statement, children who view violent TV become

1. more likely to exhibit violent and aggressive behavior
2. more likely to view violence as an effective way of settling conflicts
3. emotionally desensitized toward violence in real life
4. fearful of becoming victims of violence

Going back to Notel for a moment can shed some light on the issue. When television was brought to this previously media-free zone, the single greatest effect was increased aggression among children. The second graders studied were found to be twice as aggressive toward each other (as measured by acts of pushing or taunting) after TV was introduced. While the most aggressive acts were committed by just a few kids, the overall level rose for all children, regardless of gender. Kids who were not aggressive before TV increased as much as kids who were. The change was so dramatic that researchers wondered if there had been some change in playground policy in the two years, but the schools all had the same principals, and they all had the same basic policy: intervene only if it looks like someone will get hurt.

Another study of preschoolers and cartoons found equally disturbing results. A group of preschoolers with comparable styles of play were divided into two groups. One group watched nonviolent cartoons and the other watched cartoons that contained violence. After several weeks of exposure, the children watching violent cartoons were kicking, choking, or hitting their classmates more often than the kids from the nonviolent cartoon group.

12. Fear. Bambi's mother is shot and killed by a hunter. In *The Lion King*, Simba's father is murdered by his own brother (Simba's uncle). Nemo's mother gets eaten by a barracuda. These are supposed to be movies for children? How is playing on a child's fears of separation and abandonment appropriate for children? It is not, especially for young children.

Dr. Joanne Cantor, an internationally recognized expert on children and television and author of *Mommy, I'm Scared!*, refers to movies and television as

FROM THE EXPERTS...

Too Many Screens in the Lives of Too Many Children

While I was eating at a favorite diner a while ago I watched two families—each consisting of two parents and a toddler—cope very differently with the challenges of eating out with children at that stage of development where their delight in active exploration supersedes their delight in anything else—including eating.

One family came equipped with a bright red portable DVD player. Throughout the meal their son was immersed in *Thomas the Tank Engine*, a highly regarded television program for preschoolers. He was completely silent and oblivious to his surroundings, and absentmindedly chewed on the morsels of food his mom fed him from her fork. His parents were able to enjoy their meal uninterrupted. They were even able to carry on an extended conversation, an admittedly rare experience for parents of very young children.

The other parents had a less peaceful meal. After their toddler reached the limit of his tolerance for being confined in a high chair, his parents took turns walking him around, rather than distracting him from the urge to explore the sights and sounds of the restaurant. Clutching a plastic spoon, he spent several minutes with his nose pressed against a case of fancifully

"the number one preventable cause of nightmares and anxieties in children." In fact, most children have been frightened, sometimes very seriously, by something they have seen on TV. A random sampling of parents in Madison, Wisconsin, whose children were in kindergarten through the sixth grade, found that 43 percent of those parents reported that their children had been frightened by something on television and that the fear had outlasted the program. These fears can raise a child's level of anxiety and increase nightmares. In a survey of 150 college students, 90 percent reported experiencing a fear reaction from media during childhood. These students reported trouble sleeping and eating after watching shows, and over a quarter of the respondents said the effects lasted for more than a year. The younger the respondents were when they viewed a scary movie and TV program, the longer-lasting the effects.

In her book, Dr. Cantor mentions a long list of children's television shows and movies that have resulted in strong fright reactions from children: *Little House*

---

decorated pastries. He made shoveling gestures with his spoon and held it up to his mom. "Are you giving me a taste?" she asked. "Yum!" Laughing, he did it again. "Up," he said, pointing to the top row of cakes. "That's right," his mom said. "The pink cakes are up." "Down!" he chortled, bending his knees a little as he pointed to the bottom row. Holding his mom's hand, he trotted back to their table where he was handed over to his dad, ending up back at the pastry case while his mom finished her dinner. With his parents' help, this toddler's inborn capacity for playful exploration transformed the restaurant into a laboratory for exploring color, spatial concepts, and make-believe.

What about the little boy engrossed in his own portable DVD player? What are the primary life lessons children absorb by regularly watching DVDs while eating in a restaurant? They learn to look to screens rather than to their environment for stimulation; to expect to be entertained rather than entertaining themselves; that interacting with family during meals is so boring that they need the inducement of screen entertainment to get through dinner; and they learn that eating is something to do while you're doing something else.

—Dr. Susan Linn, director of the Campaign for a Commercial-Free Childhood and author of *Consuming Kids: The Hostile Takeover of Childhood* and *The Case for Make Believe: Saving Play in a Commercialized World*
www.commercialfreechildhood.org

[Another version of this piece first appeared in Susan Linn's *The Case for Make Believe: Saving Play in a Commercialized World.*]

on the Prairie, Bambi, Dumbo, Beauty and the Beast, The Hunchback of Notre Dame, Peter Pan, The Wizard of Oz, and *Alice in Wonderland,* to name a few. Finding appropriate movies for young children, even those over the age of three, is incredibly challenging. This is especially true because the movie rating system does not adequately inform parents. A movie that is rated G simply means that the movie does not have any sex or vulgar language. It is also supposed to mean that the movie does not have any violence, but that is not the case. Harvard researchers Fumie Yokota and Kimberly Thompson analyzed every single G-rated movie released between 1939 and 1999, only to find that *every single one* had at least one significant act of violence. Furthermore, the screen time devoted to violence rose from an average of three minutes per movie in 1940 to ten minutes per movie in 2000.

In figuring out if a movie or TV show is appropriate for your child, it is always best to err on the side of caution. One thing to be aware of when making that determination is that preschool children tend to be most influenced by the way things look, even more than they are influenced by whether or not the things are actually dangerous. For example, a young child is likely to be frightened by a movie about a person with deformities, even if the deformed character is kind and gentle, while older children are more likely to respond to situations that are actually dangerous. When trying to figure out if a specific television show or movie will be scary for your child under the age of six, always preview the material yourself with an eye toward the visual images.

13. Addictive quality of viewing. "Television is highly addictive," according to Columbia University professor Dr. Jeffrey Johnson. This is not surprising given that we know viewing results in more viewing: the more babies and toddlers watch TV, the more likely they are to become heavy watchers by the time they reach six years of age. Babies who grow up watching TV become dependent on it to self-soothe and alleviate boredom.

Television conditions children's brains to acclimate to excessive stimulus. This neurological training may prove destructive when a child tries to process stimuli from other, slower-paced sources, like day-to-day life. Television involves frequently changing images and scenarios, high-fidelity sounds, and fast-paced action. This is how TV grabs a young child's interest. Sigman makes the analogy that once you're acclimated to food with the flavor enhancer monosodium glutamate, real food doesn't taste very interesting. "Television is the flavor enhancer of the audiovisual world, providing unnatural levels of sensory stimulation," he says. "Nothing in real life is comparable to this. Television overpays the young child to pay attention to it, and in doing so it seems to physically spoil and damage his attention circuits. In effect, television corrupts the reward system that enables us to pay attention to other things in life."

Keep in mind that when your child watches television, as opposed to a DVD, the TV network is hard at work trying to maintain your little one's interest. Often commercials will show previews for the next show, and even when they don't, a parent who does not reach for the remote control fast enough is likely to have to deal with a child who has already gotten swept up in the next show. Suddenly that scheduled one hour of screen time has turned into two hours or more.

14. Harming family dynamics. Children learn how to socialize by watching our example, both with them and with each other. Mothers model to daughters how to be a mother one day, and fathers model fatherhood to their sons. Socialization starts almost immediately. I was always amazed whenever I watched my daughters talking to their baby dolls and using the same words and sentiments that I had used with them. The future of families is in big trouble when a child's model is an adult glued to the television or, worse yet, when the child is the one whose eyes are transfixed by the screen. Given the excessive number of hours adults spend watching television, experts report that parents now have more eye contact with television characters than with each other! We have to ask ourselves what kind of model this offers our children when it comes to showing them what an intimate relationship looks like.

I recently watched an episode of *The Oprah Winfrey Show* (yes, I still do watch some television, but only when my kids are sleeping) called "What Can't You Live Without?" in which Oprah challenged families to give up technology and spend time together—as a family—for seven days. The show featured a family that was so disconnected that its members hardly spoke to each other. Each member of the family watched television, emailed on their computer, or played a video game in a different room of the house. When they needed to communicate, they actually text messaged each other. When the father brought home dinner, he dropped the food on the table and everyone in the family took his or her food to a separate room to eat. In the car, the kids were too busy text messaging their friends or listening to their iPods to have an actual conversation.

While this is an extreme example of disconnection, more and more families are functioning like the family on *Oprah*. For them, media and technology had become a replacement for family interaction, and their connections, as a family, suffered. Children need to develop relationship skills, and the place they first learn the craft of verbal interaction is at home. Television can decrease communication between members of a family, as we've seen, and stunt the development of family relationships. If you are wondering why a book presumably focused on the first three years of life is taking such an in-depth look at a family with tween and teen kids, it's because I believe this family serves as a cautionary tale. As you make decisions about your family's early media habits, you can fashion your own philosophy not just about media but family life as well.

Tele-Chubbies: Four Ways Television Is Making Kids Fat

The prevalence of obesity among children aged six to eleven has more than doubled in the past twenty years, going from 6.5 percent to 17 percent, while the rates among adolescents more than tripled, increasing from 5 percent to 17.6 percent, according to the Centers for Disease Control. Overweight children are at a higher risk for health problems such as high cholesterol, high blood pressure, joint problems, sleep apnea, heart disease, type 2 diabetes, stroke, several types of cancer, and osteoarthritis. As the amount of media created and marketed to young children has mushroomed, so has the weight of toddlers and preschoolers. In just the last four years, the number of overweight children aged two to five has increased from 10 percent to 14 percent. According to a National Institutes of Health study, children who are overweight at age two are more likely to be overweight throughout childhood.

Experts warn that this may be the first generation of children who are outlived by their own parents. At an American Medical Association press briefing, Dr. William Dietz, director of the Division of Nutrition and Physical Activity, reported that six out of ten children today have a risk factor for heart disease by the time they are ten years old. "The more TV children view, the more likely they are to be overweight," he says. "Reduction in TV viewing constitutes the single most effective way for children to lose weight." A shocking study of the impact of television viewing that followed children from birth through adolescence reported that television viewing is the single biggest predictor of childhood obesity, even more so than nutritional intake or physical activity.

1. Inactivity. Obviously, when a child is sitting in front of the television, he is forgoing other, more physical activities. Some experts believe that television viewing is not necessarily replacing physical activity, arguing that viewing primarily displaces other sedentary activities. But we know that we have a generation of young children who are disturbingly sedentary. A study published in the *Lancet* revealed that three- to five-year-old children do not move for 80 percent of the day and that many are active for a total of only twenty minutes each day. When these children's activity statistics and patterns were shown to another group of researchers who were asked to profile the participants, they mistakenly assumed that the subjects were desk-bound office workers. Their conclusion was that the subjects of the study had the lifestyles of middle-aged adults and were likely to suffer from serious health risks.

A study of almost eight thousand adolescents printed in the *Journal of Adolescent Health* found that lack of physical activity is more strongly linked with TV watching than with any other type of sedentary activity including computer use, video game playing, and reading. It also revealed that children who watch TV for more than six hours a week are much more likely to be physically inactive. According to Dr. John Dwyer, a specialist in physical activity promotion and one of the study's authors, "This research confirms a universal suspicion: the more television kids watch, the less energy they expend on physical activity."

It seems apparent that reducing a child's television use will result in weight loss. Almost 200 third and fourth graders received an eighteen-lesson, six-month classroom curriculum to reduce television, videotape, and video game use. The results showed that the children who participated experienced "statistically significant relative decreases in body mass index"; in other words, they lost weight.

2. Metabolism. It is not just the fact that children are sedentary that makes them more likely to become overweight while they watch TV: television viewing actually slows down metabolic rates. A landmark study printed in *Pediatrics* shows that while viewing TV, normal-weight children experience a 12 percent decline in metabolic rates and obese children experience a 16 percent decline. The resting metabolic rate of the children in the study was so reduced that they were actually burning fewer calories watching TV than they would be if they were lying down, doing nothing. Furthermore, this slowed metabolic rate continued to some extent for twenty-five minutes after the TV was turned off.

3. Tuning out the body's signals. Eating in front of the television makes people less likely to obey their body's signals and more likely to overeat. Approximately 53 percent of children under the age of six eat at least one meal or snack while watching television. An article in the *Journal of the American Dietetic Association* revealed that the average person eats eight times more food while watching television. This is not surprising since a brain that is distracted by an entertaining show (or anything else that's distracting) is unlikely to take notice of what the mouth is doing. When we are watching the screen, it is even harder to pay attention to the body's signals of satiety.

A study of college students that examined the effects of television viewing on consumption found that, on days when the students watched a lot of television, they ate more meals, consumed more calories, and were less hungry before eating than on other days. Sigman notes that television has subliminal effects on appetite that literally cause diners to take more bites per minute, take larger mouthfuls, and eat more food. The results of these studies are applicable to both adults and children, as was discovered in the study "Television Viewing Is Associated with Increased Meal Frequency in Humans."

4. Influencing food preferences. More than 70 percent of Saturday morning commercials are about food, and 80 percent of those are about foods that are low in nutritional value. These ads obviously don't help children make healthy food choices. Young children don't understand how commercials work. For them, the television is the authority and they simply believe what they are being told.

Children trust the characters they see on TV. A study of nine- and ten-year-old children found that kids actually believe that Ronald McDonald knows what is best for children to eat. So influential are the TV characters that their mere association with a food can change a child's preference. In a study done by Sesame Workshop, children were shown a picture of broccoli and a picture of a chocolate bar and asked which they would like to eat. Of the participants, 22 percent voted for broccoli and 78 percent voted for the chocolate. When the researchers attached a picture of Elmo to the broccoli and an unknown character to the chocolate bar, the desire for chocolate dropped, while the desire for broccoli shot up 50 percent. When Elmo was attached to the chocolate, 89 percent of the children chose it.

Study after study shows that television negatively influences people, children included, regarding food choices.

- People who watch a lot of TV are more likely to rate unhealthy foods as being "good for you."
- The more children watch television commercials, the more likely they are to eat sugary cereal.
- The more TV kids view, the less likely it is that they will consume fruits, vegetables, and whole-grain cereals.

Buy, Baby, Buy: How Advertisers Influence Your Child's Thinking

We worry about so many dangers to our children—drugs, perverts, bullies—but seldom notice the biggest menace of all: the multibillion-dollar marketing effort aimed at turning the kids into oversexed, status-obsessed, attention-deficient little consumers.

—Barbara Ehrenreich,
Nickel and Dimed: On (Not) Getting By in America

Children, even the very young, have more purchasing power than ever before. In 2002 children ages four to twelve were responsible for $30 billion in purchases. This is a 400 percent increase from the decade before. It's estimated that six- to twelve-year-olds visit stores two to three times per week and on average put six items in the shopping cart each visit. Children also influence their parents' purchases, and we're not just talking cereal, but big-ticket items like cars, vacations, and even homes. It is estimated that children influence an additional $200 billion a year in spending. None of this is lost on advertisers, who are aggressively marketing to your child in ways that are unprecedented.

Children are now considered the epicenter of American consumer culture; their tastes and opinions shape marketing and brand strategies. According to one of the world's leading brand strategists, 80 percent of all brands now require a children's marketing strategy. These marketers have been very successful at their job of influencing children. According to research:

- The average American child sees 40,000 commercials a year.
- The average American child makes 3,000 requests for products and services in any given year.
- Two-thirds of mothers report that their children were "brand aware" by age three, and one-third reported this awareness by age two.
- Most kindergartners can identify 300 logos.
- The average ten-year-old knows 400 brands.

Clearly, marketing is fundamentally altering the experience of childhood. According to Juliet Schor, author of *Born to Buy,* "Corporations have infiltrated the core activities and institutions of childhood, with virtually no resistance from government or parents." Those television characters, even the "educational" ones, are being used to manipulate your child to influence you to buy everything from toothbrushes to diapers to clothing, even food and home decor. Electronic media—computer games for babies, electronic toys, and DVDs—are slowly replacing play and human interaction. Advertising has even hit the schools with McLibraries, Coca Cola vending machines, and milk cartons sporting ads. Before the CCFC stepped in, BusRadio, a corporate-sponsored TV newscast and commercialized radio, was being played on school buses where children were captive audiences every single school day. Schor says, "We have become a nation that places a lower priority on teaching its children how to thrive

The Nag Factor

Marketing professionals are coming after our children determined to teach them how to nag starting at an early age. A landmark marketing research study called "The Nag Factor" taught industry professionals the effectiveness of nagging and identified parents of young children as being most likely to give in to it. Industry professionals estimate children's nagging accounts for 46 percent of sales in key businesses that target children. Knowing that marketing executives are working day and night to undermine their authority, parents have to work that much harder to set limits.

socially, intellectually, even spiritually, than it does on training them to consume. The long-term consequences of this development are ominous."

It may seem benign when your eighteen-month-old points to a diaper and says "Sponge Bob!" or your two-year-old requests a McDonalds "Bratz-Pack" (don't even get me started on Bratz dolls!) or your three-year-old insists on wearing Dora the Explorer sneakers. But in that moment, know that your child is officially a cog in the consumerism machine. There is nothing wrong with a request for a toy or pair of shoes—I can appreciate a designer label as much as the next person—but it is disconcerting that children are now caught in a marketing web, where the diapers promote a TV show, which promotes a bottled beverage, which promotes a toy that promotes a lifestyle . . . and suddenly the brand is teaching your child values and associating its product with your child's self-worth. Studies show that American children believe that their clothes and brands describe who they are and define their social status more than children in any other country. Children's focus on consumer culture has been linked to depression, anxiety, poor self-esteem, psychosomatic complaints, and increased conflict with parents.

What's That Constant Buzzing in My Ears?

I turn the TV on while I am breastfeeding.

• • •

*I like to watch the morning news at breakfast
and when I have it on my child doesn't even notice.*

• • •

*Having the TV on while I play dolls with my child
helps me get through the monotony of kid games.*

It has been estimated that as many as 51 percent of homes in the United States have the television on most or all of the time. While such constant exposure may seem harmless, it has the potential to be extremely damaging to children on many levels. Here are just five reasons why TV background noise is bad for your child:

1. Inner speech. The constant noise and distraction of TV can prevent a child from developing "inner speech"—an inner voice—that is particularly important for kids in order for them to learn problem solving, both personally and academically. Inner speech develops as a child learns language and the process of creating internal dialogue. Inner speech is believed to strengthen what is referred to as executive functions, which are largely responsible for tasks such as planning, cognitive flexibility, abstract thinking, rule acquisition, initiating appropriate actions, and inhibiting inappropriate actions. Inner speech helps a child to remember specific things ("I am supposed to wash my hands after I use the potty"), plan ahead ("I better put dolly away before Ashley comes because I don't want her playing with it"), and work out steps in solving a problem ("When I put the puzzle piece here, it doesn't fit. If I put it there it might work better"). As children get older, they need inner language in order to sort out their thoughts and listen to others. Having the TV on prevents children from experiencing the kind of quiet needed to develop this crucial skill.

2. Decrease in quality and quantity of play. Researcher Dr. Marie Evans Schmidt studied fifty mothers and their one-, two-, and three-year-olds in her laboratory, where there was a simply furnished room with toys, magazines, and, of course, a television. The mothers were instructed not to initiate play with their children but instead to let them play on their own. For thirty minutes of the experiment, the television show *Jeopardy* was on and for another thirty minutes the television was off. Hidden cameras recorded everything. When the television was on, there was a pronounced decrease in the length of play episodes. The play duration of a one-year-old, whose play averaged eighty seconds, was reduced to less than sixty seconds during the period of background noise.

3. Reduced interactivity with parents. Another study, which focused on parent interaction, used a similar model, except the researchers told the moms to act the way they would at home and gave them freedom to choose a program from a group of prerecorded shows. On average, when the TV wasn't on, the parents were actively engaged with their kids 66 percent of the time, but once the TV was on, that number dropped to 54 percent. When the TV was off, 74 percent of their play was active, compared to 59 percent when it was on. One mom in the study was engaged 78 percent of the time without TV, but that engagement dropped to only 19 percent once the show was on. We know that parental engagement—speaking, listening, and following a child's interests—is one of the greatest gifts parents can give when it comes to their child's cognitive and emotional development.

4. Reduced language learning. Because infants have a difficult time differentiating between sounds, the background noise that television creates is particularly detrimental to language development. In a study of word recognition in the presence of background speech, it was discovered that a seven-month-old infant was not able to distinguish words he was familiar with against the background noise. In this study, a woman used key, familiar words while a monotone male voice spoke in the background. Unless the female voice was at least 10 decibels higher than the male voice, the child did not understand the familiar words. When experimenters attempted to teach toddlers new words in the presence of white noise, the children could not differentiate between "b" sounds and "ch" sounds at the end of a word, were unable to learn new words, and could not retain new words they had been taught under these conditions. Researchers concluded that the background noise not only prevented the children from hearing the different sounds in the words, but also actually prevented them from being able to pay attention and retain what they learned.

It shouldn't be a surprise to hear that television, as background noise, greatly reduces the number of words spoken by parents to children. Dr. Christakis's newest study on the subject revealed that children heard 770 fewer words from adults per additional hour of television exposure. This is more than an 80 percent decrease in language and is pretty much a guarantee of reduced language acquisition for the child, who, according to this study, utters fewer words to parents as well. According to Dr. Christakis, "Television actually reduces the number of language sounds and words babies hear, vocalize and therefore learn."

Opening Pandora's Box: Programming for kids over the age of 3

Thanks to the work of researchers, we know a lot more about the effects of specific TV shows. The following is a list of programs that are recommended by children's media experts and/or have tested well in research studies of kids over the age of three. Granted, none of them tested positively in 100 percent of the studies, so you'll have to use your best judgment with your own kids and see what works for you. The first six titles are some of the most frequently studied programs and therefore the most often mentioned by media experts. The rest are added in alphabetical order. Please note two of my personal favorites: *Signing Time!* and *The Wonder Pets*.

- *Sesame Street* (especially after 2001)
- *Dora the Explorer*
- *Mister Rogers' Neighborhood*
- *Barney & Friends*
- *Blue's Clues*
- *Arthur*
- *Animal Jam*
- *The Berenstain Bears*
- *Between the Lions*
- *Clifford the Red Dog*
- *The Doodlebops*
- *Dragon Tales*
- *Franklin*
- *Go Diego Go*
- *Higglytown Heroes*
- *It's a Big Big World*
- *The Magic School Bus*
- *Miss Spider*
- *Peep in the Big Wide World*
- *Signing Time!*
- *Timothy Goes to School*
- *The Wiggles*
- *The Wonder Pets*

5. Access to inappropriate content. When TV is on in the background, children are more likely to witness something they are not ready to see. News programs are always in the list of top ten shows that frighten children. As a matter of fact, a 1994 study of parents with children in kindergarten through sixth grade found that 37 percent of the parents reported that their children had been frightened by a news story that year. This is particularly true in the post 9/11 world we live in. You never know when a frightening story or image may appear on your TV set.

Taking Back the Remote Control

Small children have not changed over the centuries. They have always shown the same indefatigable energy, curiosity, irrationality, persistence, emotional instability, and unpredictability during their first five years of life that they exhaust us with today. It is mainly how parents deal with these difficult, though normal, aspects of development that has changed.

—MARIE WINN,
The Plug-In Drug: Television, Computers and Family Life

I am a vegetarian. For decades, I have lived my life as if meat does not exist. Eating meat is simply not an option for me. I don't feel deprived; to be honest, I don't think about eating meat at all. My attitude toward television has been very similar in that way. Once I made a decision not to expose my children to TV in their first three years, changing my mind simply wasn't an option. In many ways, it is easier never to turn on the television. Flipping that switch is like opening Pandora's box. Once you start, it's hard to regulate how much your children watch—and it's all too easy to turn on the TV in moments of need.

Before television became a universal fixture, parents somehow managed to make dinner, take care of their children, take a shower, and attend to household tasks. Parent's expectations of their children were very different and the way they parented was different, which was, in many ways, both good and bad. Parents of yesteryear expected their children to learn how to play alone and occupy themselves when they were very young. Parents went out of their way to help their children learn tasks that might occupy them long enough to allow the grown-ups to get dinner on the table and were invested in holding onto the nap for as long as possible for the same reason. I can tell you from both personal and clinical experience that if you teach your child to enjoy solitary play from the start, your life without TV will be much easier. Your child will also benefit tremendously. The television-free babies I see in my practice have longer attention spans and need less stimulation to remain interested.

It is never a good idea to leave a child unattended in front of a television set. "Would you entrust you toddler to the care of a baby sitter, even for a few minutes, who cannot hear or see your child?" asks Dr. Nancy Hall of Yale University's Bush Center in Child Development and Social Policy. I know one mom who came out of her shower only to find that her toddler, whom she had left in front of the television set in her bedroom, had taken a black crayon and drawn all over the bedroom walls. And this mom was lucky. The Consumer Product Safety Commission reports between 8,000 and 10,000 injuries every year from falling televisions and, of these, six on average result in death. You can never be too safe, and you are always best off if you put your child in a safe, childproof space that does not have a television when you need to get something done.

FROM THE EXPERTS . . .

How One Mom Kept the TV Off

The decision to keep television out of our children's lives was easy. The evidence about its adverse effects on children's development is overwhelming, and my husband and I were determined to give our twins every opportunity to thrive. The execution of our plan was much harder in reality. As a stay-at-home mom, without the benefit of a nanny or family living nearby to help out, it has been incumbent upon me to occupy and entertain my children. Often, I felt like it would be so much easier to stick them in front of the TV, just for short stints, so I could accomplish tasks that otherwise would take much longer or be impossible (e.g., make dinner, throw in a load of laundry, or make a quick phone call). Instead, I found creative, more constructive ways to occupy their time. For example, while I was cooking, the kids sat at the kitchen table with a snack and a coloring book. Since then they have come to love arts and crafts, Play Doh, Legos, and dress up, among other activities. And no matter what activity they are doing, we typically play music in the background so the kids can sing along with their favorite songs. My children are now three years old and are far more interested in interactive playing than in passive TV viewing. We know that eventually TV will be introduced into their lives, but are certain that the creative skills they have cultivated throughout early childhood by avoiding TV will be invaluable for years to come.

— Andrea Lesch Weiss, MSW, and currently a stay-at-home mom

I know that what I am suggesting is not easy, and certainly it is not what most people do. While I believe that it is ideal not to allow your children to watch any TV before the age of three, I know many families will choose to do something different. You may not choose to completely forgo TV, as I have suggested, but with all the information you now know, you can make a conscious, well-informed choice, and that only strengthens your position as a parent.

The following are ten of the most common reasons why parents turn on the TV to keep their children occupied in their first three years, along with alternative solutions that have worked for my family as well as the families with whom I have worked:

1. "I have to turn it on to make dinner." Many parents choose to make meals or at least do the prep work during naptimes. From the beginning, I made sure my children's cribs were a fun place to be—where they got to play by themselves. Often when I made dinner, I would put them in their cribs with safe toys, turn on some fun music, and take the baby monitor with me. Many families have a small baby-gated area off the kitchen where their toddlers can play safely while their parents keep an eye on them. When my kids were toddlers we started to keep boxes of toys and books in the area off the kitchen to keep them busy, and later we added an easel with crayons attached to short strings (to prevent both drawing on walls and the danger of strangulation).

If you can afford some help or if you have hands-on relatives, you may want to take meal time prep into account when you're figuring when it would be most useful to have those extra hands around the house. Mealtime prep can also be a great bonding time for a working parent. While one parent is in the kitchen cooking, the other can spend time with the children. You can also get older kids to help with the cooking, allowing them to do safe kitchen tasks. My husband, who is a great cook, got my kids cooking in the kitchen when they were about two years old. He would do the prep work and then let them do things like crack eggs, stir in spices, and put together a pizza. Involving them in making the food not only made it more likely that they would enjoy eating it, but gave them a sense of pride in their accomplishment as well.

Most kids do best if they have had some one-on-one time with a parent before the parent goes into the kitchen to cook. Also, make sure you don't let your child get too hungry before dinner. An overhungry child is a cranky one and is less likely to have patience while you are in the kitchen. Consider giving a child a small snack if it has been more than two hours since his last snack or meal.

A few other ideas you may want to try, depending on your child's age:

- Put your child in a high chair and roll it up to the counter so he can watch you make dinner while you narrate everything you are doing.

- Keep a kitchen cabinet filled with things your child can play with, like wooden spoons, unbreakable bowls, and safe containers.
- Have a special stash of toys and books that your child gets to play with only when you are cooking in the kitchen.
- Keep a stack of child-friendly magazines and catalogs in the kitchen for your child to look through.
- Play music in the kitchen that your kids love to dance to.
- Have a magnet board or art easel for your child to play with while you cook.

2. "I need a few minutes so I can take a shower." Naptime is a good time for your own personal care. I know one mom who wakes up at 5 a.m. so she can have some time to herself and take a nice long shower. Many parents of young children put a pack 'n' play in the bathroom or use a portable swing to keep their kids in sight.

3. "She loves looking at the screen." What we love isn't always good for us. When I was in college, I loved smoking cigarettes, and if the surgeon general came out with an announcement tomorrow that they are good for you I would be back up to a few packs a day before the week was through. A big part of our job as parents is to protect our children from things that might be damaging to their development. While most parents are not used to thinking of TV in these terms, it is no different.

Many parents think that the fact that their child is staring at the screen means that he is having a meaningful experience, when in fact that is not the case. It is human nature to stare at the screen. The lights and movement catch our attention. Television exploits the orienting response, which is a reflex that draws us to anything that is new or unexpected. The constantly changing themes, flashy graphics, quick cuts, and flashing lights are designed to make a baby look. Your child will sit in front of the screen, not because he is learning or even interested, but because he is biologically programmed to do so.

4. "She won't take a bottle without it." Using the television to get a child to eat teaches him to disconnect from his body's cues while eating. The distraction of the television makes it harder to focus on eating. Turning on the television during bottle time acclimates your child to media exposure during meals, which makes it more likely he'll expect to watch TV during meals as he gets older, which is likely to lead to overeating.

5. "It helps him fall asleep." Watching a lot of television can harm sleep; the more television a child watches, the more likely he is to resist going to bed, have difficulty falling asleep, have trouble staying asleep, be afraid to sleep, and wake up during the night. In fact, starting children on the tube early helps them to develop some very destructive habits. Falling asleep in front of the TV is a habit that usually starts out innocently enough. First a parent gives a child a television in his bedroom, thinking it will ease problems with the bedtime ritual. Soon parents find that their child is watching more TV than ever, delaying bedtime even further. Using television as a sleep aid and having a television set in the bedroom are two of the biggest causes of sleep problems in kids. In fact, researchers have found that watching TV is linked with increased sleepiness during the day.

6. "I don't know what else to do with him while I nurse my new baby." Exposing your infant to the background noise of television is not good for him or for you: getting distracted by the television prevents you from tuning in to your child's cues, which is especially important during a feeding. Instead, try reading a book to your older child while you nurse. This will give both of your children language exposure and keep everyone engaged. If that doesn't work, you may want to stash some special toys nearby and let your older child play with them only when you nurse (this will maintain the novelty of the toys and thus your child's interest in them). Nursing can also be a good time for the other parent to connect with and take care of an older child.

7. "My babysitter or nanny likes to let my child watch." If this is the case, then your babysitter or nanny is not doing her job. Putting a child in front of a television when she is being paid to take care of that child is abdicating her responsibility. It is important that you let your child-care provider know your stance on media viewing. Often care providers aren't aware of the detrimental effects of TV or perhaps they're simply looking after your child in a way that was acceptable to a previous employer. If your child's caregiver turns on the TV for your child despite your wishes, it's time to find a new caregiver. If you used to allow your sitter to watch TV with your kids, make sure you provide a list of other appropriate activities to do instead.

8. "I don't want my child to be a social outcast." While I have not been able to locate any studies on the topic, in my almost twenty years of clinical experience as a therapist, not to mention my experience as a parent, I have yet to see a child who was a social outcast because he did not watch television in the first three years of life. In a preschool class of twelve children, my two kids were the only ones who did not watch any television at all, and I can tell you unequivocally that it was not an issue. While my kids have never seen them on TV, they do know a few television characters like Elmo and the Cookie Monster from seeing them in books at the bookstore. If you are concerned that your child will not be up on preschool popular culture, you can always buy or check out books from the library that feature characters like Dora the Explorer.

9. "My spouse and I don't agree on how to handle the TV issue with our kids." In my experience, it tends to be the dads who are most resistant to cutting out television in the early years. Many of them have bought into the educational hype or just want to be able to relax in front of the set themselves. Often they want to share a ballgame or favorite show with their child and just don't see the harm.

That said, most fathers I speak to are very concerned about giving their children an intellectual advantage, and after reading the kind of information presented in this chapter they often change their mind. If you are having trouble negotiating this issue, I recommend finding out what is most important to your spouse about TV-viewing and work together to find a compromise. I know one father who had such fond memories of watching baseball games with his own father that it was really important to him to share that with his infant son. The parents compromised by allowing the dad to watch the last thirty minutes of any game he watched on the weekend with his son.

10. "It's educational." As the lawsuit between CCFC and the makers of "educational" DVDs has shown, there is a lot of misleading information and marketing regarding children's programming. It is disturbing that these DVDs, which claimed to help children with brain development and language acquisition, were proved to actually harm babies in those areas when they were tested. Children's media experts define educational television as "having an explicit curriculum or set of age-appropriate learning objectives and being designed around this curriculum." According to these criteria, only one quarter of the shows that claim to be educational actually are. Even for the shows that fit the criteria, the vast majority of research shows benefits only after the age of three. Children's television experts Drs. Christakis and Zimmerman refer to the period between two and three as the "gray zone" because while some children can get benefits from watching TV, others are actually harmed from the exposure. These results largely depend on the individual child and the content of the TV show or DVD. A study of two-and-a-half-year-olds who watched *Sesame Street* found that they had slower rates of language acquisition than a group of children who didn't watch the show. This was surprising to researchers since *Sesame Street* consistently tests well for children over the age of three.

Whether or not kids can learn from television continues to be a hot topic of debate. Researchers have discovered what is referred to as the "video deficit"—that is, the idea that there is something about the screen experience that may prevent children from learning. For example, when two-year-old children were shown a simple three-step task by a live adult, they were able to imitate it, but when an adult demonstrated the same task once on videotape the children were not able to master it. In a similar study, when one group of two-year-olds watched a real person hide a stuffed animal in a nearby room and another group watched a video of the person hiding the stuffed animal, only 35 percent of the children who saw the recorded video were able to find the toy compared with 69 percent who "got" the live demonstration.

The attitudes and viewing habits of parents make a big difference in how beneficial educational television is for children. In a study that examined how Israeli children differ from American children in their response to television, researcher Dr. Gavriel Salomon found that Israeli children take television much more seriously than Americans. Culturally, television is considered a source of news in Israel, and families watch it with more of a sense of purpose, which results in an increased mental effort while they watch, as well as better retention of what they've viewed. Other evidence shows that watching noneducational television with your kids can also exacerbate the negative effects, the assumption being that, by watching together, you are validating the content of what you are viewing.

The New TV Guide:
Safe Viewing Tips for Parents

So your child has turned three and you are ready to introduce some screen time, but you want to do it in the most constructive way possible. Here are some tips:

Make a family TV plan and stick to it. Devise specific rules regarding weekly screen time, content, location (no kitchen, please!), and days of the week viewing is allowed. The clearer everyone is about the rules, the more likely they will be enforced.

Avoid commercials. Stick to using the DVR or DVDs so you can protect your child from aggressive marketing campaigns that target children.

Watch together interactively. Watching a show together with your child and talking about what you're viewing has been shown to make the experience more educational—with quality children's programming, that is.

Make viewing an event. Instead of using screen time to fill holes in the day or alleviate boredom, make it a special family event. I know one family that allows only two hours a week of screen time on a special "movie night." This family gradually went from watching shows like *Barney & Friends* to two-hour documentaries over the course of the years. Because viewing time was so special for everyone, the parents did their homework to make sure the chosen shows or movies were really great.

Make the experience multidimensional. If you watch *Signing Time! Leah's Farm*, for example, read your child a book about farm animals and give him a farm-animal coloring book. If you feel adventurous, take a trip to a local farm or petting zoo.

Use television to expand on areas of interest as your child gets older. Television can give your child unusual experiences, like seeing a pride of lions basking in the sun in the Serengeti.

Be a role model. During your child's first three years, limit your own viewing to times when he is not around. When he's older and you're watching TV together, make sure you send the message that watching is a learning experience.

Take TVs out of the kitchen and your child's bedroom. As research has shown, having a TV in your child's bedroom increases the likelihood of viewing inappropriate content, excessive viewing, and poor sleep. Watching TV while eating also encourages overeating and disconnection from important bodily cues, such as satiety.

Try turning off the TV for a week. Even after you've begun to integrate media into your life, it's a good idea to take periodic breaks. The Center for Screen-Time Awareness advocates two TV turn-off weeks every year.

Media Resources for Parents

Action Coalition for Media Education, www.acmecoalition.org
Alliance for Childhood, www.allianceforchildhood.org
Campaign for a Commercial-Free Childhood, www.commercialexploitation.org
Center for Screen-Time Awareness, www.tvturnoff.org
Center on Media and Child Health, www.cmch.tv
Common Sense Media, www.commonsensemedia. org
Instead of TV, www.insteadoftv. com
Kill Your Television, www.turnoffyourtv.com
LimiTV, www.limitv.org
Media Awareness Network, www.media-awareness.ca
Parents' Choice, www.parents-choice.org
Parents Television Council, www.parentstv.org
Teachers Resisting Unhealthy Children's Entertainment (TRUCE),
    www.truceteachers.org
The TV Project, www.tvp.oirg
Trash Your TV, www.trashyourtv.com
TV Free Living, www.tvfreeliving.com
TV Smarter, www.TVsmarter.com
White Dot, www.whitedot.org

It's Easy
Being Green

Reducing Exposure to Toxic Chemicals

A year before I started trying to get pregnant, I cut out caffeine, stopped consuming artificial sweeteners, and switched primarily to organic foods. Six months later, I started taking prenatal vitamins along with DHA omega-3 supplements. I had done my homework and was determined to make my body into a vessel of health and purity for my unborn child. As the time of birth approached I ran out, or rather waddled out, to register for the baby items that I would need. As a parenting expert with many friends in the field, I was confident that I would know exactly what to get for my child, so I filled my registry with things like a name-brand mattress (bad), plastic baby bottles (bad), a bottle warmer to heat those bottles (bad), plastic teethers (bad), all kinds of toys (many of which were bad), and lots of delicious-smelling baby lotions and shampoos (bad and bad). I wanted to be prepared so I stocked up on tons of big-brand diapers, wipes, and diaper creams (yeah, those were bad too). I thought I knew so much.

I must admit, looking at the bigger picture, I was not terribly aware of chemicals in my environment in general, much less how they might affect my family. I put my trust in the big companies to only sell me things that wouldn't hurt us. I didn't think the stores I frequented would carry anything unsafe or that the government would look the other way as toxic chemicals made their way into the products I bought for my babies. Perhaps I was naive, but I believe most people think the way I did. According to a recent survey, 56 percent of people in this country agreed with the statement "Currently the government carefully tests chemicals used in all major consumer products to make sure they are safe for people to use."

Then I met Paige Goldberg Tolmach, a woman in my BABYGROUP™ class in Los Angeles. As a result of her son Jackson's severe eczema, which was not healing from conventional medical approaches, Paige became obsessed with learning about toxins in the environment and how they affect our children. Armed with this information, she made some lifestyle changes in her household, cured her son of eczema, established herself as an expert in environmental toxins, and opened The Little Seed, an eco-friendly, nontoxic store for children. Each week in class, Paige shared some new and valuable piece of information or a tip to make our babies' lives less toxic. I can still hear the horror in her voice as she said things like "You really don't want to buy pajamas with flame retardant and let me tell you why," "Before you buy another batch of those diapers, can I tell you about the chemicals in them?" and "Those bottles are leaching chemicals into your baby's milk every time you heat them up in the warmer." Paige spoon-fed us information little by little. I wish I could be as gentle on the written page, and I will do the best I can, but I want to make sure you get the information you need to know in order to start detoxifying your home.

I know that hearing the truth about what is in your baby's environment can be both terrifying and overwhelming; just learning this information can make you feel that the situation is hopeless. But the truth is that you don't have to do it all at once and that even small changes can make a big difference. For example, you can lower your child's pesticide exposure (and your own) by 90 percent simply by avoiding the twelve most contaminated fruits and vegetables. But I am jumping ahead of myself; I'll talk about pesticides, along with bovine growth hormones and mercury in fish, in Chapter 12. The point is that small changes can go a long way.

Just the Facts, Mama: Chemicals and Our Kids

We're conducting a vast toxicological experiment and we are using our children as experimental animals.

—Dr. Philip J. Landrigan,
quoted on Trade Secrets: A Moyers Report on PBS

From conception, children are exposed to an inordinate number of toxins and chemicals. In a 2004 study of umbilical cord blood performed by the American Red Cross, it was found that babies in utero had an average of 200 industrialized chemicals and pollutants in their bloodstream. Of the 287 toxins discovered in the cord blood, 180 are known to cause cancer, 217 are poisonous to the brain and nervous system, and 208 have been linked to birth defects in animals. In the last few decades, approximately 82,000 new and synthetic chemical compounds have been introduced to our environment, less than 10 percent of which have been tested for safety.

Scientists believe that it is not a coincidence that children are experiencing illnesses, disorders, and developmental problems at unprecedented levels. These conditions include cancer; asthma; rheumatoid arthritis; allergies; obesity; autism; developmental disabilities, including speech and language disorders; learning disabilities; and attention deficit disorder. Environmentalists believe that these problems are occurring because children are particularly vulnerable to toxins. Compared to adults:

- Children's metabolisms are faster and therefore they absorb toxins faster.
- Children grow so quickly that dangerous cell mutations multiply faster.
- Their developing brains and immature reproductive and immune systems are unable to detoxify the chemicals to which they are exposed.
- The blood-brain barrier is still porous and allows more chemicals to reach their brains.
- Children eat three to four times more food per pound of body weight than the average adult.
- The resting air intake of an infant is double that of an adult.
- Babies and toddlers spend most of their time on or very close to the ground and therefore are exposed to many more contaminants.
- Infants explore their world by putting things into their mouths.
- Children have a larger skin-to-surface area in relation to body weight, and their skin is thinner, resulting in greater penetration of toxins.
- Children get more cuts and rashes, leading to more exposure.
- Infants spend more time indoors, leaving them more vulnerable to unhealthy indoor air.
- Children's diets are less varied than adults', which leaves them more vulnerable to toxic exposure.
- Exposure to toxins during critical stages of growth has greater effects and can last a lifetime.

Almost all the testing done on toxins is based upon the physiology of a 180-pound adult male, which is *completely* different from the body of your developing child. Take lead, for example—the number one preventable childhood poison. Children are particularly sensitive to this toxin because their stomachs absorb 50 percent of whatever lead they encounter compared to adults, who take in "only" 11 percent. Another example is bisphenol A, commonly known as BPA, a hormone-disrupting toxin that has been found in plastic baby bottles. BPA is linked to a variety of problems, including heart disease, diabetes, liver abnormalities, problems with brain function, and mood disorders. Infants do not develop the necessary enzyme to metabolize BPA until they are at least three months old.

Combinations of toxic chemicals can also create different reactions than a single, isolated toxin. For example, a long-term study of the effects of PCB and mercury looked at the children born to mothers who ate fish from Lake Ontario, which is known to contain polychlorinated biphenyl or PCB (a carcinogen that commonly accumulates in the food chain), and were exposed to extremely low levels of mercury. The impact on the children's neurocognitive development was far more dramatic when very low mercury exposure was combined with PCB exposure.

We cannot trust the government or major corporations to eliminate toxins,

---

FROM THE EXPERTS ...

My Little Seed

Three years ago, I had a baby. A beautiful, perfect, amazing baby. Within eight weeks of birth, my perfect baby developed eczema. Extreme eczema. Every doctor on the planet told me that his skin condition was a product of genetics and a reaction to the weather. This seemed odd to me as neither my husband nor I had eczema. Though I continually insisted that my baby must be allergic to something in his environment, the doctors dismissed my notions and explained that there was absolutely nothing that I could do to help him, other than using topical and oral steroids to manage his breakouts. If we were lucky, they said, he would grow out of it by age six. They also told me to stop breastfeeding.

This wasn't good enough for me. In my heart, I knew that they were wrong. I refused to listen and kept on searching for answers. I continued to breastfeed my baby and started doing a tremendous amount of research on eczema, allergies, and environmental factors that might possibly have played a role. What I discovered was shocking—everything in my home, including the products I used to clean it, was toxic. Jackson's crib mattress off gassed toxic flame-retardant. His plastic teething toys and bottles contained phthalates and BPA, which have been linked to allergic skin conditions and worse. His cotton clothing—everything that he wore—along with his crib bedding and towels was tainted with residue from the cancer-causing pesticides that are sprayed on cotton crops. Carcinogenic

so we must take matters into our own hands. I am not telling you that exposure to certain chemicals can reduce your child's IQ and cause developmental problems and illness just to scare you. My hope is that this information will motivate you to take action to protect your child, always keeping in mind that even small changes can make a big difference on both a micro and a macro level. When you switch to a less toxic toilet cleaner, not only are you exposing your child to fewer chemicals, but you are reducing the number of chemicals that get flushed into the environment and harm sea life as well. My personal experience has taught me that awareness breeds more awareness, which makes it easier to take action on all levels.

The most significant toxic enemies you need to know about are lead, PVC and phthalates, flame retardants, and cigarette smoke.

substances such as synthetic fragrances, artificial colors, parabens, and mineral oil and/or petrolatum were in all of Jackson's body-care products— even the ones his doctors suggested that he use to help his eczema!

I immediately threw out everything in my son's nursery—his furniture, mattress, bedding, toys, bottles, clothing, and body care products. I then searched the planet looking for safe alternatives—toys without lead, clothes without pesticide residue, bottles without BPA, and a mattress without toxic flame-retardant. This was no easy task. I ordered rattles from New Zealand, bottles from Texas, stuffed animals from Sri Lanka, and clothing from England. I got rid of all chemical cleaners and started using vinegar and water to clean my house. I dressed Jackson in organic clothing and swaddled him in organic blankets. I also paid a visit to my genius acupuncturist who gave me creams to help heal Jackson's beautiful baby skin that had been ravaged by excessive scratching and bleeding. Within weeks, his eczema went away and his skin began to glow.

I was overjoyed. I wanted to shout my discovery from the rooftops and I knew just where to begin—my own backyard. With a friend, I opened a non-toxic and eco-friendly baby store called The Little Seed. I didn't want anyone else to experience what I'd gone through without help and support.

I know that every parent out there wants to make a better world for his or her little ones. With my new found knowledge I hope I can be of some assistance along the way, because, as you know, we are all in this together.

—Paige Goldberg Tolmach,
The Little Seed. www.thelittleseed.com

Lead

Lead poisoning is the number one most preventable disease among children. Lead is a heavy metal that is classified as a neurotoxin—a chemical that affects the nervous system. It is a poison that is unsafe at *any* level, so it may surprise you to learn that the Centers for Disease Control and Prevention (CDC) consider a blood level of 10 micrograms per deciliter (ug) acceptable. I guess this is progress since CDC thought 60 ug was acceptable in the 1960s. But here's the catch: a 2005 study by Dr. Bruce Lanphear found that lead harms children at much lower levels than 10 ug. There is a steeper drop in intellectual ability when a child's level of exposure goes from 5 to 10 ug than when it goes from 10 to 20 ug. More than 310,000 American children age six and under have been diagnosed with lead poisoning and as many as 3,000,000 elevated blood levels, both of which can cause lasting learning and behavior problems. In the United States, 1 million children currently exceed the current 10 mcg/dL recommended limit, and if that recommendation were to be adjusted, given what we know about IQ deficits at lower levels, it is believed that millions more children would be included, as well.

Children are at an increased risk for lead poisoning because their blood-brain-barrier, the body's built-in mechanism for protecting the brain from poisonous substances, is not as well developed as it is in an adult. Lead gets past this barrier by imitating calcium, which babies' and toddlers' brains crave. As a result, until age six, children absorb three to four times more lead than an adult absorbs, and that rate is even greater for children who are calcium-deficient.

Where is all this lead coming from? Generally children are exposed to lead by either ingesting or inhaling it. Since multiple studies have shown that kids put objects in their mouths over twenty times each hour, it shouldn't be surprising to learn that up to 80 percent of lead exposure is the result of thumb sucking and other hand-to-mouth behavior. The actual sources of the lead vary tremendously, depending on where children live and play.

1. Lead in paint. Paint containing lead is the most common source of exposure for children. In 1978 lead paint was banned for use in homes and many consumer products in the United States, but it is still on the walls and furniture of as many as 47 million homes in this country. Since

Testing for Lead

Consumer Reports mentioned Homax Lead Check ($8) and Lead Check Household Lead Test Kit ($18.45) as two of the most reasonably priced lead-testing products on the market.
For more information about testing or lead removal, call the U.S. Environmental Protection Agency Lead Hotline at 1–800–424–LEAD (5323).

the ban was passed more than thirty years ago, the paint in homes that still contain lead is undoubtedly chipping, peeling, and rubbing off, making it an even greater temptation for curious children.

If you suspect you have lead paint in your home, you should have it removed by a certified lead abatement contractor. Removing it yourself can release lead dust particles into the air, exposing your children to even greater risk. Painting over the hazard with regular paint will not solve the problem either. The Environmental Protection Agency (EPA) recommends taking the following steps:

- Clean up paint chips immediately.
- Clean floors, window frames, windowsills, and other surfaces weekly. Use a mop, sponge, or paper towel with warm water and a general all-purpose cleaner or a cleaner made specifically for lead.
- Thoroughly rinse sponges and mop heads after cleaning dirty or dusty areas.
- Wash children's hands often, especially before they eat and before naptime and bedtime.
- Keep play areas clean. Wash bottles, pacifiers, toys, and stuffed animals regularly.
- Keep children from teething on windowsills or other painted surfaces.
- Clean or remove shoes before entering your home to avoid tracking in lead from the outdoors.
- The EPA has developed extensive requirements for lead paint abatement in residences. For more information, please go to www.epa.gov/lead/pubs/leadinfo.htm.

2. Lead in water. Lead exposure from drinking water accounts for 10 to 20 percent of lead exposure. For babies this source can be much more significant than paint; the EPA estimates that non-breastfed infants can receive 40 to 60 percent of their lead exposure from drinking water used in baby formulas in the first six months of life. Lead is not usually found in source water, such as reservoirs or aquifers, but makes its way into your house through contact with pipes, solder (a filler used to connect metal pipes), fittings, fixtures, and faucets. Federal law allows pipes to contain 8 percent lead by weight and allows "lead-free" solder and fluxes (substances used in high-temperature metal joining) used for water pipes to contain 0.2 percent lead by weight. Lead pipes were commonly used before 1930, but they are not the only lead piping risk: galvanized pipes often contain lead in the compounds used to seal joining pipes. Copper pipes prior to 1988 were typically sealed with lead-based solders, and plastic pipes can also contain lead. It generally takes new pipes five years to form an effective mineral scale that helps insulate water and protect against some lead exposure.

There are some simple things you can do to reduce lead exposure in your water.

- Find out what kind of pipes you have in your home.
- Anytime the water in a particular faucet has not been used for six hours or longer, "flush" your cold-water pipes by running the water for a minute to flush out lead that may have collected in water standing in your pipes. You may want to use that water for nonconsumption uses such as watering plants, washing the car, or combining with soap to clean floors.
- Always use cold tap water for drinking, cooking, and preparing baby formula because hot water dissolves metals faster.
- Get a water filter. There are many different types of filters, ranging in price from a simple carbon filter pitcher (such as Brita water filters) to a whole house filter (a heavy-duty system that filters all the water in the house).

3. Lead in toys. In the last few years literally millions of toys have been recalled due to lead content. In 2007, 1.5 million Thomas the Train toys alone were

---

FROM THE EXPERTS . . .

Healthy Home Improvement

A home is a work in progress. You change the color of the kitchen paint, redecorate the kids' bedroom, tackle a tile job in the bathroom . . . and, oh look, it's time to repaint the kitchen again. Whether you like to DIY or call in the pros, use the project as the perfect opportunity to make your home safer and non-toxic. Here are a few easy tips to renovate more healthily:

Flooring:
Many parents opt for carpeting because it's soft for crawling and falling babies. But some carpets are better than others and all carpets take special care. Look for carpets made from pesticide-free wool or recycled fibers that have not been treated with toxic finishes. Let it air out outside for a few days before installation and tack it down instead of using fumy adhesives.

Once installed, vacuum at least once a week with a HEPA-filtered vacuum, as carpets cling to dust, pollen, and chemicals tracked in on the bottom of shoes. Deep clean annually. Visit carpet-rug.org for natural

recalled. Starting August 14, 2009, the Consumer Product Safety Improvement Act required that no "children's products" (any products intended primarily for use by children under the age of twelve) could exceed a maximum of 300 parts per million of lead. This act retroactively applies to all toys available for sale, which is a step in the right direction, and has dramatically reduced the lead risk from toys. But recalled toys continue to be available from aftermarket sources, such as eBay and Craigslist, long after they've been removed from store shelves. In addition, toys from your own childhood and antiques are also a high risk for lead. So what can you do?

- Be especially careful when buying toys from secondhand sources. If you do, consider skipping toys from China, which have accounted for the majority of lead-tainted toy recalls.
- Avoid children's jewelry and charms that are attached to shoes or clothing. These are some of the biggest lead offenders and even caused the death of a four-year-old who swallowed a charm that turned out to be made of over 99 percent lead.
- Choose wooden toys or those made with cloth, especially organic cotton.

solutions, eco-friendly product recommendations, and guidelines for cleaning that many manufacturers require in order to maintain the warranty.

Not up to the struggle of keeping carpets clean? Hard surfaces like FSC-certified hardwoods, bamboo, cork, or natural linoleum floors are easier to clean. Toss a natural fiber rug on top for comfort. Again, be aware of any toxic adhesives or finishes during installation.

Walls:
Painting is often the fastest way to give a room a facelift, but it's also a fast way to introduce unwanted airborne toxins, called volatile organic chemicals (VOCs), into your home. Look for low-VOC or no-VOC options. If low-VOC paints are too pricey, at least go with a lighter shade of conventional options: the darker the paint, the greater the VOC concentration.

Remember: If your house was built before 1978, test for lead paint. Always ventilate well by opening windows to flush fresh air inside. And keep children and pregnant women away from renovation areas.

—Christopher Gavigan, CEO and author of *Healthy Child Healthy World—Creating a Cleaner, Greener, Safer Home*
www.healthychild.org

- Use a lead testing kit (see page 278 for recommendations).
- Sign up for toy recall alerts on the Consumer Product Safety Commission website at www.cpsc.gov/cpsclist.aspx and check toy databases like HealthyToys.org to find out about toys you may own that predate 2009.

4. Lead in soil. Flaking paint, decades of use as a gasoline additive, mining operations, industrial emissions, waste incineration, pesticides, industry, and aging buildings have all resulted in elevated levels of lead in our soils. What's more disturbing is that lead remains in topsoil, increasing our children's chances of exposure. Contaminated soil in play areas greatly impacts the lead in children's blood because they are constantly exploring their world by putting things in their mouths; as a result, they ingest a lot of dirt. It has been estimated that the average child ingests two to eight times as much soil as an adult.

We may think that we've left all that lead dirt outside and that we're safe behind closed doors, but the fact is that we track lead into the house, along with other chemicals, bacteria, feces, pesticides, allergen dust, animal dander, and pollutants. But there is a simple and inexpensive solution. According to a 1991 study known as the "Door Mat Study," using a door mat reduces toxic lead dust inside the home by almost half; taking shoes off at the door reduces lead dust by 60 percent, and doing both, over a five-month period, was found to reduce toxic dust by 98.5 percent. If you don't want to keep your shoes off in every room of the house, take them off in carpeted rooms, since carpets act like dust catchers. The amount of dust in a rug can be 100 times greater than the amount of dust on the bare floors of your home. According to Dr. John Roberts, an environmental engineer who has studied the problem for nearly twenty years, a ten-year-old carpet contains two pounds of dust, on average, including lead, pesticides, and mercury. At the very least, take your shoes off before going into your child's room.

Here are a few other things you can do to keep lead soil and dust at bay:

- Invest in a good-quality vacuum cleaner with a HEPA filter. You get bonus points if you get one with a dirt finder and a power brush and/or power head, which is reported to be six times more effective than a vacuum cleaner that doesn't have one.
- Clean your house frequently and thoroughly. Because lead dust is sticky, it is best to wet wipe regularly and vacuum often.
- If you garden or need to buy soil, make sure you get clean topsoil.

5. Other sources of lead. While paint, water, and toys account for a significant portion of lead exposure for children, there are many other sources you should be aware of:

Old vinyl miniblinds. In 1996 the Consumer Product Safety Commission reported that 25 million foreign-made miniblinds containing lead had been imported into the United States. When sunlight hits these blinds, the vinyl degrades and produces lead dust. Although these blinds are no longer sold in this country, many homes and apartments may still have them. Look for blinds that have a sticker stating that no lead has been added.

Calcium supplements. Believe it or not, many calcium supplements have lead in them. A 2000 study printed in the *Journal of the American Medical Association* found that four out of seven "natural" over-the-counter calcium supplements (those made of oyster shells and bone meal) and four out of fourteen refined over-the-counter supplements contained measurable lead content. A mother named Lynn Askew learned this the hard way when, in 1996, her two-year-old daughter Destiny tested for a lead level of 10 mcg/dL. As it turned out, the culprit was the calcium supplements her pediatrician had recommended that she take. Lynn was so outraged that she started an organization called Citizens' Lead Education and Poisoning Prevention.

Dishware. The federal government prohibits the sale of dinnerware that releases lead in amounts greater than 2,000 parts per billion, which prevents direct cases of lead poisoning. However, many major manufacturers of dinnerware still use lead glazes without labeling them as such. Beware of brightly colored pottery containing lead that can leach into food you are serving, especially acidic foods like tomato sauce or orange juice. Also, keep in mind that dishware purchased abroad is unlikely to be regulated and is best used for decoration, not serving food.

PVC (Polyvinyl Chloride) and Phthalates

PVC products are everywhere: pacifiers, water bottles, shower curtains, vinyl flooring, baby bathtub books, medical tubing, and food packaging, to name a few sources. According to the Center for Health, Environment and Justice, PVC, which is commonly referred to as vinyl, "is one of the most hazardous consumer products ever created." Made from flammable gas vinyl chloride (a known carcinogen), PVC "off-gasses," which means that it releases poisonous chemicals that can be inhaled. As a result, this chemical is dangerous to your family's health and to the environment from beginning to end—in other words, from the factory, to the home, to the landfill.

This toxic chemical, which is frequently used in children's toys, is often combined with other dangerous additives such as lead, cadmium, and, when it needs to be soft and flexible, phthalates. Cadmium, which can leach out of toys, has been linked to brain damage. Phthalates are hormone disrupters, which means that they interfere with the hormone systems that regulate normal growth and reproductive development in children. It appears that these chemicals affect boys in particular. In studies of in-utero phthalate exposure, it was found that mothers with the highest levels of phthalate metabolites had sons with smaller penises and scrotums, incomplete descent of the testicles, and shorter perineums. Phthalates are used so pervasively that they can now be found literally everywhere in the world, even in subsurface snow in Antarctica and in jellyfish that live more than 300 feet below the surface of the Atlantic Ocean.

1. Toys. Phthalates in toys have already been banned since December 7, 1999, in Europe and in a number of other countries around the world, including Mexico and Japan. The U.S. Congress passed the Consumer Product Safety Improvement Act (CPSIA) in 2008, which requires pre-market safety testing for the first time for most children's products, although some of the testing requirements have been stayed. As of February 10, 2009, however, the CPSIA established limits on phthalates and lead in children's toys and child-care articles intended for children under the age of twelve. While this ban has been largely enforced, occasionally a toxic toy slips through the cracks, usually one that was purchased from a deep-discount store. Toys meant for children age twelve and older are not covered by the ban, and it's not uncommon for a young child to get her hands on, say, a plastic purse intended for her teenage sister which might contain banned substances. If you suspect a toy you own or are planning to buy may have PVC or phthalates, or if you smell that strong, toxic "shower curtain smell," you don't want it in your home. Many toy companies are now labeling their products "PVC-free," so be sure to look for the label when you're shopping.

2. Bibs. The CPSIA set limit for phthalates in childcare articles, which includes items intended for children under the age of 3 that facilitate sleeping or eating. So, baby bibs made of vinyl should not contain phthalates or lead if recently manufactured. While bibs containing phthalates and lead are banned, based on the CPSIA's regulations, many parents are still using bibs bought for older children. To keep it simple, just avoid plastic bibs altogether. Cloth bibs—ideally organic cotton ones—are your best choice.

3. Changing pads. The CPSIA ban does not apply to changing pads, which can contain PVC, particularly the portable kind that you keep in a diaper bag. If you're wondering why the CPSIA ban doesn't extend to changing pads, it's not because they contain a relatively "safe" level of PVC. On the contrary, these pads contain plenty of PVC, but they aren't included in the ban because they're not considered a toy or child-care article. The type of pad that rests on your changing table probably contains polyurethane foam, which, in addition to PVC, may contain flame retardants (see page 286-289 for more information), such as a poly-brominated diphenyl ether (PBDE) and volatile organic compounds (VOCs). The good news is that many companies have now come out with PVC-free changing pads and even ones made of organic cotton or wool (see Resources for recommendations).

4. Body-care products. A study in *Pediatrics* surveying the use of powder, talc, cornstarch, lotions, diaper creams, and shampoos, as well as plastic toys and pacifiers, found that the babies on whom these products were used the most had high concentrations of phthalates in their urine. Researchers concluded that phthalates enter children's bodies not only orally but also through the skin. What's a mommy to do?

- Avoid products with synthetic fragrances, which are likely to include phthalates.
- Look for phthalate-free products.
- Visit the Skin Deep website of the Environmental Working Group (EWG) at www.cosmeticsdatabase.com for a comprehensive personal product safety guide and to look up products you are considering buying, or already own, to see if they have unsafe toxins.

What You Need to Know about Parabens

Parabens are a widely used family of preservatives that are added to all sorts of personal products, including shampoo, soap, diaper rash ointment, baby wipes, lotions, baby oil, toothpaste, and sunscreen, to inhibit the growth of bacteria and elongate shelf life. As a matter of fact, these chemicals are so common that they show up in most of the nearly 25,000 cosmetics and personal-care products listed in the EWG's Skin Deep report of personal products. In the short term, parabens can cause skin irritation and itchiness, but the potential long-term effects are really scary: parabens are hormone disrupters that have been linked to brain and nervous system damage and cancer, particularly breast cancer. As we know, infants are more susceptible to absorbing products through their skin, since it is thinner than an adult's, and they have a greater skin surface to body weight ratio than adults. In this context, it is particularly disturbing to note that researchers found parabens in the urine of adult men only hours after parabens had been applied to their skin. Before you go shopping, check the Skin Deep report and look for paraben-free products wherever you shop.

Flame Retardants

Polybrominated diphenyl ethers (PBDEs) are compounds that are used as flame retardants to prevent fire from spreading. Sounds like something we want in order to keep our kids safe, right? Guess again. PBDEs are another hormone disrupter that have been linked to impaired memory, abnormalities of coordination, hyperactivity, and infertility.

The problem is that PBDEs are everywhere, and I mean *everywhere*. If you eat, drink, or breathe, you are exposed to them. PBDEs are in children's pajamas, mattresses, computers, TVs, furniture, upholstery, rugs, draperies, and car interiors. We know that these chemicals leak into the environment through the air, are carried by dust and water, and even enter the food chain. Like their banned relatives, the PCBs, flame retardants like PBDEs persist in the environment, are found globally, concentrate over time, and are toxic, with likely adverse effects on wildlife, marine life, and humans.

These flame retardants are bioaccumulative, which means that they accumulate in the body in fatty tissues, blood, and breast milk. Yes, breast milk. According to a 2003 study in which the breast milk of forty-seven nursing mothers was analyzed, every single sample showed PBDE in varying amounts. While expert after expert agrees that breastfeeding is still the best option for children, this exposure is disconcerting. When discussing PBDEs, Dr. David Perlmutter, neurologist and author of *Raise a Smarter Child by Kindergarten,* says, "Research indicates that they may be particularly harmful during critical windows of brain development, during pregnancy and early childhood."

1. Sleepwear. In the United States, children's sleepwear sized nine months to fourteen years must either pass flammability tests or be tight-fitting and meet certain specifications as to dimensions, according to the U.S. Consumer Product Safety Commission Office. This regulation is based on the idea that if your child is playing with fire or running out of the house to escape from a fire, it is less likely that her sleeve, or any other piece of her clothing, will catch fire if that clothing fits snugly or has been treated with a flame retardant. To avoid toxic PBDEs in flame-retardant sleepwear:

- Read labels. Most pajamas that are treated with flame retardants have labels reading "Chemically treated," "Flame resistant," or "Contains flame retardant." Pajamas that are not treated with flame retardants often have warnings that read "For child's safety, garment should fit snugly"; "This garment is not flame resistant. Loose-fitting garment is more likely to catch fire"; "Wear snug-fitting. Not flame resistant"; or "Not intended for sleepwear."
- Check fabric content. Look at the label and see what is identified as the primary fabric used. If the item is sleepwear and it is made

of a synthetic fiber, it has flame retardants. Children's pajamas that are made from these fibers either have the flame retardant woven into the fiber or are treated with chemicals after the fabric is completed. So even pajamas labels that read: "not treated with flame retardants" may have them because the flame retardant is bonded to the fiber, not applied to the fabric. It is best to assume that all pajamas containing synthetic materials have flame retardants.

- Try snug-fitting T-shirts and leggings that are made from organic cotton.
- Look for organic cotton pajamas. They don't have to cost a fortune. Costco manufactures some reasonably priced organic cotton pajamas, and many other low-cost, big-name stores are going green, too (for a list of specialty stores that manufacture organic pajamas, see Resources). Always make sure that the pajama does not claim to be flame resistant. Even organic cotton can be treated with a chemical flame retardant, since the term "organic" applies to how the cotton is grown, not processed.

2. Mattresses. In the first year of life it has been estimated that children sleep between fourteen and seventeen hours a day, although mine never seemed to sleep for more than fifteen minutes at a time. But the point is that your child will spend a lot of time on a mattress in her first years, whether she's sleeping on it or not.

In 2004 the United States voluntarily phased out certain PBDEs in mattresses due to concerns about the environment, toxicity, and the ability to bioaccumulate. This was not a federal ban, however, and imported mattresses may still have this dangerous toxin. There are other chemicals to worry about too. Today's baby crib mattresses are made with petroleum-based synthetics. Nearly all crib mattresses contain polyurethane foam, vinyl (PVC), phthalates, chemical fire retardants, and an extensive list of added industrial chemicals.

Probably the single most expensive recommendation I am going to make in this book is to buy a mattress made of natural materials like organic cotton or wool (wool is resistant to dust mites and is a natural flame retardant). I wish I had done this sooner. I was put off by the cost and, as a result, I allowed my children to spend the first two years of their lives sleeping on what I believe to have been toxic mattresses. I also recommend that you invest in an organic mattress for your bedroom, too, if your children are sharing a "family" bed. Even if you don't share a mattress with your kids, it is a really great investment in your family's health—if you can afford it.

When you are buying a mattress made of natural materials, look for the Organic Trade Association's seal and make sure that the mattress has not been treated with chemical flame retardants. If the product is stamped as 100 percent organic by federal law, it must be exactly that, which means it cannot contain any elements that harm the environment or are synthetically produced. But keep in mind that this doesn't apply to how the fiber is treated *after* the crop is grown. Also make sure that any seals or stamps clearly state that the mattress does not contain arsenic, phosphorus, or antimony.

If you are not ready or can't afford to buy an organic mattress, here are some things you can do to reduce toxic exposure:

- Air it out. Let your new mattress off-gas outside for at least three days.
- Get an organic, waterproof, fitted cover. Traditional waterproof covers contain PVCs and phthalates, but there are many different nontoxic options.
- Switch to eco-friendly bed linens made from unbleached organic cotton, linen, hemp, or bamboo. While these won't reduce PBDEs, they will reduce the amount of pesticides your child is exposed to.
- When your child is old enough for a pillow, choose one with natural fillers like wool, organic cotton, kapok, or buckwheat, and make sure the pillowcase is made with comparable materials.

3. Furniture. Some states have passed legislation to ban flame retardants, and the Washington state Departments of Ecology and Health have called for a phase-out of all forms of PBDEs, specifically those used in consumer products like furniture and televisions. When buying furniture, check the label to see whether it contains flame retardants. Often these chemicals are sprayed on foam cushions *inside* furniture upholstery. The environmental organization Friends of the Earth found that over two-thirds of the furniture in San Francisco Bay Area stores, and half of the furniture inside houses in the same area, contained flame retardants. You don't have to throw away all your furniture and completely redecorate your house, but do think about buying more eco-friendly furniture when it comes time to make a purchase in the future. It doesn't have to cost a fortune. For example, ever since 2002, IKEA has voluntarily stopped using brominated flame retardants, antimony compounds, and a long list of other toxic chemicals in its furniture.

4. Electronics. According to the Environmental Working Group, major manufacturers have taken the initiative to remove PBDEs from their electronic products, which they distribute worldwide, in response to restrictions on toxic chemicals in electronic products sold in Europe and in several U.S. states. Several companies, including Acer, Apple, Eizo Nanao, LG Electronics, Lenovo, Matsushita, Microsoft, Nokia, Phillips, Samsung, Sharp, Sony-Ericsson, and Toshiba have publicly committed to phasing out all brominated fire retardants in their products. Check out one of these companies the next time you're buying anything electronic.

5. Home. While PBDEs in food will be addressed on pages 328–329, there are a few other things you can do to avoid flame retardants in your home:

- Keep your home clean. Vacuuming frequently can reduce dust exposure. Testing by the EWG found that dust bunnies contain unusually high levels of PBDEs compared to other chemical compounds.
- Open windows to air out your home every day.
- Put a layer of protection between your baby and the floor. When you put her on the floor for tummy time, put a blanket under her so she's not directly on the floor, which is likely to have dust-containing PBDEs.

Cigarette Smoke

While it is not easy to stop smoking, it is fairly easy to take productive steps to dramatically reduce your child's exposure to cigarette smoke if you or other people who come into contact with your child do smoke. According to a 2006 surgeon general's report, 60 percent of children in the United States, nearly 22 million, are exposed to secondhand smoke. Secondhand smoke is a mixture of the smoke given off by the burning end of a cigarette, pipe, or cigar and the smoke exhaled from the lungs of smokers. Secondhand smoke contains more than 250 chemicals known to be toxic or cancer causing, including formaldehyde, benzene, vinyl chloride, arsenic, ammonia, and hydrogen cyanide. There is no "safe" exposure for you or your child. According to the Los Angeles County Public Health Department, exposure to secondhand smoke for five minutes is equivalent to smoking one cigarette.

Babies are particularly vulnerable to cigarette smoke because their lungs are still developing and their breathing rates are faster than those of adults. Compared to children who are not exposed to secondhand smoke, children who are exposed to smoke

- in utero are 20 percent more likely to be born with low birth weight.
- are more likely to die from SIDS. In 2005 an estimated 430 newborns died from SIDS as a result of secondhand smoke.
- are four time more likely to suffer from bronchitis, pneumonia, colds, and respiratory infections.
- account for over 202,000 cases of asthma per year.
- get more ear infections because exposure causes buildup of fluid in the middle ear. Middle ear infections account for 790,000 doctor

visits a year and are the most common cause of childhood surgeries and hearing loss.

- are more frequently diagnosed with attention deficit disorder (ADD). A study by Dr. Bruce Lanphear printed in *Environmental Health Perspectives* attributes one-third of ADD in the United States to exposure to tobacco smoke before birth via a smoking pregnant mother or lead exposure in early childhood.
- show deficits in reading, math, and visuospatial reasoning.
- exhibit decreased performances in tests of reasoning ability, language development, and intelligence and an increased risk of being held back a grade in school.

The impact of smoking is so catastrophic that it actually crosses generations. A 2005 study found that if a child's grandmother smoked while pregnant with the child's mother, the child's risk of asthma was doubled. It is suspected that a mother's smoking actually turns on or off genes in the DNA, resulting in the next generation's diminished immune function and therefore greater susceptibility to asthma.

Polls reveal that 95 percent of adults know not to smoke in front of their children, but many people do not realize the damage that thirdhand smoke can do to infants and children. Thirdhand smoke is a cocktail containing toxins that linger in carpets, sofas, clothes, and other materials for hours—or even days—after a cigarette is put out. A 2004 San Diego State University study published in *Tobacco Control* found that parents who smoke outside the home still subject their children to passive smoking. Children in these homes have up to eight times more nicotine in their bodies than the children of nonsmokers. Moreover, nicotine levels in babies who live in houses whose occupants smoke outside are much higher than in babies who live with nonsmokers.

If you are a smoker:

- Quit smoking and encourage all household members to quit too. I know quitting is difficult, but your child is counting on you to keep her healthy and alive for a long time. Smoking is counter to those goals. For free smoking cessation counseling on the phone, call 1-800-NO-BUTTS (1-800-662-8887).
- Do not allow smoking inside your home or car.
- After smoking, change your clothes and take a shower before spending time with your child, especially an infant.

If you are a nonsmoker:

- Do not allow guests to smoke in your home.
- Make sure to ask all child-care providers whether they smoke and if they do, opt not to work with them.
- Take your child only to smoke-free environments.

The Bottle Is Half Empty:
All about Plastic and BPA

I remember the days when I was innocent. I walked around with my bottled water, drinking all day long, thinking I was doing something good for myself, especially when I was pregnant. Later, I even carried a little plastic bottle for my daughters, in case they got thirsty at the park. I never turned a bottle upside down to check for a number. I can just hear Paige, my friend who enlightened me about toxins, screaming in horror. All that was before the Great Bottle Scare of 2008, when so many moms like me lost our toxic innocence. Now *I* am the one screaming in horror.

I remember when the news stories started trickling in about a chemical that "might" be in baby bottles that could "potentially" cause "some harm." Soon after, I started reading articles saying that these were alarmist concerns and that parents shouldn't worry about them. I trusted what I read. Once again I thought the government would never let me buy something that could harm my children, much less a toxin that could disrupt their hormones and make them more susceptible to cancer. I was wrong.

The chemical in question is bisphenol A, commonly known as BPA. It is a hormone disrupter that mimics estrogen and has been associated with cancer, heart disease, diabetes, liver abnormalities, early onset of puberty, hyperactivity, learning disorders, obesity, and neurological impairment. In 2008 it was reported that 95 percent of baby bottles contained this toxic chemical. Furthermore, warming your child's baby bottle is the quickest way to release BPA into whatever beverage your baby is drinking from that bottle! A study found that exposing a plastic bottle to boiling water releases BPA fifty-five times faster than water at room temperature.

To make matters worse, the infant formula that often goes into the bottles is contaminated. Formula containers for both powdered and liquid formula are lined with plastic that leaches BPA. According to a report on infant formula and baby bottles published by the Environmental Working Group, powdered formulas are the best choice for parents who use formula and want to avoid BPA in their baby's diet. Because powdered formula is diluted with much more water than liquid formulas, the amount of BPA that babies consume in each feeding is reduced. In addition, the metal cans have more BPA in the lining. BPA leaches into liquid formula more than powdered formulas because of the heat process used to guard against bacteria in metal cans. This is why the BPA exposure is so much higher in liquid formula in metal cans. The report found that babies fed reconstituted powdered formula receive eight to twenty times less BPA than those fed liquid formula from a metal can. An August 2007 investigation by EWG estimated that given the BPA levels found in ready-to-eat liquid formula, one of every sixteen infants fed the formula would be exposed to the chemical at doses exceeding those that caused harm in laboratory studies.

While we all know "breast is best," sometimes circumstances prevent a mother from being able to breast-feed and she must turn to formula, as I did when my daughters' reflux caused them to reject milk protein. It breaks my heart to think of the chemicals I exposed my children to. Let this serve as a cautionary tale to pay close attention to reports about chemicals that our children (and we adults) are exposed to. For this reason, I love the (free) HealthyChild.org daily newsletter, which provides up-to-date information about toxins and safety.

As of 2009 the six largest manufacturers of polycarbonate baby bottles in the United States announced that they would stop selling baby bottles made with bisphenol A. It appears that consumers spoke with their wallets. So many parents were seeking BPA-free bottles that it became a smart financial move for manufacturers to offer BPA-free options.

Keep in mind, however, that adult water bottles are still made of all sorts of toxic chemicals, and when they're left in the sun—in a hot car, for example—they can leach chemicals. Also, plastic water bottles are for the most part made from nonrenewable petroleum, much of which needs to be imported, and others cause dangerous pollution during manufacturing. I recommend using a stainless steel bottle like Klean Kanteen (www.kleankanteen.com) that does not have an inner lining. If you would like to try a reusable plastic bottle, make sure it has the number 2, 4, or 5 in the little recycling triangle on the bottom. These plastics are considered safer.

With so much information and confusing numbers out there, it's hard to keep straight which plastics are toxic and which ones are not. Christopher Gavigan of Healthy Child Healthy World has a great trick to help you remember these numbers. He suggests looking at your right hand, which represents the good plastics (he says, think "right is right"), and imagining each of your fingers is a number from one to five, minus your middle finger (personally I think giving bad plastics the middle finger is very appropriate). Numbers #6 and #7 on your left hand are bad (unless it is one of the new biobased plastics). Here is a more detailed analysis.

PLASTIC BOTTLES 101

#	Abbre-viation	Chemical	Description	Some common uses	Toxic or OK?	♻	Re-usable?
#1	PETE or PET	Polyethylene terephthalate	Thin, clear plastics	Ketchup, salad dressing, cooking oil, peanut butter, and soda containers	OK	Yes	No
#2	HDPE	High-density polyethylene	Cloudy, thick, milky-looking or opaque plastic	Milk and water jugs, juice bottles, detergent, shampoo, conditioners, yogurt containers, margarine tubs, motor oil containers, toys, plastic bags	OK	Yes	Yes
#3	PVC	Polyvinyl chloride	Varies	Bibs, mattress covers, squeeze bottles, cling wrap, peanut butter jars, detergent containers	Toxic	Yes	No
#4	LDPE	Low-density polyethylene	Soft, flexible plastics	Grocery store bags, plastic wrap, dry cleaning bags, shopping bags, garbage bags, frozen food storage bags, squeezable bottles, sandwich bags	OK	Yes	Yes

#	Abbreviation	Chemical	Description	Some common uses	Toxic or OK?	♻	Reusable?
#5	PP	Polypropylene	Hard but flexible plastics	Ice cream and yogurt containers, drinking straws, syrup bottles, salad bar containers, diapers, some baby bottles	OK	Yes	Yes
#6	PS	Polystyrene	Opaque rigid plastics	Plastic silverware, Styrofoam, including coffee cups, meat trays, egg containers, take-out containers	Toxic	No	n/a
#7*		Other, such as polycarbonate, nylon, and acrylic		Water-cooler water bottles, sports bottles, clear plastic cutlery, and the lining of food and formula cans	Toxic	No	n/a

*Note that #7 also includes some of the new, compostable green plastics, such as those made from corn, potatoes, rice, and tapioca. Gavigan recommends avoiding #7 unless it is labeled as one of these new biobased plastics.

A few more plastic-related tips:

- Buy only glass or BPA-free baby bottles.
- Do not heat baby bottles.
- Don't microwave plastic containers.
- Avoid canned foods whenever possible.
- Look for #1, #2, #4, and #5 in the recycling sign on the bottom of any plastic container or bottle you use.
- Avoid cling wrap; if you do use it, don't let it touch your food. Wrap food in wax paper first. Cut off any food that touched the cling wrap.
- Store food in glass containers instead of plastic.

Family Detox: Six Simple Things You Can Do to Reduce Toxins at Home

1. The diaper dump. The average child goes through 6,000 disposable diapers during the first two years of life. According to the Real Diaper Association, this costs the average family $1,600 a year, not including wipes or diaper cream. Aside from the cost in dollars, the environmental cost is also high. The association estimates that 92 percent of all single-use diapers end up in landfills and that it takes 250 to 500 years for a disposable diaper to decompose.

But maybe you're not ready to think globally and you just want to keep your baby away from toxins. Then you may be surprised to learn that most disposable diapers are filled with toxic chemicals. According to Gavigan, "Disposables contain chemicals that were banned in the 1980s in women's tampons, but continue to be used to improve absorbency. They can also emit gases like toluene, xylene, and styrene, and since babies inhale more air per pound of body weight than adults and are generally more affected by the toxicity or air pollutants, this is troubling." To top that off, a study published in the *Archives of Environmental Health* found that exposing mice to volatile organic compounds (VOCs)—chemicals emitted by conventional disposables—caused asthma-like reactions.

At the moment, parents have four options. The first is to seek out less chemical-laden disposable diapers. I switched my own kids to Seventh Generation, a brand that contains an absorbent gel but doesn't have bleach and a few other chemicals I was hoping to avoid. The second option is to use a disposable liner system. Liners are used between a cloth diaper and the baby's skin, theoretically letting moisture pass through to the diaper but keeping the baby's skin dry. Many of these liners are biodegradable or reusable. This can reduce waste and chemical exposure. Then there are the brave souls who opt for the third option: cloth diapers. But even cloth diapers are far from perfect. They are obviously messy. In addition, many environmentalists are concerned about the chlorine that diaper services use to clean them, the gasoline that is required for diaper pick-up and delivery, and the excessive amount of water used to wash them. One study found that families who use cloth diapers go through fifty to seventy gallons of water every three days. For more information about cloth diapers, go to www.realdiaperassociation.org; to find a diaper service, go to www.diapernet.org.

The fourth option is to encourage your child to use the toilet. As if helping the environment and saving money were not enough motivation, you'll never again have to change a dirty diaper. However, many parents opt out of the diaper-free options, also called "elimination communication," due to concerns about pushing their child too hard or the tremendous commitment it takes from parents to do this type of training. While it is important not to pressure your child to be diaper-free, the results can be fulfilling on many levels. If you are going to try this approach, pick up a copy of Dr. Jill Lekovic's book *Diaper-Free Before 3,* my favorite of all the diaper-free books.

PROTECT THE TUSH, PROTECT THE WORLD: LESS TOXIC DIAPER OPTIONS

Diaper Option	Recommendations
Less toxic diapers	Seventh Generation (www.SeventhGeneration.com) Tushies (www.tushies.com) TenderCare Diapers (www.tendercarediapers.com) Nature Baby Care (www.naty.com)
Disposable liner system	gDiapers (www.gDiapers.com) Kushies (wwww.Kushiesonline.com)
Cloth diapers	Cloth Diapers (www.clothdiaper.com) Cotton Babies (www.cottonbabies.com) Fuzzi Bunz (www.fuzzibunstore.com)

2. Lock up your keys! You're at the supermarket and your baby is getting restless but you forgot to bring some toys to distract her. What do you do? Many parents reach for their keys, dangle them in front of their child's face, or let her play with them—which means those keys are probably in her mouth right about now. What's the problem, you ask? Everyone does it. Here's the rub: Most household keys are made of brass, an alloy that contains lead, which, as you now know, is a potent neurotoxin. According to Jennifer Taggart, an environmental lawyer and author of *Smart Mama's Green Guide,* a study of brass keys led by California's attorney general determined that lead comes off keys, onto the hands, and ends up in the body through key-to-mouth and hand-to-mouth activity. This study concluded that for a high percentage of keys, there was enough potential for lead exposure to be of concern. Some of the keys that were tested left eighty times the current California standard of 0.5 micrograms of lead per day on the hands!

3. Killing germs and the environment one antibacterial pump at a time. I admit, I am a bit of a germaphobe. I hate touching doorknobs and elevator buttons, avoid shaking hands, and actually squealed with glee the first time I discovered a portable antibacterial hand sanitizer that fit in my purse. That is why I was particularly disturbed to learn that not only are my antibacterial products no better than soap and water, when it comes to getting clean, but they are harmful both to the environment and to my children's health.

To begin with, antibacterials don't kill the viruses that most of us are trying to avoid—like the common cold virus, flu viruses, and stomach bugs. In addition, by killing the "good germs" you allow the "bad germs" to flourish, which exposes your child not only to stronger germs but more of them. Dr. Allison Aiello, assistant professor of epidemiology at the University of Michigan, analyzed several studies comparing people who washed their hands with regular soap and people who washed their hands with antibacterial soap. She found that "there was no difference between groups, either in bacteria on the hands or in rates of illness."

In addition, it has been shown in tests that triclosan, one of the key chemicals in antibacterial products, actually causes bacteria to become resistant to antibiotics. Triclosan is a hormone disrupter that has also been linked to weakened immune systems, decreased fertility, altered sex hormones, birth defects, and cancer. So pervasive is this chemical in our everyday lives that a 2004 study conducted by the Centers for Disease Control and Prevention found that nearly three-quarters of adults and children older than six had detectable levels of triclosan.

When you wash your hands with an antibacterial soap, it breaks down rapidly, due to the warm, chlorinated water that you have probably been instructed to use for optimal hand-washing protocol. According to a 2005 study printed in the journal *Environmental Science and Technology,* however, using warm, chlorinated water forms toxic chemicals, including chloroform, in as little as a minute. These chemicals then travel down the drain, ending up in rivers and streams and harming wildlife. "Walk up to any two streams in the U.S., and one will contain triclosan and triclocarban," says Dr. Rolf Halden, associate professor at Arizona State University's Biodesign Institute.

If you still want your hand-sanitizer fix without the triclosan or triclocarban, try some of my favorites:

- Burt's Bees Aloe & and Witch Hazel Hand Sanitizer, www.burtsbees.com
- Clean George Hand Purifier, www.cleangeorge.com
- Cleanwell All Natural Anti Bacterial Foaming Hand Soap, www.cleanwelltoday.com
- Cleanwell Natural Hand Sanitizer Wipes, www.cleanwelltoday.com
- EO Hand Sanitizer, www.eoproducts.com
- Hand Sanz Antiseptic Hand Sanitizer, www.allterrainco.com
- Herban Essentials essential oil towelettes, www.herbanessentials.com
- Jao Hand Refresher, www.jaoltd.com
- Natures Paradise Coconut Scented Hand Sanitizer (comes in other scents too), www.naturesparadiseorganics.com
- Surya Brasil Hand Sanitizer, www.suryabrasilproducts.com

4. Let that Teflon slide right out of your kitchen. I am not a very good cook, but since my daughters were born, I have improved my cooking abilities in the hope of providing them with a healthy diet. There is one culinary skill that I have really perfected: I make a great stir-fry, sautéing organic vegetables and fresh garlic in a heart-healthy olive oil. But I've recently found out that the nonstick Teflon wok I had been using was, very likely, releasing toxins.

An EWG study found that, within five minutes on a conventional stovetop, cookware coated with Teflon and other nonstick surfaces can exceed temperatures at which the coating breaks apart and emits toxic particles and gases. These pans release at least six toxic gases, including two carcinogens, two global pollutants, and MFA, a chemical lethal to humans at low doses. The EWG report was appropriately titled "Canaries in the Kitchen: Teflon Toxicosis." For centuries, coal miners used to take canaries, which respond very quickly to toxic gases, into the mines with them. As long as the canary kept singing, the miners knew their

FROM THE EXPERTS . . .

Baby Gear

Can toxic chemicals lurk in baby gear? Unfortunately, yes. High chairs, car seats, portable cribs, and similar baby gear often contain phthalates, flame retardants, formaldehyde, lead, and other potentially harmful chemicals. Whether the chemicals in baby gear can harm your child is subject to debate, but many concerned parents choose to limit their children's exposure to them and seek alternative products.

How to choose nontoxic baby gear? Skip polyvinyl chloride (aka PVC plastic), which is frequently used to cover pads on high chairs, and for mattress covers in portable cribs. PVC can contain hormone-disrupting phthalates. Phthalates make PVC plastics soft and flexible, but they can be mobilized by saliva, when, for example, a baby mouths a PVC-covered portable crib rail. The Consumer Product Safety Improvement Act (CPSIA) limits phthalates in children's toys and child care articles, meaning articles for children under 3 intended to facilitate sleeping and eating. Some children's gear is included but other items are not. PVC also usually contains a metallic salt so it may have lead, cadmium, manganese, or organotin. The CPSIA now prohibits lead in children's products, so PVC in children's products bought today should have lead below 300 ppm—but older PVC-containing products may not be compliant. Instead, choose natural fibers for covers or a safer plastic, such as polypropylene. Wool pads shed water, so

air supply was safe, but a dead canary signaled the need for immediate evacuation. We now use fire alarms in our homes and office buildings the way canaries were used in mines.

Veterinarians have known for a long time that Teflon-coated and other nonstick cookware can produce fumes that are highly toxic to birds. So common is this type of bird poisoning that it actually has a name, "Teflon toxicosis." According to one expert, this phenomenon is a "leading cause of death among birds." It is estimated that hundreds of birds are killed by the fumes and particles emitted by Teflon-coated products each year. What does this mean for us? And more importantly, what does this mean for our children? As Dr. Alan Greene recently asked at a lecture on toxic chemicals, "Are our children the new canary in the coal mine?"

As a result of government pressure, eight companies that make nonstick pans using PFOA, the chemical that makes the surface slippery and is considered

---

they can be used in place of PVC waterproof covers. If you have PVC covers, then consider covering them to reduce contact with your baby.

Flame retardants serve an important purpose by reducing the risk of injuries caused by fire. Unfortunately, flame retardants are linked to a host of adverse health effects. They off-gas from products to which they are added, resulting in toxic exposure. However, flame retardants only need to be applied to items that are not naturally flame resistant, such as polyurethane foam. So avoid flame retardants by skipping polyurethane foam in padded products. Look for materials that are naturally flame-retardant, such as wool, cotton, coconut husks, and similar materials.

Formaldehyde is linked to cancer, allergies, and asthma. Formaldehyde off-gases from products that use formaldehyde glues, including pressed wood products. When it comes to baby gear, formaldehyde is most likely to be found in cribs, changing tables, and wood high chairs. Formaldehyde off-gassing from just one piece of furniture can elevate indoor air concentrations of formaldehyde above levels considered safe. Instead, buy solid wood or look for formaldehyde-free pressed wood products. When buying wood, consider the environment and choose certified, sustainably harvested wood.

—Jennifer Taggart, environmental attorney
and author of *Smart Mama's Green Guide:*
Simple Steps to Reduce Your Child's Toxic Chemical Exposure
www.thesmartmama.com

to be a "likely human carcinogen," have agreed to eliminate its use by 2015. Until then, try to use cookware that is stainless steel; anodized aluminum; copper-coated, especially with a stainless steel interior; cast iron; enamel-coated iron; steel with chromium and nickel; or Cuisinart's Green Gourmet Hard Anodized Eco-Friendly Nonstick Cookware.

Another thing to be aware of is that PFOA is also found in fast-food packaging, such as Chinese food takeout containers and pizza boxes, and in microwave popcorn bags (one of the biggest offenders). So when you order take-out food, try to get it onto the plate or into different containers as soon as you can, and you may want to skip the microwave popcorn altogether.

5. Green is the new black in baby fashion. Putting together your baby's first wardrobe, also known as the layette, can be a lot of fun. Most parents are inundated with gifts of clothes, hats, and receiving blankets from generous friends and relatives. It is important to remember that all these adorable items will be in direct contact with your child's vulnerable new skin.

To protect your child, there are a few things to keep in mind. First, some cheap kid's clothing is made from petroleum-based synthetic fabric. Many of these outfits, especially those made in China, may be colored with toxic aromatic amine dyes, which are banned in the European Union but sometimes show up in the United States. Second, beware of fabric finishes; if that cute outfit on the hanger looks a little stiff or smells like chemicals, it has probably been sprayed to make it look nice on the display. The most common fabric finish—formaldehyde—is commonly used to preserve dead bodies, but it is also a known allergen, respiratory irritant, chemical sensitizer, neurotoxin, skin irritant, and carcinogen. Be especially wary of clothes from China, where it is standard practice to use formaldehyde on cotton permanent press, all polyester, cotton woven, and 100 percent cotton fabrics. Finally, it is worth noting that cotton, which accounts for 10 percent of the world's farmland, accounts for 25 percent of the world's insecticide use. Many of the pesticides used on cotton crops are considered by the EPA to be the most dangerous pesticides in common use today. It has been estimated that 20,000 people die each year due to pesticide poisoning in cotton agriculture. Buying clothing made from organic, pesticide-free cotton is one of those opportunities where the micro benefit helps your child and the macro benefit helps the world. I don't think it is reasonable for most people to buy only organic cotton, but there are a lot of other eco-friendly options for clothing out there, like bamboo, soy, hemp, and linen.

Inspired by the desire to have more positive messages on shirts worn by both kids and adults, in 2009 I started a clothing company called Retail Therapy (www.ShopRetailTherapy.net). Our feel-good messages say things like "I make a difference," "Embrace change," and "Take responsibility." Along with my design partner, Stefanie Lain, I have worked hard to make sure that our clothing line is eco-friendly by using materials like organic cotton and recycled fabrics. We even use 100 percent recycled paper, embedded with seeds, for our hang tags: people can plant the tags and grow wild flowers. Our motto is "Take care of yourself, take care of the world." We are not the only company that is conscious of these issues. To find eco-friendly fabrics, check out these sources:

Baby Naturopathics, www.babynaturopathics.com
Best Baby Organic, www.bestbabyorganics.com
Fuzzy Green Monster, www.fuzzygreenmonster.com
Go Green Baby Co., www.gogreenbabyshop.com
Green Edge Kids, www.greenedgekids.com
Hanna Andersson, www.hannaandersson.com
Kid Bean, www.kidbean.com
The Little Seed, www.thelittleseed.com
Mother Earth & Baby, www.motherearthandbaby.com
Nubius Organics, www.nubiusorganics.com
Oscar & Belle, www.oscarandbelle.com
Pur Bebe, www.purbebe.com
Soul Flower, www.soul-flower.com
Under the Nile, www.underthenile.com
Wild Dill, www.wilddill.com

6. Green house, clean house.

Cleaning with nontoxic ingredients is one of the most important things you can do for you and your family's health. It's also one of the easiest.

—CHRISTOPHER GAVIGAN, *Healthy Child Healthy World*

You know that lemony, floral, or pine scent that we've come to associate with clean? That scent probably indicates chemicals that are toxic to your child and to you. According to Sloan Barnett, author of *Green Goes with Everything,* "We need to rethink what is clean—our idea of clean may actually be hurting us." If a label says "fragrance," the bottle is likely to have phthalates in it, so beware. We have been brainwashed into believing that "clean" has an odor when, in fact, clean is the absence of dirt, scum, mold, and germs so technically it should have no smell at all.

The most obvious risk for your child from household cleaners is accidental poisoning. You may tend to think that if you keep all the cleaning chemicals locked up or behind a childproof cabinet, your child will be safe. But what about when you spray your counter with one of those chemical agents? It may clean away microorganisms, but you have probably just coated that surface with invisible toxic residue, polluting your indoor air. Many common household cleaners contain volatile organic compounds (VOCs). Don't let the word "organic" fool you. VOCs are carbon-based chemicals that evaporate into the air, causing off-gassing, and are linked to everything from neurological and organ damage to cancer. According to the EPA, concentrations of many VOCs are consistently up to ten times higher indoors than outdoors. No wonder indoor air has been shown to be two to five times more polluted than outdoor air!

One British study found that infants born to mothers who frequently used chemical-based cleaners while pregnant were more than twice as likely to develop breathing problems. Now, what woman doesn't go crazy cleaning her home during the "nesting stage" of pregnancy? It is hard not to think about these things once you know about them. A study funded by the California Resources Board found that a person who cleans a shower stall with a cleaning product containing glycol ethers for fifteen minutes may be exposed to three times the

FROM THE EXPERTS . . .

Household Cleaners

There are simple ways to clean your home effectively while avoiding harmful chemicals. Clean often to reduce the need for harsh chemicals and extra scrubbing, and use natural substitutes for conventional cleaners when possible.

In the kitchen:
- Use a baking soda and water paste instead of oven cleaners—a major source of indoor air pollution.
- Mix equal portions of vinegar and water for a great surface cleaner. Add lemon juice for a nice smell.
- To clear clogged drains, pour in baking soda, then vinegar. For stubborn clogs, use a mechanical snake.
- Wet sponges and microwave them for two minutes to keep them free of bacteria.
- Don't use antibacterial hand or dish soaps. Regular soap is just as effective and doesn't contain as many toxic agents.

In the bathroom:
- A baking soda and water mixture works on toilets, too. Avoid acidic toilet-bowl cleaners, which are full of dangerous chemicals.

recommended one-hour exposure limit. I can't smell that "lemony fresh scent" or do a load of laundry without thinking about the 2008 Environmental Impact Assessment Review that tested six best-selling products (cloth dryer sheets, a fabric softener, a laundry detergent, and three air fresheners) only to find that they off-gassed nearly 100 VOCs, of which ten are considered toxic or hazardous by federal law and three are classified as hazardous air pollutants.

Once you start looking, you will find toxins everywhere. It can be hard to know where to start. Experts say that some of the most hazardous products are oven and drain cleaners, acid-based toilet bowl cleaners, metal polishes, and adhesive removers, followed by disinfectants, furniture and floor polish, carpet cleaners, laundry softeners, spot removers, all-purpose cleaners, automatic dishwashing detergent, chlorine bleach, mold and mildew removers, scouring cleaners, spray starch, and tile, tub, and sink cleaners. It seems that most mainstream products have something in them that you don't want to have near your baby.

- Store the toilet brush where no one will touch it. Wash cleaning rags right away to avoid spreading germs.
- Wipe down showers frequently to avoid mold and mildew.
- Use baking soda and vinegar for drains, vinegar and water for surfaces, and plain soap and water for hands.
- Air fresheners create indoor air pollution. Go with natural ventilation, fans, or a box of baking soda.

Floors:
- Use a vacuum cleaner with a HEPA filter.
- Mop floors with a diluted vinegar and water solution and use a microfiber mop.
- Take shoes off at the door to avoid tracking in dirt.

When using conventional cleaners:
- Follow all directions.
- Dilute the mixture as directed.
- Open windows and run a fan to keep air fresh.
- Keep the kids away.
- Never mix bleach with ammonia, vinegar, or other acids.
- Use certified green products, such as EcoLogo and Green Seal.
- Skip pine and citrus oil cleaners, especially on smoggy days.

—Rebecca Sutton, PhD, senior scientist, Environmental Working Group
www.ewg.org

But you don't need to make yourself crazy. If you want to rid your home of these toxins, start small. If you are not ready to throw everything out (please call your local sanitation department to find out the safest way to do this), then just replace your laundry and cleaning products with greener options as you run out. These days there are many companies that make green cleaning products:

- Begley's Best, www.begleysbest.com
- Eco Mist, www.ecomistsolutions.com
- Ecover, www.ecover.com
- Mrs. Meyers Clean Day, www.mrsmeyers.com
- Seventh Generation, www.seventhgeneration.com
- Shaklee, www.shaklee.com
- Sun & Earth, www.sunandearth.com
- Toni Natural, www.toninatural.com

Some families save a lot of money and avoid a ton of toxins by making their own cleaning solutions from basic household products such as baking soda, lemon juice, soap, vinegar, cornstarch, and salt. I admire these families. I am just not that Martha Stewart about it. A thorough Google search can lead you to home-made cleaning recipes, or you can check out these books:

- *The Complete Idiot's Guide to Green Cleaning* by Mary Findley and Linda Formichelli
- *Green Clean: The Environmentally Sound Guide to Cleaning Your Home* by Linda Mason Hunter and Mikki Halpin
- *Green Cleaning for Dummies* by Elizabeth B. Goldsmith with Betsy Sheldon
- *Knack Clean Home, Green Home: The Complete Illustrated Guide to Eco-Friendly Homekeeping* by Kim Delaney
- *The Naturally Clean Home* by Karyn Siegel-Maier
- *Nontoxic Housecleaning* by Amy Kolb Noyes

Sometimes I feel like the little boy in *The Sixth Sense,* except instead of seeing dead people, "I see toxins." While removing toxins from my home can some-times seem overwhelming and discouraging, I am glad I know about them. I believe that becoming greener and less toxic is a process, probably one I will be working on my whole life. I am constantly taking baby steps and I hope you will too. I have exposed my children to more toxins that I would have liked, but I have also eliminated many of them. Being proactive helps to empower us and protects our babies.

Food for Thought

Eating and Nutrition

When it comes to nutrition, the first three years of your child's life are particularly important. This significant window can influence good eating habits, lifelong health, and even lifespan. One study found that as many as two-thirds of cancer cases are linked to the kind of food people consume. Early childhood is the best time to help your child develop healthy eating habits since young children are particularly malleable when it comes to taste preferences.

Young children utilize half of all energy they consume to fuel brain activity. Since food is considered by many to be the architect of a child's brain, early food choices can have a great impact on intelligence. New research has revealed that specific nutrients may actually activate the genes responsible for enhancing and refining brain development. In addition to affecting IQ, nutritional choices can have long-term effects on your child's immune system, growth, body weight, strength, and vulnerability to allergies.

Feeding children for good health is not just about vitamins and minerals. It is also about avoiding the toxins and chemicals that are pervasive in our children's food. In the United States we are fortunate to be able to purchase inexpensive food, but the downside to this mass-produced cornucopia is that it has created a virtual minefield of genetically modified organisms, pesticides, growth hormones, excitotoxins (common food additives that can literally excite brain cells to death), and food coloring, none of which is beneficial to your child's health. According to the

Environmental Working Group, every day nine out of ten American children between the ages of six months and five years are exposed to combinations of thirteen different neurotoxic insecticides in the foods they eat. Young children are particularly vulnerable to the effects of these chemicals.

But eating is also about emotion, connection, and creating memories. For most new parents, moms in particular, feeding can be a source of great anxiety. Is my child eating enough? Will I be able to breastfeed? How can I get him to eat a vegetable? Is he going to have a weight problem? Parents who know how to introduce foods and avoid mealtime power struggles and who are well educated about age- and developmentally appropriate childhood nutrition can have a dramatic impact on their children's health, well-being, and relationship with food.

More Than Baby Fat: The Obesity Epidemic

Many experts in nutrition and obesity believe that today's children are eating themselves to death. According to the Centers for Disease Control and Prevention, over the past three decades the childhood obesity rate has more than doubled for preschool children aged two to five and more than tripled for children aged six to eleven. Besides more children becoming overweight, the heaviest children are getting even heavier. Overweight is the most common problem that pediatricians address everywhere in the United States. This is not surprising when you look at the statistics on childhood nutrition in America:

- 25 percent of toddlers eat no fruits and vegetables at all.
- French fries are the most common vegetable consumed in America.

- On a given day nearly one-third of children are eating fast food.
- 69 percent of nineteen- to twenty-four-month-old kids eat candy or dessert.
- 44 percent of toddlers drink sweetened beverages.
- 46 percent of seven- to eight–month-old babies consume some type of sweetened drink, dessert, or sweets daily.
- 27 percent eat hot dogs, bacon, or sausage on a typical day.
- Children typically get less than 2 percent of their diet from fruits and vegetables.
- On average, kids get 90 percent of their caloric intake from dairy products, white flour, sugar, and oil.

All these nutritional deficits leave children vulnerable to a host of medical and emotional problems ranging from depression and eating disorders to diabetes and heart disease. Weight problems in children have even been linked to early puberty, which is associated with cancers later in life. Pediatricians are reporting early signs of heart disease more frequently. Results from the Bogalusa Heart Study, the largest long-term study of children's health, found fatty deposits in the coronary arteries of three-year-old children; 70 percent of the twelve-year-olds examined had coronary fatty deposits.

The good news is that parents have a huge influence on their children's relationship with food and dietary habits, especially in the first three years—a great window of opportunity.

Metabolic Programming and Food Preferences

The most recent scientific evidence is both overwhelming and shocking—what we feed (or don't feed) our children as they grow from birth to early childhood has a greater total contributory effect on the dietary contribution to cancers than dietary intake over the next fifty years.

—Dr. Joel Fuhrman, *Disease-Proof Your Child: Feeding Kids Right*

Young children's growing bodies, with all their dividing cells, are particularly vulnerable to negative influences, whether they are dietary, chemical, or toxic. According to the U.S. Environmental Protection Agency, infants and toddlers have a ten times greater risk for cancer than adults when exposed to gene-damaging chemicals. It makes sense that food would also have a significant impact that could have long-lasting effects for young children.

In a study funded by the American Institute for Cancer Research, animals that were susceptible to cancer were divided into two groups: one was fed a high-fat diet and a second group was switched to a low-fat diet at various stages of their lives. The data showed the same results researchers report in human studies: adults who were fed a high-fat diet had more cancer, and the cancer spread more, whereas adults whose diet changed early to lower-fat foods fared better. Of course babies and toddlers need more and different kinds of fats than adults do—and their energy needs should be fueled with "good fats."

Starting a child's life with healthy, nutritious foods does two key things: it helps prevent disease and it creates healthy food preferences that can last a lifetime. Nutrition experts and researchers studying "metabolic programming" have found that foods eaten in childhood can have long-lasting effects on the way a child's body grows. In *The Healthiest Kid in the Neighborhood,* the authors note that what children eat creates a cellular blueprint that can make them more resistant to disease in adulthood.

It is believed that metabolic programming takes place because growth and cell division in many parts of the body occur only in childhood. During this time individual cells are particularly sensitive to the availability of nutrients, the body's basic building blocks. In their book *Feeding Your Child for Lifelong Health,* Drs. Susan Roberts and Melvin Heyman, along with Lisa Tracey, note, "The nutrients physically present at this crucial time for cell division and growth determine how large or small each cell within the different body components ultimately becomes and how efficiently and well it functions in the future." Metabolic programming can have an especially significant impact in promoting healthy body weight, preventing allergies, optimizing bone strength and height, increasing intelligence, and reducing disease, particularly childhood cancers.

In addition to starting children on the road to good health, exposing children to high-nutrient foods helps them develop a preference for these beneficial choices for a lifetime. Children are not born preferring Cheetos to carrots. Kids who grow up eating natural, unprocessed foods will often shun their first Cheeto because it tastes strange to them. On the other hand, children who grow up eating processed foods have a heightened sense of what food is supposed to taste like and are often unsatisfied by "real" foods or, even worse, refuse to eat them.

Research shows that food preferences are learned through a combination of exposure and repetition. This begins very early, as early as in utero, where fetuses are exposed to the same flavors ingested by the mother. One study that used carrots as a test food found that intake during pregnancy or breastfeeding influenced whether or not a child liked carrots by the age of five or six months. When it comes to taste preferences, breastfed infants have a major advantage because they are constantly exposed to new tastes, based on the diet of their mother, whereas formula-fed babies become accustomed to the same taste every time. A 1994 study by Drs. Susan Sullivan and Leann Lipps Birch found that breastfed babies more readily accepted new foods and ate more of them than their formula-fed counterparts.

It is largely up to parents to shape their children's food tastes because the foods they grow up with become their default choices later in life. Alexandra, for example, grew up eating lots of fruits, vegetables, and whole grains. As a college freshman she ate the usual cafeteria cuisine, fast food, vending machine fare, and soda, but as time went by she intuitively veered back to the foods she'd grown up with. Beside the fact that she didn't feel very well after eating the less nutritious food, the foods that she associated with comfort were the ones she'd eaten as a child.

Taking advantage of the first three years is paramount for parents, and luckily during those years children are largely in a familial bubble when it comes to feeding. Children this age are fed at home for the most part, and many daycare centers will accommodate food preferences. Once children start preschool, they become more influenced by peers ("Logan has blue yogurt in her lunch, I want that too!" "I want cookies in my lunch like Ben!"). Although peer influence is usually considered negative, studies show that it can work in your favor too. Another study by Dr. Leann Lipps Birch found that children as young as three and four could be persuaded to change their selection and consumption of vegetables as a result of eating meals with friends whose preferences differed from their own. Furthermore, peer influence was strongest for the younger children in the group.

Divide and Conquer: Parent-Child Eating Responsibilities

New parents typically have two major initial feeding concerns: "Is my child eating enough?" and "Is my child eating too much?" These two concerns can make feeding time an unpleasant, anxiety-filled experience for parent and child. The good news is that children's bodies are miraculously capable. When kids are hungry, the drive to eat is powerful. Your child's body knows how much to eat in order to grow and gain weight properly. Forcing your child to eat when he is not hungry only teaches him to disconnect from his body's signals, making it more likely that he will have a weight problem in the future. Furthermore, forcing him to eat things he does not want can frighten him and make him feel out of control. It is important to trust your child's body to do its job. By sending the message that you believe in your child's ability to regulate his own intake and by allowing him to control what goes into his mouth, you avoid setting up food power struggles.

Ellyn Satter, dietician and author of *Child of Mine: Feeding with Love and Good Sense,* recommends a "division of responsibility" in feeding: parents take responsibility for the *what, when,* and *where* of feeding and let children be responsible for the *how much* and *whether or not* to eat. This division allows you to feed your child in the most helpful and supportive way possible, while allowing him to regulate his appetite. The burden of providing nutritious food, making meals, and helping your child come to the table falls on the parent. The child gets to decide how much to eat, if he wants to eat at all.

Listening to Their Bodies: Children and Intuitive Eating

In their book *Intuitive Eating,* registered dieticians Evelyn Tribole and Elyse Resch point out that the typical toddler is indeed an intuitive eater. He plays until he is hungry and then goes inside to eat lunch. He often leaves food on his plate, even his favorite cookies, and then goes back to play when his physical hunger has been satiated. Children come into this world eating to satisfy their energy needs and self-regulate their calorie intake. In a study in which infants were fed both diluted and concentrated baby formulas, researchers found that the babies consumed more of the diluted formula in comparison to the concentrated one, which showed that they were able to adjust and maintain a relatively consistent level of caloric intake over the course of a single feeding in order to meet their needs.

Children's intake can vary greatly from day to day; however, over a week or even a month, children have an innate ability to supply their energy and nutrition needs. When they're teething and during times of illness or stress, children tend to eat less, but their bodies compensate for the deficit as soon as the situation has passed. Sometimes children go through periods when they have a much greater appetite, especially during growth spurts. There were times when it seemed like my own kids were eating double or triple their body weight in food. These extremes can sometimes panic parents, but it is important to trust your child's body.

There are two parent-created situations that can disrupt a child's natural ability to be an intuitive eater:

When a child consumes a lot of processed foods in the early years. The gist of the problem here is that technology has bypassed nature, meaning that children's bodies are not set up to handle the excessive chemicals, additives, fats, and huge quantities of sugar that are contained in much of today's food. As a result, kids have a difficult time processing these artificial items and compensating for the excessive calories and fat. Dr. Susan Johnson, director of the University of Colorado Health and Science Center, sees a dangerous trend in the making: young children who are increasingly less capable of self-regulation. She reports that, in the 1980s, two- to four-year-old children in her lab were able to compensate for 90 percent of the extra calories in their intake after eating more energy-dense food, but by the 1990s they were compensating for only 45 percent of intake. Children who grow up eating lots of processed foods also have a harder time accepting and enjoying healthier foods. According to Dr. Fuhrman, "the unnaturally high level of sugar, salt, and artificially heightened flavors in processed (fake) foods will lesson or deaden the sensitivity of the taste buds to more subtle flavors, making natural foods taste flat."

When a parent deprives or withholds food from a child. Teaching a child to ignore his own hunger or to deprive himself of food when he is hungry sends a powerful message to the child that he cannot trust his own body. This disconnect, the cessation of his innate ability to hear and obey his body's hunger and satiety signals, is likely to be the beginning of a lifetime of eating and weight problems. This also explains why studies have shown that dieting in childhood is actually a predictor of later obesity.

Building a Better Intuitive Eater

If you want to support your child's natural intuitive eating abilities, try doing the following:

1. Breastfeed for as long as possible. Studies have shown that breastfeeding helps protect babies from becoming overweight or obese later in life. One analysis of seventeen studies found that every month of breastfeeding reduced the risk of childhood overweight by 4 percent. Babies breastfed for nine months had a 31 percent overall reduction in risk. According to Martha and Dr. William Sears in *The Breastfeeding Book,* the fat content of breast milk changes during feedings to meet the needs of a baby, allowing him to control his own intake of fat. In addition, breastfed babies eat smaller meals and are reported to eat more slowly, both healthy eating habits.

2. Focus on your child during feedings. When your child is an infant, it is crucial that you learn to read his hunger cues, be responsive to them, and create a positive feeding experience that makes you both feel connected. He needs your help to focus on eating so that he can listen to his body's cues—a task that can be accomplished only in a quiet environment. Studies show that when a mother is responsive to her baby's signals, the feeding process is a positive experience. Because of the importance of one-on-one focus during feedings, avoid feeding more than one infant at a time whenever possible and never prop feed. In addition to being a choking hazard, prop feeding—using an object to prop up a bottle so a child can feed himself—prevents parents from accurately reading their child's signals.

3. Let your child's hunger overrule the clock. Structured, regular feedings or meals can help regulate hunger and prevent low blood sugar in infants and toddlers, but children should never be prevented from eating when they are hungry simply because it is not the scheduled time to eat. Always support your child's natural hunger.

4. Turn off the television. TV makes children more likely to tune out their body's signals of hunger and satiation. (For more information, see page 257.) As a result, the average person eats eight times more food when watching television. At the same time, watching TV slows down the body's metabolic rate by 12 percent in normal-weight children and 16 percent in overweight children. A study that correlated TV watching to childhood obesity, conducted by the Children's Nutrition Research Center, found that children who were overweight ate 50 percent of their dinners in front of the television, whereas normal-weight kids ate only 35 percent in front of the tube.

5. Create reliable eating times. Children should not have to worry about when they will be fed again. This creates anxiety and a sense of scarcity. Make meals and snacks predictable and pleasant.

6. Restrict between-meal and snack-time munching. Most dieticians agree that starting in toddlerhood, children should be offered three meals and two snacks each day. In order to come to the table with an appetite and eager to eat, they should not be eating at other times. I, too, recommend that you do not allow your toddler or preschooler to rummage through the refrigerator or kitchen cabinets in search of snacks.

7. Provide balanced and nutritious meals. Once your child is able to eat solid foods, it is especially important to give him well-balanced meals in order to create a blueprint for what a "normal" meal should look like—an image that often lasts a lifetime. In addition, you want your child to eat food that will provide him with adequate energy for his body. Most nutritionists recommend that every meal contain the following:

- A source of calcium
- A carbohydrate
- Protein
- Fruit
- Vegetables (not always necessary for breakfast)
- Good fats (like olive oil or nuts)

FROM THE EXPERTS . . .

Peanuts, Peanut Butter, and Jelly

It was previously recommended that parents hold off on giving their children highly allergenic foods, such as peanuts and nuts, until after one year of age. Then the recommendation was to wait until a child was two years old, or even older, depending on a child's family history of allergies. Although further studies need to be done, current research shows that there is little evidence that holding off on introducing your infant to peanuts and nuts has any effect on whether or not he will develop a nut allergy. In fact, some experts suggest that early introduction of allergenic foods may even decrease the chance that your child may become allergic later. Therefore, the American Academy of Pediatrics Nutrition Committee has changed its recommendation. It now says that infants over six months of age can try a variety of foods, including peanut and other nut products.

Before you offer your six-month-old a peanut butter and jelly sandwich, however, remember that peanut butter is sticky and can easily get stuck in an infant or toddler's mouth or throat. Your baby has an entire lifetime in which to enjoy all kinds of foods, so what's the rush to introduce peanut butter now? Start off slowly with pureed foods and gradually work your way to a lumpier consistency until your child is ready for solid finger foods. Don't forget that whole nuts are a serious choking hazard and should never be given to infants and toddlers.

Food allergies are more common in children whose families have a history of food allergies, asthma, hay fever, and eczema. If your child falls into this category, talk to your pediatrician about the best time to introduce nuts into your child's diet. Food allergies cause symptoms such as facial swelling, hives, eczema, vomiting, wheezing, or trouble breathing. Call your doctor right away if you notice any of these symptoms. If your infant is having trouble breathing, call 911.

—Dr. Tanya Remer Altmann, pediatrician, author of *Mommy Calls: Dr. Tanya Answers Parents' Top 101 Questions About Babies and Toddlers,* editor in chief of *The Wonder Years,* and associate medical editor of *Caring for Your Baby and Young Child, Birth to Age 5*
www.drtanya.com

8. Do not use food to reward, bribe, or punish. Using food to manipulate, control, or coerce a child, even when the intentions are good (e.g., "I know he'll be hungry later if he doesn't eat now," "He is so thin and I don't want him to lose weight," or "He hasn't eaten a vegetable all day!") will always backfire. Food-related rewards, bribes, and punishments cause a child to disconnect from his body's signals and eat only in order to please you. The more neutral or seemingly disinterested you are in the outcome (how much he eats), the more likely he is to follow his own body's cues.

9. Eat together as a family. Family meals allow children to learn from their parents' behaviors and attitudes about food and nutrition. If you have a positive body image and a healthy relationship with food, there's a good chance your child will pattern his attitudes after yours. It's even likely that he'll get more complete nutrients from his meals if you supervise or cook the family dinner. Study after study shows that children who eat with their parents take in more folate, fiber, calcium, iron, and vitamins A, B6, B12, C, and E. They consume fewer soft drinks, less fat, and fewer fried foods and also tend to have a lower body mass index (BMI). A 1996 Harvard Medical School study found a strong correlation between a lack of family dinners and obesity. The researchers found that the more dinners that children ate with their family, the lower were the children's BMIs.

10. Let go of your ideas about what your child's body is "supposed" to look like. You can trust your child's body to grow the way it was meant to. Your job is to support your child in listening to his body's cues. You never want your child to feel that your love is conditional or get the sense that there is something "wrong" with his body. This creates a preoccupation with food and eating that leads to eating disorders and body dissatisfaction. The thin child who is pushed to eat is likely to become disgusted by food, and the heavy child who is restricted is likely to develop a sense of scarcity that makes it more likely he will overeat.

Be a Super Model: Setting an Example

When she looked in the mirror, she'd squint her eyes and curl her lip in disapproval. Then she would gently but desperately try to fluff her hair. Finally she'd groan and throw her arms up in the air. I would look in the mirror next to her and imitate her expressions and gestures to make the "mirror face" I had seen so many times. I learned at a young age that when you look in the mirror, you do not like what you see.

—PSYCHOTHERAPY CLIENT
talking about watching her mother get ready for work

The greatest gift you can give your child is to model a healthy relationship with food: giving your body the food it needs to be healthy and feel good, trusting and obeying your body's signals, treating your body with respect (including how you talk about and even look at your body), and, at the same time, avoiding food restrictions that make you binge because you feel deprived.

A study of mothers who engage in unhealthy dieting behaviors found that their five-year-old daughters had more weight concerns than the daughters of nondieting moms and were twice as likely to possess awareness of and knowledge about dieting, one of the biggest triggers for eating disorders later in life. Another study of mothers who did not follow their own body cues found that their daughters' eating habits mirrored their mothers'. In addition, the girls' eating habits were more likely to be triggered by external cues. In other words, if one of the girls saw a cookie (even if she wasn't hungry and hadn't wanted a cookie previously), she was more likely to eat one. A recent study done by Boston University School of Medicine found that parents who reported the two eating extremes—food restricting and overeating—in their own behavior had overweight children compared to families where only one or none of the parents scored high on eating extremes.

Eating practices, neurosis, and disorders are often handed down from generation to generation. If you are a mother and have issues with food, as many women

---

FROM THE EXPERTS . . .

Intuitive Eating

If you've ever tried to get an infant to eat when she's not hungry or taken the breast or bottle away before she's full, you know that you've attempted an almost impossible task. Infants are born with all the internal wisdom they need in order to know when and how much to eat. The earliest developmental task they must accomplish is that of self-trust, and eating is the arena where this task is best practiced. If there is a direct attunement between an infant's hunger and satiety signals and her caregiver's response, a reinforcement of those signals begins to develop. The infant soon learns not only to trust that her signals are accurate, but develops a sense of self-trust as well. If, however, her parent or caregiver is driven by an agenda of anxiety that her child is either not gaining enough weight or might be gaining too much weight, the potential for a disconnected attunement to her signals is created.

do, you owe it to the next generation to resolve your issues before you pass them on. Keep in mind that the messages your child absorbs from you are not just from what you eat but also from how you talk about your own body and food.

Ideally, you want your children to eat fruits, vegetables, and other nutrient-dense foods because they enjoy them and see your whole family enjoying them. This may sound delusional, but I have seen it firsthand, not only in my own household but also in the homes of clients and friends. Just this morning my own children were telling me, completely unsolicited, how much they love mushrooms, broccoli, and tomatoes—not surprising, since these are foods that my husband and I love, too. Mothers are particularly influential when it comes to children's food preferences. In fact, studies show that children tend to develop food preferences and eating habits that are similar to their mothers'.

But fathers are not off the hook! A Pennsylvania State University study found that five-year-olds who ate the most fruits and vegetables came from households in which both parents did the same. Not surprisingly, another study that looked at adults who ate a lot of fruits and vegetables found that they consumed a lot of the same foods when they were children.

For messages about food to be most powerful, both parents need to agree about family nutrition and believe in the advice and philosophy they pass on to their kids. Ideally, everyone in the family should eat the same things, and there

---

A child's inborn internal wisdom about eating is the foundation for a life of intuitive eating. If a wide variety of foods are introduced to her when she begins to eat, and as she becomes a toddler, she will develop the ability to appreciate different tastes and textures and will learn what pleases her palate and what does not. Her ability to tap into internal wisdom will progress beyond hunger and satiety to include food preferences. If no judgments are placed on food, the child will have the opportunity to further strengthen self-trust and drastically reduce the risk of disordered eating. A parent's job is to provide her child with opportunities to taste many foods. The child's need is to have her food preferences and hunger and fullness signals respected. With this opportunity, she will grow at an appropriate pace and have balance and satisfaction in her eating.

—Elyse Resch, MS, RD, FADA,
Registered dietitian, nutrition therapist, and co-author of
Intuitive Eating: A Revolutionary Program That Works and the CD *Intuitive Eating: A Practical Guide to Make Peace with Food, Free Yourself from Chronic Dieting, Reach Your Natural Weight*
www.ElyseResch.com, www.IntuitiveEating.org

shouldn't be any "kids only" rules about food. I recognize that this can be challenging but I believe it is a worthy goal, nonetheless.

Starting Off on the Right Foot—or Breast

The American Academy of Pediatrics (AAP) strongly recommends breastfeeding: "Epidemiologic research shows that human milk and breastfeeding of infants provide advantages with regard to general health, growth, and development, while significantly decreasing risk for a large number of acute and chronic diseases." The AAP adds, "breastfeeding has also been related to possible enhancement of cognitive development." It recommends exclusive breastfeeding for the first six months, then breastfeeding in combination with solid foods through at least twelve months, and then continuing for as long as mutually desired by mother and child. Research has shown that the benefits gained are greater the longer a baby is breastfed.

Breastfeeding can be difficult for some moms, as it was for me. For many mothers (and babies), the breastfeeding process is not as easy or as "natural" as they had imagined. Breast pain, sore nipples and infections, latching issues, and fatigue can challenge even the most determined mom. A study done by the New Mexico Department of Health found that three things help breastfeeding mothers: confidence in the process of breastfeeding, confidence in their ability to breastfeed, and commitment to making breastfeeding work despite obstacles. If I were to add a fourth point, it would be "good support." In my practice I see the best outcomes from mothers who have a group of people—family and friends and compassionate health-care providers—who encourage them to meet their breastfeeding goals. A partner who supports breastfeeding and is willing to help in any way possible makes a huge difference, as well as access to a lactation consultant (whose expertise is often provided by hospitals and frequently covered by insurance) and breastfeeding support groups.

Breastfeeding Hotlines

International Lactation Consultant Association, 1-888-ILCA-IS-U

La Leche League, twenty-four-hour breastfeeding hotline, 1-877-4-LA LECHE

The National Women's Health Information Center, National Breastfeeding Hotline (Monday through Friday, 9 a.m. to 6 p.m. Eastern Standard Time), 1-800-994-9662, TDD 1-888-220-5446

Study after study shows that drinking breast milk can actually make kids smarter. A 1992 British study examined the cognitive development of two groups of preemies that were being fed through feeding tubes due to their prematurity. One group was given breast milk while the other was given formula. Tests done eight years later showed that the breast milk group scored more than eight points higher in IQ than the formula-fed group. Even babies who were raised on donor breast milk have been shown to be more developmentally advanced than their formula-fed counterparts at eighteen months. Researchers from New Zealand found that babies who were breastfed for eight months or more had higher IQs, better reading comprehension and math skills, and overall increases in scholastic ability than babies who were not breastfed. The effects are long-lived, the study says, extending through childhood and adolescence.

The benefits of breastfeeding go beyond intelligence, however. Research has shown that breastfeeding may help

- Strengthen children's immune system
- Lower the risk of SIDS
- Protect against allergies and eczema
- Prevent the development of type 1 diabetes
- Protect against some cancers, especially leukemia and Hodgkin's lymphoma
- Reduce the chance of getting meningitis
- Prevent gastroenteritis
- Aid visual development
- Prevent ear infections
- Diminish respiratory infections
- Reduce urinary tract infections
- Make obesity less likely
- Prevent high blood pressure later in life

As if these benefits were not valuable enough, studies show that breastfeeding also benefits mothers in a number of significant ways:

- Helps take off pregnancy weight
- Reduces postpartum bleeding
- Helps shrink the uterus to its prepregnancy size
- Decreases stress levels
- Reduces the risk of cancers, especially breast cancer
- Protects against osteoporosis
- Aids in general weight loss

Despite the statistics, some mothers are unable to breastfeed or choose not to. Personally, I was very disappointed that I was not able to breastfeed as long as I would have liked. While breast is clearly best, not being able to breastfeed does not mean that your child is doomed. For parents who have opted to use formula, the American Academy of Pediatrics recommends an iron-fortified formula for the baby's first year, a recommendation that is supported by a University of Michigan study that found that children who had severe and chronic iron deficiency in infancy scored lower than their peers on cognitive and motor tests in their teens.

If you are unsure if you want to breastfeed, I urge you to try it. You can always change your mind and switch to formula later. At the very least, you will have provided the initial colostrum, or "first milk," that gives your baby valuable nutrients in a very concentrated, low-volume form and also gives his vulnerable immune system a boost from the start. You may even find that you enjoy the process more than you expected.

FROM THE EXPERTS . . .

Tips for Moms Who Are Having Trouble Breastfeeding

Corky Harvey and Wendy Haldeman have consulted with new breastfeeding moms for thirty years and share a common concern over the number of women who needlessly abandon breastfeeding within the first few weeks. Here are some of their recommendations to ensure a successful experience.

- Know where to get breastfeeding help before you give birth and get the help as soon as you need it. Most difficult nursing situations can be solved with the assistance of a qualified lactation consultant.
- Find a supportive, knowledgeable pediatrician who understands breastfeeding management.
- If you are having breastfeeding difficulty, concentrate on nursing your baby, resting, eating healthy food, and drinking water.
- Surround yourself with family and friends who are knowledgeable and supportive of your decision to breastfeed.
- Join a breastfeeding support group in your area. Ask moms you meet where you can find resources to support you.
- Protect your milk supply. Milk must be removed from your breast in order for you to produce more. If your baby isn't able to nurse effectively, it is

From Breast to Fork:
Utilizing Windows of Opportunity

Where food is concerned, there are two key areas for parents to pay attention to in the first three years: (1) nutrition, and (2) the developing relationship between your child and eating. In the beginning, your job revolves around learning your child's cues and meeting his needs, but, as he gets older, the focus shifts to presenting your child with wholesome meals and helping him develop a sense of mastery in regard to food. For the early eater, mastery might be the newly found ability to pick up a Cheerio and put it in his mouth; for the preschooler, it might mean the use of utensils. Most of the battles that involve food—which tend to start in a child's second year and escalate from there—deal with issues of control. If you follow Ellyn Satter's division of responsibility (where parents are responsible for what is presented to eat and the manner in which it is presented, and

important that you pump eight to ten times in twenty-four hours (around the clock) until the baby can take over.

- Sore nipples are a common challenge during the first few weeks of breastfeeding. Finessing the latch and the positioning of the infant may solve the problem. A lactation consultant can assess the situation and help find solutions.
- Educate yourself about the normal feeding patterns of breastfed infants. Most newborns have at least one "marathon" feeding a day and will have many growth spurts throughout infancy. Frequent feedings during these times are normal and necessary. Formula use will decrease rather than increase milk supply.
- Avoid books and the advice of well-meaning family or friends who advocate scheduled feedings during the newborn period. Infants need to feed very often during the first weeks of life to establish a good milk supply. Milk supplies vary from woman to woman; some babies will need to eat more often than others.
- Wait at least two weeks before introducing a bottle.

Time and patience go a long way in solving many breastfeeding issues—and it will be worth the wait.

—Corky Harvey, MS, RN, and Wendy Haldeman, MN, RN,
board certified lactation consultants and co-owners of The Pump Station
www.PumpStation.com

children are responsible for whether they eat and how much), you turn that control over to your child and as a result avoid many of these fights.

As children get older, their primary task becomes individuation—learning to be separate from you. But in the post-toddler era this is still a huge conflict. There is a constant swing between "I can do it myself" and "Mommy, help me!" Kids at this age want control, yet too much control is scary for them. In her book *Just Tell Me What to Say,* Betsy Brown Braun points out that post-toddler power struggles tend to fall into four general areas: eating, sleeping, talking, and eliminating. Children intuitively know that you can't make them eat. By not investing in "how much" and "whether or not" your child eats, you will in effect remove yourself from these battles.

All parents want their children to eat healthily, but not all parents know how to take advantage of the developmental windows that help make their children's healthy food experience a positive one. In his book *Feeding Baby Green,* Dr. Alan Greene talks about helping children develop "nutritional intelligence," or the ability to be smart about what they eat in order to support good health. He asserts

FROM THE EXPERTS . . .

Colic: Still Fuzzy After All These Years

Is the word "colic" dead? If not, perhaps it should be. Or perhaps our view of this comfortable, overused term should be modified to something with more historical relevance. Consider this: since colic represents a pattern of behavior and not a disease, a baby cannot be "diagnosed" with colic. To use the word "diagnosis" with colic suggests that intelligent, established criteria, backed up by clinical research, were used to come to that conclusion. Unfortunately, such criteria don't exist. Despite the complete absence of consensus on what constitutes colic, it remains nonetheless a convenient wastebasket diagnosis for pediatricians.

But our experience tells us that the screaming baby screams for a reason. Advances in technology, immunology, and nutrition have allowed us to rethink why babies cry. New studies have shown that in many cases a baby may be suffering from acid reflux, a milk protein allergy, or an imbalance in intestinal bacteria. Acid reflux—which refers to the movement of stomach contents up into the swallowing tube and throat—represents one treatable cause of infant misery.

that, just as some children have fine motor or language delays, we have created an environment that fosters developmental delays in children learning to like vegetables, fruits, and whole grains. Having a home full of delicious and nutritious foods and knowing how and when to present them to your child can go a long way toward developing the nutritional intelligence they'll need later in life.

Feeding Tips for the First Three Years:

FOUR TO SIX MONTHS

At this stage, your child has a powerful drive to put everything in his mouth. While this creates an imperative for parents to be hypervigilant and makes your job a lot more exhausting, it does make the transition to solid foods easier. When you give your baby his first solids, open your mouth as you bring the spoon to his so he knows what to do. Don't forget, no one has ever given him a spoonful

---

Here are six signs that your baby may be suffering with acid reflux:

1. Spitting and vomiting—Spitting up is the sine qua non of reflux.
2. Hiccups—All babies have hiccups, but they may be worse with reflux.
3. Irritability and positional preference—Babies with reflux prefer to be upright.
4. Feeding disturbance—Reflux will often lead to painful feeding and pulling from the breast.
5. Sleep disturbance—Reflux can be worse in the nighttime hours, leading to crying and disorganized sleep.
6. Congestion—The throat irritation experienced by the refluxing baby can create noisy breathing, often mistaken for a cold or allergy.

Ask your doctor to help you determine whether your baby's misery may represent a treatable condition. And think twice when your baby is "diagnosed" with colic.

—Bryan Vartabedian, MD, pediatric gastroenterologist and author of
*Colic Solved: The Essential Guide to Infant Reflux
and the Care of Your Crying, Difficult-to-Soothe Baby*
www.ColicSolved.com

of food before so he doesn't necessarily know what to do. Take advantage of your child's active mirror neurons, those special cells that get him to imitate what you do (the same cells that operate, for example, when you see someone yawn and you are compelled to yawn too). Demonstrating shows the baby what to do and also makes for a fun interaction. Around this age your baby will start to lose the "extrusion reflex," which makes him push everything out of his mouth with his tongue. The disappearance of this previously necessary and life-saving reflex is one of the many signs that your child is ready for solid food.

Many parents are eager to start their children on solids; I know I was. Some are working under the mistaken belief that solids will get a baby to sleep through the night faster or make reflux go away; some parents think that babies need "real food" to be healthy. While you may notice small changes as your child begins eating sold foods, breast milk (or formula) is still going to be his primary source of nutrition for a while. Keep in mind that your baby's intestinal lining is immature. Introducing solids too early, usually before four months, can result in an increased likelihood of food allergies and even obesity, while introducing solids too late, after six months, has been linked to the development of gluten sensitivity. Look for the following signs to determine if your baby is ready for solids:

- He is at least four months old.
- He sits up in a high chair unassisted.
- He has sufficient head control to keep his head in a steady upright position.
- He has lost the tongue-thrust reflex.
- His appetite has increased and he seems unsatisfied after a milk feeding.
- He has made significant weight gains—most pediatricians recommend introducing solids after a child has doubled his birth weight.
- He shows interest in what grown-ups are eating.
- He is able to coordinate his mouth and tongue effectively to chew and to move food to the back of his mouth when he is ready to swallow.
- He can close his lips over a spoon.

SIX TO TWELVE MONTHS

The ideal diet for an older baby who has already tried a variety of foods is a diverse one that allows him to get all the micronutrients he needs. Once again your baby's biology works in his favor by making him an inconsistent diner. The peas that thrilled him yesterday may revolt him today. According to Roberts, Heyman, and Tracy, "Most children older than about eight months instinctively seek variety unless discouraged by bad food experiences. They push their parents to provide variety by refusing to eat what they ate two days ago." Take advantage of this opportunity to expand your child's culinary horizons, but don't overwhelm him by giving him a plate of entirely new foods. Combine tried favorites with a single new food. Take advantage of foods that are well received to introduce similar-looking ones. For example, if your child likes oranges, try introducing tangerines. If he likes mashed potatoes, try mashed yams.

Sometime between seven and nine months, you may notice your baby reaching for the spoon you are using to feed him with, trying to pick up his pureed carrots, or even grabbing food off your plate. At first, he may just rake food into his hand and bring it to his mouth, but eventually he will figure out how to use his thumb and forefinger to pick up food. This early use of the pincer grasp is an important milestone that signifies the development of fine motor skills. It is important for parents to support this autonomous step toward self-feeding, no matter how messy it may be. This sense of mastery is important for your child, and the self-feeding process allows him to start to feel in charge of his own eating, which can also reduce power struggles.

ONE TO TWO YEARS

At the end of your child's first year, as Roberts, Heymen, and Tracy point out, he demonstrates the perfect convergence of physical development, metabolic maturity, and natural instinct that encourages adventurous eating. Your child wants to be like you and is now physically capable of eating the way you do, while not yet becoming the cautious eater he is likely to become at age two. Your biggest obstacle is likely to be that, sometime around eighteen months, when the emergence of will occurs, your sweet angel will begin screaming "No!" and testing you at every meal. This is a time when it becomes increasingly important to your child to be independent. It is also a time when there is the potential for those natural urges for individuation to get played out at the dinner table in the form of power struggles. But don't despair. You will want to play off this new desire for independence as much as you can. At this point, that pincer grasp is likely to be much more developed and your child will want to feed himself, not just with his fingers but also with utensils. Letting him do it by himself is the way to avoid battles at this stage and allow him to have a feeling of mastery at the table.

Another instinct that works in your favor around this time is your child's desire to be just like you. As children get closer to the two-year mark, they are pretty much programmed to imitate everything their parents do, including eating. Animal studies suggest that even a single experience of watching an adult eat a specific food can increase the odds of a child wanting to eat that food a year later. Use this instinct to your advantage by letting your child see you eat foods that you want him to eat. If you ask your toddler to try something new, you are almost guaranteed to get an emphatic "No!" but if he sees you eating it he is likely to show interest. A helpful tip I learned from pediatric nutritionist Cynthia Epps of MotherWork is to act surprised and then say, "This is my tofu," and after hesitating for a moment say, "I'll share it with you." This response allows the child to maintain control while opening the door to try new foods.

By the way, this tactic also works in reverse. If your child sees you eating a less nutritious food, he'll want that, too. I can, shamefully, share my own experience on this one. While writing this very book and staying up way too late, I found myself drinking coffee, which I had previously sworn off. My increasing need for caffeine overcame my better parenting judgment and I began to bring my daily caffeine fix, which often came in the form of a caffeine-filled coffee shake loaded with whipped cream, into the house where my daughters observed the drinks. They now regularly tell me, "Mommy, when I am a big girl I want to drink coffee!" Needless to say, this was not the best nutritional example I could model for my kids.

Studies show that it is not uncommon for a child to have as many as fifteen exposures to a new food before he accepts it. Most parents are not that patient. In a large-scale study, researchers found that approximately 25 percent of parents gave up offering their child a new food after only one or two tries if the child rejected it, and only 6 percent were willing to continue to try it six to ten times. This is unfortunate because familiarity promotes acceptance when it comes to kids and food. In a study in which moms offered their babies a disliked vegetable every other day, over 70 percent ate it happily by the time they had been presented with the vegetable seven or eight times, and nine months after the study ended 75 percent of the children were still eating that vegetable.

Another thing that can throw parents off at this stage is a child's tendency to chew and spit foods out or make a face. While this looks like food rejection, often it is not. Sometimes a child just wants to examine the food in its newly chewed form. This natural skepticism is nature's way of making sure your toddler rules out food that might be harmful. Make sure you avoid a big reaction. This can be hard to do when your child makes a really funny face, but the less attention you give it, the better off everyone will be. As gross as this sounds, let your child leave the chewed-up food on his plate so he can revisit it later. I know—"Eww yuck!" I felt the same way. Just remind yourself that you are helping your child expand his palate.

Because kids' stomachs are small, but their nutritional needs are big, most pediatric dieticians recommend that children start to incorporate two snacks into their diet at some point between twelve and fifteen months. This prevents a child's blood levels from dipping too low during the day and ensures that his growing brain receives a steady supply of glucose throughout the day, according to Dr. David Perlmutter, author of *Raise a Smarter Child by Kindergarten*. Just make sure those snacks are nutritious, so your child can get the greatest benefit.

FROM THE EXPERTS . . .

Veggie Kids

More and more children today are vegetarians, either because their parents raised them that way or because they chose a vegetarian lifestyle on their own—sometimes at a very early age! Plenty of research has found that a vegetarian lifestyle has enormous health benefits. Compared to meat-eaters, vegetarians tend to consume more fiber, vitamins, and minerals from a variety of sources. They also have lower cholesterol levels and are less likely to develop chronic illnesses, such as obesity, atherosclerosis, asthma, and diabetes. Vegetarian foods are a more efficient energy source than animal products because they are easier for the body to break down and leave a smaller carbon footprint. Often there are concerns that children might not be getting the nutrients they need for proper growth and development if they've omitted meat from their diet. Essentially, without meat, poultry, and fish, we need to ensure that a child receives sufficient protein, iron, and zinc. There are plenty of veggie-based protein- and iron-rich foods like tofu, lentils, chickpeas, and beans. Zinc can be found primarily in whole grains, wheat germ, lima beans, soy, and nuts. As you would with any other child, offer your veggie little ones three meals and two or three snacks daily so that they have many opportunities to receive the nutrition they need. If you have any concern about your child's growth or nutritional intake, discuss it with your pediatrician or pediatric dietician.

—Nicole Meadow, MPN, RD,
pediatric dietician, founder of NutritionWise
www.nicolemeadow.com

TWO TO THREE YEARS

Beginning at around age two, children suddenly express extremely strong opinions about food. They can also be a bit quirky about it, developing what I call a "Food of the Month" mentality. They may insist on having the same food for every meal for weeks and then suddenly refuse to eat it and develop a new favorite. Don't cater to this quirk by serving macaroni and cheese three times a day. At each meal you should be serving food from all the food groups and let your child pick what he likes. Once you start cooking special meals or replacing foods that your child refuses to eat, you are walking down a slippery slope. If you put a selection of foods on the table that includes protein, carbohydrates, vegetables, fruit, a source of calcium, and so on, there is bound to be something your child will eat. The urge to satisfy his hunger will ultimately override his desire to control the meal. If your child continues to refuse a healthy variety of foods after a few days, be sure to consult your pediatrician.

At the same time, you should not force food on your child. One of the reasons why you should offer your child foods from all the different food groups is that it is important to respect your child's food preferences and make sure there are some things on the table you know he will like. You should still obey the division of responsibility (where parents controls the *what* and *when* while the child decides *how much,* if any, he will eat) and never push your child to eat (not even the old "just one bite" gambit). Children have individual food preferences, just as adults do. You wouldn't force your husband to eat a plateful of spinach if you knew he didn't like it, and you shouldn't force your child to eat it either. The attempt will not be well received and the outcome will be the opposite of what you are trying to accomplish. Although it is a good idea to introduce your child to a variety of new foods, once those efforts have been made, your child's food preferences should be honored.

Fueling the Fire: Flame Retardants in Meat

In the fall of 2009 the American Academy of Pediatrics Committee on Nutrition revised its recommendations on first solid foods for babies. Rice cereal has traditionally been a first food for infants in the United States, but newer thinking is that the emphasis in first foods should be on naturally nutrient-rich foods such as vegetables, fruits, and meats.

But before you pull out that meat cleaver, you may want to check with your pediatrician. A study in the journal *Environmental Health Perspectives* revealed that people who frequently eat poultry and beef have higher levels of polybrominated diphenyl ethers (PBDEs), a common flame retardant, in their blood (for more information about PBDEs, go to page 286). These known endocrine disrupters, which accumulate in the liver, kidneys, and thyroid gland, have been linked to impaired memory, abnormalities of coordination, hyperactivity, and reproductive and nervous system impairments.

In a study of thirty-two food samples sold in major supermarkets in Dallas, researchers reported PBDE contamination in *all* food containing animal fats. According to Arnold Schecter, an environmental sciences professor at the

University of Texas School of Public Health and co-author of the study, "That's because PBDEs are easily absorbed by fatty tissues. Nonfat milk, on the other hand, had no detectable PBDE levels."

Americans and Canadians have ten to twenty times higher levels of PBDEs than people in Europe, where PBDEs have been banned since 2004, and Japan, where their use and production have been voluntarily restricted. The highest levels have been detected in U.S. children between the ages of two and five. Studies show that vegetarians have PBDE concentrations that are 23 to 27 percent lower than omnivores.

The Toxic Plate: What's Really in Our Children's Food

Our children are exposed to a toxic alphabet soup of BGH, MSG, OPs, GMOs, and other harmful chemicals and additives. While these harmful chemicals are not good for adults either, children are far more vulnerable because of their small body size, fast metabolism, less varied diet, immature immune system, and more porous blood-brain barrier. According to a report issued by the Environmental Working Group called *How 'Bout Them Apples?*, some apples are literally so toxic to a child under five that just one bite can deliver an unsafe dose of organophosphate (OP) insecticides.

We want to believe that our government is protecting us and that it wouldn't sanction the sale of certain foods if they weren't safe. But this is just not the case. To protect our kids, we have to take matters into our own hands: Knowledge is power. In the area of nutrition, research shows that even small changes make an especially large difference for our children. Take a look at eight of their biggest food enemies:

1. PESTICIDES

Things that by their very nature are designed to kill come with risks. And they don't always disappear after doing the job. Pesticides can remain in the air, food, and soil; contaminate water; and accumulate in plants, animals, and people.

—Allan Magaziner, Linda Bonvie, and Anthony Zolezzi,
Chemical-Free Kids: How to Safeguard Your Child's Diet and Environment

If your child took a swig from a bottle of garden pesticide, you would be on the phone with poison control or 911 immediately. So what would you say if I told you that you have been unknowingly feeding your child pesticides every day?

- There are currently 600 chemicals that farmers are legally allowed to use on produce and at least fifty of these are classified as carcinogenic, according to the U.S. Food and Drug Administration (FDA).
- Twenty pounds of pesticides are used per person per year in the United States.
- Pesticides are present not only in conventionally grown fruits and vegetables but also in processed products like cookies, cereals, and crackers.
- Nine out of ten kids under the age of five are exposed to thirteen different neurotoxic insecticides in baby foods, according to the EWG.
- OPs in apple, peach, grape, and pear baby food that is consumed by 85,000 children every day exceed the federal safety standard by a factor of ten or more.
- 20 million children age five and under consume an average of eight pesticides a day.
- Drinking nonorganic apple juice may expose your two-year-old to as many as eighty different pesticides, an exposure that is twenty times that of his mother on a body-weight basis.

Although pesticides have been linked to cancers, birth defects, kidney and liver damage, reproductive disorders, and asthma, they are still present in our children's foods. The current regulatory system assumes that chemicals are not harmful until proved otherwise. According to Cindy Burke, author of *To Buy or Not to Buy Organic,* this proof is almost impossible to supply for three reasons. First, pesticides are too dangerous to be tested directly on humans. Second, because people are contaminated with trace levels of hundreds or even thousands of chemicals, it is impossible to attribute a specific health effect to any one chemical. Third, most safety tests performed for regulatory agencies like the FDA are not intended to determine if low-dose exposure to pesticides is safe; they only measure the effect of high doses. Another problem is the poor system of regulation. Take, for example, the EPA, whose job is to regulate and establish tolerances (acceptable levels of toxic substances in food). Toxicity testing is actually left to the manufacturers to carry out and then report to regulators at their discretion. Furthermore, according to Burke, "the EPA almost never bans a pesticide that is presently in use."

The EPA estimates that 80 percent of our pesticide exposure comes from food, and the remaining 20 percent comes from drinking water and pesticides that are used in and around our homes. So it shouldn't be surprising to hear that by feeding your children organic food you eliminate nearly 90 percent of their pesticide exposure. Not only does this switch make a tremendous difference, but the change in detected pesticides is dramatic and immediate. A University of Washington study that was funded by the EPA measured the pesticide levels in the urine of twenty-three children before and after switching to an organic diet. Prior to the switch, every single child tested showed the presence of pesticides, but after only five straight days on an organic diet, researchers found that pesticide levels were undetectable. They remained that way until the children returned to eating conventionally grown foods. This result really speaks to the power of making a few small changes in a child's diet.

Based on an analysis of more than 87,000 tests for pesticide residues in produce collected by the U.S. Department of Agriculture and the U.S. Food and Drug Administration, researchers at the EWG developed a list they call the "dirty dozen" of especially pesticide-laden fruits and vegetables. The analysis led the EWG to recommend that consumers always buy organic if possible. According to the EWG, "nearly all the studies used to create these lists assume that people rinse or peel fresh produce." Rinsing reduces, but does not eliminate pesticides; despite the loss of valuable nutrients contained in the peel, peeling does reduce exposure. Not everyone can afford the expense of buying organic food, although many parents consider it an early investment in their children's health as well as a way to reduce medical bills over the long term. If you can't buy everything organic, at least do it for the "dirty dozen":

1. Celery
2. Peaches
3. Strawberries
4. Apples
5. Blueberries
6. Nectarines
7. Bell peppers
8. Spinach
9. Kale
10. Cherries
11. Potatoes
12. Grapes (imported)

The fruits and vegetables that were shown to have the fewest pesticides are identified by the EWG as the "clean fifteen." These conventionally grown products are considered the safest to buy:

1. Onions
2. Avocados

3. Sweet corn
4. Pineapples
5. Mangos
6. Sweet peas
7. Asparagus
8. Kiwis
9. Cabbages
10. Eggplants
11. Cantaloupes
12. Watermelons
13. Grapefruit
14. Sweet potatoes
15. Honeydew melons

Here's what you can do to cut down your family's pesticide intake:

- After peeling and discarding the skins of bananas, melons, pineapples, mangos, and similar fruits, wash your hands.
- Wash and peel conventionally grown fruits and vegetables.
- Remove and discard outer leaves of cabbage and lettuce.
- Rotate foods so your child is not eating the same things every day.
- Buy organic whenever possible (for a list of companies that ship organic produce to your door, see Resources).
- Get information about pesticide exposure in your food at the EWG's website Foodnews.org or the Pesticide Action Network's site whatsonmyfood.org.
- Make your own baby food using organic ingredients (see Resources).
- Purchase organic baby food. Organic baby food has become mainstream and less expensive over the years (see Resources).

2. BOVINE GROWTH HORMONES

My image of my healthy toddlers happily eating a grilled cheese sandwich and drinking a glass of milk faded into the distance when I learned about bovine growth hormone (BGH). BGH is a bioengineered variant of growth hormone that is now frequently injected into cows on conventional dairy farms in order to increase milk production. It is estimated that this drug increases milk production by up to 25 percent.

What is the problem with BGH? A lot—for both cows and people, especially children, since they typically drink a lot of milk and eat so much cheese. Cows that are injected with BGH have up to an 80 percent incidence of mastitis and infections of the udder, which results in an increase in pus and bacterial contamination of the milk. Consequently, these infections create a greater need for and use of antibiotics, which passes into the milk as well. According to the Cancer Prevention Coalition and many other experts, milk from cows that have been injected with these hormones contains two to ten times as much IGF-1 (insulin-like growth factor) as milk from other cows. IGF-1 has been linked to multiple cancers, specifically breast, colon, and prostate cancers.

Several countries, including Australia, New Zealand, Canada, Japan, and the countries of the European Union, have banned bovine growth hormone because of its impact on humans and animals. "There are a lot of unknowns" about BGH, says Michael Hansen, a research associate with Consumer Policy Institute, a division of Consumers Union, "and if you look at it in terms of risks and benefits, there's absolutely no benefit for humans." Dr. Hansen further points out, "Children drink a lot more milk per unit of body weight than adults."

Here's what you can do:

- Buy dairy products for your family that do not have BGH. This is the only way to be sure you are avoiding BGH in your children's dairy foods. You should assume that milk, cheese, yogurt, and other dairy products contain BGH unless they are labeled otherwise. If they do not have these hormones, they are usually labeled as "Organic," "No rBGH", "No BGH," or something similar.

- Consider reducing dairy products in your child's diet. In *Disease-Proof Your Diet,* Dr. Joel Fuhrman recommends reducing or eliminating dairy products in children's diets. He advises switching from full or low-fat milk to non-fat as early as possible. Make sure you discuss any dietary changes you plan to make with your pediatrician. These suggestions are very controversial and not all pediatricians agree with them. If you do make these switches, you will want to make sure your child is getting proper nutrition from other nondairy sources.

- Let your local supermarket know that you will only buy dairy products that come from untreated sources. Find out if the store has a policy regarding BGH and milk. Make clear that you would like the store to carry BGH-free milk.

- Write or email the FDA to express your concerns about bovine growth hormones. You can contact the agency through its website at www.fda.gov or send a letter to:

Food and Drug Administration
10903 New Hampshire Avenue, Silver Spring, MD 20993-0002

Dr. Scott Cohen's Rule of Two & Four

Most infants will breastfeed every *two to four hours* for the first *two to four months* of life and when they take a bottle take around *two to four ounces.*

MILK TO SOLIDS FROM ZERO TO THREE

Age	Formula	Breast Milk	Cow's Milk	Solids
Birth to 2 weeks	16–24 oz (1–3 oz per bottle*)	About 8 feedings** (every 2–4 hours around the clock)	None	None
2 weeks to 2 months	24–32 oz (2–4 oz per bottle*)	About 8 feedings** (every 2–4 hours around the clock)	None	None
2 to 4 months	24–32 oz (2–4 oz per bottle*)	About 8 feedings** (every 2–4 hours around the clock)	None	None
4 to 6 months	28–32 oz (2–4 oz per bottle*)	5 to 6 feedings** (every 2–4 hours during the day)	None	1 meal per day (optional)
6 to 9 months	20–32 oz (3–4 oz per bottle*)	4 to 6 feedings**	None	1 to 3 meals per day
9 to 12 months	16–24 oz (3–4 oz per bottle*)	3 to 5 feedings**	None	3 meals per day +/– snacks
12 to 18 months		1 to 3 feedings per day if still nursing	Whole milk 16–24 oz per day	3 meals per day +/– snacks
18 to 24 months			Whole milk 16–24 oz per day	3 meals per day +/– snacks
2 to 3 years			Nonfat milk	3 meals per day +/– snacks
3 to 4 years			Nonfat milk	3 meals per day +/– snacks

* Some infants may take larger volumes (4–6 oz per bottle) and fewer feedings.
** The number of feedings may vary—some days more and other days less. The key is to follow your child's clues. Healthy babies will not starve themselves and they will let you know when they are hungry.

—Scott W. Cohen, MD, FAAP,
cofounder of Beverly Hills Pediatrics and author of
Eat, Sleep, Poop: A Common Sense Guide to Your Baby's First Year
www.commonsensepediatrics.com

3. MERCURY

Because fish is known to be a fantastic source of brain-boosting omega-3 acids, lean protein, vitamins, and minerals, parents tend to be especially pleased when their children are willing to eat it. Although fish are considered to be allergens, especially shellfish and "bony" types, the American Academy of Pediatrics no longer recommends waiting to give your child fish.

It is important to note, however, that mercury-contaminated fish is the main source of human exposure to this toxic heavy metal. Freshwater fish and large, long-lived fish like shark, swordfish, king mackerel, and tilefish generally accumulate the highest levels. How do fish get contaminated with mercury? It's released into the air every day from coal-burning power plants and waste incinerators that burn products that contain mercury (batteries, fluorescent light bulbs) as well as from chlor-alkali plants (plants that use mercury cell technology to produce chlorine products). Power plants and waste incinerators account for 85 percent of the mercury pollution in the United States and release over 150 tons of mercury into the atmosphere per year. Airborne mercury vapor can be carried for thousands of miles and absorbed by oceans and lakes, where it poisons fish habitats. According to Jennifer Taggart, author of *Smart Mama's Green Guide,* microorganisms in the water convert mercury to methyl mercury (the most toxic form that most people are exposed to), which then washes over the fish's gills and is ingested when it eats smaller fish that have been contaminated. Because it is stored in fatty tissue, methyl mercury bioaccumulates, which explains why long-lived fish have the highest concentrations.

Here's what you can do:

- Look for other sources of omega-3 for your kids. Other sources include flax seed, walnuts, canola oil, and kiwi, to name a few.
- Avoid large, long-lived fish and bottom feeders, since they tend to contain more mercury.
- Avoid farmed fish. In addition to containing mercury, these fish are often treated with pesticides and fed antibiotics.
- Be wary of feeding canned tuna to your child, since it can be particularly high in mercury. Check out the EWG's tuna calculator at www.ewg.org/tunacalculator so you can figure out how much tuna is safe to feed your children.
- Look up your fish. Two websites that provide up-to-date information about fish and pollutants are Kid Safe Seafood (kidsafeseafood.org) and the Environmental Defense Network's Seafood Selector (www.edf.org/page.cfm?tagID=1521).
- Check local advisories before eating fish caught by friends or family.

- Consider an omega-3 supplement. My kids love Yummi Bears Fish Free Omega 3-6-9 dietary supplements. Always check with your pediatrician before adding any vitamins or supplements to your child's diet.

4. MSG (MONOSODIUM GLUTAMATE) AND GLUTAMIC ACID

You may be thinking that if your baby doesn't eat Chinese food, you don't need to worry about MSG. Guess again. Unfortunately, MSG has a lot to do with feeding kids today. MSG is so pervasive that writing a list of all the foods that contain it would fill volumes. You may want to think twice when your toddler dips that chicken nugget in barbecue sauce, when he eats canned soup, or when you drop one of those packaged kid lunches into the diaper bag. MSG is present in a multitude of such foods, including, but not limited to, crackers, bread, barbecue sauce, snack foods, canned foods, dressings, dried foods, soups, and, of course, fast food.

In the early 1970s, manufacturers voluntarily removed MSG and glutamic acid from baby food after Dr. John Olney, a Washington University neurosurgeon, disclosed to Congress the potential damage MSG can do to developing

FROM THE EXPERTS . . .

Alphabet Soup Nutrition:

EFA, ALA, EPA, DHA

Babies need healthy fats for their rapid growth and development—typically a baby's weight triples and her brain doubles in size during the first year of life! There are many types of fats, from saturated to monounsaturated, but babies especially need the fats known as EFAs or essential fatty acids.

Whereas most fats can be manufactured in our bodies, EFAs must be obtained from food and, therefore, are considered essential. Omega-3s and omega-6s are the two EFAs. They should be eaten in almost equal quantities for optimal health; however, the typical American diet is far too heavy in omega-6s and far too light in omega-3s. This imbalance contributes to heart disease, obesity, inflammation, depression, and a host of other problems. Perhaps more omega-3s in the American diet would help our current health crisis!

brains. According to Dr. Allan Magaziner, Linda Bonvie and Anthony Zolezzi, authors of *Chemical-Free Kids,* manufacturers have managed to sneak it back into baby foods and even ones labeled "contain no MSG" because they have used other forms such as glutamic acid. According to the FDA, MSG falls into their "generally recognized as safe" (GRAS) category. But some experts don't think it is so benign. Dr. William Sears, author of *The NDD Book,* says that, "MSG should absolutely be banned from the brains of children."

MSG is commercially used as a flavor enhancer, most notably for foods that are shortchanged of natural ingredients during processing before being frozen, canned, or vacuum sealed. By enhancing the flavor of food, it generally makes people—including the under-age-three set—eat more of it. According to Carol Hoernlein, a former food process engineer and food scientist who created the website MSGtruth.org, food companies continue to use MSG for several reasons. For one, it tricks you into thinking a food with MSG is high in protein. According to Hoernlein, free glutamic acid is detected by the taste buds as a simple way to signal the presence of protein in a food, changing your perception of not simply the taste but the nutritional qualities of what you put into your mouth. If your child's body craves protein and is "fooled" into being satisfied by food with MSG, his nutritional need for protein is still not being met. Second, using

---

Some food sources of omega-6s are corn oil and other vegetable oils, cereals, and breads. Omega-3s can be found in salmon and other cold-water oily fish and the microalgae that they eat, meat and dairy from grass-fed (not feedlot) cows, flax seeds, walnuts, and other foods.

One important omega-3 is ALA. ALA from both fish and plants contributes significantly to overall health. But only the ALA from fish is good for our brain and eyes, which can use ALA only after it is converted to EPA and then to DHA. ALA from fish converts efficiently to DHA; ALA from plants does not. Many baby foods are fortified with EPA and DHA, specifically for the health of babies' brains and eyes.

Omega-3 supplements now abound and can be found not only in natural foods stores, but also the average supermarket. There are several brands of flax seed oils and fish oil supplements. The price range of fish oil varies greatly, with the expensive brands claiming to contain only minute amounts of ocean-water toxins such as mercury and PCBs. Vegetarians can buy omega-3 products formulated from algae, without having to eat the fish that ate the algae.

—Ruth Yaron, author of *Super Baby Food*
www.SuperBabyFood.com

MSG allows food producers to cut down on quality and cost while making up for the loss of flavor caused by the omission of "real" ingredients by adding this flavor enhancer. Third, MSG stimulates the pancreas to produce insulin, causing blood sugar levels to drop, which means your child will be hungry again within a short period of time. The illusion of fullness created by adding MSG to a product enables the manufacturer to use less "real" food in that product and, ultimately, to deliver less nutrition to the consumer.

Glutamic acid, which is a key component of MSG that triggers adverse reactions, is what scientists call an excitotoxin. According to the authors of *Chemical-Free Kids,* excitotoxins quite literally "excite" brain cells to death, and once the cells have died they do not regenerate. Here's a simple explanation of the process. When the brain receives glutamate, the neurons of the hypothalamus become overexcited and fire repetitively. In infants, this is of particular concern because the blood-brain barrier is not fully developed. This overstimulation allows in too much calcium, which triggers an influx of free radicals that cause cell death. The tricky part about avoiding MSG is that it is everywhere, including in food that's available for babies and toddlers.

Studies have shown that giving animals low-dose shots of MSG over the course of eleven days resulted in shorter, fatter, and more hyperactive animals with reduced intelligence. We are seeing increasing behavioral problems in children (uncontrollable outbursts of anger and hyperactivity, for example), starting at younger ages, and some experts, like Dr. Russell Blaylock, author of *Excitotoxins,* believe this problem is related to the consumption of additives like glutamic acid. MSG has also been linked to conditions such as Alzheimer's, Parkinson's disease, Huntington's disease, amyotrophic lateral sclerosis (ALS), autism, diabetes, fibromyalgia, irritable bowel syndrome, migraines, multiple sclerosis, and vision problems.

Here's what you can do:

- Avoid processed foods as much as possible.
- Steer clear of foods with long lists of additives.
- Buy organic whenever possible.
- When reading a food label, make sure that the product does *not* contain MSG, hydrolyzed proteins, or any form of glutamic acid.
- Check product labels for ingredients that might contain MSG or glutamic acid.
- Bring the list of food additives in the box on the next page to the market so you can avoid products that include them.

The MSG Hiding in Your Child's Food

Food manufacturers frequently disguise the MSG added to foods. In his book *Excitotoxins: The Taste That Kills,* Dr. Russell Blaylock points out the following hidden sources of MSG.

Food Additives That Always Contain MSG

Autolyzed yeast
Calcium caseinate
Hydrolyzed oat flour
Hydrolyzed plant protein
Hydrolyzed protein
Hydrolyzed vegetable protein
Monosodium glutamate
Plant protein extract
Sodium caseinate
Textured protein
Yeast extract

Food Additives That Frequently Contain MSG

Bouillon
Broth
Flavoring
Malt extract
Malt flavoring
Natural beef or chicken flavoring
Natural flavoring
Seasoning
Spices
Stock

Food Additives That May Contain MSG or Excitotoxins

Carrageenan
Enzymes
Soy protein concentrate
Soy protein isolate
Whey protein concentrate

5. ASPARTAME

Many parents who hope to avoid giving their toddlers and young children foods high in sugar turn to products labeled "sugar-free" or "light," thinking they might provide a healthier option. But most of these products contain aspartame, a noncaloric sweetener, sold under the brand name NutraSweet or Equal. This ingredient, which is also an excitotoxin, is present in many foods, such as instant breakfasts, cereals, gelatin, juice beverages, milk drinks, supplements, soft drinks, yogurts, tea beverages, and even some multivitamins.

Thousands of reports to the FDA show adverse reactions to aspartame, most of which involve brain functioning, such as depression, insomnia, vision problems, hearing loss, loss of sense of taste, vertigo, and memory loss. Other serious conditions that have been linked to aspartame include chronic illnesses and conditions such as brain tumors, multiple sclerosis, chronic fatigue, Parkinson's disease, Alzheimer's, fibromyalgia, and diabetes.

According to Carol Simontacchi, author of *The Crazy Makers: How the Food Industry Is Destroying Our Brains and Harming Our Children,* when aspartame is heated above eighty-six degrees Fahrenheit it is converted into methanol—or wood alcohol—and when consumed it is absorbed into the bloodstream. It is common for many of these aspartame-containing foods to undergo high temperatures—for example, when you make Jell-O or hot chocolate or even when food is stored in a warm warehouse.

Here's what you can do:

- Read labels and avoid products that contain NutraSweet or aspartame.
- Be wary of products labeled "sugar-free," "light," or "low-cal."
- Avoid products that have warnings for people who are suffering from phenylketonuria (PKU) because such products are likely to contain this sweetener.
- Check the labels on your children's medications, vitamins, and supplements to make sure they don't contain aspartame.

6. FOOD COLORING

Sure, you know those brightly colored goldfish crackers couldn't possibly be bright orange, pink, green, or purple without some food dye, right? But did you know that the juice you give your toddler probably has red or orange dye to make it look sweeter and that the waffles you feed him probably have yellow food coloring to make them look golden brown? And did you know that the "blueberries" in those waffles are most likely not real blueberries at all but made from Red 40 and Blue 2? Indeed, food dyes—Blue 1, Blue 2, Green 3, Red 2,

Red 3, Red 40, Orange B, Yellow 6, and Yellow 5—most of which are petroleum-derived, are everywhere. According to data from the Food and Drug Administration, Americans consume five times as much food dye as they did thirty years ago.

Food dyes have been linked to hyperactivity, even in kids who don't normally exhibit this kind of behavior. The *Archives of Disease in Childhood* published a study of 277 three-year-old children who were given a diet that was free of artificial coloring and benzoate preservatives for one week and then given drinks containing yellow and red colorings, along with benzoate or a placebo mixture, for three weeks. The children's hyperactive behavior was significantly reduced during the week when their diets did not contain the colorings. Parents also reported worsening behavior during the three-week period when the children were exposed to the dyes. In addition to hyperactivity, these synthetic dyes have been linked to aggressive behavior, cognitive disturbances, asthma, hives, low-serum iron and zinc, irritability, poor sleep, and tumors.

Despite these problems, the FDA considers the nine synthetic colors allowed in food to be safe as long as each batch has been certified to meet composition standards. In the United Kingdom, however, the Food Standards Agency recommended that, by the end of 2009, food manufacturers should stop using six of those synthetic colors; the agency also called for a ban on their use in foods in Europe. As a result, companies that sell products in both countries now make dye-free versions of the same food for sale in the UK. For example, in the UK, Fanta orange soda gets its bright color from pumpkin and carrot extract, but in the U.S. it comes from Red 40 and Yellow 6. Nutri-Grain cereal bars in the UK are made with beet root, annatto, and paprika extract for color but those sold in the U.S. contain Red 40, Yellow 6, and Blue 1. In the U.S., McDonald's strawberry sundaes are colored with Red 40; in the UK real strawberries are used. Because the United States has not demanded dye-free versions of foods and it is cheaper to use artificial dyes, US companies are not motivated to provide healthier versions.

The Center for Science in the Public Interest has called on the FDA to ban eight of the artificial dyes (all but Citrus Red 2, which is used predominantly in the skins of oranges to make them look more appealing) or at least affix a warning label to products that contain artificial dyes—for example, "Warning: The artificial coloring in this food causes hyperactivity and behavioral problems in some children."

Here's what you can do:

- Read labels and avoid processed foods with artificial colors.
- Avoid brightly colored kids' foods. Many toddler foods like crackers and cereals come in unnaturally bright colors in order to visually excite children.

- Try to shop at stores like Whole Foods and Trader Joe's that carry a selection of natural and organic products that contain no artificial dyes.
- If you don't have access to a health food store, check online for bulk orders of foods without food coloring.
- To learn which of your child's favorite foods contain unhealthy food dyes, go to the Institute for Agriculture and Trade Policy's Brain Food Selector at www.iatp.org/brainfoodselector/.
- If you think your child has been affected by food dyes, file a report with the Center for Science in the Public Interest at www.cspinet.org/fooddyes.

7. GENETICALLY ALTERED FOODS

The children of North America have now become the world's lab animals on whom to study the long-term effects of eating GM products.

—JANE GOODALL in *Harvest for Hope: A Guide to Mindful Eating*

The terms "genetically modified organisms" (GMOs) and "genetic engineering" (GE) refer to human interference with plant or animal reproduction by the artificial manipulation of DNA. This is done by injecting the DNA from one species into another, thus creating genetic combinations that do not occur in nature or as the result of typical crossbreeding methods. There are no regulatory restraints, labeling requirements, medical testing, or scientific protocol for these new, altered foods that your child is eating. Currently, over 75 percent of processed foods contain at least one GE ingredient. In the United States, GE foods account for the following:

- 87 percent of soybeans
- 79 percent of cotton (used for cottonseed oil)
- 55 percent of canola
- 52 percent of corn
- 50 percent of Hawaiian papayas

In addition, meat may not come from GE animals, but unless it is certified organic the livestock may have been raised on GE feed.

Scientists warn that genetically modified foods could cause serious allergies, make formerly nontoxic food toxic, increase antibiotic resistance, compromise our immune systems, and reduce nutrition in our foods. This is of particular concern for infants, whose intestinal barrier functions and immune systems are not fully developed.

How does GE work? A bioengineer takes genes from an arctic flounder, for example—because it has natural "antifreezing" properties that protect it from cold water—and injects them into tomato DNA to make a new variety that is highly resistant to frost damage. While this genetic manipulation sounds reasonable enough, it can lead to negative results.

- In 1996, for example, researchers in Nebraska inserted a Brazil nut gene into a soybean in an attempt to make the soybean more nutritious, but found that it could induce potentially fatal allergies in people who are sensitive to Brazil nuts. One of the many concerns about GMOs is the potential for allergic reactions that can range from mild to fatal when people consume unlabeled genetically altered ingredients in common products. Currently 8 percent of children suffer from food allergies and that number appears to be growing.

- According to internal documents at the FDA that were made public as a result of a lawsuit, the overwhelming consensus among the FDA's scientists was that genetically modified (GM) foods are so substantively different, in fact, from natural products that their consumption might result in unpredictable and hard-to-detect allergens, toxins, new diseases, and nutritional problems. For example, an estimated 10,000 sheep died in India within five to seven days of grazing on GM plants engineered to produce their own pesticide.

- British researcher Dr. Arpad Pusztai found that GE potatoes are poisonous when fed to mammals, causing damage to the vital organs, compromising the immune system, harming the stomach lining, and causing severe viral infections.

- In 2000, Kraft Foods recalled millions of dollars' worth of taco shells after scientists discovered that they contained StarLink corn, a GE crop that failed to meet EPA standards for human consumption.

- In 1989, thirty-seven Americans died after consuming a genetically engineered brand of l-tryptophan dietary supplement, and 5,000 more were permanently disabled or stricken with a potentially fatal blood disorder after taking the same supplement.

Despite the fact that polls show that 90 percent of Americans want GMO foods identified, the United States is virtually alone in failing to demand the labeling of such foods. According to the Non-GMO Project, a nonprofit, independent verification program, more than thirty countries around the world, including Australia, Japan, and all of the countries in the European Union, have significant restrictions or outright bans on the production of GMOs because they have not been proved to be safe. In Europe, any approved products containing more than 0.9 percent GMO are labeled by the government as GMO products.

Here's what you can do:

- Choose organic foods, which cannot legally be genetically modified, for your family.
- Look for foods marked "GMO-free" or "GE-free."
- Avoid nonorganic products made with corn and soy, two of the largest genetically engineered crops.
- If you are unable to get organic baby food, buy from baby food companies, like Gerber, that have pledged to avoid GE ingredients in all their baby foods.
- If you buy animal products, make sure they are 100 percent certified organic or labeled "100% grass fed."
- To avoid eggs from GE egg-laying chickens (yes, they're out there), look for certified organic eggs, which also ensures that the chickens have not been fed GE grain.
- Buy locally grown produce from farmers' markets and community supported agriculture (CSA) farms, where you can speak directly to the producer.
- Visit the Non-GMO Project website at www.nongmoproject.org for more information about non-GMO foods.
- Look for the Non-GMO Project sticker on foods to ensure they are not GMO.
- According to the International Federation of Produce Coding, price look up (PLU) codes on produce indicate how a piece of produce was grown. The system is voluntary, so you cannot count on it, but when available it may provide helpful information. The code consists of several digits:

  four digits = conventional produce
  five digits starting with 9 = organic produce
  five digits starting with 8 = genetically engineered produce

Although there are a lot of scary things in the environment and in the food our families eat, knowledge goes a long way, not only toward keeping our children healthy and happy, but mitigating some of our own anxieties, as parents, about our children's future and well-being. It's astonishing how far a few small changes can go.

Appendix A

Child Care

In the United States, well over 50 percent of new mothers return to work within four months of giving birth to their first child, and 70 percent of mothers with children under the age of six are in the workforce. Some mothers return to work because of financial need and others because they find their work fulfilling, but, regardless of the reason for returning to work, leaving their child in the care of someone else is challenging in the best of circumstances.

Next to a parent, babysitters, nannies, and other child-care providers are often the most influential people in a child's life—which makes it all the more essential to choose the right person to help nourish your child's physical, emotional, and psychological development. One-on-one care, if it's a financial option, or a "nanny share" are the best child-care options in the first year because they can provide the focused attention and bonding that are optimal for children's development. However, since providing your child with a loving caretaker or day-care experience is not only about optimal development but about quality of life as well, make sure that the environment you choose for your child is as pleasing to you as it is to her.

THE OPTIONS: CHILD CARE FROM A TO Z

There are many viable child-care options, each with its strengths and weaknesses. The key to great child care is making sure that you choose the right option for your family and finances and do your homework regarding screening, interviewing, and background checks.

Type of Care	Pros	Cons
Au pair	• Exposes your child to other cultures and languages • Often young and energetic • Personalized attention for your child • Expected to provide up to forty-five hours of child care a week (up to ten hours a day)	• Young • May not have any child-care experience • Allowed by the State Department to stay only for one year • Loss of privacy because au pair lives with the family

Type of Care	Pros	Cons
Au pair continued	• Many au pair programs provide screening and child-care training • Live-in child care • Very cost-effective • No per child cost increase	• Must be provided with a room • Must be enrolled in at least six hours of course work • Must have two weeks of paid vacation and one weekend off a month • Must have use of a vehicle • It is unlikely you will get to meet your au pair before she moves into your house to take care of your child
Day-care center	• Reliable care. Someone will always be available even if your child's caregiver gets ill • If it is licensed, there are minimum standards • Some staff have specialized training in child development • May have educational materials, toys, and play equipment not available to most families • Rules and procedures are usually well spelled out, providing structure and an established means to resolve conflicts	• Good centers often have waiting lists to get in • Quality varies tremendously • Increased exposure to a variety of children and therefore more germs and illness • Limited flexibility in scheduling; late pickups are often an additional charge • Staff turnover can be problematic • Care is not individualized • Can be costly • Difficult to regulate because it is not in your own home
Family run day-care center	• Family atmosphere • Can accommodate children of different ages, enabling siblings to attend the same facility • Often offers access to individualized care • Tends to have small groups • Usually able to offer flexible scheduling options • Tends to be a less expensive option than traditional day-care center	• Many home day-care centers are illegal, unlicensed, do not meet minimum state safety requirements (always ask to see the license) • Less likely to have specialized training in child development • Primary caregiver does not always offer backup care in the event of illness

Type of Care	Pros	Cons
Nanny	• Individualized, one-on-one care • Activities are tailored to your child's needs, interests, and schedule • You can hire someone with the same child-care philosophies as you have • Conveniently located in your own home, which avoids transportation issues • Because care is in your home, it is easier to drop in and visit your child • Works around your schedule and needs • Available even if your child is ill • Your child is in a comfortable, familiar setting	• Can be prohibitively expensive • Quality of care varies tremendously • Because most nannies are home alone, there is no one to check on the level of care on a daily basis • Turnover can be high • In the event of illness or vacation, backup is not always available • You are dependent on the nanny's promptness and reliability to start your day • Loss of privacy in your own home • You may need to manage personality issues • You will need to act as boss and manager
Relative taking care of child	• Someone you know and love is caring for your child • Likely to be invested in your child's well-being • May be willing to come to your home • Individualized attention • Often no cost	• Is not an employee so making demands or suggestions can cause conflict depending on the relative's personality • Paying a family member can create sticky situations • If relative is not paid, resentments can develop • Generally is not schooled in child development • May have different philosophies about child rearing

FROM THE EXPERTS . . .

Eleven Things Your Nanny Wishes You Would Do

1. **Respect the schedule.** Once you have a regular set schedule, make your best attempt to respect it. Of course with children you need to be flexible, but be careful of taking advantage of this flexibility—it may just cost you your nanny.

2. **Talk to your nanny.** Communication is key. Set up a regular time to touch base about the kids and job details. Sometimes employers assume the nanny should just know everything. However, she is not a mind reader and needs you to inform her how things are done, especially in the beginning.

3. **Allow your nanny some break time on vacation.** When you are on vacation and your nanny travels with you, she is not on vacation. Utilize the hotel babysitting service for a day or two or give your nanny a night off (or two). She deserves some respite as much as you do, and she'll be a better nanny for it.

4. **Pay your nanny on time and hassle-free.** Counting hours and trying to track you down can be tough. Having a discussion about money can be even tougher. Set up a regular system for paying your nanny.

5. **Do not blame your nanny for your private troubles.** Your nanny understands that she works in your private home, embedded in your

PUTTING QUALITY CHILD CARE UNDER THE MICROSCOPE

There is an extraordinary international consensus among child care researchers and practitioners about what quality child care is: It is warm, supportive interactions with adults in a safe, healthy, and stimulating environment, where early education and trusting relationships combine to support individual children's physical, emotional, social, and intellectual development.

—Sandra Scarr,
president of the Society for Research in Child Development

private life. Try not to take it out on her. She doesn't deserve it and if it happens enough, you may drive a good nanny away.

6. **Give your nanny respect.** Your nanny is a professional caring for your child. Ask her opinion. Listen to her guidance. She has done this before and may have a lot of wisdom to share.

7. **Encourage your nanny to connect you to your child.** Your nanny can help you stay connected with your baby. She can take pictures of your child, log her daily activities, and update you on anything new that happened that day.

8. **Avoid changing your mind.** When you change your mind at the last minute, it slows things down and you need to be patient and understanding to get things back on track.

9. **Show appreciation.** Your nanny needs to know she is doing a good job and will do an even better job if she knows you appreciate her.

10. **Collaborate.** Your nanny is doing the best job she knows how, but she needs your help.

11. **Don't change the job requirements without warning.** If the job description is changing, take care to sit down and discuss the changes and your family's specific needs with your nanny.

—Lindsay Heller, PsyD, is a licensed clinical psychologist
and former nanny and is known as The Nanny Doctor
www.TheNannyDoctor.com

Studies have shown a wide variety of benefits for children in *quality* child care. A landmark study by the National Institute of Child Health and Human Development Study of Early Child Care found that children in high-quality day-care environments have larger vocabularies and more complex language skills. A University of Miami study concluded that children in out-of-home care learned to get along with others, developed leadership abilities, and had a strong sense of worth. A German study found that children with affectionate caregivers demonstrated more compassionate behavior. According to Drs. Alison Clarke-Stewart and Virginia D. Allhusen, authors of *What We Know About Childcare*, children are more likely to learn social and intellectual skills when caregivers are good at being teachers, managers, and nurturers, traits that, researchers have found, continue to benefit the children into their early school years.

But what makes a good caregiver or day-care program? Here are a few qualities parents should look for in a nanny or day-care worker:

Interactions with children should be frequent and positive. Good caregivers get down on the ground so they can speak at a child's eye level. They are warm and affectionate and respond promptly to a child's noises, questions, and requests. In group settings, caregivers should interact with children one-on-one and in small groups, not just with the whole group.

Communication should be fostered. Quality caregivers encourage children to talk about their experiences, feelings, and ideas. They listen attentively, ask open-ended questions, reflect children's feelings, and extend children's verbalizations. They are responsive and present. With infants, they converse through eye contact, touch, noises, and words.

Sensitivity is extremely necessary for working with children. Caregivers must be sensitive to children's moods, level of exhaustion, boundaries, and needs. Good caregivers are never intrusive or suffocating but are able to read a child's cues and act appropriately.

FROM THE EXPERTS . . .

Tips for Working with Nanny Agencies

1. Find out how long the agency has been in business. Recent start-ups can be vulnerable, and the last thing you need is an agency that won't be there for you in the long run.

2. Connect personally with the people in charge of helping you. If you have your assistant call the agency, information can get lost in translation, and you'll never know whether or not you like the people you're dealing with.

3. Ask whether the agents are on commission. You want people who are interested in helping you for the sake of doing so, not because they're desperate to make ends meet.

4. Check out the agency's website. Look for descriptions of the agents to get a sense of them as people and for examples of the types of nannies they represent.

Patience is crucial. Great caregivers never lose their cool. They are able to tolerate testing, tantrums, screaming, crying, hitting, and all kinds of acting out without losing their temper.

Teaching should be developmentally appropriate and sensitive to the child's age, level, and interest. Caregivers should spend a lot of time talking, reading, and playing. They should encourage appropriate independence and help children learn age-appropriate self-care skills such as self-feeding and toileting.

When assessing programs, here are a few things to consider:

Continuity of care. A child needs to form strong attachments to caregivers in order to develop a sense of safety, security, and well-being. She should be cared for by the same person every day, not a rotating group of different care providers. This is crucial for your child's ability to form attachments. If this is not the case at a day-care center you are considering, you should look elsewhere.

Staff turnover. The annual turnover rate for child-care professionals is approximately 30 percent, one of the highest of any profession. Having caregivers who

5. Ask what makes the agency stand out from others.

6. Don't assume you will be paying the same salary your friends are paying. Every household has different needs. A good agency should be able to guide you in this respect.

7. Try to have an idea of what hours you need covered, whether or not you require travel, and what your "Mary Poppins" might look like before you call.

8. If you're not sure about any of the things in #7, be open to ideas from the agent.

9. If you have special circumstances or needs in your household, be upfront with the agency about them so the agents can help you choose the best fit for your family.

10. Once you have chosen an agency, trust that the agents are on your side, doing their best to help you be as happy as possible with your choice of nanny!

—Amy E. Giles, The Elizabeth Rose Agency
www.elizabethroseagency.com

stick around for the long term is especially important because it allows the employees to hone their skills and become more confident and skilled, as well as more responsive and attuned to the children, who, in turn, become more attuned to them. In a national staffing study, children in centers with the highest turnover rates spent the most time wandering aimlessly and did the poorest on IQ tests.

Child-to-caregiver ratios. Having too many children for each caregiver to look after is extremely detrimental. Studies show that caregivers with high child to staff ratios are less sensitive, responsive, and positive. Children in their care have less contact with the caregiver, spend more time playing with other children, have fewer of their questions answered, have shorter conversations, engage in fewer intellectual activities, and are more likely to be given prohibitions, commands, and corrections. Research has found that children who received more attention and stimulation from their caregivers were less likely to have increased cortisol levels over the course of the day. Their cortisol levels looked just like the levels in kids who stayed at home in their own familiar environment.

HELPING YOUR SUPERBABY BOND WITH YOUR SUPERNANNY

The attachment literature does not demand exclusive parental care. There will be a hierarchy of attachments....

—Dr. Penelope Leach,
Child Care Today: Getting It Right for Everyone

It can be difficult to leave your precious child in the care of a nanny. Many parents, especially moms, feel anxious that the caregiver will somehow replace them. But you *want* to see your child fall "in love" with the caregiver. Forming strong attachments only helps her to form more strong attachments, an ability that will last a lifetime.

It is crucial that you are comfortable with the person you hire because your child will sense any ambivalence you have and be more anxious about the transition. For a list of nanny interview questions and tips, check out my first book, *The A to Z Guide to Raising Happy, Confident Kids.*

FROM THE EXPERTS . . .

Attachment in Day Care

When babies and toddlers are cared for on a daily basis by a consistent secondary attachment figure such as a father, grandmother, babysitter, or nanny, the outcome for children is usually positive. But when they are cared for by people to whom they are not attached—and when they are unable to reach any of their established attachment figures—babies and toddlers will sense danger and be afraid. The absence of attachment figures is sensed as increasing the risk of danger and it triggers separation anxiety, which continues until they are reunited with an attachment figure. Although the importance of the primary attachment relationship has been known for many years, it's only recently been recognized that in order to avoid *emotional* neglect, babies and toddlers always need access to a secondary attachment figure when their primary attachment figure is not available.

Babies and toddlers who do not have secure attachments at home are especially vulnerable when being cared for by strangers in day care. They have multiple disadvantages—they have insecure attachments at home and then in day care they suffer separation anxiety, plus fear of strangers caring for them in unfamiliar surroundings. By contrast, a baby or toddler who develops a secure secondary attachment to a skilful and consistent caregiver can have their insecure attachment partially compensated for.

If separation anxiety is to be avoided during day care, babies and toddlers need to develop a secure secondary attachment to a new caregiver before being left with them. It takes a baby a month or two of frequent and regular visits to develop a secure secondary attachment to a caregiver who, in turn, must develop a bond with the baby. The baby's secondary attachment needs to be sufficiently robust that their attachment seeking response is not activated when they are left with the caregiver. One way to achieve this is for the primary attachment figure to stay with the baby and caregiver until they become friends and, only then, start leaving them together for just a short period of time.

—Sir Richard Bowlby, author of *Fifty Years of Attachment Theory: Recollections of Donald Winnicott and John Bowlby*

Holding onto Mommy: Easing Separation

To make the transition from home to a new child-care center easier for your child, try some of these ideas:

- Let your child get familiar with other children in the center by planning a playgroup.

- Visit the facility with your child and spend some time there together so that it becomes familiar.

- If possible, have the child-care provider come to your house for a visit.

- Talk with your child about her feelings.

- Keep the schedule consistent in order to create a sense of security and predictability.

- Avoid big changes at home, such as getting a new pet, having visitors, starting potty training, switching to a big bed, or redecorating your child's room.

- Let your child bring a transitional object like a lovey, pacifier, blanket, or stuffed animal.

- Give your child a book of family photos to take with her.

- If you cannot stay around until your child is comfortable in the new situation, see if you can get another family member to go in your place.

- Make sure to let your child know when you are coming back, when she will go home, who will feed her, who will take care of her, and so on.

- Read lots of books about day care and transitions (for recommendations, see page 191).

- Always say good-bye. Never sneak away from your child!

- Once you do say good-bye, leave right away. Do not hover anxiously by the door. Show your child that you have confidence in the new arrangement.

FINDING THE GOOD ONES: GETTING GOOD DAY CARE

In a study of day-care centers, researchers ranked only one in seven centers as "good" while rating most of the rest as "poor" to "mediocre," concluding that 40 percent of children in day care were receiving substandard care. In a different study, performed by the Cost, Quality and Child Outcomes team, researchers found that parents were not well informed about the care their children were receiving and consistently rated it as being better quality than the trained observers did. It is hard to know if parents rated the centers higher because they, themselves, were not trained in child care or because they wanted to believe their children were getting great care. It is necessary to observe a child-care setting in order to assess it and become a more critical consumer. While it may seem like great quality care is out of the financial reach of most families, according to Child Care Aware, a program of the National Association of Child Care Resource and Referral Agencies, which provides high-quality care referrals nationwide, 99 percent of all families in the United States have access to high-quality, affordable child care. For information about day care near you, go to www.ChildCareAware. org or call 800-424-2246.

Tips:

- Start your search early. Many sites have waiting lists.
- Visit several sites before making a decision. Observe how caregivers interact with the children.
- Ask lots of questions about the philosophy and policies of the staff.
- Trust your instincts.
- Speak directly with the person who would be taking care of your child.
- Once your child is attending, drop by the day-care center unannounced to visit and observe. You should not consider using a day-care center that does not allow parents to drop in and observe.
- Avoid centers that use televisions to occupy children.
- Ask to see licensing and accreditation paperwork.
- Watch your child's responses, reactions, and moods in response to the child care.

WHO KNOWS WHAT EVIL LURKS: SAFETY

When working with a nanny, day-care center, or any other type of child-care provider, the two most important things you can do are to implement your own investigation and to trust your instincts. Reports say that one in twenty children is being cared for by someone who has committed a crime and 15 percent of background checks turn up some sort of criminal history not mentioned in an interview. In this age of Internet access and Google searches, there is so much free information at your fingertips. Make sure to use it. Above all, trust your instincts: if something makes you uncomfortable, your child will be uncomfortable too.

FROM THE EXPERTS . . .

Safety & Background Checks

Q What are the best background checks parents can do without paying a private investigator?
A Finding a child-care provider such as a babysitter or nanny can be challenging. I often tell parents that the most difficult part of being a parent is finding people they can trust to help take care of their children. Beside my own concerns as a parent, I need to find someone my child will like and trust as well. At some point, you will need to rely on other people to assist you with child care. If you don't have a parent, sibling, or other family member you trust to watch your child, here are items to request when hiring a babysitter, nanny, or other caretaker:

- A driver's license (or other government-issued photo ID)

- A social security card or work permit

- A printout of their driving record (if the position requires driving), with proof of auto insurance

- A resume

- The names and numbers of at least three references

With these documents you can do a preliminary background check using an online company (like US-Search, www.ussearch.com). You can call the Childcare Trustline Registry at 800-822-8490 for information on how to have your caregiver fingerprinted.

Q What information should parents look for online about day-care providers?
A When the time comes to hire a nanny and/or babysitter, parents should make a candidate-recruiting plan for searching both on and offline.

Security expert and author of *Protecting the Gift,* Gavin De Becker says that "intuition about your children is always right in at least two ways: It is always based on something, and it always has your child's best interest at heart."

Recruiting requires research, both into the type of help you realistically need and an awareness of the going rates for that help. Who is your ideal? Are you looking for Mary Poppins, Fran from *The Nanny,* or someone who can cook and clean? To help determine what kind of assistance you need, you must consider the age of your children, the hours of help required, and your family's priorities. While having one person who can do it all seems ideal, it is unrealistic for one person to watch a couple of toddlers and cook and clean at the same time. A comprehensive checklist for what to look for is available here: www.ladpss.org/dpss/child_care/checklist.cfm.

Q Where can I find lists of licensed day-care centers?

A Sources within your community, such as the local law enforcement office, a social service agency, or even schools may help parents in their search for lists of recommended child-care providers. If you are a part of a religious community, your church, temple, or the YMCA or YMHA is another good way to find reliable and trustworthy people. Asking coworkers and friends for references can help identify care providers with previous experience with whom you can, with some confidence, feel safe. For example, here is a list of licensed child-care centers from the City of Los Angeles: www.laparks.org/dos/childcare.htm.

Q Where should you look to find out if there is a pedophile living near an unlicensed family-run day care?

A Go to the following URL: http://familywatchdog.us/ and enter the street address of the day care. You will then see if a registered sex offender is living in that area. In addition, most states maintain their own sex offender registry. To find yours, google "megans law + (your state's name)".

—Robin Sax is a former Los Angeles County deputy district attorney who specialized in prosecuting sex crimes against children and the author of *Predators and Child Molesters: A Sex Crimes DA Answers Parents' 100 Most Asked Questions to Keep Kids Safe* and other books regarding parenting and criminal justice
www.RobinSax.com

Appendix B

Preschool

When you are holding your infant in your arms, cuddling in a rocking chair, it is hard to imagine the day your little angel will be ready to go to preschool. I don't know if school separation is harder for the parent or the child, but after reading this book and trying out the suggestions I have given you, your child is likely to be ready for that experience. He will be showing up for school with a mind that is ready and able to learn. Having structure, secure attachments, and lots of books and playtime will have prepared him to be intellectually ready for school. The separation process is often a little more tricky, but you can ease the situation by finding the right school for your child's temperament and your family's philosophy.

NOT YOUR ABCS: **THE REAL PURPOSE OF PRESCHOOL**

Contrary to what many parents think, the purpose of preschool is not for children to acquire information, have an academic experience, or "get smarter." Here are the eight most important learning experiences that preschool can provide—and you may find the real reasons are far more significant than learning his ABCs:

1. **Separation.** Being away from their parents helps children continue the process of becoming independent and learning to manage the world. This can be very empowering for children.

2. **Independence.** At school, kids get to choose whom they play with, whether they want to paint or play dress-up, and what they keep in their cubby. All these choices are self-defining. In addition, children work on mastering self-care skills like toileting, washing hands, and cleaning up after lunch.

3. **Loving school.** Preschool is a child's first experience with being in a school environment, and a positive association can set into motion a lifelong love of learning.

4. **Socialization.** In preschool, kids learn how to be part of a group, which teaches them how their behavior and words affect others. They learn about manners, impulse control, cooperation, and conflict resolution.

5. **Making friends.** In preschool, children learn how to forge friendships and settle differences. They learn how to approach other

children, have one-on-one interactions, and work with different personalities.

6. **Asking for help.** Learning how to get their needs met by asking for help facilitates the growth of a child's confidence. Doing this in the context of a group of children who are also vying for the teacher's attention is a learned skill.

7. **Developing a teacher-student relationship.** Research shows that having a caring, responsive relationship with their first teacher helps children form productive relationships with subsequent teachers and other adults.

8. **New kinds of play.** Preschools generally provide kids with a variety of toys, books, and playground equipment they might not have access to at home. This helps them to develop fine motor skills, spatial skills, and coordination, not to mention that it can be a lot of fun.

THE PROBLEM WITH ACADEMIC PRESCHOOLS

In recent years there has been a real push toward more academic preschools, increasing traditional learning methods, reducing playtime, and adding regular testing. This type of prekindergarten, high-stress school experience is a huge mistake. It has the potential to burn kids out, generate too much stress, and create a dislike of school that can last a lifetime.

When you're assessing preschools for your child, I urge you to avoid schools that push academic skills over play-based learning. Academic schools tend to require kids to perform daily schoolwork, complete worksheets, and be tested. They follow a teacher-directed approach as opposed to following the interests of the children. Concerned that their children will somehow fall behind, some parents seek out preschools with a curriculum that includes teaching letters, numbers, and even computer skills. But studies show that this provides no short-term or long-term academic advantages and that, in fact, children who have been through academic preschools were more anxious, less creative, and had a more negative attitude toward school than children in play-based programs. Another study that observed children in a traditional play-based preschool, a Montessori preschool, and an academic preschool found that the nonacademic programs fostered math and reading achievement far more than the academic one and that the benefits were still evident years later in eighth grade.

SCHOOLS DAZE: UNDERSTANDING THE
DIFFERENT TYPES OF PRESCHOOL PROGRAMS

Type	Philosophy	Distinguishing Features
Academic	• Clear structure and curriculum that generally involves teaching letters, numbers, shapes, reading, writing, and math • Worksheets and testing may be used • Children encouraged to raise their hands when they have questions	• Teacher-directed • Children often sit at desks • Formal learning environment • Early exposure to academic skills like reading, writing, and math
Bank Street	• Child-centered education • Focuses on diverse opportunities for physical, emotional, cognitive, and social growth • Based on the belief that children are active learners, explorers, experimenters, and artists • Based on the idea that learning should encompass several subjects at once and occur in collaborative groups.	• Focuses on five key social studies subjects: cultural anthropology, history, political science, economics, and geography • Children play with toys and materials that leave a lot to the imagination—blocks, water, art materials, clay, puzzles
Cooperative (co-op)	• Philosophy varies but is often developmental • Parents are instrumental to the functioning of the school and must be prepared to donate their time	• Parents may be responsible for everything from hiring teachers to fund-raising to cleaning classrooms to teaching • Many provide parent education • There are minimum requirements for parent participation • Close-knit community
Developmental/ Whole Child	• Most preschools fall under this umbrella • Children learn by doing, not from listening to lectures • Teacher is a facilitator rather than dispenser of knowledge • Children learn at their own pace • Play focused approach • Focus on process over product • Problem solving encouraged	• Play stations • Flexible environment

Type	Philosophy	Distinguishing Features
Head Start	• Comprehensive parent-involved preschool program that provides school for low-income children and education for parents • Aims to improve the lives of low-income children by providing comprehensive, family-focused, child development services, including education, health, nutrition, and mental health • Parents are the primary educators of their children and must be directly involved • Supports the growth of children, families, and staff through encouragement, nurturing, education, and empowerment	• Multicultural and anti-bias education • Active involvement with materials, peers, and adults • Involves parents in the total operation and administration of the program
High Scope	• Active learning through engaging all five senses • Adults seen as supporters of child's learning • Children are encouraged to solve their own problems • Conflict is seen as a learning opportunity	• Play areas set out to support children's choices and interests • Outside areas seen as extensions of the indoor learning environment • Teachers record their observations grouped into ten specific areas through High Scope Observation Records • Consistent daily routine and schedule
Montessori	• Based on the works of Maria Montessori • Emphasizes learning through all five senses • Believes in "sensitive periods" of development when learning specific tasks is easiest • Children learn through discovery	• Traditional Montessori schools are associated with either the American Montessori Internationale or the American Montessori Society • Children direct their own learning, choosing among the sections of a well-structured, well-stocked classroom **continued**

Type	Philosophy	Distinguishing Features
Montessori *continued*	• The first six years are considered a stage of the "absorbent mind," a time of enormous potential • Allowing child room for repetitious play helps mastery • Children learn best alone during periods of intense concentration and should not be interrupted • Teaches children life skills such as dressing themselves and washing hands • Children learn at their own, individual pace and according to their own choice of activities	• Teacher is an observer and guide to the child instead of a lecturer • Play with "manipulative materials" such as Pink Tower, Smelling Jars, Red Rods, colored cylinders, etc. • Often uses mixed-age classrooms with up to a three-year age span • Order, attention to detail, and aesthetic focus in the classroom environment
Reggio Emelio	• Based on the principles of respect, responsibility, and community through exploration and discovery in a supportive and enriching environment • Curriculum emerges from the interests of the children • The teacher is a teacher-researcher, a resource and guide lending expertise to children • Children undertake long-term projects • Environment supports child's creativity • Creative children encouraged to express themselves by talking, dancing, singing, painting, drawing, performing, etc.—the "hundred languages of children"	• Strong belief in parents and community involvement • Emphasis on aesthetics • Documentation is an important part of the approach; teachers act as recorders (documenters) for the children, helping them put their words and actions to paper, thereby making learning visible. Videotaping and photography are also frequently used to document.
Religious-Based	• Usually developmental approach but can vary widely • Typically has a religious focus	• Takes place at a church, synagogue, or other religious institution • Preschool restricted to children of families who are members of the religious institution

Type	Philosophy	Distinguishing Features
Waldorf	• Based on the works of Rudolf Steiner • Emphasis on the oral tradition; the curriculum is taught verbally through conversation and song • Focus on imagination, imitation, experiential learning, consistency, creativity, and practical activities • Early experiences of daily and annual rhythms are valued; seasonal festivals drawn from a variety of traditions are celebrated • Use of simple toys like cloth dolls, wooden blocks, plain wooden toys, pots and pans • Children are engaged through "head, heart, and hands."	• Nontraditional activities such as knitting, sewing, whittling, cooking, gardening, etc. • No commercial posters or toys in classrooms • Parents are often asked to commit to not letting their children watch television or severely limiting viewing • Clothing sporting commercial characters is discouraged • Use of nature tables with natural objects like twigs, shells, and pinecones • Classrooms use natural light instead of fluorescent lighting

SCHOOL HOUSE ROCK:
WHAT TO LOOK FOR IN A ROCKIN' PRESCHOOL

Quality care is the key to a positive experience for your child and great brain-boosting results. Check out the suggestions on finding quality care listed in Appendix A, since they apply to preschool as well.

Ask other parents about their experiences with preschools in your area. You can learn a lot about how a school works with parents, how kids feel about their experience, and what the teachers and administration are like, through word of mouth. While you don't want to base your decision completely on what other parents say, it should be taken into account.

When visiting a school (and you should not consider a school without making a visit yourself), try to plan your visit so you can watch the school in action. Many schools will allow parents to sit in on a class, which is the ideal way to learn about that school. If the school will not allow you to observe a class in session, you can show up early for your tour or hang out afterward for a while to take a closer look. Watch and listen closely, and ask yourself the following questions:

- How do the teachers talk to the children?
- Do the children seem happy and engaged or do they wander around aimlessly?

- Are the teachers constantly directing the children's activities and reprimanding them?
- Does there seem to be some kind of predictable structure to the day (most schools have a child-friendly version of the day's events posted on the wall)?
- Do the teachers seem to recognize the children's individuality or do the kids get treated as a group?
- Is the facility safe and secure or do people wander in and out with little accountability?
- Is there a good variety of toys, art supplies, puzzles, books, blocks, and other equipment or are kids fighting over a few playthings?
- Does all the children's artwork on the wall look the same, as if the teacher had instructed them how to do it "right," or have kids

---

FROM THE EXPERTS ...

Tips for Applying to Preschool

In many cities, choosing a preschool, and being chosen, has come to feel like a competitive sport. However, despite what some overachieving parents think, admission to the "right" preschool will not set your child on the road to Harvard. What is vastly more important to find is the preschool that fits your child and your family. The following tips will point you in the right direction.

1. Do you want your child in a half-day or a full-day program? How much flexibility do you need in terms of number of days and hours your child is in school?

2. How far do you want to drive? There are many outstanding preschools; unless you have a pathological desire to listen to Elmo during long car rides, the closer the better.

3. How much do you want to spend on preschool? Don't forget hidden costs like the annual fund drive, capital campaigns, endowment funds, and galas.

4. What is the educational philosophy you are most comfortable with (remembering, of course, that you are looking for the best fit for your child)?

been allowed to explore their creativity by drawing purple trees and people with three arms?

- Is there an open-door policy? Can parents come and visit when they want to? Does the school seem to be hiding anything from parents?

Make sure to get all available printed materials on the school and check out its website. What is the school's philosophy? Is it consistent with your family's approach to children and your beliefs? Check with your local Better Business Bureau for complaints. Make sure that the school is licensed. The government classifies preschools as day-care centers rather than educational institutions, so they have to meet the same licensing requirements that day-care centers do. Keep in mind that licensing does not guarantee quality, only that the school has met the minimum health, safety, and teacher training standards set by the state.

---

5. Would you consider sending your child to a preschool affiliated with a church or a temple? Joining the congregation can give you an advantage in the admissions process.

6. What is the school's policy on toilet training? Some preschools have a very strict requirement that a child must be toilet trained before starting preschool, while others are far more lenient and realize that peer modeling will probably accomplish the task.

7. After preschool, do you plan to send your child to public or private school? Some preschools send all their graduates on to private elementary schools. There are also many excellent preschools whose graduates attend public schools.

8. Apply to the toddler program of the preschool you are interested in. Many preschools have once-a-week toddler programs that start when the child is about eighteen months old. These programs are an excellent way of getting to know a preschool, and attending the toddler program in some preschools gives your child an advantage in admission.

Finally, try to remember that although these first decisions regarding your child's education are important, no preschool can ever replace you. There are no golden tickets—no preschool will guarantee success. It is far more important to be a loving, involved, present parent.

—Dr. Michelle Nitka, psychologist and author of
Coping with Preschool Panic: The Los Angeles Guide to Private Preschools

---

FROM THE EXPERTS...

Ten Things Parents Need to Know about School Food

1. Does your school have an active wellness committee?

2. Does your school have a wellness policy that includes school food guidelines? Does the policy limit sugary and diet beverages, sports drinks, and fruit drinks? Does the policy address party and holiday celebrations, fundraisers, sports events, vending machines, snack sales, and field trips?

3. Is your school's wellness policy part of an overall sustainability plan?

4. Is your school's meal program self-operated or run by an outsourced food service management company?

5. How much of the food being served is real and freshly prepared? Is your child being fed processed, brand-named packaged food items? Does the food in your child's school contain so-called "natural" and artificial

TOURING SCHOOLS: QUESTIONS TO ASK

At the end of most preschool tours, parents have the opportunity to ask a few questions. Watching how a school director or teacher handles questions can be very telling about how the school treats parents. Here are a few questions that I have found to be very revealing:

Q How do you handle a child who doesn't want to participate in an activity, like circle time?

A You are looking for a school that knows how to respect your child's boundaries, but will also help him move past his reservations. A caring teacher will take the time to find out why the child doesn't want to participate (did he just get teased by another child? is he afraid to speak in a group?) so she can help him. When my husband and I asked this question at one school, the answer was, "I would tell the child, 'Everyone else is sitting in the circle; don't you want to go too?'" Just what a kid needs—peer pressure and coercion from a teacher . . . I don't think so.

flavorings, colorings, artificial sweeteners, preservatives, binders, and unpronounceable ingredients? Ask to see a list of ingredients for everything in the cafeteria and vending machines.

6. How much of the food is sourced locally?

7. Does your school have a schoolyard garden where the children can learn about growing, preparing, and eating fresh fruits, vegetables, grains, and legumes?

8. Are the school district's administrators, teachers, and food service staff setting a good example for students by drinking water and eating lots of fresh foods instead of soda, energy bars, and chips?

9. Does the school provide your child with a source of good quality drinking water?

10. How much time does your child have to eat lunch? Is lunchtime combined with recess time?

—Amy Kalafa, award-winning filmmaker, television producer, writer, and creator of the documentary *Two Angry Moms,* about parents working to improve their children's school food environment · www.angrymoms.org

Q How do you handle conflict resolution?

A If you have not had the chance to observe a teacher resolving conflict on your tour, it's important to ask questions about it. Conflict between kids is a normal part of preschool, but it is also an opportunity for your child to learn problem-solving and social skills. Avoid schools that use time-outs, punishments, or reprimands. Look for schools that will teach your child the necessary skills to work through conflicts with his peers.

Q How do you handle separation?

A There are a lot of effective ways to handle separation, and many of them have merit, though the true effectiveness of any plan depends upon you, your child, and your specific needs. In some schools, teachers visit children at home, and in some the parents stay in the classroom for the first week or two. In other schools, the parents wait in a different room, where the children cannot see them, and in some schools parents are able to watch their kids through a one-way mirror. The most important thing to divine from your tour is that the school will work with you and your child if he is having a difficult time.

Q How long have your teachers been with the school? What kind of education do they have?

A High staff turnover is indicative of an underpaid and overworked staff that may not have the patience needed to deal with a room of rowdy preschoolers. As mentioned in Appendix A, having long-term teachers on staff is important because this allows the teachers to hone their skills and get to know and become attuned to the children. Experienced teachers are confident in their abilities in the classroom, skilled in working with children, and responsive to their needs.

While there are many terrific teachers who do not have an advanced degree, take additional continuing education classes, or get certified in child development, taking those steps shows a level of dedication, commitment, and passion for children that raises the odds for quality teaching. Compared to less educated teachers, studies show that teachers who receive specialized training are more involved, more responsive, more affectionate, more encouraging, more stimulating, less authoritarian, less restrictive, and more able to provide high-quality, developmentally appropriate care and rich literary experiences.

Appendix C

Sample Baby Schedules

When my newborn daughters first came home from the hospital, we had them on a three-hour feeding schedule. Due to their reflux, medication requirements, and the length of time it took to feed them, we had to switch to a four-hour feeding schedule sooner than expected. At the advice of our pediatrician we continued to "dream feed" (a nighttime feed while the baby is asleep) Quincy and Mendez until they were approximately seven months old due to weight gain issues. We also introduced solid food at about six months, instead of the more usual four. I have always been resistant to dropping naps and as a result I chose to replace naps with "quiet time" in the girls' cribs before transitioning to actually dropping the nap. This is not a traditional method to handle the transition, but it worked for us. Our experience indicates that parents should consider all times listed in the following schedules to be "suggested times," not absolute laws.

Below are some samples of the schedules that worked for us as well as those that worked for other families. When making your child's schedule, keep in mind that formula-fed babies are generally able to go longer between feedings than breastfed babies.

But above all, make sure that you individualize your child's schedule based on her physical and development needs, preferably with the help of your pediatrician.

Schedule for twins Quincy and Mendez, age three months

8 am	feeding
9–11	nap
12 noon	feeding
1–3 pm	nap
4	feeding
5–6	nap
7	bath and mini baby massage
8	feeding
11	dream feed

Six months

8 am	feeding
9–11	nap
12 noon	feeding
1–3	nap
4	feeding
5–6	nap
6–7	bath and mini baby massage
7:30	feeding
11	dream feed

Seven months

8 am	breakfast
9–10:30	nap in crib
10:30–12 noon	playtime
12 noon–1 pm	lunch
1–2:30	nap in crib
2:30–4	playtime
4–5	dinner
5–5:30	nap
5:30–6:30	bath
6:30–7	playtime
7–7:30	wind-down time (quiet music, no stimulating toys)
7:30–8:30	feed
9	bedtime
11	dream feed for only one child

Ten months

8–8:30 am	breakfast
9–10:30	nap in crib
10:30–12noon	playtime
12–12:30	lunch
1–2:30	nap in crib
2:30–4	playtime
4–4:30	dinner
5–5:30	quiet time in crib in place of third nap
5:30–6:30	bath
6	wind-down time
6:30	music and cuddles
6:45–7	feed
7:20	bedtime

Fifteen months

    8–8:30 am .... breakfast
    9–10:30 .... nap in crib
    10:30–12noon .... playtime
    12–12:30pm .... lunch
    1–2:30 .... nap in crib
    2:30–4 .... playtime
    4–4:30 .... dinner
    4:30–5 .... playtime
    5:00–5:45 .... bath
    6:00–6:15 .... snack
    6:15–6:30 .... brush teeth, story time, music and cuddle
    6:30 .... bedtime

Twenty-one months

    8–8:30 am .... breakfast
    9–9:30 .... quiet time in crib
    10:30 .... snack
    9:30–12 noon .... activity time
                          (park, class, play at home or outside, etc.)
    12–12:30 .... lunch
    12:30–2:30/3 .... nap in crib
    3:00–4 .... playtime
    4–4:30 .... snack
    4:30–5 .... playtime
    5:00–5:45 .... bath
    5:50–6:20 .... dinner
    6:20–6:45 .... brush teeth, story time, music and cuddle
    6:50 .... bedtime, no later than 7 pm

Twenty-six months

    8–8:30 am .... breakfast
    9–11:30 .... activity
                          (class, playdate, park, visit with grandparents)
    10:30 .... snack
    12 noon–12:30pm .. lunch
    12:30–2:30/3 .... nap in crib
    3:00–4 .... playtime
    4–4:20 .... snack
    4:30–5 .... playtime
    5:00–5:45 .... bath

5:50–6:20 .... dinner
6:20–6:45 .... brush teeth, story time, music and cuddles
6:50 .... bedtime, no later than 7 pm

Thirty months

8–8:30 am .... breakfast
9–11:30ish .... activity
                            (class, playdate, park, visit with grandparents)
10:30 .... snack
12 noon–12:30pm .. lunch
1:00–3 .... nap in crib
3:00–4 .... playtime
4–4:30 .... snack
4:30–5 .... playtime
5:00–5:45 .... bath
5:50–6:20 .... dinner
6:20–7:00 .... story time, music and cuddles
7:00 .... bedtime

Here are a few schedules that have worked for other families with children at different ages and stages:

Schedule for triplets Ben, Sophia, and Max, age two months

6 am .... first feeding
6:30–9 .... play in house
                            (swings, bouncy seats, tummy time)
9 .... second feeding
9:30–10 .... nap
11 .... walk in stroller
12 noon .... third feeding
12:30–3 pm .... play inside
3 .... fourth feeding
4:30–5 .... second walk in stroller
6 .... fifth feeding
7 .... bath
7:30 .... bedtime
10:30–11 .... last feeding

Schedule for triplets Chase, Juliet, and Chloe, age four months

7 am .... wake up, bottle
8–9 .... playtime
9–11 .... nap

11 .... wake up, bottle
12 noon–1 pm........ playtime
1–3 .... nap
3 .... wake up, bottle
4 .... playtime (third nap until four months)
6:30 .... bath
7 .... bottle, bedtime
11 .... feed (eliminated at three and a half months)
3 am .... feed (eliminated at four months)

Schedule for twins Raj and Krish, age eight months

6:30 am .... wake up
7 .... bottle
7:45 .... breakfast
8:30 .... first nap
10:45 .... bottle
11:30 .... lunch
12 noon .... second nap
2 .... bottle
3:30 .... third nap
5 .... dinner, play, bath
6:30 .... bottle, book, bed

Schedule for twins Brandon and Rachael, age thirteen months

6:45–7 am .... wake up, bottle
7–7:45 .... playtime and reading books
7:45–8:30 .... neighborhood walk
8:30–9 .... breakfast
9–1 .... playtime and reading books
1–11:30 .... bottle, nap
11:30–12 noon....... lunch
12–1:30 .... playtime
1:30–3 .... nap
3–4:30 .... playtime
4:30–5 .... dinner
5:30–6 .... bath
6–6:15 .... PJs, bottle, sleep

Thirty months

7–8 am .... wake up
8:30–9:30 .... breakfast
9:30–12:30 pm....... playtime

```
12:30–1 ................... lunch
1–2:30 .................... nap
3 ............................ play in their room
4:30 ....................... snack
6 ............................ dinner
6:30 ....................... bath
7 ............................ bedtime
```

Looking for More Sample Schedules?

Try these books:

Secrets of the Baby Whisperer by Tracy Hogg

The New Contented Little Baby Book by Gina Ford

On Becoming Baby Wise by Gary Ezzo and Robert Bucknam

Appendix D

Reducing the Risk of SIDS

As new research comes out, the American Academy of Pediatrics (AAP) is constantly updating its position regarding recommendations to reduce the risk of sudden infant death syndrome (SIDS). While there is some new research that SIDS may be caused by deficiencies in a serotonin receptor in the brain, an abnormally high number of neurons that produce serotonin, or an insufficient amount of a brain protein that "recycles" serotonin, there are many things you can do (or make sure not to do) in order to reduce your child's risk.

Here are a dozen things you can do to reduce the risk of SIDS:

1. Always put your infant to sleep on his back. Since the beginning of the Back to Sleep campaign, which encourages parents to put their babies to sleep on their backs, the rate of SIDS has been reduced by more than 50 percent.

2. Put your baby to sleep on a firm mattress with a fitted sheet that cannot be pulled off.

3. Keep soft objects and loose bedding out of the crib. Things like pillows, quilts, comforters, sheepskins, stuffed toys, and other soft objects should be kept out of an infant's sleeping environment.

4. Do not expose your child to any smoke. In normal birth-weight infants, the risk for SIDS is increased about twofold with passive smoke exposure and about threefold when the mother smokes during the pregnancy and the baby continues to be exposed to tobacco smoke after birth.

5. Sleep separately but near your child. The AAP recommends that infants sleep in the same room as parents without sharing a bed in order to reduce the risk of SIDS. This can be accomplished by keeping a bassinet, co-sleeper, or crib in the parent's room.

6. Avoid co-sleeping. The AAP issued the following statement: "Several cases of accidental suffocation or death from undetermined cause suggest that bed sharing is hazardous." This risk increases with multiple bed sharers, smokers, exhaustion (what new parent isn't exhausted?), and the consumption of alcohol.

7. Let your child use a pacifier when sleeping. Consider offering a pacifier at naptime and bedtime. The pacifier should be used when placing infants down for sleep but should not be reinserted if it falls out while the infant sleeps.

8. Avoid overheating. Make sure your child is lightly clothed for sleep. The bedroom temperature should be kept comfortable for a lightly clothed adult. It is believed that 68 to 72 degrees Fahrenheit is ideal for SIDS prevention.

9. Use a fan in your infant's room. A recent study found that using a fan in a child's room can reduce incidence of SIDS by 72 percent. Opening a window has been shown to reduce risk slightly, as well.

10. Avoid home monitors and commercial devices to monitor or reduce the incidence of SIDS. According to the AAP reports, none have been tested sufficiently to show efficacy or safety.

11. Make sure that other caregivers are aware of these recommendations. Two-thirds of parents of children under the age of one rely on other caregivers to help take care of their children. A study of licensed child-care facilities found that 43 percent were unaware of the relationship between SIDS and infant sleep position. To make matters worse, babies who are used to sleeping on their backs and then are suddenly placed on their stomachs to sleep are eighteen times more likely to die of SIDS.

12. Breastfeed your baby. In 2005 the AAP acknowledged that sleep studies of infants have shown that breastfed infants are more easily roused from sleep than formula-fed babies, but it reported mixed findings regarding the relationship between breastfeeding and SIDS prevention. A 2009 study printed in *Pediatrics* compared more than 300 infants who died of SIDS and almost 1,000 age-matched "control" infants: at two weeks of age, 83 percent of the controls were being breastfed compared to only 50 percent of the SIDS infants. At one month of age, the corresponding rates were 72 percent versus 40 percent.

Poisonous Mattress?

Another more controversial theory about SIDS has emerged. New Zealand chemist and forensic scientist Dr. Jim Sprott hypothesizes that crib death is caused by toxic gases generated from conventional baby mattresses. He says chemical compounds containing phosphorus, arsenic, and antimony have been added to mattresses as fire retardants and for other purposes. He believes that a fungus that commonly grows in bedding can interact with these chemicals to create poisonous gases, which become concentrated in a thin layer on the baby's mattress. He claims that if a baby breathes in a lethal dose of the gases, the central nervous system shuts down, stopping breathing and then heart function. Most American pediatricians believe that much more research must be done to prove that this hypothesis has any merit.

That said, prior to New Zealand's crib death prevention campaign, that country had the highest rate of SIDS in the world, and now it boasts a 100 percent successful campaign. Parents in New Zealand are advised to wrap their child's mattress in a BabeSafe mattress cover, a special cover that has been tested to block gases.

A study in the Journal of the American Medical Association found that infants who die of SIDS have brainstem abnormalities that may impair the child's ability to sense high carbon dioxide and low oxygen levels. This impairment would put an infant at risk in situations in which they breathe in their own exhaled breath, depriving them of oxygen. According to Dr. Duane Alexander, director of the NIH's National Institute of Child Health and Human Development, "This finding lends credence to the view that SIDS risk may greatly increase when an underlying predisposition combines with an environmental risk."

A few precautions you might want to consider:

- Use only an organic mattress for your child.
- Get a BabeSafe mattress cover if you are using a conventional mattress.
- Avoid hand-me-down mattresses, which have been shown to triple the risk of SIDS due to the proliferation of fungus.

SIDS and Pacifiers: Thumbs Up or Thumbs Down?

In 2005 the American Academy of Pediatrics issued a statement recommending that infants use pacifiers in order to prevent SIDS. A study in the *British Medical Journal* found that babies who sucked their thumbs had a 57 percent decreased chance of SIDS, while those who used pacifiers had a 92 percent decrease.

The AAP makes the following recommendations:

- A pacifier should be used when placing an infant down to sleep and not reinserted once the infant falls asleep. If the infant refuses the pacifier, he should not be forced to take it.
- Pacifiers should not be coated in any sweet solution.
- Pacifiers should be cleaned often and replaced regularly.
- For breastfed infants, delay introducing a pacifier until your child is one month old to ensure that breastfeeding is firmly established.

However, pacifier use and thumb sucking can still negatively impact speech. According to Patricia McAleer-Hamaguchi, pediatric speech pathologist and author of *Childhood Speech, Language, and Listening Problems: What Every Parent Should Know,* sucking on a pacifier locks a child's mouth in an unnatural position, making it more difficult for the tongue and lip muscles to develop normally.

Psychologically speaking, many children turn to thumb sucking and pacifiers for self-soothing and for use as a transitional object. Personally, I would rather pay for braces than therapy as a result of taking away my child's comfort object. According to pediatric dentist Dr. Lidieth Libby, "For most children there is no reason to worry about a sucking habit until the permanent front teeth are ready to come in." Every parent has to figure out her own comfort zone with these self-soothing activities. If you do allow your child to continue to use a pacifier beyond the first year, speech therapists recommend limiting its use to sleep time only. Use a newborn-size pacifier, which has less impact on speech, and don't allow your child to speak with a pacifier in his mouth.

Swaddling and SIDS

Some information about the association between overbundling, overheating, and SIDS has made many professionals apprehensive about swaddling. One study even suggests that swaddling may increase the SIDS risk for infants sleeping on their stomach. It is currently believed that SIDS is caused by a number of factors occurring at the same time, one of which may be swaddling. A later study found that the association between swaddling and SIDS was not significant in infants who were sleeping on their backs.

Dr. Harvey Karp, pediatrician and author of *The Happiest Baby on the Block*, asserts that swaddling reduces the risk of SIDS for four reasons:

1. Swaddling prolongs sleep and makes babies sleep more lightly, which has been shown to lower the risk of SIDS.
2. Swaddling prevents babies from rolling onto the stomach, which would dramatically increase the risk of SIDS.
3. Research shows that swaddled babies sleep as well on their backs as unswaddled babies sleep on their stomachs.
4. Because swaddling makes babies less mobile, it may prevent many bed-sharing risks for families that choose the "family bed."

If you choose to swaddle your baby, Dr. Karp recommends the following precautions:

1. Swaddled babies should be dressed lightly in warm weather, and babies with hot ears and sweaty necks should wear only a diaper when wrapped (if wrapped at all).
2. Suffocation hazards, such as bulky or thick blankets, should be avoided.
3. Loose sheets or thin blankets should never be allowed to cover a baby's face.
4. Parents should swaddle their babies in a big, light blanket that is large enough to allow a secure wrap all around the body so it does not unravel during sleep.

References

In addition to the numerous interviews conducted, the following is a list of significant research materials that directly inform the text.

Introduction

Bouchez, Colette. "How to Raise a Smart Baby." WebMD Children's Health Center. August 2008. http://children.webmd.com/features/how-to-raise-smart-baby.

Eliot, Lise. *What's Going On in There? How the Brain and Mind Develop in the First Five Years of Life.* New York: Bantam, 2000.

Fowler, William. *Talking from Infancy: How to Nurture & Cultivate Early Language Development.* Cambridge, MA: Center for Early Learning and Child Care, 1995.

Gerhardt, Sue. *Why Love Matters: How Affection Shapes a Baby's Brain.* Hove, East Sussex, UK: Brunner-Routledge, 2004.

Gordon, Jay, and Brenda Adderly. *Brighter Baby: Boost Your Child's Intelligence, Health, and Happiness through Infant Therapeutic Massage.* Washington, DC: LifeLine, 1999.

Greenspan, Stanley I., and Nancy Breslau Lewis. *Building Healthy Minds: The Six Experiences That Create Intelligence and Emotional Growth in Babies and Young Children.* Cambridge, MA: Perseus, 2000.

Hall, Susan L., and Louisa Cook Moats. *Straight Talk about Reading: How Parents Can Make a Difference during the Early Years.* Lincolnwood, IL: Contemporary, 1999.

Heller, Sharon. *The Vital Touch: How Intimate Contact with Your Baby Leads to Happier, Healthier Development.* New York: Henry Holt, 1997.

Matthiessen, Connie. "Top 5 Parenting Fears and What You Can Do about Them." BabyCenter. June 2008. www.babycenter.com/0_top-5-parenting-fears-and-what-you-can-do-about-them_3656609.bc.

Perlmutter, David, and Carol Colman. *Raise a Smarter Child by Kindergarten: Build a Better Brain and Increase IQ Up to 30 Points.* New York: Morgan Road, 2006.

Siegel, Daniel J., and Mary Hartzell. *Parenting from the Inside Out: How a Deeper Self-Understanding Can Help You Raise Children Who Thrive.* New York: J.P. Tarcher/Penguin, 2004.

Sigman, Aric. *Remotely Controlled: How Television Is Damaging Our Lives—and What We Can Do about It.* London: Vermillion, 2005.

Stamm, Jill, and Paula Spencer. *Bright from the Start: The Simple, Science-Backed Way to Nurture Your Child's Developing Mind, from Birth to Age 3.* New York: Gotham, 2007.

Steinberg, Laurence D. *The Ten Basic Principles of Good Parenting.* New York: Simon & Schuster, 2004.

Trelease, Jim. *The Read-Aloud Handbook.* New York: Penguin, 2006.

Zigler, Edward, Dorothy G. Singer, and Sandra J. Bishop-Josef, eds. *Children's Play: The Roots of Reading.* Washington, DC: Zero to Three, 2004.

1. Talk the Talk: Respectful Communication

Adler, Alfred, and Colin Brett. *What Life Could Mean to You.* Oxford: Oneworld, 1992.

Berman, Jenn. *The A to Z Guide to Raising Happy, Confident Kids.* Novato, CA: New World Library, 2007.

———. "The Problem with Praise." *Los Angeles Family,* November 2008.

Branden, Nathaniel. *The Six Pillars of Self-Esteem.* New York: Bantam, 1994.

Braun, Betsy Brown. *Just Tell Me What to Say: Sensible Tips and Scripts for Perplexed Parents.* New York: Collins, 2008.

Bronson, Po. "How Not to Talk to Your Kids: The Inverse Power of Praise." *New York,* February 12, 2007.

Brooks, Robert B., and Sam Goldstein. *Raising a Self-Disciplined Child: Help Your Child Become More Responsible, Confident, and Resilient.* New York: McGraw-Hill, 2007.

Chen, Xiaoli, May A. Beydoun, and Youfa Wang. "Is Sleep Duration Associated With Childhood Obesity? A Systematic Review and Meta-Analysis." *Obesity* 16 (2008): 265–274.

Cohen, Scott W. *Eat, Sleep, Poop: A Complete Common Sense Guide to Your Baby's First Year from a Pediatrician/Dad.* New York: Scribner, 2010.

Culbertson, Brian. *Golden Slumbers: A Father's Lullabye.* CD. Warner Brothers, 2002.

Dreikurs, Rudolf, and Vicki Soltz. *Children: The Challenge.* New York: Penguin, 1964.

Dr. Sears. "Spanking: 10 Reasons Not to Hit Your Child." www.askdrsears.com/html/6/T062100.asp.

Dweck, Carol S. "Caution: Praise Can Be Dangerous." *American Educator* 23.1 (1999): 4–9.

Dweck, Carol S., and N.D. Reppucci. "Learned Helplessness and Reinforcement Responsibility in Children." *Journal of Personality and Social Psychology* 25 (1973): 109–116.

Eisenmann, Joey C., Panteleimon Ekkekakis, and Megan Holmes. "Sleep Duration and Overweight Among Australian Children and Adolescents." *Acta Paediatrica* 95.8 (2006): 956–963.

Erikson, Erik H. *Childhood and Society.* New York: W.W. Norton, 1993.

Faber, Adele, and Elaine Mazlish. *Liberated Parents, Liberated Children: Your Guide to a Happier Family.* New York: Avon, 1990.

Finkelstein, Alix. "Why Toddlers Misbehave (And What You Can Do About It)." *Child* (1997): 75–79.

Foote, Donna. "The War of Wills." *Newsweek,* Fall 2000.

Ganske, Mary Garner. "Beyond 'No.'" *Parenting,* October 2003.

Gardner, Amanda. "Spanking Raises Chances of Risky, Deviant Sexual Behavior." *U.S. News & World Report.* February 28, 2008. http://health.usnews.com/usnews/health/healthday/080228/spanking-raises-chances-of-risky-deviant-sexual-behavior.htm.

Gerber, Magda, and Allison Johnson. *Your Self-Confident Baby: How to Encourage Your Child's Natural Abilities—from the Very Start.* New York: Wiley, 1998.

Ginott, Haim G., Alice Ginott, and H. Wallace Goddard. *Between Parent and Child: The Bestselling Classic That Revolutionized Parent-Child Communication.* New York: Three Rivers, 2003.

Gonzalez-Mena, Janet, and Dianne Widmeyer Eyer. *Infants, Toddlers, and Caregivers: A Curriculum of Respectful, Responsive Care and Education.* New York: McGraw-Hill, 2009.

Harder, Ben. "Spanking: When Parents Lift Their Hands." *Los Angeles Times,* February 19, 2007.

Hart, Betty, and Todd R. Risley. *Meaningful Differences in the Everyday Experience of Young American Children.* Baltimore: Paul H. Brookes, 1995.

HealthDay News. "Moms Who Spank More Likely to Abuse." BabyCenter. August 27, 2008. www.babycenter.com/204_study-moms-who-spank-more-likely-to-abuse_10218815.bc.

Kohn, Alfie. *Unconditional Parenting: Moving from Rewards and Punishments to Love and Reason.* New York: Atria, 2005.

Kurcinka, Mary Sheedy. *Kids, Parents, and Power Struggles: Winning for a Lifetime.* New York: HarperCollins, 2001.

McGraw, Phillip C. *Family First: Your Step-by-Step Plan for Creating a Phenomenal Family.* New York: Free Press, 2004.

Medhus, Elisa. *Hearing Is Believing: How Words Can Make or Break Our Children.* Novato, CA: New World Library, 2004.

Nelsen, Jane. *Positive Time-Out: And Over 50 Ways to Avoid Power Struggles in the Home and the Classroom.* Rocklin, CA: Prima, 1999.

Nelsen, Jane, Cheryl Erwin, and Roslyn Duffy. *Positive Discipline: The First Three Years from Infant to Toddler—Laying the Foundation for Raising a Capable, Confident Child.* New York: Three Rivers, 2007.

Parents. "Mine! Can You Really Teach Your Toddler to Share?" August 1995.

Walsh, David Allen. *No: Why Kids—of All Ages—Need to Hear It and Ways Parents Can Say It.* New York: Free Press, 2007.

2. You Got Me! Responding to Cues

Ainsworth, Mary D. Salter. *Patterns of Attachment: A Psychological Study of the Strange Situation.* Hillsdale, NJ: Erlbaum, 1978.

Bennett, Shoshana S. *Postpartum Depression for Dummies.* Hoboken, NJ: Wiley, 2007.

Bennett, Shoshana S., and Pec Indman. *Beyond the Blues: A Guide to Understanding and Treating Prenatal and Postpartum Depression.* San Jose, CA: Moodswings, 2006.

Berman, Jenn. *The A to Z Guide to Raising Happy, Confident Kids.* Novato, CA: New World Library, 2007.

——. "Personality Theory: What You Need to Know in Order to Better Understand Yourself and Your Loved Ones." *Los Angeles Family,* May 2005.

——. "Postpartum Depression: Part 1." *Los Angeles Family,* April 2003.

——. "Postpartum Depression: The Mind Body Connection: Part 2." *Los Angeles Family,* May 2003.

——. "Toilet Training by Numbers." *Los Angeles Family,* August 2008.

——. "What Your Baby's Telling You: Infant Cues." *Parenting,* October 2002.

Biederman, Jerry, and Lorin Biederman, eds. *Parenting School: Simple Lessons from the Leading Experts on Being a Mom.* New York: M. Evans, 2004.

Boucke, Laurie, and Linda Carlson. *Infant Potty Training: A Gentle and Primeval Method, Adapted to Modern Living.* Lafayette, CO: White-Boucke, 2000.

Bowlby, John. *A Secure Base: Parent-Child Attachment and Healthy Human Development.* New York: Basic Books, 1988.

Brazelton, T. Berry, and Bertrand G. Cramer. *The Earliest Relationship: Parents, Infants, and the Drama of Early Attachment.* Reading, MA: Perseus, 1990.

Brazelton, T. Berry, and Stanley I. Greenspan. *The Irreducible Needs of Children: What Every Child Must Have to Grow, Learn, and Flourish.* Cambridge, MA: Perseus, 2000.

Briggs, Dorothy Corkille. *Your Child's Self-Esteem.* New York: Broadway, 2001.

Brooks, Robert, and Sam Goldstein. *Raising Resilient Children: Fostering Strength, Hope, and Optimism in Your Child.* New York: McGraw-Hill, 2001.

Chess, Stella, and Alexander Thomas. *Know Your Child: An Authoritative Guide for Today's Parents.* Northvale, NJ: Jason Aronson, 1996.

Cohen, Lawrence J. *Playful Parenting: A Bold New Way to Nurture Close Connections, Solve Behavior Problems, and Encourage Children's Confidence.* New York: Ballantine, 2001.

Conner, Bobbi. *Everyday Opportunities for Extraordinary Parenting.* Naperville, IL: Source, 2000.

Cozolino, Louis J. *The Neuroscience of Human Relationships: Attachment and the Developing Social Brain.* New York: W.W. Norton, 2006.

Davidson, Richard J. "Affective Style, Psychopathology, and Resilience: Brain Mechanisms and Plasticity." *American Psychologist* 55.11 (2000): 1196–1214.

Dawson, Geraldine, Karin Frey, David Hess, Julie Osterling, and Heracles Panagiotides. "Infants of Depressed Mothers Exhibit Atypical Frontal Brain Activity: A Replication and Extension of Previous Findings." *Journal of Child Psychology & Psychiatry* 38 (1997): 179–186. NCBI. www.ncbi.nlm.nih.gov/pubmed/9232464.

Dunstan, Priscilla. *Dunstan Baby Language.* DVD. 2006.

Gerber, Magda, and Allison Johnson. *Your Self-Confident Baby: How to Encourage Your Child's Natural Abilities—from the Very Start.* New York: Wiley, 1998.

Gerhardt, Sue. *Why Love Matters: How Affection Shapes a Baby's Brain.* Hove, East Sussex, UK: Brunner-Routledge, 2004.

Gottman, John Mordechai, and Joan DeClaire. *Raising an Emotionally Intelligent Child.* New York: Simon & Schuster, 1997.

Greenspan, Stanley I., and Nancy Breslau Lewis. *Building Healthy Minds: The Six Experiences That Create Intelligence and Emotional Growth in Babies and Young Children.* Cambridge, MA: Perseus, 2000.

Greenspan, Stanley I., and Nancy Thorndike Greenspan. *First Feelings: Milestones in the Emotional Development of Your Baby and Child.* New York: Penguin, 1989.

Gurian, Michael. *Nurture the Nature: Understanding and Supporting Your Child's Unique Core Personality.* San Francisco: Jossey-Bass, 2007.

Herold, Shelly. *Seven Secrets of Perfect Parenting.* Hollywood, FL: Frederick Fell, 2004.

Hirsh-Pasek, Kathy, Roberta M. Golinkoff, and Diane E. Eyer. *Einstein Never Used Flash Cards: How Our Children Really Learn—and Why They Need to Play More and Memorize Less.* Emmaus, PA: Rodale, 2003.

Karen, Robert. *Becoming Attached: First Relationships and How They Shape Our Capacity to Love.* New York: Oxford University Press, 1994.

Kurcinka, Mary Sheedy. *Kids, Parents, and Power Struggles: Winning for a Lifetime.* New York: HarperCollins, 2001.

Nelsen, Jane, Cheryl Erwin, and Roslyn Duffy. *Positive Discipline: The First Three Years from Infant to Toddler—Laying the Foundation for Raising a Capable, Confident Child.* New York: Three Rivers, 2007.

Oldham, John M., and Lois B. Morris. *The New Personality Self-Portrait: Why You Think, Work, Love, and Act the Way You Do.* New York: Bantam, 1995.

Pregnancy Info. "Postpartum Psychosis." www.pregnancy-info.net/postpartum_psychosis.html.

Schore, Allan N. *Affect Regulation and the Origin of the Self: The Neurobiology of Emotional Development.* Hillsdale, NJ: Lawrence Erlbaum, 1994.

Sears, William, Martha Sears, and Elizabeth Pantley. *The Successful Child: What Parents Can Do to Help Kids Turn Out Well.* Boston: Little, Brown, 2002.

Sebastian, Linda. *Overcoming Postpartum Depression & Anxiety.* Omaha, NE: Addicus, 1998.

Seifert, Ariane. "Over-Stimulated Children: Is Your Baby Over-Stimulated?" Essortment.com. 2002. www.essortment.com/all/overstimulated_rflg.htm.

Seligman, Martin E.P., and Steven F. Maier. "Failure to Escape Traumatic Shock." *Journal of Experimental Psychology* 74 (1967): 1–9.

Siegel, Daniel J. *The Developing Mind: How Relationships and the Brain Interact to Shape Who We Are.* New York: Guilford, 1999.

Siegel, Daniel J., and Mary Hartzell. *Parenting from the Inside Out: How a Deeper Self-Understanding Can Help You Raise Children Who Thrive.* New York: J.P. Tarcher/Penguin, 2004.

Stamm, Jill, and Paula Spencer. *Bright from the Start: The Simple, Science-Backed Way to Nurture Your Child's Developing Mind, from Birth to Age 3.* New York: Gotham, 2007.

Steinberg, Laurence D. *The Ten Basic Principles of Good Parenting.* New York: Simon & Schuster, 2004.

Sunderland, Margot. *The Science of Parenting: Practical Guidance on Sleep, Crying, Play, and Building*

Emotional Well-Being for Life. New York: Dorling Kindersley, 2006.

Talaris Institute. "Getting in Tune with Baby." www.talaris.org/spotlight_tune.htm.

Tronick, Edward Z., and Jeffrey F. Cohn. "Infant-Mother Face-to-Face Interaction: Age and Gender Differences in Coordination and the Occurrence of Miscoordination." *Child Development* 60 (1989): 85–92.

Winnicott, Donald Woods. *Babies and Their Mothers.* Reading, MA: Addison-Wesley, 1992.

Zigler, Edward, Dorothy G. Singer, and Sandra J. Bishop-Josef, eds. *Children's Play: The Roots of Reading.* Washington, DC: Zero to Three, 2004.

3. Tick-Tock: Creating Security and Predictability

AAP Task Force on Infant Sleep Position and Sudden Infant Death Syndrome. "The Changing Concept of Sudden Infant Death Syndrome: Diagnostic Coding Shifts, Controversies Regarding the Sleep Environment, and New Variables to Consider in Reducing Risk." *Pediatrics* 116.5 (2005).

Andruss, Paula. "The Best Schedule for Your Baby." *Parents,* May 2006.

BabyCenter. "Eleven Reasons Babies Cry and How to Soothe Them." June 2009. www.babycenter.com/0_eleven-reasons-babies-cry-and-how-to-soothe-them_9790.bc.

Bamroo. "The Importance of Naps." www.bamroo.com/Article.aspx/15.

Berman, Jenn. *The A to Z Guide to Raising Happy, Confident Kids.* Novato, CA: New World Library, 2007.

_____. "Sleep Training: Everything You Need to Know to Get a Great Night's Rest for You and Your Family." *Los Angeles Family,* June 2005.

Bronson, Po. "Snooze or Lose." *New York,* October 8, 2007.

Chen, Xiaoli, May A. Beydoun, and Youfa Wang. "Is Sleep Duration Associated with Childhood Obesity? A Systematic Review and Meta-Analysis." *Obesity* 16 (2008): 265–274.

Cohen, George J. *American Academy of Pediatrics' Guide to Your Child's Sleep: Birth through Adolescence.* New York: Villard, 1999.

Cohen, Scott W. *Eat, Sleep, Poop: A Complete Common Sense Guide to Your Baby's First Year from a Pediatrician/Dad.* New York: Scribner, 2010.

Culbertson, Brian. *Golden Slumbers: A Father's Lullabye.* CD. Warner Brothers, 2002.

Eisenmann, Joey C., Panteleimon Ekkekakis, and Megan Holmes. "Sleep Duration and Overweight Among Australian Children and Adolescents." *Acta Paediatrica* 95.8 (2006): 956–963.

Elston, Christina. "AAP Revises SIDS Prevention Guidelines." Parenthood.com. www.parenthood.com/article-topics/aap_revises_sids_prevention_guidelines.html.

Ezzo, Gary, and Robert Bucknam. *On Becoming Baby Wise: Giving Your Infant the Gift of Nighttime Sleep.* Louisiana, MO: Parent-Wise Solutions, 2006.

Ferber, Richard. *Solve Your Child's Sleep Problems.* New York: Fireside Book, 2006.

Fierro, Pamela. *The Everything Twins, Triplets, and More Book: From Seeing the First Sonogram to Coordinating Nap Times and Feedings—All You Need to Enjoy Your Multiples.* Avon, MA: Adams Media, 2005.

Ford, Gina. *The Complete Sleep Guide for Contented Babies and Toddlers.* London: Vermillion, 2003.

_____. *The New Contented Little Baby Book: The Secret to Calm and Confident Parenting.* London: Vermillion, 2006.

Gerber, Magda, and Allison Johnson. *Your Self-Confident Baby: How to Encourage Your Child's Natural Abilities—from the Very Start.* New York: Wiley, 1998.

Greenman, James T. *What Happened to My World: Helping Children Cope with Natural Disaster and Catastrophe.* Watertown, MA: Comfort for Kids, 2005.

Hagan, Carolyn. "The Art of the Nap." *Child,* February 1998.

Harrison, Yvonne. "The Relationship between Daytime Exposure to Light and Night-Time Sleep in 6–12-Week-Old Infants." *Journal of Sleep Research* 13 (2004): 345–352.

Herold, Shelly. *Seven Secrets of PERFECT Parenting.* Hollywood, FL: Frederick Fell, 2004.

Hogg, Tracy, and Melinda Blau. *The Baby Whisperer Solves All Your Problems (by Teaching You How to Ask the Right Questions): Sleeping, Feeding, and Behavior—Beyond the Basics from Infancy through Toddlerhood.* New York: Atria, 2005.

_____. *Secrets of the Baby Whisperer: How to Calm, Connect, and Communicate with Your Baby.* New York: Ballantine, 2001.

Karp, Harvey, and Paula Spencer. *The Happiest Toddler on the Block: How to Eliminate Tantrums and Raise a Patient, Respectful and Cooperative One- to Four-Year-Old.* New York: Bantam, 2008.

Kurcinka, Mary Sheedy. *Sleepless in America: Is Your Child Misbehaving or Missing Sleep?* New York: HarperCollins, 2006.

Lieberman, Alicia F. *The Emotional Life of the Toddler.* New York: Free Press, 1993.

Malenfant, Nicole. *Routines & Transitions: A Guide for Early Childhood Professionals.* St. Paul, MN: Redleaf, 2006.

Martin, Julia. "Why Babies Need Private Time: Nurturing Independence Now Will Pay Off Later." *Parents,* September 1997.

Mindell, Jodi A. *Sleeping through the Night: How Infants, Toddlers, and Their Parents Can Get a Good Night's Sleep.* New York: Collings Living, 2005.

National Institute of Health. "NICHD Back to Sleep Campaign." NICHD. May 1, 2009. www.nichd.nih.gov/sids/.

National Childbirth Trust. "Info Centre—Crying Baby." www.nct.org.uk/info-centre/information/view-78.

Nelsen, Jane, Cheryl Erwin, and Roslyn Duffy. *Positive Discipline: The First Three Years from Infant to Toddler—Laying the Foundation for Raising a Capable, Confident Child.* New York: Three Rivers, 2007.

Owens, Judith. "Should I Put My Baby on a Schedule?" BabyCenter. www.babycenter.com/404_should-i-put-my-baby-on-a-schedule_3174.bc.

Owens, Judith, and Jodi A. Mindell. *Take Charge of Your Child's Sleep: The All-in-One Resource for Solving Sleep Problems in Kids and Teens.* New York: Marlowe, 2005.

Pantley, Elizabeth. *The No-Cry Sleep Solution: Gentle Ways to Help Your Baby Sleep Through the Night.* New York: McGraw-Hill, 2002.

——. *The No-Cry Sleep Solution for Toddlers and Preschoolers: Gentle Ways to Stop Bedtime Battles and Improve Your Child's Sleep.* New York: McGraw-Hill, 2005.

Parents. "The Best Schedule for Your Baby." www.parents.com/baby/sleep/basics/the-best-schedule-for-your-baby/.

Persing, John, Hector James, John Kattwinkel, and Jack Swanson. "Prevention and Management of Positional Skull Deformities in Infants." *Pediatrics* 112.1 (2003): 199–202. American Academy of Pediatrics Policy.

Ryan, Amy. "Naps Are Good for Kids Even When They Don't Think So." *Everest Herald,* June 19, 2009.

Schaefer, Charles E., and Theresa Foy DiGeronimo. *Ages and Stages: A Parent's Guide to Normal Childhood Development.* New York: Wiley, 2000.

Sears, William. *The Baby Sleep Book: The Complete Guide to a Good Night's Rest for the Whole Family.* New York: Little, Brown, 2005.

Sunderland, Margot. *Science of Parenting: Practical Guidance on Sleep, Crying, Play, and Building Emotional Well-Being for Life.* New York: Dorling Kindersley, 2006.

Vanderijt, Hetty, and Frans X. Plooij. *The Wonder Weeks: Eight Predictable, Age-Linked Leaps in Your Baby's Mental Development.* Arnhem, Netherlands: Kiddy World Promotions, 2008.

Vennemann, Mechtild M., Thomas Bajanowski, Bernd Brinkmann, Gerhard Jorch, Edwin A. Mitchell, Cristina Sauerland, K. Yücesan, and GeSID Study Group. "Does Breastfeeding Reduce the Risk of Sudden Infant Death Syndrome?" *Pediatrics* 123.3 (2009): E406–410.

Waldburger, Jennifer, and Jill Spivack. *The Sleepeasy Solution: The Exhausted Parent's Guide to Getting Your Child to Sleep—from Birth to Age Five.* Deerfield Beach, FL: Health Communications, 2007.

Weber, Elsa L. "Back to Sleep? What's a Parent to Do?" *SIDS Horizon* (1996). SIDS Network. http://sids-network.org/experts/elsa.htm.

Weissbluth, Marc. *Healthy Sleep Habits, Happy Child: A Step-by-Step Program for a Good Night's Sleep.* New York: Ballantine, 2005.

Zigler, Edward, Dorothy G. Singer, and Sandra J. Bishop-Josef. *Children's Play: The Roots of Reading.* Washington, DC: Zero to Three, 2004.

4. Let Your Fingers Do the Walking: The Importance of Touch

Adamson-Macedo, Elvidina, and J. Werner. "Very Early Tactile Stimulation and Later Cognitive Development." *Infant Behaviour and Development* 17 (1994): 259.

Anisfeld, Elizabeth, Virginia Casper, Molly Nozyce, and Nicolas Cunningham. "Does Infant Carrying Promote Attachment? An Experimental Study of the Effects of Increased Physical Contact on the Development of Attachment." *Child Development* 61.5 (2008): 1617–1627.

Bagshaw, Joanne, and Ilene Fox. *Baby Massage for Dummies.* New York: Wiley, 2005.

Bakalar, Nicholas. "Mother's Touch Helps Cut Newborns' Pain." *New York Times,* May 13, 2008.

Cozolino, Louis J. *The Neuroscience of Human Relationships: Attachment and the Developing Social Brain.* New York: W.W. Norton, 2006.

Dieter, John N.I., Eugene K. Emory, Tiffany Field, Maria Hernandez-Reif, and Mercedes Redzepi. "Stable Preterm Infants Gain More Weight and Sleep Less after Five Days of Massage Therapy." *Journal of Pediatric Psychology* 28.6 (2003): 403–411.

Eliot, Lise. *What's Going On in There? How the Brain and Mind Develop in the First Five Years of Life.* New York: Bantam, 2000.

Erikson, Erik H. *Childhood and Society.* New York: W.W. Norton, 1993.

Ferber, Sari Goldstein, Jacob Kuint, Moshe Laudon, Aron Weller, and Nava Zisapel. "Massage Therapy by Mothers Enhances the Adjustment of Circadian Rhythms to the Nocturnal Period in Full-Term Infants." *Journal of Developmental & Behavioral Pediatrics* 23.6 (2002): 410-15

Field, Tiffany. "Massage Therapy for Infants and Children." *Journal of Developmental & Behavioral Pediatrics* 16.2 (1995): 105–111.

——. *Touch.* Cambridge, MA: MIT, 2003.

——. *Touch in Early Development.* Mahwah, NJ: Lawrence Erlbaum, 1995.

——. "Young Children's Adaptations to Repeated Separations from Their Mothers." *Child Development* 62 (1991): 539–547.

Field, Tiffany, Sonya Abrams, Nancy Grizzle, Cynthia Kuhn, Sarah Richardson, Frank Scafidi, and Saul Schanberg. "Massage Therapy for Infants of Depressed Mothers." *Infant Behavior & Development* 19 (1996): 109–114.

Field, Tiffany, Charles R. Bauer, Robert Garcia, Cynthia M. Kuhn, Jerome Nystrom, Frank Scafidi, Saul M. Schanberg, and Nitza Vega-Lahr. "Tactile/Kinesthetic Stimulation Effects on Preterm Neonates." *Pediatrics* 77.5 (1986): 654–658.

Field, Tiffany, and Martin Reite. "Children's Responses to Separation from Mother during the Birth of Another Child." *Child Development* 55 (1984): 1308–1316.

Gerhardt, Sue. *Why Love Matters: How Affection Shapes a Baby's Brain.* Hove, East Sussex, UK: Brunner-Routledge, 2004.

Gordon, Jay, and Brenda Adderly. *Brighter Baby: Boost Your Child's Intelligence, Health, and Happiness through Infant Therapeutic Massage.* Washington, DC: LifeLine, 1999.

Gundersen, Judith P. "Kangaroo Care: High Touch in a High Tech World." *Perinatal Nursing Link* 5.1: 8–9.

Heath, Alan, Nicki Bainbridge, and Julie Fisher. *Baby Massage.* New York: Dorling Kindersley, 2000.

Heller, Sharon. *The Vital Touch: How Intimate Contact with Your Baby Leads to Happier, Healthier Development.* New York: Henry Holt, 1997.

Klaus, Marshall J., and John H. Kennell. "Parent-Infant Bonding: Setting the Record Straight." *Journal of Pediatrics* 102.4 (1982): 575–576.

Lam, Tina, Clare Mundy, and Glenda Taylor. *Your Happy Baby: Massage, Yoga, Aromatherapy, and Other Gentle Ways to Blissful Babyhood.* Ed. Sheena Meredith. London: Ryland Peters & Small, 2006.

Ludington-Hoe, Susan M., and Susan K. Golant. *Kangaroo Care: The Best You Can Do to Help Your Preterm Infant.* New York: Bantam, 1993.

Ludington-Hoe, Susan M., Robert Hosseini, and Deborah L. Torowicz. "Skin-to-Skin Contact (Kangaroo Care) Analgesia for Preterm Infant Heel Stick." *AACN Clinical Issues* 16.3 (2005): 373–387.

Ludington-Hoe, Susan M., Kathy Morgan, and Amel Abouelfettoh. "A Clinical Guideline for Implementation of Kangaroo Care With Premature Infants of 30 or More Weeks' Postmenstrual Age." *Advances in Neonatal Care* 8.3 (2008): S3–S23.

Ludington-Hoe, Susan M., Barbara Morrison, and Gene C. Anderson. "A Comprehensive Review of Skin-to-Skin Contact (Kangaroo Care) Research with Full-Term Infants." 2010. Available from Susan.ludington@case.edu.

McClure, Vimala Schneider. *Infant Massage: A Handbook for Loving Parents.* New York: Bantam, 2000.

McKenzie, Catherine. "Car Seat Are for Cars." *Mothering*, May & June 2006.

Montagu, Ashley. *Touching: The Human Significance of the Skin.* New York: Perennial Library, 1986.

Moore, Diana. "StorkNet Interview with Diana Moore, Founder and Leading Teacher of the Loving Touch Foundation in Oregon." Interview by StorkNet. www.storknet.com/guests/babymassage.htm.

Morris, Desmond. *Amazing Baby: The Amazing Story of the First Two Years of Life.* Richmond Hill, Ontario: Firefly, 2008.

Neal, Mary. "Vestibular Stimulation and Developmental Behavior in the Small Premature Infant." *Nursing Research Report* 3 (1967): 1–5.

Persing, John, et al. "Prevention and Management of Positional Skull Deformities in Infants." *Pediatrics* 112.1 (2003): 199–202.

Peterson-DeGroff, Maren. "Developmental Care: Overstimulation and Your Premature Baby." Prematurity.org. www.prematurity.org/overstimulation.html.

Reese, Suzanne P., and Bill Milne. *Baby Massage: Soothing Strokes for Healthy Growth.* New York: Viking Studio, 2006.

Rosenthal, Elisabeth. "Kangaroo's Pouch Inspires Care for Premature Babies." *New York Times*, June 10, 1992.

Sachs, Jessica Snyder. "What Your Baby's Telling You." *Parenting*, October 2002.

Sears, William, and Martha Sears. *The Attachment Parenting Book: A Commonsense Guide to Understanding and Nurturing Your Baby.* Boston: Little, Brown, 2001.

Slater, Lauren. "Monkey Love." *Boston Globe.* www.boston.com/news/globe/ideas/articles/2004/03/21/monkey_love/.

Stamm, Jill, and Paula Spencer. *Bright from the Start: The Simple, Science-Backed Way to Nurture Your Child's Developing Mind, from Birth to Age 3.* New York: Gotham, 2007.

Sullivan, Karin Horgan. "Kudos for Cuddling." *Prevention,* May 2005.

Uvnäs, Moberg Kerstin, and Roberta W. Francis. *The Oxytocin Factor: Tapping the Hormone of Calm, Love, and Healing.* Cambridge, MA: Da Capo, 2003.

5. More than Chitchat: Promoting Language Development

Abbasi, Jennifer. "Kids' Health." *Parenting,* June 2007.

ABC1. "Talk Enough? Interaction Crucial to Child's Development." October 3, 2007. http://abclocal.go.com/kabc/story?section=health&id=5681064.

Ackerman-Ross, Susan, and Prabha Khanna. "The Relationship of High Quality Day Care to Middle-Class Three-Year-Olds' Language Performance." *Early Childhood Research Quarterly* 4 (1989): 407–432.

Agin, Marilyn C., Lisa F. Geng, and Malcolm J. Nicholl. *The Late Talker: What to Do If Your Child Isn't Talking Yet.* New York: St. Martin's, 2003.

Apel, Kenn, and Julie Masterson. *Beyond Baby Talk: From Sounds to Sentences: A Parent's Complete Guide to Language Development.* New York: Three Rivers, 2001.

Associated Content. "Three Potential Problems If Your Child Uses a Sippy Cup." www.associatedcontent.com/article/149540/three_potential_problems_if_your_child.html?cat=51.

BabyCenter. "How Can I Tell If My Child Has a Stuttering Problem?" www.babycenter.com/404_how-can-i-tell-if-my-child-has-a-stuttering-problem_2486.bc.

_____. "Pacifiers and Your Toddler." www.babycenter.com/0_pacifiers-and-your-toddler_12254.bc?page=1.

Berman, Jenn. *The A to Z Guide to Raising Happy, Confident Kids.* Novato, CA: New World Library, 2007.

_____. "How Big Business Has Let Parents Down." *Los Angeles Family,* October 2007.

_____. "Parent's Guide to Better Baby Talk: Language Development in the First Three Years." *Los Angeles Family,* August 2007.

Blakeslee, Sandra. "Studies Show Talking With Infants Shapes Basis of Ability to Think." *New York Times,* April 17, 1997.

Bowen, Caroline. "Speech Intelligibility from 12 to 48 Months." Speech-language-therapy.com. www.speech-language-therapy.com/intelligibility.htm.

CNN.com. "Your Baby: 10 Milestones for the First 2 Years." www.cnn.com/2007/HEALTH/parenting/06/07/par.baby.milestones/index.html.

Chomsky, Noam. *Knowledge of Language: Its Nature, Origin, and Use.* New York: Praeger, 1986.

Conture, Edward G., and Jane H. Fraser. *Stuttering and Your Child: Questions and Answers.* Memphis, TN: Stuttering Foundation of America, 2007.

Cooper, Robin Panneton, and Richard N. Aslin. "Developmental Differences in Infant Attention to the Spectral Properties of Infant-Directed Speech." *Child Development* 65 (1994): 1663–1677.

_____. "Preferences for Child Directed Speech in the First Month After Birth." *Child Development* 61 (1990): 1584–1595.

Dyer, Laura. *Look Who's Talking! How to Enhance Your Child's Language Development, Starting at Birth.* Minnetonka, MN: Meadowbrook, 2004.

Eliot, Lise. *What's Going On in There? How the Brain and Mind Develop in the First Five Years of Life.* New York: Bantam, 2000.

Feit, Debbie. "Talking Trouble: If Your Child Doesn't Say Much or Is Hard to Understand, Don't Assume That She'll Eventually Catch Up Without Help." *Parents,* March 2008.

Fowler, William. *Talking from Infancy: How to Nurture & Cultivate Early Language Development.* Cambridge, MA: Center for Early Learning and Child Care, 1995.

Gilkerson, Jill, and Jeffrey A. Richards. *The Power of Talk: Adult Talk and Conversational Turns During the Critical 0–3 Years of Child Development.* Boulder, CO: Infoture, 2007.

Golinkoff, Roberta M., and Kathy Hirsh-Pasek. *How Babies Talk: The Magic and Mystery of Language in the First Three Years of Life.* New York: Plume, 2000.

Guitar, Barry, and Jane Fraser. *If Your Child Stutters: A Guide for Parents.* Memphis, TN: Stuttering Foundation of America, 2006.

Hamaguchi, Patricia McAleer. *Childhood Speech, Language, and Listening Problems: What Every Parent Should Know.* New York: Wiley, 2001.

Hart, Betty, and Todd R. Risley. *Meaningful Differences in Everyday Experiences of Young American Children.* Baltimore: P.H. Brookes, 1995.

_____. *The Social World of Children Learning to Talk.* Baltimore: P.H. Brookes, 1999.

Heilbeck, Tracy H., and Ellen M. Markman. "Word Learning in Children: An Examination of Fast Mapping." *Child Development* 58.4 (1987): 1021–1034.

Hirsh-Pasek, Kathy, Roberta M. Golinkoff, and Diane E. Eyer. *Einstein Never Used Flash Cards: How Our Children Really Learn—and Why They Need to Play More and Memorize Less.* Emmaus, PA: Rodale, 2003.

Howes, Carrollee. "Children's Experiences in Center-Based Child-Care as a Function of Teacher Background and Adult:Child Ratio." *Merrill-Palmer Quarterly* 43 (1997): 404–425.

Hurt, Jeanette. "Late Talkers." *Parenting,* October 2007.

Kegl, Judy. "The Nicaraguan Sign Language Project: An Overview." *Signpost* 7.1 (1994): 24–31.

Language Log. "Word Counts." November 28, 2006. http://itre.cis.upenn.edu/~myl/languagelog/archives/003831.html.

Lawton, Joseph T., and Nancy Fowell. "A Description of Teacher and Child Language in Two Preschool Programs." *Early Childhood Research Quarterly* 4 (1989): 97–116.

Lotus, Jean. "It's Official: TV Linked to Attention Deficit." WhiteDot.org. www.whitedot.org/issue/iss_story.asp?slug=ADHD%20Toddlers.

Mandel, Denise R., Peter W. Jusczuk, and David B. Pisoni. "Infant's Recognition of the Sound Patterns of Their Own Names." *Psychological Science* 6 (1995): 314–317.

March of Dimes Foundation. "Multiples: Twins, Triplets and Beyond." www.marchofdimes.com/professionals/14332_4545.asp.

McCartney, Kathleen. "Effect of Quality Day Care Environment on Children's Language Development." *Developmental Psychology* 20 (1984): 244–259.

McCathern, Rebecca B., Paul J. Yoder, and Steven F. Warren. "The Role of Directives in Early Language Intervention." *Journal of Early Intervention* 19 (1995): 91–101.

Mommy Speech Therapy. "Do Pacifiers and Sippy Cups Cause Speech Delay?" http://mommyspeechtherapy.com/?p=12.

NICHHD Early Child Care Research Network. "The Relation of Child Care to Cognitive and Language Development." *Child Development* 71.4 (2000): 960.

Owens, Robert E., and Leah Feldon. *Help Your Baby Talk: Introducing the Shared Communication Method to Jump-Start Language and Have a Smarter, Happier Baby.* New York: Perigee, 2004.

Parenting. "Late Talker: Read This." May 2008.

Parents. "Dr. Alan Greene on Toddler Stuttering." www.parents.com/toddlers/development/intellectual/toddler-stuttering/.

Parents Connect. "Pacifiers & Teeth Damage." www.parentsconnect.com/questions/pacifier_bad_for_teeth.jhtml.

Paul, Pamela. *Parenting, Inc.: How We Are Sold on $800 Strollers, Fetal Education, Baby Sign Language, Sleeping Coaches, Toddler Couture, and Diaper Wipe Warmers—and What It Means for Our Children.* New York: Times/Henry Holt, 2008.

Peisner-Feinberg, Ellen S., Margaret R. Burchinal, R.M. Clifford, M.L. Culkin, C. Howes, Sharon Lynn Kagan, and Noreen Yazejian. "The Relation of Preschool Child-Care Quality to Children's Cognitive and Social Development Trajectories Through Second Grade." *Child Development* 72.5 (2001): 1534.

Pinker, Steven. *The Language Instinct: How the Mind Creates Language.* New York: HarperPerennial ModernClassics, 2007.

Remer Altmann, Tanya. *Mommy Calls: Dr. Tanya Answers Parents' Top 101 Questions about Babies and Toddlers.* New York: American Academy of Pediatrics, 2009.

Schaefer, Charles E., and Theresa Foy DiGeronimo. *Ages and Stages: A Parent's Guide to Normal Childhood Development.* New York: Wiley, 2000.

Schiff, Donald, and Steven P. Shelov. *American Academy of Pediatrics Guide to Your Child's Symptoms: The Official Home Reference, Birth through Adolescence.* New York: Villard, 1997.

Shonkoff, Jack P., and Deborah Phillips. *From Neurons to Neighborhoods: The Science of Early Child Development.* Washington, DC: National Academy, 2000.

Stamm, Jill, and Paula Spencer. *Bright from the Start: The Simple, Science-Backed Way to Nurture Your Child's Developing Mind, from Birth to Age 3.* New York: Gotham, 2007.

Treiber, Patricia M. *Keys to Dealing with Stuttering.* Hauppauge, NY: Barrons, 1993.

Walker, Dale, Charles Greenwood, Betty Hart, and Judith Carta. "Prediction of School Outcomes Based on Early Language Production and Socioeconomic Factors." *Child Development* 65.2 (1994): 606–621.

Wall Street Journal. "Toddlers Who Watch TV Risk Attention Problems, Study Finds." April 5, 2004.

Ward, Sally. *Baby Talk: Strengthen Your Child's Ability to Listen, Understand, and Communicate.* New York: Ballantine, 2001.

WebMD Children's Health Center. "So Long Sippy Cups, Hello Straws." http://children.webmd.com/news/20080212/so-long-sippy-cups-hello-straws.

Wetherby, Amy M., and Gary P. Rodriguez. "Measurement of Communicative Intentions in Normally Developing Children During Structured and Unstructured Contexts." *Journal of Speech and Hearing Research* 35 (1992): 130–138.

Wikipedia. "Nicaraguan Sign Language." http://en.wikipedia.org/wiki/Nicaraguan_Sign_Language.

Yoder, Paul J., and Steven F. Warren. "Maternal Responsivity Mediates the Relationship between Prelinguistic Intentional Communication and Later Language." *Journal of Early Intervention* 22.2 (1999): 126–136.

6. Talk to the Hand: Sign Language

ABCNews.com. "Baby Sign Language May Boost IQ." February 22, 2005. http://abcnews.go.com/GMA/TurningPoints/story?id=521213&page=1.

Acredolo, Linda P., and Susan Goodwyn. *Baby Signs: How to Talk with Your Baby before Your Baby Can Talk.* New York: McGraw-Hill, 2009.

Agin, Marilyn C., Lisa F. Geng, and Malcolm J. Nicholl. *The Late Talker: What to Do If Your Child Isn't Talking Yet.* New York: St. Martin's, 2003.

Anthony, Michelle, and Reyna Lindert. *Signing Smart with Babies and Toddlers: A Parent's Strategy and Activity Guide.* New York: St. Martin's Griffin, 2005.

Apel, Kenn, and Julie Masterson. *Beyond Baby Talk: From Sounds to Sentence: A Parent's Complete Guide to Language Development.* New York: Three Rivers, 2001.

Berman, Jenn. "Teaching Babies Sign Language." *Los Angeles Family,* November 2007.

Beyer, Monica. *Baby Talk: A Guide to Using Basic Sign Language to Communicate with Your Baby.* New York: Jeremy P. Tarcher/Penguin, 2006.

_____. *Teach Your Baby to Sign: An Illustrated Guide to Simple Sign Language for Babies.* Beverly, MA: Fair Winds, 2007.

Brady, Diane. "Look Who's Talking with Their Hands." *Business Week,* August 14, 2000.

Charbonneau, Nicolle. "Early Childhood Critical Time to Learn Sign Language." *Tri-Med.* January 8, 2002. www.freelists.org/post/tri-med/FYI-Early-Childhood-Critical-Time-to-Learn-Sign-Language.

Daniels, Marilyn. *Dancing with Words: Signing for Hearing Children's Literacy.* Westport, CT: Bergin & Garvey, 2001.

_____. "The Effect of Sign Language on Hearing Children's Language Development." *Communication Education* 43.4 (1994): 291–298.

_____. "Happy Hands: The Effect of ASL on Hearing Children's Literacy." *Reading Research and Instruction* 44.1 (2004): 86–100.

Dennis, Kirsten, and Tressa Azpiri. *Sign to Learn: American Sign Language in the Early Childhood Classroom.* St. Paul, MN: Redleaf, 2005.

Dyer, Laura. *Look Who's Talking! How to Enhance Your Child's Language Development, Starting at Birth.* Minnetonka, MN: Meadowbrook, 2004.

Easton-Waller, Linda. "Baby Signs in Bilingual Settings." *SignShine: Signing with Babies and Children.* www.babysignshine.com/bilingual.shtml.

Eliot, Lise. *What's Going On in There? How the Brain and Mind Develop in the First Five Years of Life.* New York: Bantam, 1999.

Feit, Debbie, and Heidi M. Feldman. *The Parent's Guide to Speech and Language Problems.* New York: McGraw-Hill, 2007.

Garcia, W. Joseph. *Sign with Your Baby: How to Communicate with Infants before They Can Speak.* Seattle: Sign2Me, 2001.

ITV BabySign. "Baby Sign Research: Does It Improve Language Skills and IQ?" www.itvbabysign.com/about/language.aspx.

Leit, Etel. *FAQ.* SignShine: Parenting Sign Language Advanced Classes. Handout, page 28.

Paul, Pamela. *Parenting, Inc.: How We Are Sold on $800 Strollers, Fetal Education, Baby Sign Language, Sleeping Coaches, Toddler Couture, and Diaper Wipe Warmers—and What It Means for Our Children.* New York: Times/Henry Holt, 2008.

Ryan, Diane. *The Complete Idiot's Guide to Baby Sign Language.* Indianapolis, IN: Alpha, 2006.

Sign2Me. "Signs with Hearing Babies of Hearing Parents." www.sign2me.com/index.php?option=com_content&task=view&id=17&Itemid=33.

Simpson, Teresa R. *The Everything Baby Sign Language Book: Get an Early Start Communicating with Your Baby!* Avon, MA: Adams Media, 2008.

Stamm, Jill, and Paula Spencer. *Bright from the Start: The Simple, Science-Backed Way to Nurture Your Child's Developing Mind, from Birth to Age 3.* New York: Gotham, 2007.

Thompson, Stacy A., and Val Nelson-Metlay. *Teach Your Tot to Sign: The Parents' Guide to American Sign Language.* Washington, DC: Gallaudet University Press, 2005.

University of Washington. "Hearing Infants Show Preference for Sign Language over Pantomime." June 4, 2002. www.washington.edu/newsroom/news/2002archive/06-02archive/k060402.html.

Watson, Jennifer Hill. *Baby Signing for Dummies.* Hoboken, NJ: Wiley, 2006.

7. Babies without Borders: **Foreign Language**

Barron-Hauwaert, Suzanne. *Language Strategies for Bilingual Families: The One-Parent-One-Language Approach.* Clevedon, UK: Multilingual Matters, 2004.

Berman, Jenn. "Foreign Language Learning: Unlock Your Child's Global Potential." *Los Angeles Family,* September 2007.

Bialystok, Ellen. *Bilingualism in Development: Language, Literacy, and Cognition.* Cambridge, UK: Cambridge University Press, 2001.

Bialystok, Ellen, and Kenji Hakuta. *In Other Words: The Science and Psychology of Second-Language Acquisition.* New York: Basic Books, 1994.

Bichachi, Olga. "Is English Enough for Your 21st Century Baby?" BlueSuitMom.com. www.bluesuitmom. com/family/education/bilingual.html.

Boston Children's Music. "5 Amazing Ways Music Can Teach Your Child a Foreign Language." May 4, 2009. www.bostonchildrensmusic.com/foreign-language-music/.

Clark, D.R. "Visual, Auditory, and Kinesthetic Learning Styles (VAK)." Performance Juxtaposition Site. April 11, 2008. www.nwlink.com/~Donclark/hrd/styles/vakt.html.

Cunningham-Andersson, Una, and Staffan Andersson. *Growing Up with Two Languages: A Practical Guide.* London: Routledge, 1999.

Eliot, Lise. *What's Going On in There? How the Brain and Mind Develop in the First Five Years of Life.* New York: Bantam, 2000.

Foust, Linda. "Earlier Is Better." Parents' Press. 2003. www.parentspress.com/edulanguages.html.

Fuller, Cheri. *Talkers, Watchers, and Doers: Unlocking Your Child's Unique Learning Style.* Colorado Springs, CO: Pinon, 2004.

Genesee, Fred, Johanne Paradis, and Martha B. Crago. *Dual Language Development and Disorders: A Handbook on Bilingualism and Second Language Learning.* Baltimore: Paul H. Brookes, 2004.

Golinkoff, Roberta M., and Kathy Hirsh-Pasek. *How Babies Talk: The Magic and Mystery of Language in the First Three Years of Life.* New York: Plume, 2000.

King, Kendall A., and Alison Mackey. *The Bilingual Edge: Why, When, and How to Teach Your Child a Second Language.* New York: Collins, 2007.

Kuhl, Patricia K., Feng-Ming Tsai, and Huei-Mei Liu. "Foreign-Language Experience in Infancy: Effects of Short-Term Exposure and Social Interaction on Phonetic Learning." *Proceedings of the National Academy of Sciences* 100.15 (2003): 9096–9101.

Lee, Patrick. "Cognitive Development in Bilingual Children: A Case for Bilingual Instruction in Early Childhood Education." *Bilingual Research Journal* 20.3 & 4 (1996): 499–522.

Linn, Susan. *The Case for Make Believe: Saving Play in a Commercialized World.* New York: New Press, 2008.

McCardle, Peggy D., and Erika Hoff. *Childhood Bilingualism: Research on Infancy through School Age.* Clevedon, UK: Multilingual Matters, 2006.

Medical News Today. "Bilingualism Has Protective Effect in Delaying Onset of Dementia by Four Years, Canadian Study Shows." January 12, 2007. www.medicalnewstoday.com/articles/60646.php.

Merrill, Jane. *Bringing Up Baby Bilingual.* New York: Facts on File, 1984.

National Center for Research on Cultural Diversity and Second Language Learning. "Myths and Misconceptions about Second Language Learning." Center for Applied Linguistics. www.cal.org/resources/Digest/myths.html.

Neergaard, Lauran. "How Do Kids Become Bilingual So Easily?" AP Newswire. July 21, 2009. http://news.aol.com/article/bilingual-children/581917.

Paradowski, Michal B. "The Benefits of Multilingualism." Bilingual/Bicultural Family Network. www.biculturalfamily.org/benefitsofmultilingualism.html.

Parenting. "Too Young for Two Languages? Ages + Stages." March 1, 2007.

Patterson, Janet L. "Relationships of Expressive Vocabulary Development to Frequency of Reading and Television Experience Among Bilingual Toddlers." *Applied Psycholinguistics* 23 (2002): 493–508.

Paul, Pamela. "Extract One: Parenting Inc." Telegraph.co.uk. May 10, 2008. www.telegraph.co.uk/education/3356199/Extract-one-Parenting-Inc.-by-Pamela-Paul.html.

Peal, Elizabeth, and Wallace Lambert. "The Relation of Bilingualism to Intelligence." *Psychological Monographs* 76: 1–23.

Pearson, Barbara Zurer. *Raising a Bilingual Child: A Step-by-Step Guide for Parents.* New York: Living Language, 2008.

Pearson, Barbara Zurer, Sylvia C. Fernandez, Vanessa Lewedeg, and D. Kimbrough Oller. "The Relation of Input Factors to Lexical Learning by Bilingual Infants." *Applied Psycholinguistics* 18 (1997): 41–58.

Simms, Patricia. "Baby Einsteins or Baby Couch Potatoes?" Campaign for a Commercial-Free Childhood. February 3, 2006. http://commercialfreechildhood.org/news/babycouchpotato.htm.

Steiner, Naomi, Susan L. Hayes, and Steven Parker. *7 Steps to Raising a Bilingual Child.* New York: AMACOM, 2008.

Tabors, Patton O. *One Child, Two Languages: A Guide for Early Childhood Educators of Children Learning English as a Second Language.* Baltimore: Paul H. Brookes, 2008.

———. *One Child, Two Languages: A Guide for Preschool Educators of Children Learning English as a Second Language.* Baltimore: Paul H. Brookes, 1997.

Zigler, Edward, Dorothy G. Singer, and Sandra J. Bishop-Josef, eds. *Children's Play: The Roots of Reading.* Washington, DC: Zero to Three, 2004.

8. Baby Got Book: Reading

Adams, Marilyn Jager. *Beginning to Read: Thinking and Learning about Print.* Cambridge, MA: MIT, 1990.

Bankson, Nicholas W. *Bankson Language Screening Test.* Baltimore: University Park, 1977.

Bardige, Betty, Lynn Segal, and Marilyn M. Segal. *Building Literacy with Love: A Guide for Teachers and Caregivers of Children from Birth through Age 5.* Washington, DC: Zero to Three, 2005.

Barone, Diane M., and Lesley Mandel Morrow, eds. *Literacy and Young Children: Research-Based Practices.* New York: Guilford, 2003.

Berman, Jenn. "Raising Lifetime Readers from the Start." *Los Angeles Family,* November 2009.

Biemiller, Andrew. "Oral Comprehension Sets the Ceiling on Reading Comprehension." *American Educator,* Spring/Summer 2003.

Biemiller, Andrew, and Paula Menyuk. *Language and Reading Success.* Newton Upper Falls, MA: Brookline, 1999.

Birckmayer, Jennifer, Anne Kennedy, and Anne Stonehouse. *From Lullabies to Literature: Stories in the Lives of Infants and Toddlers.* Washington, DC: NAEYC, 2008.

Blakemore, Caroline, and Barbara Weston-Ramirez. *Baby Read-Aloud Basics: Fun and Interactive Ways to Help Your Little One Discover the World of Words.* New York: AMACOM, 2006.

Burns, M. Susan, Peg Griffin, and Catherine E. Snow. *Starting Out Right: A Guide to Promoting Children's Reading Success.* Washington, DC: National Academy, 1999.

Codell, Esmé Raji. *How to Get Your Child to Love Reading.* Chapel Hill, NC: Algonquin of Chapel Hill, 2003.

Coronato, Helen. *The Complete Idiot's Guide to Reading with Your Child.* Indianapolis, IN: Alpha, 2007.

Cunningham, Anne E., and Keith E. Stanovich. "What Reading Does for the Mind." *American Educator,* Spring/Summer 1998.

Emery, Olga, and Mihalyi Csikszentmihalyi. "The Socialization Effects of Cultural Role Models in Ontogenetic Development and Upward Mobility." *Child Psychiatry and Human Development* 12.1 (Fall 1981): 3–18.

Fox, Mem. *Reading Magic: Why Reading Aloud to Our Children Will Change Their Lives Forever.* New York: Harcourt, 2008.

Gelman, Judy, and Vicki Levy Krupp. *The Kids' Book Club Book: Reading Ideas, Recipes, Activities, and Smart Tips for Organizing Terrific Kids' Book Clubs.* New York: Penguin, 2007.

Hall, Susan L., and Louisa Cook Moats. *Straight Talk about Reading: How Parents Can Make a Difference during the Early Years.* Lincolnwood, IL: Contemporary, 1999.

Hamilton, Emma Walton. *Raising Bookworms: Getting Kids Reading for Pleasure and Empowerment.* Sag Harbor, NY: Beech Tree, 2009.

Hayes, Donald P., and Margaret G. Ahrens. "Vocabulary Simplification for Children: A Special Case for 'Motherese'" *Journal of Child Language* 15 (1988): 395–410.

Kailing, Timothy D. *Native Reading: How to Teach Your Child to Read, Easily and Naturally, before the Age of Three.* CreateSpace, 2008.

Krashen, Stephen D. *The Power of Reading: Insights from the Research.* Englewood, CO: Libraries Unlimited, 1993.

Lee Pesky Learning Center. *Every Child Ready to Read: Literacy Tips for Parents.* New York: Ballantine, 2004.

Lee, Sy-Ying, and Stephen D. Krashen. "Writing Apprehension in Chinese as a First Language." *Review of Applied Linguistics* 115–116: 27–37.

McGuinness, Diane. *Growing a Reader from Birth: Your Child's Path from Language to Literacy.* New York: W.W. Norton, 2004.

Miller, Donalyn. *The Book Whisperer: Awakening the Inner Reader in Every Child.* San Francisco: Jossey-Bass, 2009.

Morrow, L. "Home and School Correlates of Early Interest in Literature." *Journal of Education Research* 75: 339–344.

Multnomah County Library. "Dialogic Reading: How We Read to Children Is as Important as How Frequently We Read to Them." 2009. www.multcolib.org/birthtosix/elitdialogic.html.

Munson-Benson, Carolyn. *Playful Reading: Positive, Fun Ways to Build the Bond between Preschoolers, Books, and You.* Minneapolis: Search Institute, 2005.

Nell, Victor. *Lost in a Book: The Psychology of Reading for Pleasure.* New Haven, CT: Yale University Press, 1988.

Neuman, Susan B. "The Home Environment and Fifth-Grade Students' Leisure Reading." *Elementary School Journal* 86: 335–343.

Prescott, Orville. *A Father Reads to His Children.* New York: E.P. Dutton, 1965.

Rosenkoetter, Sharon E., and Joanne Knapp-Philo. *Learning to Read the World: Language and Literacy in the First Three Years.* Washington, DC: Zero to Three, 2006.

Stamm, Jill, and Paula Spencer. *Bright from the Start: The Simple, Science-Backed Way to Nurture Your Child's Developing Mind, from Birth to Age 3.* New York: Gotham, 2007.

Straub, Susan, and K.J. Dell'Antonia. *Reading with Babies, Toddlers, and Twos: A Guide to Choosing, Reading, and Loving Books Together.* Naperville, IL: Source, 2006.

Trelease, Jim. *The Read-Aloud Handbook.* New York: Penguin, 2006.

U.S. Department of Education. "Start Early, Finish Strong: How to Help Every Child Become a Reader." www.ed.gov/pubs/startearly/ch_1.html.

Warwick, Elley B. "Vocabulary Acquisition from Listening to Stories." *Reading Research Quarterly* 24 (Spring 1989): 174–187.

Woodward, Amanda L. "Infants' Developing Understanding of the Link Between Looker and Object." *Developmental Science* 6.3 (2003): 297–311.

9. A Different Kind of Toy Story: The Importance of Play

American Academy of Pediatrics. "Injuries Associated with Infant Walkers." 108.3 (2001): 790–792.

Aubert, Emilie J. "Adaptive Equipment and Environmental Aids for Children with Disabilities." *Pediatric Physical Therapy.* Ed. Jan Stephen Tecklin. Philadelphia: Lippincott Williams & Wilkins, 2008. 389–414.

Auerbach, Stevanne. *Dr. Toy's Smart Play Smart Toys: How to Raise a Child with a High PQ (Play Quotient).* Rancho Dominguez, CA: Educational Insights, 2004.

Barnett, Lynn A. "Research Note: Young Children's Resolution of Distress Through Play." *Journal of Child Psychology and Psychiatry* 25 (1984): 477–483.

Barnett, Lynn A., and B. Storm. "Play, Pleasure and Pain: The Reduction of Anxiety through Play." *Leisure Sciences* 4.2 (1981):161–175.

Berk, Laura E. *Awakening Children's Minds: How Parents and Teachers Can Make a Difference.* New York: Oxford University Press, 2001.

Berman, Jenn. *The A to Z Guide to Raising Happy, Confident Kids.* Novato, CA: New World Library, 2007.

——. "The Importance of Play." *Los Angeles Family,* June 2009.

Bodrova, Elena, and Deborah J. Leong. "The Importance of Being Playful." *First Years of School* 60.7 (2003): 50–53.

——. *Tools of the Mind: The Vygotskian Approach to Early Childhood Education.* Upper Saddle River, NJ: Pearson/Merrill Prentice Hall, 2007.

Bronson, Martha. *The Right Stuff for Children Birth to 8: Selecting Play Materials to Support Development.* Washington, DC: NAEYC, 1995.

Brown, Pei-San, John Sutterby, and Candra Thorton. "Combating Childhood Obesity With Physical Play Opportunities." *PTO Today.* www.ptotoday.com/pto-today-articles/article/67-combating-childhood-obesity-with-physical-play-opportunities.

Burton, Roger V. "Baby Walkers May Impede Child Development." *Bio-Medicine,* October 12, 1999. http://news.bio-medicine.org/medicine-news-2/Baby-walkers-may-impede-child-development-10211-2/.

Carlo, George Louis, and Martin Schram. *Cell Phones: Invisible Hazards in the Wireless Age: An Insider's Alarming Discoveries about Cancer and Genetic Damage.* New York: Carroll & Graf, 2002.

Carlson, Ginger. *Child of Wonder: Nurturing Creative & Naturally Curious Children.* Eugene, OR: Common Ground, 2008.

Child. "Hi-Tech Toys: How Are They Really Affecting Your Child?" February 2001.

Child Development Perspectives. "Improving the Numerical Understanding of Children from Low-Income Families." 3.2 (2009): 118–124.

Child's Genius. "Developing the Child Brain: Children Endangered by Cell Phone Radiation." www.internationalparentingassociation.org/BrainDevelopment/cellphones.html.

Christakis, Dimitri A., Frederick J. Zimmerman, and Michelle M. Garrison. "Effect of Block Play on Language Acquisition and Attention in Toddlers: A Pilot Randomized Controlled Trial." *Archives of Pediatrics & Adolescent Medicine* 161.10 (2007): 967–971.

Conner, Bobbi. *Unplugged Play: No Batteries, No Plugs, Pure Fun.* New York: Workman, 2007.

Connolly, Jennifer A., and Anna-Beth Doyle. "Relations of Social Fantasy Play to Social Competence in Preschoolers." *Developmental Psychology* 20 (1984): 797–806.

Diaz, Rafael M., and Laura E. Berk. *Private Speech: From Social Interaction to Self-Regulation.* Hillsdale, NJ: Lawrence Erlbaum, 1992.

Dolan, Deirdre. "Do Cell Phones Harm Unborn Babies?" *Daily Green.* May 30, 2008. www.thedailygreen.com/living-green/blogs/organic-parenting/cell-phones-55053901.

Early Learning World. "Good Toys, Bad Toys: How Your Child Can Develop by Having Good Toys." www.earlylearningworld.com.au/articles/art_toys.asp.

Elkind, David. *Power of Play: How Spontaneous, Imaginative Activities Lead to Happier, Healthier Children.* Cambridge, MA: Da Capo Lifelong, 2008.

——. "Thinking About Children's Play: Play Is Not Work, Nor Is Work Play." *Child Care Information Exchange* (2001): 27–28.

EM Radiation Research Trust. "Cellphones and Brain Tumors: 15 Reasons for Concern: Science, Spin and the Truth Behind Interphone." www.radiationresearch.org/pdfs/15reasons.asp.

Feldman, Ruth, and Charles W. Greenbaum. "Affect Regulation and Synchrony in Mother-Infant Play as Precursors to the Development of Symbolic Competence." *Infant Mental Health Journal* 18 (1997): 4–23.

Fiese, Barbara. "Playful Relationships: A Contextual Analysis of Mother-Toddler Interaction and Symbolic Play." *Child Development* 61 (1990): 1648–1656.

FOXNews.com. "Parents Use Cell Phones as Modern Baby Rattles." May 20, 2009. www.foxnews.com/story/0,2933,520892,00.html.

Fromberg, Doris Pronin, and Doris Bergen. *Play from Birth to Twelve: Contexts, Perspectives, and Meanings.* New York: Routledge, 2006.

Frost, Joe L., Sue Clark Wortham, and Stuart Reifel. *Play and Child Development.* Upper Saddle River, NJ: Pearson, 2007.

Furrow, D. "Developmental Trends in the Differentiation of Social and Private Speech." In *Private Speech: From Social Interaction to Self-Regulation,* ed. Rafael M. Diaz and Laura E. Berk, 143–158. Hillsdale, NJ: Lawrence Erlbaum, 1992.

Gerber, Magda, and Allison Johnson. *Your Self-Confident Baby: How to Encourage Your Child's Natural Abilities—from the Very Start.* New York: Wiley, 1998.

Google Answers. "Developmental Impact of Walkers, Exersaucers, and Jumpers on Babies / Infants." http://answers.google.com/answers/threadview/id/745582.html.

Greenspan, Stanley I. *Great Kids: Helping Your Baby and Child Develop the Ten Essential Qualities for a Happy, Healthy Life.* Cambridge, MA: Da Capo, 2007.

——. *The Secure Child: Helping Our Children Feel Safe and Confident in a Changing World.* Cambridge, MA: Da Capo, 2003.

Greenspan, Stanley I., and Nancy Breslau Lewis. *Building Healthy Minds: The Six Experiences That Create Intelligence and Emotional Growth in Babies and Young Children.* Cambridge, MA: Perseus, 2000.

HealthyChildren.org. "Baby Walkers: A Dangerous Choice." March 30, 2010. www.healthychildren.org/English/safety-prevention/at-home/Pages/Baby-Walkers-A-Dangerous-Choice.aspx

Helen DeVos Children's Hospital. *Walkers, Exersaucers and Jumpers: Why They Won't Teach Your Child to Walk.* Handout. 2008. http://applications.spectrum-health.org/education/document.aspx?url=Patient+Education%2Fx11470.pdf.

Hirsh-Pasek, Kathy, Roberta M. Golinkoff, and Diane E. Eyer. *Einstein Never Used Flash Cards: How Our Children Really Learn—and Why They Need to Play More and Memorize Less.* Emmaus, PA: Rodale, 2003.

Holloran, Donna. *Tummy Time: Respectfully and Naturally.* Handout. BabyGroup, 2003.

Hope, Jenny. "Background TV 'Can Harm Children's Speech.'" DailyMail Online. June 2, 2009. www.dailymail.co.uk/health/article-1190183/Background-TV-harm-childrens-speech.html.

Iovinelli, Beth M. "Tummy Time Explained for Baby Development." BabyZone. www.babyzone.com/askanexpert/tummy-time-101.

Isenberg, Joan Packer, and Nancy Quisenberry. "Play: Essential for All Children: A Position Paper of the Association for Childhood Education International." Association for Childhood Education International. http://acei.org/action/acei-positions/positions-papers/.

Jenkinson, Sally. *The Genius of Play: Celebrating the Spirit of Childhood.* Stroud, UK: Hawthorn, 2001.

Jenner, Sue. *The Parent-Child Game: The Proven Key to a Happier Family.* New York: Bloomsbury, 2000.

Jones, Elizabeth, and Renatta M. Cooper. *Playing to Get Smarter.* New York: Teachers College, 2006.

Leinkauf, Von Simone. "Intelligence? A Child's Play: Making Mud Pies or Building Sand Castles Increases Intelligence According to the American Psychologist Dr. Toy." Dr. Toy. August 5, 2003. www.drtoy.com/about_drtoy/tagesspielgel_english.html.

Levin, Diane E., and Barbara Rosenquest. "The Increasing Role of Electronic Toys in the Lives of Infants and Toddlers: Should We Be Concerned?" *Contemporary Issues in Early Childhood* 2.2 (2001): 242–247.

Linn, Susan. *The Case for Make Believe: Saving Play in a Commercialized World.* New York: New Press, 2008.

McCarthy, Claire. "Tummy-Time Makeover, Q+A: Kid's Health." *Parenting,* July 2008.

MediaWise. "Children and Advertising." www.mediafamily.org/facts/facts_childadv.shtml.

Medical News Today. "Cellphones Cause Brain Tumors, Says New Report by International EMF Collaborative." August 26, 2009. www.medicalnewstoday.com/articles/161960.php.

Mercer, Jean. "Child's Play: How They Do the Math." *Psychology Today.* July 29, 2009. www.psychologytoday.com/blog/child-myths/200907/childs-play-how-they-do-the-math.

Moyles, Janet. *The Excellence of Play.* Maidenhead, UK: Open University Press, 2005.

Neighmond, Patti. "U.S. Childhood Obesity Rates Level Off." NPR: National Public Radio. www.npr.org/templates/story/story.php?storyId=90880182.

Oppenheim, Joanne, and Stephanie Oppenheim. *Oppenheim Toy Portfolio: The Best Toys, Books, & DVDs for Kids.* New York: Oppenheim Toy Portfolio, 2006.

Parenting. "Benefits of Blocks." January 2008.

Parenting. "Tummy Time! Ages and Stages, Birth to Age 12." October 2003.

Parents. "Tummy Time." August 2001.

Perlmutter, David, and Carol Colman. *Raise a Smarter Child by Kindergarten: Build a Better Brain and Increase IQ Up to 30 Points.* New York: Morgan Road, 2006.

Piaget, Jean. *Play, Dreams and Imitation in Childhood.* New York: W.W. Norton, 1962.

Pitamic, Maja. *Teach Me to Do It Myself: Montessori Activities for You and Your Child.* Hauppauge, NY: Barron's Educational Series, 2004.

Pleshette, Murphy Ann. *The Secret of Play: How to Raise Smart, Healthy, Caring Kids from Birth to Age 12.* New York: F.A.O Schwarz, 2008.

Ramseyer, Viola. "Stages of Play." EzineArticles. http://ezinearticles.com/?Stages-of-Play&id=900253.

Rectenwald, Traci, and Alan Greene. "Baby Walkers." DrGreene.com. April 15, 2009. www.drgreene.com/21_810.html.

Schaefer, Charles E., and Theresa Foy DiGeronimo. *Ages and Stages: A Parent's Guide to Normal Childhood Development.* New York: Wiley, 2000.

Siegler, Robert S. "Improving the Numerical Understanding of Children from Low-Income Families." Carnegie Mellon Psychology. www.psy.cmu.edu/~siegler/siegler09-inpress.pdf.

Singer, Dorothy G., Roberta M. Golinkoff, and Kathy Hirsh-Pasek. *Play = Learning: How Play Motivates and Enhances Children's Cognitive and Social-Emotional Growth.* Oxford: Oxford University Press, 2006.

Springen, Karen. "A Faltering First Step: Can Exercise Saucers Hinder Development?" *Newsweek,* June 23, 1997.

Stamm, Jill, and Paula Spencer. *Bright from the Start: The Simple, Science-Backed Way to Nurture Your Child's Developing Mind, from Birth to Age 3.* New York: Gotham, 2007.

Stilson, Stephanie R., and Carol Gibb Harding. "Early Social Context As It Relates to Symbolic Play: A Longitudinal Investigation." *Merrill-Palmer Quarterly* 43 (1997): 682–693.

Striker, Susan. *Please Touch: How to Stimulate Your Child's Creative Development.* New York: Fireside, 1986.

Sunderland, Margot. *Science of Parenting: Practical Guidance on Sleep, Crying, Play, and Building Emotional Well-Being for Life.* New York: Dorling Kindersley, 2006.

Szymanski, Marianne M., and Ellen Neuborne. *Toy Tips: A Parent's Essential Guide to Smart Toy Choices.* San Francisco: Jossey-Bass, 2004.

UCLA School of Public Health. "Study Questions Safety of Children's Exposure to Cell Phones during Prenatal and Early Childhood Period." May 21, 2008. www.ph.ucla.edu/pr/newsitem052108.html.

Weaver, Jon. "Play Is Serious Business for Children's Intelligence." IQ Test Labs. www.intelligencetest.com/articles/article6.htm.

Winerman, Lea. "Playtime in Peril." *Monitor on Psychology,* September 2009.

Winn, Marie. *The Plug-in Drug: Television, Computers, and Family Life.* New York: Penguin, 2002.

Wolfgang, Charles H. *Child Guidance through Play: Teaching Positive Social Behaviors (Ages 2–7).* Boston: Allyn and Bacon, 2004.

Zigler, Edward, Dorothy G. Singer, and Sandra J. Bishop-Josef. *Children's Play: The Roots of Reading.* Washington, DC: Zero to Three, 2004.

10. Thinking Outside the Box: Screen Time

ABC Science. "Daily Dose of TV Doubles Asthma Risk." www.abc.net.au/science/articles/2009/03/03/2505813.htm.

Acuff, Dan S., and Robert H. Reiher. *Kidnapped: How Irresponsible Marketers Are Stealing the Minds of Your Children.* Chicago: Dearborn Trade, 2005.

American Academy of Child & Adolescent Psychiatry. "Children and Watching TV." March 2001. www.aacap.org/cs/root/facts_for_families/children_and_watching_tv.

_____. "Obesity in Children and Teens." May 2008. www.aacap.org/cs/root/facts_for_families/obesity_in_children_and_teens.

American Academy of Pediatrics. "Joint Statement on the Impact of Entertainment Violence on Children: Congressional Public Health Summit." July 26, 2000. www.aap.org/advocacy/releases/jstmtevc.htm.

_____. "Policy Statement: Children, Adolescents, and Television." *Pediatrics* 107.2 (2001): 423–426. http://aappolicy.aappublications.org/cgi/content/full/pediatrics;107/2/423.

_____. "TV and Your Family." www.aap.org/publiced/BR_TV.htm.

BabyCenter. "Two Hours of TV Doubles Kids' Asthma Risk." www.babycenter.com/204_two-hours-of-daily-tv-doubles-kids-asthma-risk_10310208.bc.

Belton, Teresa. "The 'Face at the Window' Study: A Fresh Approach to Media Influence and to Investigating the Influence of Television and Videos on Children's Imagination." *Media, Culture, and Society* 22 (2001): 629–643.

_____. "Television and Imagination: An Investigation of the Medium's Influence on Children's Story-Making." *Media, Culture, and Society* 23 (2001): 799–820.

Berman, Jenn. *The A to Z Guide to Raising Happy, Confident Kids.* Novato, CA: New World Library, 2007.

_____. "Television and Your Child: What Every Parent Needs to Know." *Los Angeles Family,* November 2004.

_____. "TV's Attack on Your Children's Health." *Los Angeles Family,* May 2007.

Blakemore, Caroline, and Barbara Weston Ramirez. *Baby Read-Aloud Basics: Fun and Interactive Ways to Help Your Little One Discover the World of Words.* New York: AMACOM, 2006.

Brock, Barbara J. *Living Outside the Box: TV-Free Families Share Their Secrets.* Spokane: Eastern Washington University Press, 2007.

Bronson, Po, and Ashley Merryman. *Nurture Shock: New Thinking About Children.* New York: Twelve, 2009.

Cantor, Joanne. *Mommy, I'm Scared: How TV and Movies Frighten Children and What We Can Do to Protect Them.* New York: Harcourt Brace, 1998.

Carlsson-Page, Nancy. *Taking Back Childhood: Helping Your Kids Thrive in a Fast-Paced, Media-Saturated, Violence-Filled World.* New York: Hudson Street, 2008.

CBC.ca. "Refunds Offered on Baby Einstein DVDs." October 25, 2009. www.cbc.ca/consumer/story/2009/10/25/waltdisney-babyeinstein-refunds.html?ref=rss.

Cederquist, Caroline J. *Helping Your Overweight Child: A Family Guide.* Naples, FL: Advance Medical, 2002.

Centers for Disease Control and Prevention. "Childhood Obesity." www.cdc.gov/HealthyYouth/obesity/.

Chmielewski, Dawn C. "Kids Watch More Than a Day of TV Each Week." *Los Angeles Times,* October 27, 2009.

Christakis, Dimitri A., and Frederick J. Zimmerman. "Children's Viewing and Cognitive Outcomes: A Longitudinal Analysis of National Data." *Archives of Pediatrics & Adolescent Medicine* 159 (2005): 619.

_____. *The Elephant in the Living Room: Make Television Work for Your Kids.* Emmaus, PA: Rodale, 2006.

CNN.com. "Study: Want a Smart Baby? TV's Not Going to Help." www.cnn.com/2009/HEALTH/03/03/babies.watch.TV/index.html.

Common Sense Media. "New Study: Exposure to Media Damages Children's Long-Term Health." www.commonsensemedia.org/about-us/press-room/press-releases/study-reveals-media-damages-child-health.

Dance, Amber. "Video as a Baby Brain Drain." *Los Angeles Times,* August 7, 2007.

Elkind, David. *The Power of Play: Learning What Comes Naturally.* Cambridge, MA: Da Capo, 2007.

Fisch, Shalom M. *Children's Learning from Educational Television: Sesame Street and Beyond.* Mahwah, NJ: Lawrence Erlbaum, 2004.

Garrison, Michelle M., and Dimitri A. Christakis. *A Teacher in the Living Room? Educational Media for Babies, Toddlers, and Preschoolers.* The Henry J. Kaiser Family Foundation. www.kff.org/entmedia/upload/7427.pdf.

Goddard, Sally. *What Babies and Children Really Need.* Stroud, UK: Hawthorn, 2008.

Graaff, John de, Thomas H. Naylor, and David Wann. *Affluenza: The All-Consuming Epidemic.* San Francisco: Berret-Koehler, 2001.

Guernsey, Lisa. *Into the Minds of Babes: How Screen Time Affects Children from Birth to Age Five.* New York: Basic Books, 2007.

Hancox, Robert J., and Richie Poulton. "Watching Television Is Associated with Childhood Obesity: But Is It Clinically Important?" *International Journal of Obesity* 30 (2006): 171–175.

Harrison, Kristen, and Joanne Cantor. "Tales from the Screen: Enduring Fright Reactions to Scary Media." *Psychology* 1.2 (1999): 97–116.

Healy, Jane M. *Endangered Minds: Why Our Children Don't Think.* New York: Simon & Schuster, 1990.

Hope, Jenny. "Background TV 'Can Harm Children's Speech.'" DailyMail Online. June 2, 2009.www.dailymail.co.uk/health/article-1190183/Background-TV-harm-childrens-speech.html.

Johnson, Jeffrey G., Judith S. Brook, Patricia Cohen, Michael B. First, and Stephanie Kasen. "Association between Television Viewing and Sleep Problems during Adolescence and Early Adulthood." *Pediatrics* 116 (2004): 562–568.

Klesges, Robert C., Mary L. Shelton, and Lisa M. Klesges. "Effects of Television on Metabolic Rate: Potential Implications for Childhood Obesity." *Pediatrics* 91.2 (1993): 281–286.

Koezuka, Naoko, Kenneth R. Allison, Edward M. Adlaf, John J.M. Dwyer, Guy Faulkner, Jack Goodman, and Malcolm Koo. "The Relationship between Sedentary Activities and Physical Inactivity among Adolescents: Results from the Canadian Community Health Survey." *Journal of Adolescent Health* 39.4 (2006): 515–522.

Krcmar, Marina. *Living without the Screen: Causes and Consequences of Life without Television.* New York: Routledge, 2009.

Kubey, Robert, and Mihaly Csikszentmihalyi. "Television Addiction Is No Mere Metaphor." ScientificAmerican.com. February 23, 2002. www.shenet.org/high/hsacaddept/English/ddayton/Documents/Media/Television%20Addiction%20is%20no%20Mere%20Metaphor.pdf.

Landhuis, Carl Erik, Richie Poulton, David Welch, and Robert John Hancox. "Does Childhood Television Viewing Lead to Attention Problems in Adolescence? Results From a Prospective Longitudinal Study." *Pediatrics* 120.3 (2007): 532–537.

Linn, Susan. *The Case for Make Believe: Saving Play in a Commercialized World.* New York: New Press, 2008.

——. *Consuming Kids: The Hostile Takeover of Childhood.* New York: Anchor, 2005.

Lipper, Ari. *Buy, Buy, Baby: The Complete Sourcebook of Products for Your New Baby.* Chicago: Contemporary, 1996.

Los Angeles Times. "Study: TV Affects Toddlers." April 16, 2004.

Lotus, Jean. "It's Official: TV Linked to Attention Deficit." White Dot. www.whitedot.org/issue/iss_story.asp?slug=ADHD%20Toddlers.

Mander, Jerry. *Four Arguments for the Elimination of Television.* New York: Perennial, 2002.

Marans, Steven. *Listening to Fear: Helping Kids Cope, from Nightmares to the Nightly News.* New York: Owl, 2005.

Martinez-Gomez, David, Joey C. Eisenmann, Kate A. Heelan, Jared Tucker, and Gregory J. Welk. "Associations Between Sedentary Behavior and Blood Pressure in Young Children." *Archives of Pediatrics & Adolescent Medicine* 163.8 (2009): 724-730.

Mishori, Ranit. "TV and Asthma." *Parade,* May 3, 2009.

Msnbc.com. "Even Background TV May Delay Infants' Speech." June 1, 2009. www.msnbc.msn.com/id/31051013.

New York Post. "Study: Kids Who Watch 2 Hours of TV a Day Twice as Likely to Develop Asthma." March 3, 2009. www.nypost.com/p/news/international/tv_linked_to_kids_asthma_CuQvD4GQkIH4Z9aHAdnvLK.

Oppenheimer, Todd. *The Flickering Mind: The False Promise of Technology in the Classroom, and How Learning Can Be Saved.* New York: Random House, 2003.

Oprah.com. "Take Oprah's 'What Can You Live Without?' Challenge." www.oprah.com/oprahshow/What-Can-You-Live-Without-Experiment-Steps.

Ostrov, Jamie M., Douglas A. Gentile, and Nicki R. Crick. "Media Exposure, Aggression and Prosocial Behavior During Early Childhood: Longitudinal Study," *Social Development,* 15.4 (2006): 612–627.

Owens, Judy. "Television-Viewing Habits and Sleep Disturbance in School Children." *Pediatrics* 104.3 (1999): E27.

Parents. "Too Much Television?" July 2008.

Park, Alice. "Baby Einsteins: Not So Smart After All." *Time,* August 6, 2007.

——. "Watching TV: Even Worse for Kids Than You Think." *Time,* August 4, 2009.

Pecora, Norma Odom, John P. Murray, and Ellen Wartella. *Children and Television: Fifty Years of Research.* Mahwah, NJ: Lawrence Erlbaum, 2007.

Peterson, Gayle. "How Can TV Affect Your Family?" iVillage. http://parenting.ivillage.com/mom/structure/0,3wpc,00.html.

Redford, John. "The Impact of Television." Tannis MacBeth Williams, ed. TheWorld.com. January 1995. http://world.std.com/~jlr/comment/tv_impact.htm.

Reilly, John, Stan Grant, Diane M. Jackson, Louise A. Kelly, Colette Montgomery, James Y. Paton, and Christine Slater. "Total Energy Expenditure and Physical Activity in Young Scottish Children: Mixed Longitudinal Study." *Lancet* 363.9404 (2004): 211–212.

Rideout, Victoria J., and Elizabeth Hamel. *The Media Family: Electronic Media in the Lives of Infants, Toddlers, Preschoolers, and Their Parents.* The Henry J. Kaiser Family Foundation, May 24, 2006. www.kff.org/entmedia/7500.cfm.

Rideout, Victoria J., Elizabeth A. Vandewater, and Ellen A. Wartella. *Zero to Six: Electronic Media in the Lives of Infants, Toddlers and Preschoolers.* The Henry J. Kaiser Family Foundation, October 28, 2003. www.kff.org/entmedia/3378.cfm.

Robinson, Thomas N. "Reducing Children's Television Viewing to Prevent Obesity: A Randomized Controlled Trial." *JAMA* 282.16 (1999): 1561–1567.

Ruskin, Gary. "Why They Whine: How Corporations Prey on Our Children." *Mothering,* November & December 1999.

Schmidt, Marie Evans, and Elizabeth A. Vandewater. "Media and Attention, Cognition, and School Achievement." *JSTOR.* www.jstor.org/pss/20053120.

Schor, Juliet. *Born to Buy: The Commercialized Child and the New Consumer Culture.* New York: Scribner, 2004.

Shute, Nancy. "Television and Adolescent Depression." *US News & World Report,* February 3, 2009. http://health.usnews.com/blogs/on-parenting/2009/02/03/television-and-adolescent-depression.html.

Sigman, Aric. *Remotely Controlled: How Television Is Damaging Our Lives.* London: Vermillion, 2005.

Singer, Dorothy G., and Jerome L. Singer. *Imagination and Play in the Electronic Age.* Cambridge, MA: Harvard University Press, 2005.

Society for the Advancement of Education. "Scary Movies and TV Programs Have Long-Lasting Effects." *USA Today.* http://findarticles.com/p/articles/mi_m1272/is_2659_128/ai_61586768/.

Spock, Benjamin, and Steven Parker. *Dr. Spock's Baby and Child Care.* New York: Dutton, 1998.

Starr, Belle. "Prevent Falling Television Injuries to Children or Child-Proof Your TV." *Helium.* www.helium.com/items/1166444-preventing-falling-tv-injuries.

Stein, Jeannine. "Hours Sitting in Front of TV Found to Shorten Life." *Los Angeles Times,* January 12, 2010.

Steyer, James P. *The Other Parent: The Inside Story of the Media's Effect on Our Children.* New York: Atria, 2002.

Strasburger, Victor C., and Barbara J. Wilson. *Children, Adolescents, & the Media.* Thousand Oaks, CA: Sage, 2002.

Sunderland, Margot. *Science of Parenting: Practical Guidance on Sleep, Crying, Play, and Building Emotional Well-Being for Life.* New York: Dorling Kindersley, 2006.

Thaindian News. "TV Damaging Children's Eyesight." December 10, 2007. www.thaindian.com/newsportal/health/tv-damaging-childrens-eyesight_1008379.html.

Thompson, D.A., and Dimitri A. Christakis. "The Association Between Television Viewing and Irregular Sleep Schedules Among Children Less Than 3 Years of Age." *Pediatrics* 116 (2005): 851–856.

Trelease, Jim. *The Read-Aloud Handbook.* New York: Penguin, 2006.

Troseth, Georgene, and Judy DeLoache. "The Medium Can Obscure the Message: Young Children's Understanding of Video." *Child Development* 69.4 (1998): 950–965.

U.S. Department of Health and Human Services. "Overweight in Early Childhood Increases Chances for Obesity at Age 12." National Institutes of Health. September 5, 2006. www.nih.gov/news/pr/sep2006/nichd-05.htm.

Vandewater, Elizabeth A., David S. Bickham, and June H. Lee. "Time Well Spent? Relating Television Use to Children's Free-Time Activities." *Pediatrics* 117.2 (2006): 181–191.

Vandewater, Elizabeth A., David S. Bickham, June H. Lee, Hope M. Cummings, Victoria J. Rideout, and Ellen A. Watella. "When the Television Is Always On." *American Behavioral Scientist* 48.5 (2005): 562–577.

Van Evra, Judith Page. *Television and Child Development.* Mahwah, NJ: Lawrence Erlbaum, 2004.

Wall Street Journal. "Toddlers Who Watch TV Risk Attention Problems, Study Finds." April 5, 2004.

Winn, Marie. *The Plug-In Drug: Television, Computers, and Family Life.* New York: Penguin, 2002.

Yale-New Haven Hospital. "Too Much TV Can Disrupt Sleep." October 1999. www.ynhh.org/healthlink/pediatrics/pediatrics_10_99.html.

11. It's Easy Being Green: Reducing Exposure to Toxins

American Lung Association. "Secondhand Smoke." www.lungusa.org/stop-smoking/about-smoking/health-effects/secondhand-smoke.html.

Barnett, Sloan. *Green Goes with Everything: Simple Steps to a Healthier Life and a Cleaner Planet.* New York: Atria, 2008.

Berman, Jenn. *The A to Z Guide to Raising Happy, Confident Kids.* Novato, CA: New World Library, 2007.

_____. "How Big Business Has Let Parents Down." *Los Angeles Family,* October 2007.

Best-in-Bedding. "Why You Absolutely Must Use an Organic Crib Mattress for Your Baby." www.best-in-bedding.com/babybedding/use-an-organic-crib-mattress.htm.

Blanchard, Tamsin. *Green Is the New Black: How to Change the World with Style.* London: Hodder & Stoughton, 2007.

Brockovich, Erin. "Wake Up America." *The Brockovich Report.* September 10, 2007. www.brockovichblog. com/2007/09/wake_up_america.html#.

CBS 5. "Fire Retardants Linked With Health Problems." http://cbs5.com/local/consumer.watch. flame.2.661700.html.

CBS News. "FDA Issues Warning About BPA Exposure." January 18, 2010. www.cbsnews.com/ stories/2010/01/18/earlyshow/health/main6110716.shtml?tag=cbsnewsTwoColUpperPromoArea.

Center for Health, Environment & Justice. "PVC: The Poison Plastic." www.chej.org/BESAFE/pvc/.

Centers for Disease Control and Prevention. "Children and Secondhand Smoke Exposure." www.cdc. gov/features/childrenandsmoke/.

Cik, Barry A. "Five Problems with Baby Crib Mattresses." *Naturepedic.* www.naturepedic.com/research/ fiveproblems.php.

Dadd, Debra Lynn. "Is Formaldehyde in Children's Clothing from China?" *Healthy Child Healthy World.* December 25, 2009. http://healthychild.org/blog/comments/is_formaldehyde_in_childrens_ clothing_from_china/.

Dolan, Deirdre, and Alexandra Zissu. *The Complete Organic Pregnancy.* New York: Collins, 2006.

Eco Child's Play. "Baby Lotion Linked to Phthalates." February 4, 2008. http://ecochildsplay. com/2008/02/04/baby-lotion-linked-to-phthalates/.

_____. "When 'Getting the Lead Out' Is Not Enough." January 22, 2008. http://ecochildsplay. com/2008/01/22/when-%e2%80%9cgetting-the-lead-out%e2%80%9d-is-not-enough/.

Environmental Working Group. "BodyBurden? The Pollution in Newborns." 2005. www.ewg.org/ reports/bodyburden2/.

_____. "Canaries in the Kitchen: Teflon Toxicosis." May 14, 2003. www.ewg.org/book/export/html/8296.

_____. "EWG's Guide to Infant Formula and Baby Bottles." January 2001. www.ewg.org/book/export/ html/25570.

_____. "Reducing Your Exposure to PBDEs in Your Home." October 2008. www.ewg.org/pbdefree.

Evans, Lynette. "What's in a Fragrance? Labels Aren't Required to Say." *SFGate.* August 10, 2008. www. sfgate.com/cgi-bin/blogs/chrongreen/detail?entry_id=28990.

FindLaw's Common Law. "Phthalates Ban from Toys Starts Today While Amount in Existing Inventory Remains Unknown." February 2009. http://commonlaw.findlaw.com/2009/02/phthalates-ban-from- toys-starts-today-while-amount-in-existing-inventory-remains-unknown.html.

FoxNews.com. "ADHD Linked to Tobacco Smoke, Lead Exposure." September 19, 2006. www.foxnews. com/story/0,2933,214523,00.html.

Gavigan, Christopher. *Healthy Child, Healthy World: Creating a Cleaner, Greener, Safer Home.* New York: Dutton, 2008.

Ginsberg, Gary, and Brian Toal. *What's Toxic, What's Not.* New York: Berkley, 2006.

Glaser, Aviva. "Ubiquitous Triclosan: A Common Antibacterial Agent Exposed." *Pesticides and You* 24.3 (2004).

Green America. "The Best Toys for Your Tots." www.greenamericatoday.org/pubs/realgreen/articles/toys.cfm.

_____. "Ten Simple Ways to Clean Green." www.greenamericatoday.org/pubs/realgreen/articles/ greencleaners.cfm.

Greene, Alan R. *Raising Baby Green: The Earth-Friendly Guide to Pregnancy, Childbirth, and Baby Care.* San Francisco: Jossey-Bass, 2007.

GreenYour.com. "Choose Organic Cotton or PVC-Free Bibs." www.greenyour.com/lifestyle/baby/baby- feeding/tips/choose-organic-cotton-or-pvc-free-bibs.

Grinning Planet. "Triclosan." October 4, 2005. www.grinningplanet.com/2005/10-04/triclosan-article.htm.

Grossman, Elizabeth. "Toxic Flame Retardant Is Out: Will What Follows Be Safe?" *Healthy Child Healthy World.* December 28, 2009. http://healthychild.org/blog/comments/toxic_flame_retardant_is_out_ will_what_follows_be_safe/#ixzz0hehSAwBa.

Gutierrez, David. "Drinking From Plastic Raises BPA Levels 70 Percent." *Natural News.* October 14, 2009. www.naturalnews.com/027236_BPA_health_disease.html.

Hktdc.com. "EU Ban on Phthalates in Toys Is Renewed." September 15, 2000. www.hktdc.com/info/ mi/a/baeu/en/1X00PQ6O/1/Business-Alert-%E2%80%93-EU/EU-ban-on-phthalates-in-toys-is- renewed.htm.

Hoffman, Matthew. "Antibacterial Soap Alternatives." WebMD. www.webmd.com/health-ehome-9/ antibacterial-soap-cleaners.

IKEA Fans. "Pbde-Free Furniture." www.ikeafans.com/forums/green-living-building/31306-pbde-free- furniture.html.

Imus, Deirdre. *Growing Up Green: Baby and Child Care.* New York: Simon & Schuster, 2008.

Jones, Ashby. "Retailers 'In a Panic' Over Recent Consumer-Safety Ruling." *Wall Street Journal,* February 10, 2009. http://blogs.wsj.com/law/2009/02/10/retailers-in-a-panic-over-recent-consumer-safety- ruling/.

Landrigan, Philip J., Herbert L. Needleman, and Mary M. Landrigan. *Raising Healthy Children in a Toxic World: 101 Smart Solutions for Every Family.* Emmaus, PA: Rodale, 2001.

Layton, Lyndsey. "No BPA for Baby Bottles in US: 6 Makers Announce Decisions on Chemical." *Washington Post,* March 6, 2009.

Lekovic, Jill M. *Diaper-Free Before 3: The Healthier Way to Toilet Train and Help Your Child Out of Diapers Sooner.* New York: Three Rivers, 2006.

Lipton, Eric S., and David Barboza. "As More Toys Are Recalled, Trail Ends in China." *New York Times.* www.nytimes.com/2007/06/19/business/worldbusiness/19toys.html.

Magaziner, Allan, Linda Bonvie, and Anthony Zolezzi. *Chemical-Free Kids: How to Safeguard Your Child's Diet and Environment.* New York: Kensington, 2003.

Marriott, Susannah. *Green Baby.* New York: Dorling Kindersley, 2008

McDonald, Libby. *The Toxic Sandbox: The Truth about Environmental Toxins and Our Children's Health.* New York: Penguin, 2007.

Medscape. "Tobacco Smoke Exposure & Cognitive Abilities in Adolescence: Discussion." www.medscape.com/viewarticle/497383_4.

Minnesota Department of Health. "Removing Exterior Lead Paint." www.health.state.mn.us/divs/eh/lead/homes/exterior.html.

Moninger, Jeannette. "Lead Astray." *Parents,* September 2007.

Natterson, Cara Familian. *Dangerous or Safe? Which Foods, Medicines, and Chemicals Really Put Your Kids at Risk.* New York: Hudson Street, 2009.

Natural Resources Defense Council (NRDC). "Court Upholds Congressional Ban on Toxic Toys." www.nrdc.org/media/2009/090205a.asp.

New Jersey GASP. "Protecting Children." www.njgasp.org/pc_main.htm.

New Parents Guide. "Diapers? Cloth Diapers vs. Disposable Diapers." http://thenewparentsguide.com/diapers.htm.

Oak Ridge National Laboratory. "Reducing Risk from Lead in Soil." January 4, 2004. www.esd.ornl.gov/research/earth_sciences/images/2004ryan_esd_38_10A-24A.pdf.

Office of the Surgeon General. "The Health Consequences of Involuntary Exposure to Tobacco Smoke: A Report of the Surgeon General." www.surgeongeneral.gov/library/secondhandsmoke/report/.

Pechman, Rachel Rabkin. "Surprising Lead Hazards." *Parenting,* September 2007.

Perlmutter, David, and Carol Colman. *Raise a Smarter Child by Kindergarten: Build a Better Brain and Increase IQ Up to 30 Points.* New York: Morgan Road, 2006.

Perron, Celeste. "Safe House: How to Avoid the Chemicals That Could Hurt Your Kids—Inside Your Home and Out." *Parenting,* August 2008.

Planet Green. "Green Glossary: Volatile Organic Compounds." http://planetgreen.discovery.com/home-garden/green-glossary-volatile-compounds.html.

Pollution in People. "Toxic Flame Retardants: A Burning Problem in Our Bodies." www.pollutioninpeople.org/toxics/pbdes.

Rabin, Roni Caryn. "A New Cigarette Hazard: 'Third-Hand Smoke.'" *New York Times,* January 2, 2009. www.nytimes.com/2009/01/03/health/research/03smoke.html.

Ross, Edward A., Nancy J. Szabo, and Ian R. Tebbett. "Lead Content of Calcium Supplements." *JAMA* 284.11 (2000): 1425–1429.

Ryan, James A., William R. Berti, Sally L. Brown, Stan W. Casteel, Rufus L. Chaney, Mark Doolan, Petere Grevatt, Judith Hallfrisch, Mark Maddaloni, Dave Mosby, and Kirk G. Scheckel. "Reducing Children's Risk from Lead in Soil." *Environmental Science & Technology* (2004).

Sathyanarayana, Sheela, Catherine J. Karr, Paula Lozano, Elizabeth Brown, Antonia M. Calafat, and Shanna H. Swan. "Baby Care Products: Possible Sources of Infant Phthalate Exposure." *Pediatrics* 121.2 (2008): E260–268.

Schecter, Arnold, Marian Pavuk, Olaf Päpke, John Jake Ryan, Linda Birnbaum, and Robin Rosen. "Polybrominated Diphenyl Ethers (PBDEs) in U.S. Mothers' Milk." *Environmental Health Perspectives* 111.14 (2003): 1723–1729.

Shabecoff, Philip, and Alice Shabecoff. *Poisoned Profits: The Toxic Assault on Our Children.* New York: Random House, 2008.

Skipton, Sharon, and DeLynn Hay. "Drinking Water: Lead." N.C. Division of Pollution Prevention and Environmental Assistance. Cooperative Extension, Institute of Agriculture and Natural Resources, University of Nebraska-Lincoln. www.p2pays.org/ref/20/19711.htm.

Small Property Owners of America. "Lead Paint: No One Talks about the Door Mat Study." www.spoa.com/pages/lead3.html.

Steinemann, Anne C. "Fragranced Consumer Products and Undisclosed Ingredients." *Environmental Impact Assessment Review* (2008). July23, 2008. www.ce.washington.edu/people/faculty/bios/documents/Steinemann2008.pdf.

Taggart, Jennifer. *Smart Mama's Green Guide: Simple Steps to Reduce Your Child's Toxic Chemical Exposure.* New York: Center Street, 2009.

Terressentials. "The Truth About Parabens." www.terressentials.com/truthaboutparabens.html.

Thompson, John. "Poison in the Air." *Parents,* September 2007.

TripletsMommy.com. "BPA-Free Baby Bottles: What You Need to Know." August 8, 2008. http://tripletsmommy.com/bpa-free-baby-bottles-what-you-need-to-know#.

U.S. Consumer Product Safety Commission. "Children's Sleepwear Regulations." Office of Compliance. www.cpsc.gov/businfo/regsumsleepwear.pdf.

_____. "Section 108: Products Containing Certain Phthalates—Consumer Product Safety Improvement Act (CPSIA)." www.cpsc.gov/ABOUT/Cpsia/faq/108faq.html.

U.S. Environmental Protection Agency. "Furniture Flame Retardancy Partnership." http://epa.gov/dfe/pubs/projects/flameret/index.htm.

_____. "Lead in Paint, Dust, and Soil." www.epa.gov/lead/pubs/leadinfo.htm#protect.

_____. "Lead in Your Drinking Water Fact Sheet." June 1993. www.epa.gov/safewater/lead/lead1.html.

_____. *Supplemental Environmental Projects in Administrative Enforcement Matters Involving Section 1018 Lead-Paint Cases.* Office of Enforcement and Compliance Assurance. November 23, 2004. www.epa.gov/compliance/ressources/policies/civil/seps/sepssection1018-leadbasedpaint112304.pdf.

_____. "Volatile Organic Compounds." www.epa.gov/iaq/voc.html.

U.S. Food and Drug Administration. "Bisphenol A (BPA)." www.fda.gov/NewsEvents/PublicHealthFocus/ucm064437.htm.

_____. "Database of Select Committee on GRAS Substances (SCOGS) Reviews: L-Glutamic Acid Hydrochloride. 1980. www.accessdata.fda.gov/scripts/fcn/fcnDetailNavigation.cfm?rpt=scogsListing&id=188.

YES! Magazine. "Yes! But How? Practical Ideas for Saving the Earth." May 20, 2004. www.yesmagazine.org/issues/art-and-community/yes-but-how.

Yolton, Kimberly, et al. "Exposure to Environmental Tobacco Smoke and Cognitive Abilities among U.S. Children and Adolescents." *Environmental Health Perspectives* 113.1 (2005). http://ehp.niehs.nih.gov/members/2004/7210/7210.html.

12. Food for Thought: Eating and Nutrition

Action on Additives. "Action on Additives." www.actiononadditives.com/.

Attwood, Charles R. "Tender Is the Heart." Vegsource.com. www.vegsource.com/attwood/heart.htm.

Avery, Alexis, Kristine Zimmerman, Patricia W. Underwood, and Jeanette H. Magnus. "Confident Commitment Is a Key Factor for Sustained Breastfeeding." *Birth* 36.2 (2009): 141–148.

BabyCenter. "Finger Foods." November 2008. www.babycenter.com/0_finger-foods_105.bc#articlesection2.

_____. "How Breastfeeding Benefits You and Your Baby." June 2005. www.babycenter.com/0_how-breastfeeding-benefits-you-and-your-baby_8910.bc?print=true.

_____. "Introducing Solid Foods." October 2006. www.babycenter.com/0_introducing-solid-foods_113.bc#articlesection2.

Berman, Jenn. *The A to Z Guide to Raising Happy, Confident Kids.* Novato, CA: New World Library, 2007.

Birch, Leann Lipps. "Experiential Determinants of Children's Food Preferences." *Current Topics in Early Childhood Education,* ed. Lilian Katz. Vol. 3. Norwood, NJ: Ablex, 1980.

Birch, Leann Lipps, and Kirsten Krahnstoever Davison. "Family Environmental Factors Influencing the Developing Behavioral Controls of Food Intake and Childhood Overweight." *Pediatric Clinics of North America* 48.4 (2001). MD Consult. www.Mdconsult.Com/Das/Article/Body/182388530-2/Jorg=Journal&Source=Mi&Sp=11920321&Sid=0/N/233741/1.Html?Issn=0031-3955.

Blaylock, Russell L. *Excitotoxins: The Taste That Kills.* Santa Fe, NM: Health, 1998.

Boyles, Salynn. "Breastfed Babies Less Overweight." WebMD. September 26, 2006. www.webmd.com/parenting/news/20060926/breastfed-babies-less-overweight.

Braun, Betsy Brown. *Just Tell Me What to Say: Sensible Tips and Scripts for Perplexed Parents.* New York: Collins, 2008.

Breastfeeding.com. "Higher IQ Connected to Breastfeeding." www.breastfeeding.com/all_about/all_about_iq.html#FIRST.

Burke, Cindy. *To Buy or Not to Buy Organic: What You Need to Know to Choose the Healthiest, Safest, Most Earth-Friendly Food.* New York: Marlowe, 2007.

Campbell, T. Colin, and Thomas M. Campbell. *The China Study: The Most Comprehensive Study of Nutrition Ever Conducted and the Startling Implications for Diet, Weight Loss and Long-Term Health.* Dallas: BenBella, 2006.

Cancer Prevention Coalition. "Milk: America's Health Problem." www.preventcancer.com/consumers/general/milk.htm.

Center for Science in the Public Interest. "Brits Get Treats, Americans Get Tricks From Food Companies, Says Nutrition Action Healthletter." October 22, 2008. www.cspinet.org/new/200810221.html.
_____. "Food Dyes and Behavior Report." http://cspinet.org/fooddyes/.
Centers for Disease Control and Prevention. "Prevalence of Overweight and Obesity Among Children and Adolescents: United States, 1999–2002." October 6, 2004. www.cdc.gov/nchs/data/hestat/overwght99.htm.
Conners, C. Keith. *Feeding the Brain: How Foods Affect Children.* New York: Plenum, 1989.
Cordes, Nancy. "The Truth About Food (Dyes)." CBS News. June 3, 2008. www.cbsnews.com/blogs/2008/06/03/couricandco/entry4151130.shtml.
Curl, Cynthia L., Richard A. Fenske, and Kai Elgethun. "Assessment of Organophosphorus Pesticide Exposures in the Diets of.Preschool Children in Washington State." *Environmental Health Perspectives* 111.3 (2003): 377–382.
Edelstein, Sari, and Judith Sharlin. *Life Cycle Nutrition: An Evidence-Based Approach.* Sudbury, MA: Jones and Bartlett, 2009.
Eliot, Lise. *What's Going On in There? How the Brain and Mind Develop in the First Five Years of Life.* New York: Bantam, 2000.
Environmental Working Group. "Pesticides Pose Health Risks for Children." *Healthy Child.* www.healthychild.com/toxic-food/pesticides-pose-health-risks-for-children/.
_____. "Shopper's Guide to Pesticides." www.foodnews.org/EWG-shoppers-guide-download-final.pdf.
Epstein, Samuel S. *What's in Your Milk? An Exposé of Industry and Government Cover-Up on the Dangers of the Genetically Engineered (rBGH) Milk You're Drinking.* Victoria, British Columbia: Trafford, 2006.
Escobar, Alyson. "Factors Influencing Children's Dietary Practices: A Review." *Family Economics and Nutrition Review.* Winter 1999. http://findarticles.com/p/articles/mi_m0EUB/is_1999_Winter/ai_67583128/.
Ewall, Mike. "Bovine Growth Hormone: Milk Does Nobody Good..." EJnet.org. www.ejnet.org/bgh/nogood.html.
Family Farm Defenders. "Concerned Farmers and Consumers Warn FDA Commissioner Hamburg and Sen. Kohl Against Unsafe Dairy Products!" www.familyfarmdefenders.org/pmwiki.php/BovineGrowthHormone/BovineGrowthHormone?action=print.
Fenske, Richard A. *Children's Pesticide Exposure in the Seattle Metropolitan Area.* Report no. 190. Agrichemical and Environmental News, February 2002. www.aenews.wsu.edu/Feb02AENews/FenskePDF.pdf.
Fisher, Jennifer Orlet, Diane C. Mitchell, Helen Smiciklas-Wright, and Leann Lipps Birch. "Parental Influences on Young Girls' Fruit and Vegetable, Micronutrient, and Fat Intake." *Journal of American Dietetic Association* 102.1 (2002): 58–64.
Fomon, Samuel J. *Nutrition of Normal Infants.* St. Louis: Mosby, 1993.
Fraser, Alicia J., Thomas F. Webster, and Michael D. McClean. "Red Meat and Poultry: Two Major Sources of PBDE Exposure in the US." *Environmental Health News.* 2009. www.environmentalhealthnews.org/ehs/newscience/red-meat-and-poultry-sources-of-pbde.
Fuhrman, Joel. *Disease-Proof Your Child: Feeding Kids Right.* New York: St. Martin's Press, 2005.
Gavigan, Christopher. *Healthy Child, Healthy World: Creating a Cleaner, Greener, Safer Home.* New York: Dutton, 2008.
Goodall, Jane, Gary McAvoy, and Gail E. Hudson. *Harvest for Hope: A Guide to Mindful Eating.* New York: Warner, 2005.
Greene, Alan R. *Feeding Baby Green: The Earth-Friendly Program for Healthy, Safe Nutrition during Pregnancy, Childhood, and Beyond.* San Francisco: Jossey-Bass, 2009.
Greer, Beth. *Super Natural Home: Improve Your Health, Home, and Planet—One Room at a Time.* Emmaus, PA: Rodale, 2009.
Hood, Maggie Y., Landon L. Moore, Anuradha Sundarajan-Ramamurti, L. Adrienne Cupples, and R. Curtis Ellison. "Parental Eating Attitudes and the Development of Obesity in Children." *Journal of Related Metabolic Disorders* 24.10 (2000): 1319–1325.
Institute for Agriculture and Trade Policy. "Smart Guide to Food Dyes: Buying Foods That Can Help Learning." Docstoc. February 2009. www.docstoc.com/docs/25391612/Smart-GuideTo-Food-Dyes.
Kimbrell, Andrew. *Your Right to Know: Genetic Engineering and the Secret Changes in Your Food.* San Rafael, CA: Earth Aware, 2007.
Klingberg, H., Jurij Brankack, and Fritz Klingberg. "Long-Term Effects on Behaviour after Postnatal Treatment with Monosodium-L-Glutamate." *Biomedica Biochimica Acta* 46.10 (1987): 705–711.
Leavitt, Kathryn Perrotti. "Hormones in Our Food." *Healthy Child Healthy World.* May 24, 2007. http://healthychild.org/blog/comments/hormones_in_our_food/.
Llanos, Miguel. "Flame Retardants Found in U.S. Food Test." Msnbc.com. September 1, 2004. www.msnbc.msn.com/id/5887631.

Lu, Chensheng, Kathryn Toepel, Rene Irish, Richard A. Fenske, Dana B. Barr, and Roberto Bravo. "Organic Diets Significantly Lower Children's Dietary Exposure to Organophosphorus Pesticides." *Journal of Exposure Analysis and Environmental Epidemiology* 12.1 (2002): 21–28.

Lubick, Naomi. "PBDEs in Diet: Meat Fat a Leading Source." *Environmental Health Perspectives.* http://ehsehplp03.niehs.nih.gov/article/info:doi%2F10.1289%2Fehp.117-a455b.

Magaziner, Allan, Linda Bonvie, and Anthony Zolezzi. *Chemical-Free Kids: How to Safeguard Your Child's Diet and Environment.* New York: Kensington, 2003.

McDonald, Libby. *The Toxic Sandbox: The Truth about Environmental Toxins and Our Children's Health.* New York: Penguin, 2007.

Meek, Joan Younger, and Sherill Tippins. *American Academy of Pediatrics New Mother's Guide to Breastfeeding.* New York: Bantam, 2006.

MSGTruth.org. "MSG Truth." www.msgtruth.org/.

Napoli, Maryann. "The Bogalusa Heart Study of 14,000 Children." http://findarticles.com/p/articles/mi_m0815/is_n8_v23/ai_21155460/.

National Pesticide Information Center. "Organophosphate Insecticides." http://npic.orst.edu/RMPP/rmpp_ch4.pdf.

Natural Resources Defense Council. "Healthy Milk, Healthy Baby? Chemical Pollution and Mother's Milk." March 25, 2005. www.nrdc.org/breastmilk/.

Neifert, Marianne R. *Great Expectations: The Essential Guide to Breastfeeding.* New York: Sterling, 2009.

Nestle, Marion. *What to Eat.* New York: North Point, 2006.

NewsInferno. "Is It Time to Ban Controversial Food Dyes?" June 4, 2008. www.newsinferno.com/archives/3202.

Nwaru, Bright I., et al. "Age at the Introduction of Solid Foods During the First Year and Allergic Sensitization at Age 5 Years." *Pediatrics* 125.1 (2010): 50–59.

Obesity Society. "Childhood Overweight." www.obesity.org/information/childhood_overweight.asp.

Organic Consumers Association. "OCA: Genetically Engineered Bovine Growth Hormone (Posilac, Also Known as RBGH or RBST)." www.organicconsumers.org/rbghlink.cfm.

Perlmutter, David, and Carol Colman. *Raise a Smarter Child by Kindergarten: Build a Better Brain and Increase IQ up to 30 Points.* New York: Morgan Road, 2006.

Perron, Celeste. "Rock Your Body: Where's the Beef." *Whole Life Times,* December–January 2009–2010.

Perry, Luddene, and Dan Schultz. *A Field Guide to Buying Organic.* New York: Bantam, 2005.

Pesticide Action Network UK. "Organophosphate Insecticides Fact Sheet." www.pan-uk.org/pestnews/Actives/organoph.htm.

Pizzorno, Joseph. "Genetically Modified Foods: Just Say No!" Web MD. November 20, 2007. http://blogs.webmd.com/integrative-medicine-wellness/2007/11/genetically-modified-foods-just-say-no.html.

Pollan, Michael, and Eric Schlosser. *Food, Inc.* DVD. Directed by Robert Kenner. New York: Magnolia Home Entertainment, 2008.

Robbins, John. *The Food Revolution: How Your Diet Can Help Save Your Life and Our World.* Berkeley, CA: Conari, 2001.

Roberts, Susan B., Melvin B. Heyman, and Lisa Tracy. *Feeding Your Child for Lifelong Health: Birth through Age Six.* New York: Bantam, 1999.

Roberts, Susan B., and Roger McDonald. "The Evolution of a New Research Field: Metabolic Programming by Early Nutrition." *Journal of Nutrition* 128.2 (1998): 400S.

Satter, Ellyn. *Child of Mine: Feeding with Love and Good Sense.* Palo Alto, CA: Bull, 2000.

Sears, Martha, and William Sears. *The Breastfeeding Book: Everything You Need to Know about Nursing Your Child from Birth through Weaning.* Boston: Little, Brown, 2000.

Sears, William, Martha Sears, James Sears, and Robert Sears. *The Healthiest Kid in the Neighborhood: Ten Ways to Get Your Family on the Right Nutritional Track.* Boston: Little, Brown, 2006.

Sears, William. *The NDD Book: How Nutrition Deficit Disorder Affects Your Child's Learning, Behavior, and Health, and What You Can Do about It—without Drugs.* New York: Little, Brown, 2009.

Sears, Martha, William Sears, James Sears, and Robert Sears. *The Family Nutrition Book: Everything You Need to Know about Feeding Your Children—from Birth through Adolescence.* Boston: Little, Brown, 1999.

Simontacchi, Carol N. *The Crazy Makers: How the Food Industry Is Destroying Our Brains and Harming Our Children.* New York: Jeremy P. Tarcher/Penguin, 2007.

Sorensen, Janelle. "Animals Don't Want to Eat GMOs, So Why Are We?" *Healthy Child Healthy World.* July 18, 2009. http://healthychild.org/blog/comments/animals_dont_want_to_eat_gmos_so_why_are_we/.

Sullivan, Susan A., and Leann L. Birch. "Infant Dietary Experience and Acceptance of Solid Foods." *Pediatrics* 93.2 (1994): 271–277. http://pediatrics.aappublications.org/cgi/content/abstract/93/2/271.

Taggart, Jennifer. *Smart Mama's Green Guide: Simple Steps to Reduce Your Child's Toxic Chemical Exposure.* New York: Center Street, 2009.

Tamborlane, William V., and Janet Z. Weiswasser. *The Yale Guide to Children's Nutrition.* New Haven, CT: Yale University Press, 1997.

Tribole, Evelyn and Elyse Resch. *Intuitive Eating: A Revolutionary Program That Works.* New York: St. Martin's Griffin, 2003.

Vartabedian, Bryan S. *Colic Solved: The Essential Guide to Infant Reflux and the Care of Your Crying, Difficult-to-Soothe Baby.* New York: Ballantine, 2007.

Wachter, Kerri. "Rice Cereal Can Wait, Let Them Eat Meat First: AAP Committee Has Changes in Mind." *Pediatric News* 43.11 (2009): 1–5.

Weber, Karl. *Food, Inc.: How Industrial Food Is Making Us Sicker, Fatter and Poorer—and What You Can Do about It.* New York: PublicAffairs, 2009.

Wiles, Richard, Christopher Campbell, Kenneth A. Cook, and Todd Hettenbach. "How 'Bout Them Apples? Pesticides in Children's Food Ten Years after Alar." *Environmental Working Group.* February 2009. www.ewg.org/files/apples.pdf.

Yaron, Ruth. *Super Baby Food: Absolutely Everything You Should Know about Feeding Your Baby and Toddler from Starting Solid Foods to Age Three Years.* Archbald, PA: F.J. Roberts, 1998.

Appendix A. **Child Care**

Berman, Jenn. *The A to Z Guide to Raising Happy, Confident Kids.* Novato, CA: New World Library, 2007.

Bowlby, Richard, and Pearl King. *Fifty Years of Attachment Theory.* London: Karnac on Behalf of the Winnicott Clinic of Psychotherapy, 2004.

Clarke-Stewart, Alison, and Virginia D. Allhusen. *What We Know about Childcare.* Cambridge, MA: Harvard University Press, 2005.

Connell, Linda H. *The Childcare Answer Book.* Naperville, IL: Sphinx, 2005.

Cryer, Debby, and Margaret Burchinal. "Parents as Child Care Consumers." *Early Childhood Research Quarterly* 12.1 (1997): 35–58.

de Becker, Gavin. *Protecting the Gift: Keeping Children and Teenagers Safe (and Parents Sane).* New York: Dial, 1999.

Douglas, Ann. *Choosing Childcare for Dummies.* Hoboken, NJ: Wiley, 2004.

——. *The Unofficial Guide to Childcare.* New York: Macmillan, 1998.

Ehrich, Michelle. *The Anxious Parents' Guide to Quality Childcare: An Informative, Step-by-Step Manual on Finding and Keeping the Finest Care for Your Child.* New York: Berkley, 1999.

Fowler, William, Karen Oqston, Gloria Roberts-Fiati, and Amy Swenson. "The Effects of Enriching Language in Infancy on the Early and Later Development of Competence." *Early Child Development and Care* 135 (1997): 41–77.

Golinkoff, Roberta M., and Kathy Hirsh-Pasek. *How Babies Talk: The Magic and Mystery of Language in the First Three Years of Life.* New York: Plume, 2000.

Howes, Carrollee, Deborah A. Phillips, and Marcy Whitebook. "Thresholds of Quality: Implications for the Social Development of Children in Center-Based Child Care." *Child Development* 63.2 (1992): 449–460.

Kindy, Kimberely, Tony Saavedra, and Natalya Shulyakovskaya. "Who's Watching the Children: Ex-Convicts Abound in Child Care." *Orange County Register,* March 17, 2002.

Leach, Penelope. *Child Care Today: Getting It Right for Everyone.* New York: Alfred A. Knopf, 2009.

Lee, Allison. *The Parent's Guide to Childcare: How to Choose and Manage the Right Care for Your Child.* Oxford, UK: How To, 2008.

NICHD Early Child Care Research Network. *Child Care and Child Development: Results from the NICHD Study of Early Child Care and Youth Development.* New York: Guilford, 2005.

Pruissen, Catherine M. "Choosing Care on Blind Faith." ChildCare.net. www.childcare.net/library/choosingcare.shtml.

Raffin, Michele. *The Good Nanny Book: How to Find, Hire, and Keep the Perfect Nanny for Your Child.* New York: Berkley, 1996.

Sax, Robin. *Predators and Child Molesters: What Every Parent Needs to Know to Keep Kids Safe: A Sex Crimes DA Answers 100 of the Most Asked Questions.* Amherst, NY: Prometheus, 2009.

Scarr, Sandra. "American Child Care Today." *American Psychologist* 53 (1998): 95–110.

Stamm, Jill, and Paula Spencer. *Bright from the Start: The Simple, Science-Backed Way to Nurture Your Child's Developing Mind, from Birth to Age 3.* New York: Gotham, 2007.

Whitebook, Marcy, Carrollee Howes, and Deborah A. Phillips. *Who Cares? Child Care Teachers and the Quality of Care in America.* Final Report, National Child Care Staffing Study. Oakland, CA: Child Care Employee Project, 1989.

Appendix B. Preschool

BabyCenter. "What Preschool Licensing Means." www.babycenter.com/0_what-preschool-licensing-means_64623.bc.

Baty, Christy Gordon. "Working Together: Is a Co-op Preschool Right for You?" *Parents' Press.* 2005. www.parentspress.com/educooppreschools.html.

Boyd, Hannah. "Academic Preschools: Too Much Too Soon?" Education.com. www.education.com/magazine/article/Ed_Academic_Preschools/.

Bozdech, Betsy. "Signs of a Bad Preschool." BabyCenter. www.babycenter.com/0_signs-of-a-bad-preschool_64639.bc.

Clarke-Stewart, Alison, and Virginia D. Allhusen. *What We Know about Childcare.* Cambridge, MA: Harvard University Press, 2005.

Elkind, David. *Miseducation: Preschoolers at Risk.* New York: Knopf, 2000.

———. *The Power of Play: How Spontaneous, Imaginative Activities Lead to Happier, Healthier Children.* Cambridge, MA: Da Capo Lifelong, 2007.

Fliess, Sue Douglass. "Preschool Accreditation: What It Means." Education.com. www.education.com/magazine/article/accredited_Preschool/.

Hertzog, Nancy B. *Ready for Preschool: Prepare Your Child for Happiness and Success at School.* Waco, TX: Prufrock, 2008.

Hirsh-Pasek, Kathy, Roberta M. Golinkoff, and Diane E. Eyer. *Einstein Never Used Flash Cards: How Our Children Really Learn—and Why They Need to Play More and Memorize Less.* Emmaus, PA: Rodale, 2003.

Holloran, Donna. *Preschool Programs at a Glance.* Handout. BabyGroup, 2000.

Holt, Nicky. *Bringing the High/Scope Approach to Your Early Years Practice.* London: Routledge, 2007.

Isaacs, Barbara. *Bringing the Montessori Approach to Your Early Years Practice.* London: Routledge, 2007.

Loh, Andrew. "Reggio Emilia Approach." Brainy-Child.com. December 2006. www.brainy-child.com/article/reggioemilia.html.

Montessori, Maria. *The Absorbent Mind.* New York: Henry Holt, 1995.

Montessori Method. "Montessori FAQ's." http://michaelolaf.net/FAQMontessori.html.

NICHD Early Child Care Research Network. *Child Care and Child Development: Results from the NICHD Study of Early Child Care and Youth Development.* New York: Guilford, 2005.

Nicol, Janni. *Bringing the Steiner Waldorf Approach to Your Early Years Practice.* London: Routledge, 2007.

Nitka, Michelle. *Coping with Preschool Panic: The Los Angeles Guide to Private Preschools.* Beverly Hills, CA: Michelle Nitka, 2007.

Parents. "Picking the Right Preschool." March 1998.

Petrash, Jack. *Understanding Waldorf Education: Teaching from the Inside Out.* Beltsville, MD: Gryphon House, 2002.

Pregnancy Info. "What to Look For: Finding the Right Preschool for Your Child." www.pregnancy-info.net/finding_a_preschool.html.

Robledo, S. Jhoanna. "The Top Preschool Programs and How They Differ." BabyCenter. www.babycenter.com/0_the-top-preschool-programs-and-how-they-differ_64635.bc.

Sacramento SETA Head Start. "Head Start." www.headstart.seta.net/index2.htm.

Schulman, Nancy, and Ellen Birnbaum. *Practical Wisdom for Parents: Demystifying the Preschool Years.* New York: Alfred A. Knopf, 2007.

Solomon, Barbara. "What Kids Really Learn in Preschool." *Parents,* September 2000.

Appendix D. Reducing the Risk of SIDS

AAP Task Force on Infant Sleep Position and Sudden Infant Death Syndrome. "The Changing Concept of Sudden Infant Death Syndrome: Diagnostic Coding Shifts, Controversies Regarding the Sleep Environment, and New Variables to Consider in Reducing Risk." *Pediatrics* 116.5 (2005).

Ariagno, Ronald. "Smoking and the Risk for SIDS." *Horizons* 1.3 (1994). SIDS Network. http://sids-network.org/experts/smok.htm.

Elston, Christina. "AAP Revises SIDS Prevention Guidelines." Parenthood.com. http://www.parenthood.com/article-topics/aap_revises_sids_prevention_guidelines_1.html.

Ferber, Richard. *Solve Your Child's Sleep Problems.* New York: Fireside Book, 2006.

Gordon, Serena. "Bedroom Fan Cuts SIDS Risk by 72%." *U.S. News & World Report,* October 6, 2008.

Greene, Alan. "Pacifiers and Sids?" DrGreene.com. December 11, 2005. www.drgreene.com/21_2051.html.

Karp, Harvey. *The Happiest Baby on the Block: The New Way to Calm Crying and Help Your Baby Sleep Longer.* New York: Bantam, 2002.

Naik, Gautam. "Study Suggests SIDS Is Linked to Brain Defect: Findings Come Closer to Unlocking One of Biggest Medical Mysteries." *Wall Street Journal,* November 1, 2006.

National Institutes of Health. "NICHD Back to Sleep Campaign." NICHD. May 1, 2009. www.nichd.nih.gov/sids/.

National Institutes of Health. "SIDS Infants Show Abnormalities In Brain Area Controlling Breathing, Heart Rate: Serotonin-Using Brain Cells Implicated In Abnormalities." October 31, 2006. www//nih.gov/news/pr/oct2006/nichd-31.htm

Sheppard, Jane. "Has the Cause of Crib Death (SIDS) Been Found?: Toxic Gases in Baby Crib Mattresses." HealthyChild.org. 2009. www.healthychild.com/toxic-sleep/has-the-cause-of-crib-death-sids-been-found/.

Sprott, Jim. *The Cot Death Cover Up?* Auckland, New Zealand: Penguin Books, 1996.

Vennemann, Mechtild M., Thomas Bajanowski, Bernd Brinkmann, Gerhard Jorch, Edwin A. Mitchell, Cristina Sauerland, K. Yücesan, and GeSID Study Group. "Does Breastfeeding Reduce the Risk of Sudden Infant Death Syndrome?" *Pediatrics* 123.3 (2009): E406–410.

Waldburger, Jennifer, and Jill Spivack. *The Sleepeasy Solution: The Exhausted Parent's Guide to Getting Your Child to Sleep—from Birth to Age Five.* Deerfield Beach, FL: Health Communications, 2007.

Weber, Elsa L., ed. "Back to Sleep—What's a Parent to Do?" *SIDS Horizons* (1996).

Resources

Baby Food (Organic)

It is amazing to see how many companies are now making organic baby food. While organic baby food was popular when my kids were babies, the options were much more limited. We fed our daughters a lot of Earth's Best, Healthy Times, and, my personal favorite, Homemade Baby. Organic baby food can now be purchased in mainstream grocery stores, specialty shops, online retailers, "healthy food" stores, and stores like Whole Foods.

The following companies make organic baby food:

Earth's Best: www.earthsbest.com
Ella's Kitchen: www.ellaskitchen.com
Gerber Organics: www.gerber.com
Happy Baby: www.happybabyfood.com
Healthy Times: www.healthytimes.com
Homemade Baby: www.homemadebaby.com
Jack's Harvest: www.jacksharvest.com
Mom Made Foods: www.mommadefoods.com
Wild Harvest Organic: www.wildharvestorganic.com
Petite Palate: www.petitepalate.com
Plum Organics: www.PlumOrganics.com
Pomme Bébé: www.pommebebe.com
Sprout Baby Food: www.SproutBabyFood.com
Taste Bud Organic Baby Food: www.tastebudbaby.com
Tasty Baby: www.tastybaby.com
Wild Harvest: www.wildharvestorganic.com
Yummy Spoonfuls: www.YummySpoonfuls.com

Making Your Own Baby Food

Thanks to people like Ruth Yaron, author of *Super Baby Food,* making your own baby food is becoming mainstream. While some recipes can take a long time to prepare, others can be put together relatively quickly. A great website to check out for information and recipes is Wholesome Baby Food (www.whole-somebabyfood.com). There are a lot of wonderful books on the market about making your own baby food, which allows you to know exactly what is going into your child's mouth.

Keep in mind that in January 2010 the American Academy of Pediatrics changed its food introduction guidelines and now recommends introducing almost all foods, including those considered to be high-allergen, at four to six months, along with foods that were previously considered to be starter foods. It has also changed what used to be its "three-day rule" (only introduce one food at a time and wait at least three days before introducing another new one). Make sure to check with your pediatrician before introducing a new food to your child— and make sure those introductory foods do not pose any choking hazards.

If you are looking to make your own baby food, you may want to check out these resources:

Baby & Toddler Meals for Dummies by Dawn Simmons, Curt Simmons, and Sallie Warren
Best Food for Your Baby & Toddler: From First Foods to Meals Your Child Will Love (Great Expectations series) by Jeannette L. Bessinger with Tracee Yablon-Brenner
The Big Book of Recipes for Babies, Toddlers & Children: 365 Quick, Easy, and Healthy Dishes by Bridget Wardley and Judy More
The Everything Organic Cooking for Baby and Toddler Book: 300 Naturally Delicious Recipes to Get Your Child Off to a Healthy Start by Kim Lutz and Megan Hart
First Meals: Fast, Healthy, and Fun Foods to Tempt Infants and Toddlers by Annabel Karmel
Mommy Made and Daddy Too! Home Cooking for a Healthy Baby & Toddler by Martha Kimmel and David Kimmel, with Suzanne Goldenson
Organic Baby and Toddler Cookbook: Easy Recipes for Natural Food by Lizzie Vann and Daphne Razazan
The Petit Appetit Cookbook: Easy, Organic Recipes to Nurture Your Baby and Toddler by Lisa Barnes

Simply Natural Baby Food: Easy Recipes for Delicious Meals Your Infant and Toddler Will Love by Cathe Olson
Super Baby Food by Ruth Yaron
Superfoods: For Babies and Children by Annabel Karmel
Top 100 Baby Purees: 100 Quick and Easy Meals for a Healthy and Happy Baby by Annabel Karmel

Changing Pads

Whether you need a non-toxic changing pad for your diaper table at home or a portable one for your diaper bag, finding less toxic options is becoming easier. Here are a few to check out:

Portable Changing Pads:

Baby OHM Diaper Changing Mat: www.zo-li.com
Backwoods Babies: www.backwoodsbabies.com
OopC! I'm Still Me Organic Changing Pad: www.imstillme.com
Patemm Pad Organic Line: www.patemm.com

Diaper Table Changing Pads:

Costco L.A. Baby Organic Changing Pad: www.costco.com
Holy Lamb Organics Changing Table Pad: www.holylamborganics.com
Naturepedic Organic Changing Pad: www.naturepedic.com
Moonlight Slumber Naturals Changing Pad: www.moonlightslumber.com

Food Delivery Services (Organic)

In some areas of the country it can be difficult to get organic fruits and vegetables. Fortunately, there are a number of terrific companies that ship organic foods directly to your front door.

Boxed Greens: www.boxedgreens.com
Diamond Organics: www.diamondorganics.com
Farm Fresh to You: www.farmfreshtoyou.com
The Fruit Guys: www.fruitguys.com
Greenling: www.greenling.com
Harry and David (organic fruit of the month club): www.harryanddavid.com
Local Harvest: www.localharvest.org
Planet Organics: www.planetorganics.com
Urban Organics: www.urbanorganic.com

Mattresses (Organic)

For reviews of organic mattresses:
Organic Crib Mattresses: www.Organic-Crib-Mattress.org

To buy an organic mattress:
Absolutely Organic Baby: www.absolutelyorganicbaby.com
Dax Stores: www.DaxStores.com
Eco Bedroom: www.EcoBedroom.com
The Little Seed: www.TheLittleSeed.com
Naturepedic: www.naturepedic.com
Nirvana Safe Haven: www.NonToxic.com
Nook Sleep Systems: www.nooksleep.com
Pure-Rest Organics: www.purerest.com

Pajamas (Organic)

While organic cotton pajamas have become increasingly popular, they can still be hard to find. These companies make their own sleepwear for children and much of it is certified organic.

Garden Kids: www.gardenkidsclothing.com
Green Babies www.greenbabies.com
Hanna Andersson: www.hannaandersson.com
Kid Bean: www.kidbean.com
New Jammies: www.newjammies.com

Nuno Organics: www.nunoorganic.com
Polarn O. Pyret (ECO collection only): www.polarnopyretusa.com/eco
Snug Organics: www.snugorganics.com
Under the Nile: www.underthenile.com

For less expense options check out stores like Wal-Mart, Costco, and Kohl's, all of whom manufacture organic pajamas.

Signing Board Books

Finding Fido the Feline: Flipbook with American Sign Language by Barbara A. Palmer
Happy Birthday! A Beginner's Book of Signs by Angela Bednarczyk and Janet Weinstock

Signing Time! Series by Rachel de Azevedo Coleman & Emilie de Azevedo Brown
    Signing Time! My First Signs
    Signing Time! Playtime Signs
    Signing Time! Everyday Signs

Early Sign Language Series by Garlic Press
    An Alphabet of Animal Signs: First Signs
    First Signs at Home
    First Signs at Play
    Food Signs for Pets and Animals
    Young Signers Series: Colors
    Young Signers Series: Go-Togethers
    Young Signers Series: Opposites

Sign About Series by Child's Play, illustrated by Anthony Lewis
    Getting Ready
    Going Out
    Mealtime

Other Signing Books

I Can Sign My ABCs by Susan Gibbons Chaplin
Handsigns: A Sign Language Alphabet by Kathleen Fain
My ABC Signs of Animal Friends by Ben Bahan and Joe Dannis
Sabuda & Reinhart PopUps: Baby Signs by Kyle Olmon and Jacqueline Rogers
Where is Baby? A Lift-the-Flap Sign Language Book by Michelle Cryan
Winnie-the-Pooh's ABC: Sign Language Edition by A. A. Milne and Ernest S. Shepard

Story Time with Signs & Rhymes Series by Dawn Babb Provnic and Stephanie Bauer:
    The Best Day in the Room: Sign Language for School Activities
    The Big Blue Bowl: Sign Language for Food
    Famous Fenton Has a Farm: Sign Language for Farm Animals
    The Nest Where I Like to Rest: Sign Language for Animals
    See the Colors: Sign Language for Colors
    Silly Sue: Sign Language for Actions
    Watch Me Go: Sign Language for Vehicles
    Wear a Silly Hat: Sign Language for Clothes

Sign Language Web Sites

American Sign Language Browser: www.aslbrowser.commtechlab.msu.edu
ASL Pro: www.aslpro.com
Babies and Sign Language: www.babies-and-sign-language.com
Hand Speak www.HandSpeak.com
My Baby Can Talk Dictionary of Signs: www.MyBabyCanTalk.com
My Smart Hands: www.mysmarthands.com
Sign Babies: www.SignBabies.com
Sign Shine: www.BabySignShine.com and www.SignShine.com
Sign2Me: www.Sign2me.com
Signing Time: www.SigningTime.com
Signing with Your Baby: www.signingbaby.com
Wee Signs: www.weesign.ca

Cool Signing Flashcards

The English Alphabet with American Sign Language (Volumn Two) Flash of Brilliance
Signing Time! Flashcards (Set 3): Everyday Signs
Signing Time! Flashcards (Set 1): My First Signs
Signing Time! Flashcards (Set 2): Playtime Signs
Sign2Me (Beginner Series) Actions & Opposites
Sign2Me (Beginner Series) Animals & Colors
Sign2Me (Beginner Series) Family, Clothing & Toileting
Sign2Me (Beginner Series) Objects & Emotions
Sign2Me (Beginner Series) Quick Start
Touch and Feel Picture Cards (DK) Animals
Touch and Feel Picture Cards (DK) Colors & Shapes
Touch and Feel Picture Cards (DK) Farm
Touch and Feel Picture Cards (DK) First Words
Touch and Feel Picture Cards (DK) Numbers and Counting
Touch and Feel Picture Cards (DK) Things That Go

Great Places to Get Foreign Language Books

Adopted from Russia: www.adoptedfromrussia.com
Alien Languages: www.alien-languages.com
Amazon Foreign Language: www.amazon.com/Foreign-Language-Books/b?ie=UTF8&node=3118571
Asian Parent: www.asianparent.com
Bilingual Books for Kids: www.bilingualbooks.com
China Sprout: www.chinasprout.com
Chinese Mall: www.chinesemall.com
Culture for Kids www.cultureforkids.com
French Books Online: www.frenchbooksonline.com
Global Language Books: www.globallanguage.com.au/index.php
Innovative Educators: www.innovative-educators.com
International Children's Books: www.internationalchildbook.com/home
Language Lizard: www.languagelizard.com
Mantra Lingua: www.mantralingua.com
Me+Mi Publishing: www.memima.com
Multilingual Books: www.multilingualbooks.com
Oui for Kids: www.ouiforkids.com
Powell's Books: www.powells.com/psection/ForeignLanguages.html
Pukeko Books: www.pukekobooks.com.au/index.html
Schoenhof's Foreign Books: www.schoenhofs.com
Star Bright Books: www.StarBrightBooks.com
You Are Special: www.youarespecial.com

Web Sites for Going Green

Center for Health, Environment & Justice: www.chej.org
The Daily Green: www.TheDailyGreen.com
Dr. Greene: www.drgreene.com
Ecorazzi: www.ecorazzi.com
Environmental Protection Agency: www.epa.gov
Environmental Working Group: www.ewg.org
Green Guide: www.thegreenguide.com
Greener Choices: www.greenerchoices.org
Greenopia: www.greenopia.com
Healthy Child Healthy World: www.healthychild.org
Healthy Toys: www.HealthyToys.org
Lead Toy Recalls: www.LeadToyRecalls.com
Safe Mama: www.SafeMama.com
Safer Chemicals, Healthy Families: www.ecorazzi.com
Skin Deep: www.cosmeticsdatabase.com
The Smart Mama: www.TheSmartMama.com
Toy Recall Alert: www.RecalledToyAlert.com
Treehugger: www.treehugger.com

Acknowledgements

I would like to thank Jerry Levin and Dr. Laurie Ann Levin for introducing me to the powers that be at Sterling Publishing. I am enormously grateful for your belief in me, your faith in my work, and your friendship. I am forever grateful.

Thank you, Marcus Leaver and Michael Fragnito, for your great appreciation of *SuperBaby* and my written word. Your response to my original proposal and the enormous encouragement you have given me throughout this process gave me the freedom and the courage to dig deeper and reach new levels as a writer. Jason Prince, your constant support and belief in this project has helped this book flourish. From the content to the layout to the illustrations, you made my dreams come true. This book would not be what it is today were it not for the three of you. Thank you for finding such a special place at Sterling for my *SuperBaby*.

Jennifer Williams, you are my editing soulmate. You are a joy to work with. You have a deep understanding of how precious a writer's words are to her and a great ability to mold those words and make them clearer, smoother, and better. Your hand-holding, great sense of humor, and brilliant insight made all the sleepless nights of writing a little easier. Thank you for taking such good care of my SuperBaby and being my greatest literary advocate.

Elizabeth Mihaltse, thank you for your patience, creativity, and perseverance with the cover. You did such a beautiful job and I love how you captured the feel of *SuperBaby*. Lary Rosenblatt and Fabia Wargin, I don't think I have ever seen a more beautifully designed book. You made *SuperBaby* with all its depth and complexities visual candy that is fun and easy to read. Laurie Lieb, thank you for your fine eye for detail, incredible memory, and copy-editing genius.

I am very grateful to Leign Ann Ambrosi and Anwesha Basu for working so hard to get the word out about *SuperBaby*. Thank you, Megan Murphy, for your creativity and your passion to help me reach new readers. Karen Patterson, thank you for having my back and for sharing my enthusiasm for SuperBaby.

I want to thank those experts and organizations who were so kind and generous, contributing "From the Experts..." sidebars. Thank you so much for contributing your time, energy, and expertise: The Alliance for Childhood, Dr. Joan Almon, Dr. Tanya Remer Altmann, Kenn Apel, BabyGroup™, Sir Richard Bowlby, Dr. Nathaniel Brandon, Betsy Brown Braun, Leeann Brown, Dr. Scott Cohen, Rachael Coleman & Emelie Brown, Campaign for a Commercial-Free Childhood, Sue Darrison, The Elizabeth Rose Agency, Environmental Working Group, Jim and Charles Fay, Christopher Gavigan, Amy Giles, Wendy Haldeman, Corky Harvey, Healthy Child Healthy World, Dr. Lindsay Heller, Donna Holloran, Sharon Huang, Dr. Harvey Karp, Dr. Kendall King & Dr. Alison Mackey, Allison LaTona, Etel Leit, Susan Linn, Love and Logic, Nicole Meadows, Donalyn Miller, Ed Miller, Dr. Jane Nelsen, Dr. Michelle Nitka, Angelika Putintseva of

WorldSpeak, Positive Discipline, Elyse Resch, Robin Sax, Dr. Bob Sears, Signing Time!, SignShine, Sleepy Planet, Jill Spivack, Dr. Rebecca Sutton, Jennifer Taggart, Paige Goldberg Tolmach, Dr. Bryan Vartabedian, Jennifer Waldberger, Andrea Lesch Weiss, and Ruth Yaron.

A special thank you to Dr. Alan Greene for going through the book with a fine-tooth comb and giving me feedback. Thank you for sharing your thoughts and insights but most of all for writing such an insightful and meaningful foreword, despite difficult and unusual circumstances.

I want to thank the many experts who shared their expertise, allowed me to interview them, sent advance drafts of papers and research projects, answered my never-ending questions, and were kind enough to read through my work for accuracy. Thank you so much: Jennifer Taggart, Dr. Tanya Remer-Altmann, Ruth Yaron, Dr. Jane Nelsen, Dr. Joseph Garcia, Marie Field, RN, Dr. Susan Ludington-Hoe, Shirley Munro, RN, Marion Nestle, Janet Nudelman of the Breast Cancer Fund, Margie Kelly at Safer States, Kathy Curtis at Clean NY, Dr. Heather Stapleton at Duke University, Lynne Oyama, RN, Jill Spivack, Jennifer Waldberger, Dr. Michelle Nitka, and Paige Goldberg Tolmach.

I want to thank my SuperHusband, Joshua Berman. Since the moment we met, you have been my greatest supporter. Thank you for editing and formatting all 462 pages of my doctoral dissertation and everything I have written since we first met, for all the laughter you bring into my life, for your friendship and your tremendous support, and for loving me the way you do. But most of all...thank you for being such a spectacular father to our SuperBabies, Quincy and Mendez.

This book would not exist were it not for my SuperParents, who served as extraordinary role models for parenting. You always made me feel heard and loved. You taught me to follow my ambition and let me know that I could achieve anything I put my mind to. In writing this book and approaching experts I admire so much to ask for expert sidebars, I became especially grateful that you taught me to ask for what I want.

I want to thank my friends who have supported me through this writing process, listened to me complain, and shared in my passion for parenting. Thank you to my twin mommy support system and dear friends Andrea Barnow and Andrea Weiss. I am especially grateful for my SSBG friends—Paige Goldberg Tolmach, Leslie Grossman, and Kellie Martin. You ladies are my mommy lifeline. Thank you to my great friends and neighbors Lisa and Jason Leopold. Your support has been invaluable. Thank you, Lisa Weiner, for your friendship and support and for always showing such love and interest for both my SuperBabies and my *SuperBaby* book. Thank you to Jennifer Simpson for being the best friend I could ever ask for. I bask in the light of your friendship.

I also want to give a special thanks to Allison LaTona. Next to my own parents, you have been my greatest influence as a parent. Many of the messages and ideas you have imparted to me over the years me are woven throughout this book. I cannot thank you enough for all the support, guidance, and wisdom you have shared.

Index